THE FLASH UNWRAPPED BY
FRANCIS MANAPUL

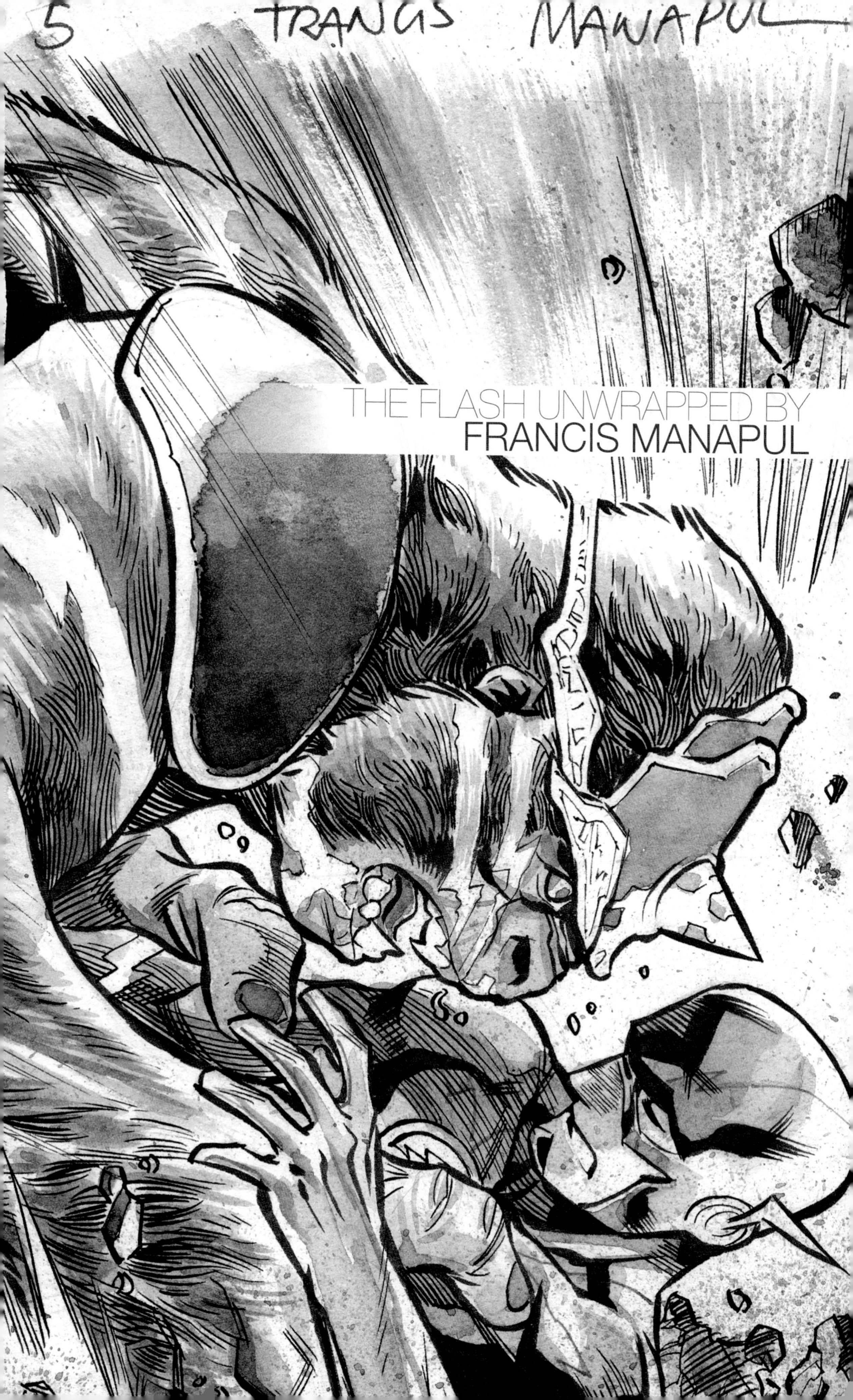
5 FRANCIS MANAPUL

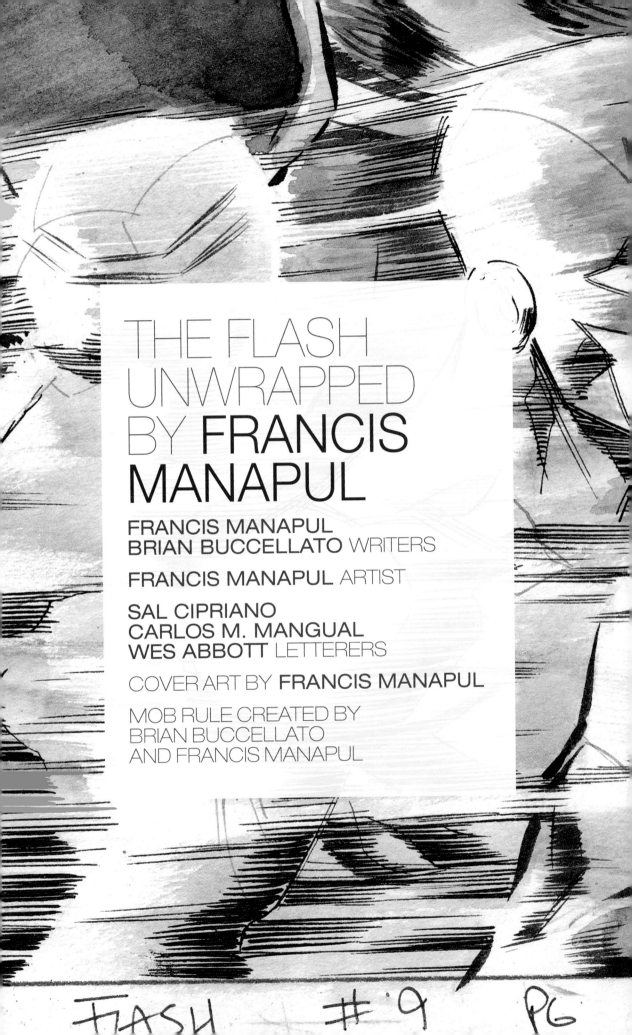

THE FLASH UNWRAPPED
BY FRANCIS MANAPUL

FRANCIS MANAPUL
BRIAN BUCCELLATO WRITERS

FRANCIS MANAPUL ARTIST

SAL CIPRIANO
CARLOS M. MANGUAL
WES ABBOTT LETTERERS

COVER ART BY **FRANCIS MANAPUL**

MOB RULE CREATED BY
BRIAN BUCCELLATO
AND FRANCIS MANAPUL

FLASH #9 PG

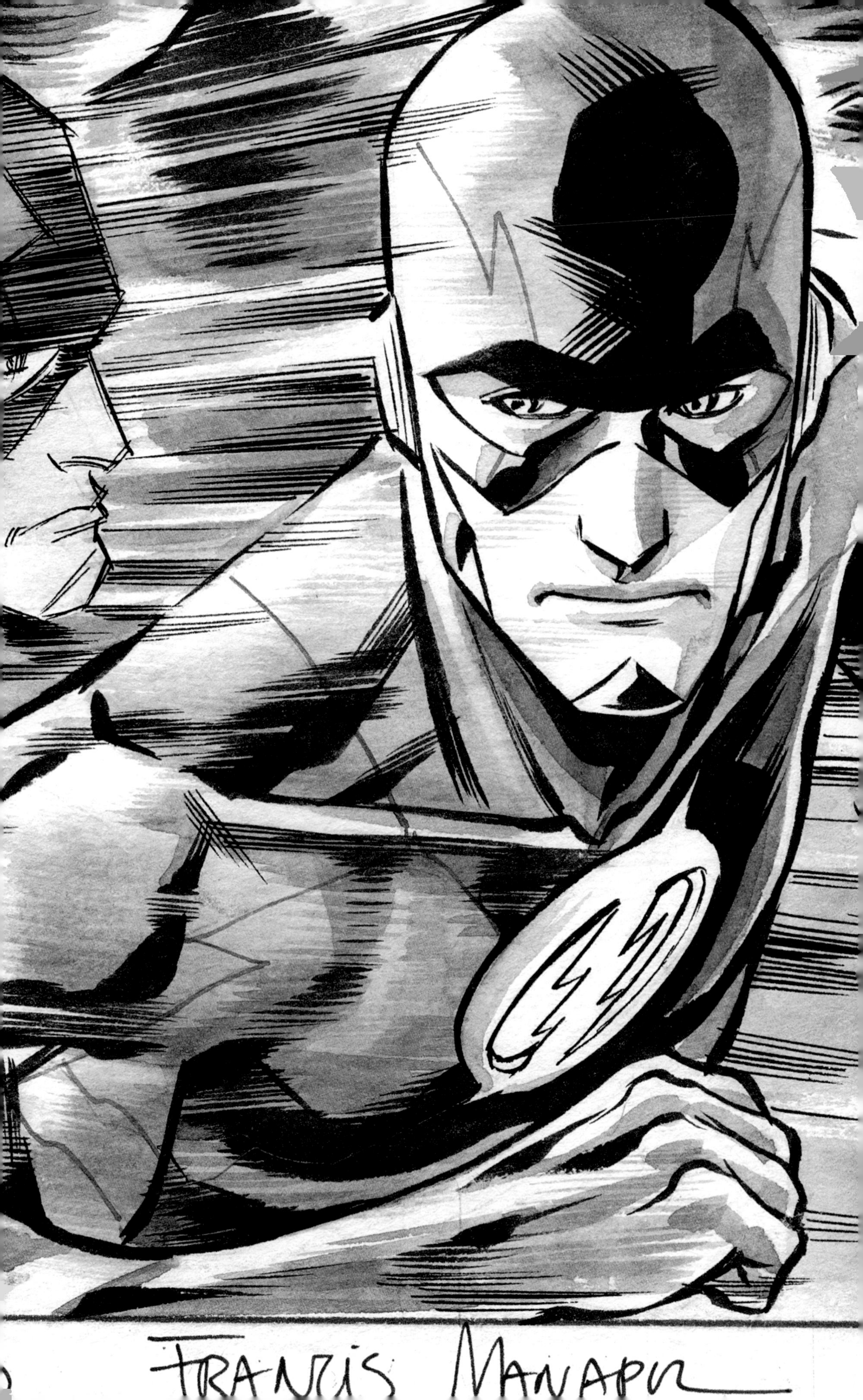
FRANCIS MANAPUL

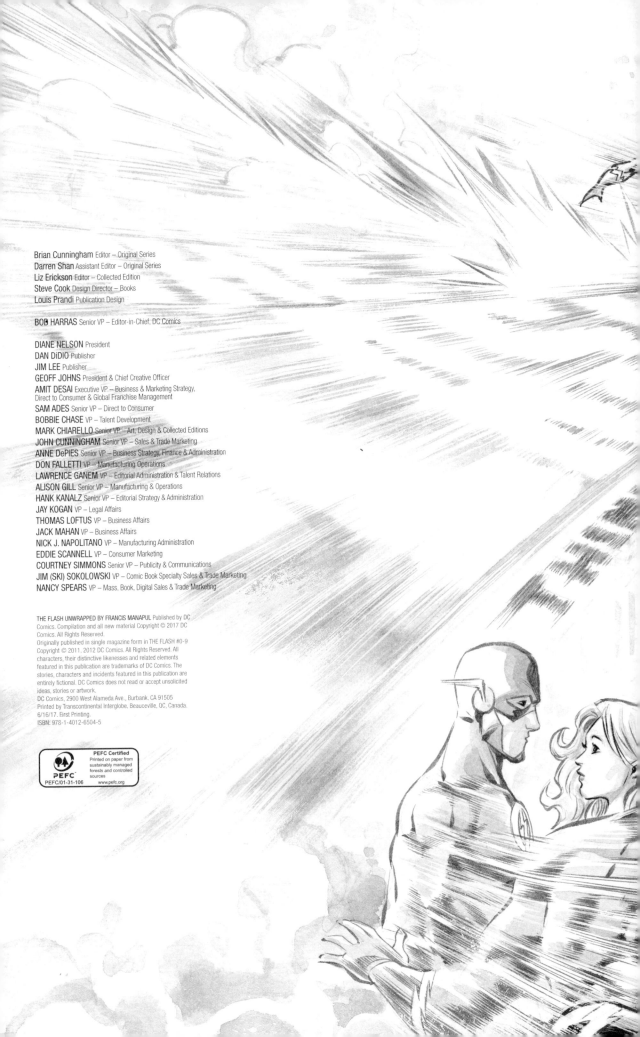

Brian Cunningham Editor – Original Series
Darren Shan Assistant Editor – Original Series
Liz Erickson Editor – Collected Edition
Steve Cook Design Director – Books
Louis Prandi Publication Design

BOB HARRAS Senior VP – Editor-in-Chief, DC Comics

DIANE NELSON President
DAN DiDIO Publisher
JIM LEE Publisher
GEOFF JOHNS President & Chief Creative Officer
AMIT DESAI Executive VP – Business & Marketing Strategy, Direct to Consumer & Global Franchise Management
SAM ADES Senior VP – Direct to Consumer
BOBBIE CHASE VP – Talent Development
MARK CHIARELLO Senior VP – Art, Design & Collected Editions
JOHN CUNNINGHAM Senior VP – Sales & Trade Marketing
ANNE DePIES Senior VP – Business Strategy, Finance & Administration
DON FALLETTI VP – Manufacturing Operations
LAWRENCE GANEM VP – Editorial Administration & Talent Relations
ALISON GILL Senior VP – Manufacturing & Operations
HANK KANALZ Senior VP – Editorial Strategy & Administration
JAY KOGAN VP – Legal Affairs
THOMAS LOFTUS VP – Business Affairs
JACK MAHAN VP – Business Affairs
NICK J. NAPOLITANO VP – Manufacturing Administration
EDDIE SCANNELL VP – Consumer Marketing
COURTNEY SIMMONS Senior VP – Publicity & Communications
JIM (SKI) SOKOLOWSKI VP – Comic Book Specialty Sales & Trade Marketing
NANCY SPEARS VP – Mass, Book, Digital Sales & Trade Marketing

DC Comics, 2900 West Alameda Ave., Burbank, CA 91505
Printed by Transcontinental Interglobe, Beauceville, QC, Canada. 6/16/17. First Printing.
ISBN: 978-1-4012-6504-5

PEFC Certified
Printed on paper from sustainably managed forests and controlled sources
PEFC
PEFC/01-31-106 www.pefc.org

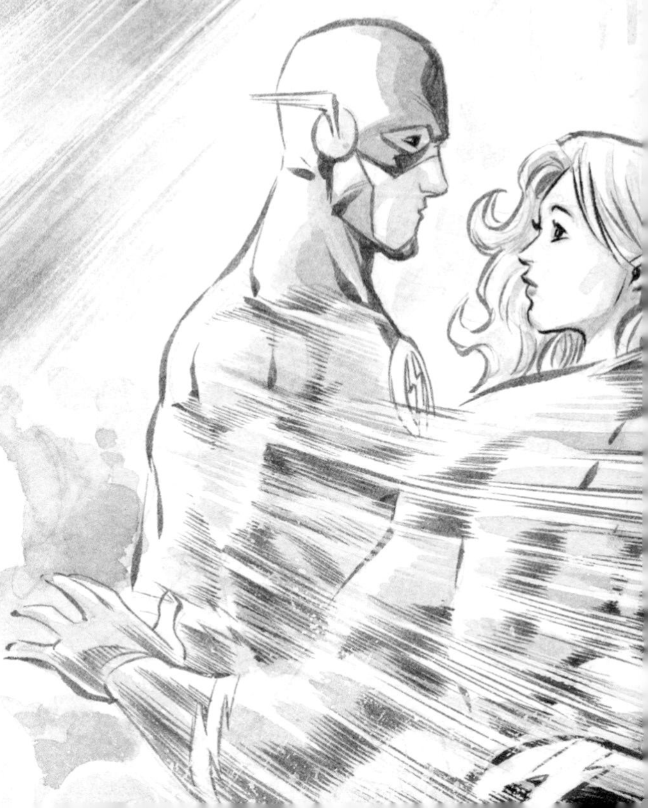

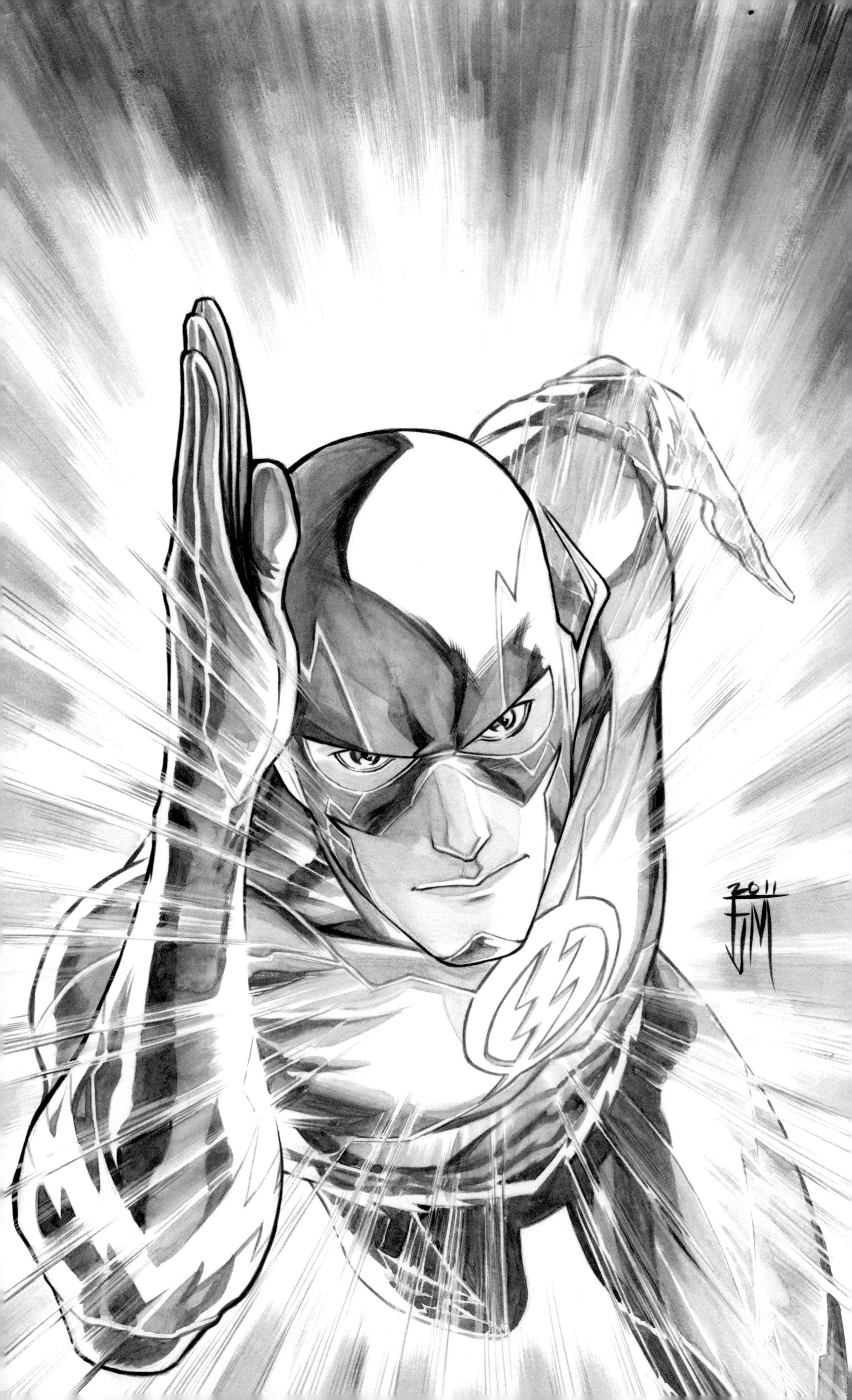
2011

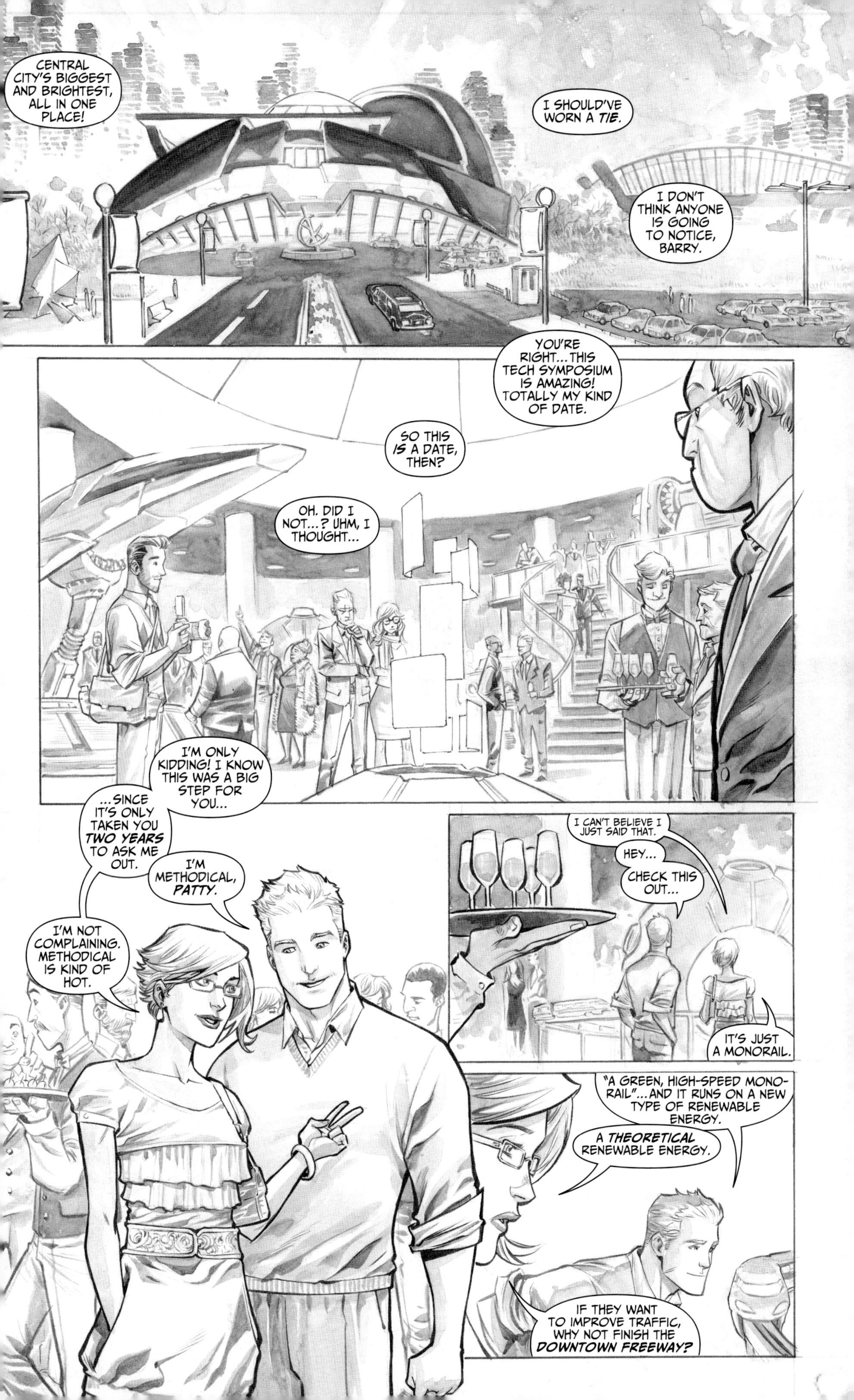
CENTRAL CITY'S BIGGEST AND BRIGHTEST, ALL IN ONE PLACE!
I SHOULD'VE WORN A TIE.
I DON'T THINK ANYONE IS GOING TO NOTICE, BARRY.
YOU'RE RIGHT... THIS TECH SYMPOSIUM IS AMAZING! TOTALLY MY KIND OF DATE.
SO THIS IS A DATE, THEN?
OH. DID I NOT...? UHM, I THOUGHT...
I'M ONLY KIDDING! I KNOW THIS WAS A BIG STEP FOR YOU...
...SINCE IT'S ONLY TAKEN YOU TWO YEARS TO ASK ME OUT.
I'M METHODICAL, PATTY.
I'M NOT COMPLAINING. METHODICAL IS KIND OF HOT.
I CAN'T BELIEVE I JUST SAID THAT.
HEY...
CHECK THIS OUT...
IT'S JUST A MONORAIL.
"A GREEN, HIGH-SPEED MONO-RAIL"... AND IT RUNS ON A NEW TYPE OF RENEWABLE ENERGY.
A THEORETICAL RENEWABLE ENERGY.
IF THEY WANT TO IMPROVE TRAFFIC, WHY NOT FINISH THE DOWNTOWN FREEWAY?

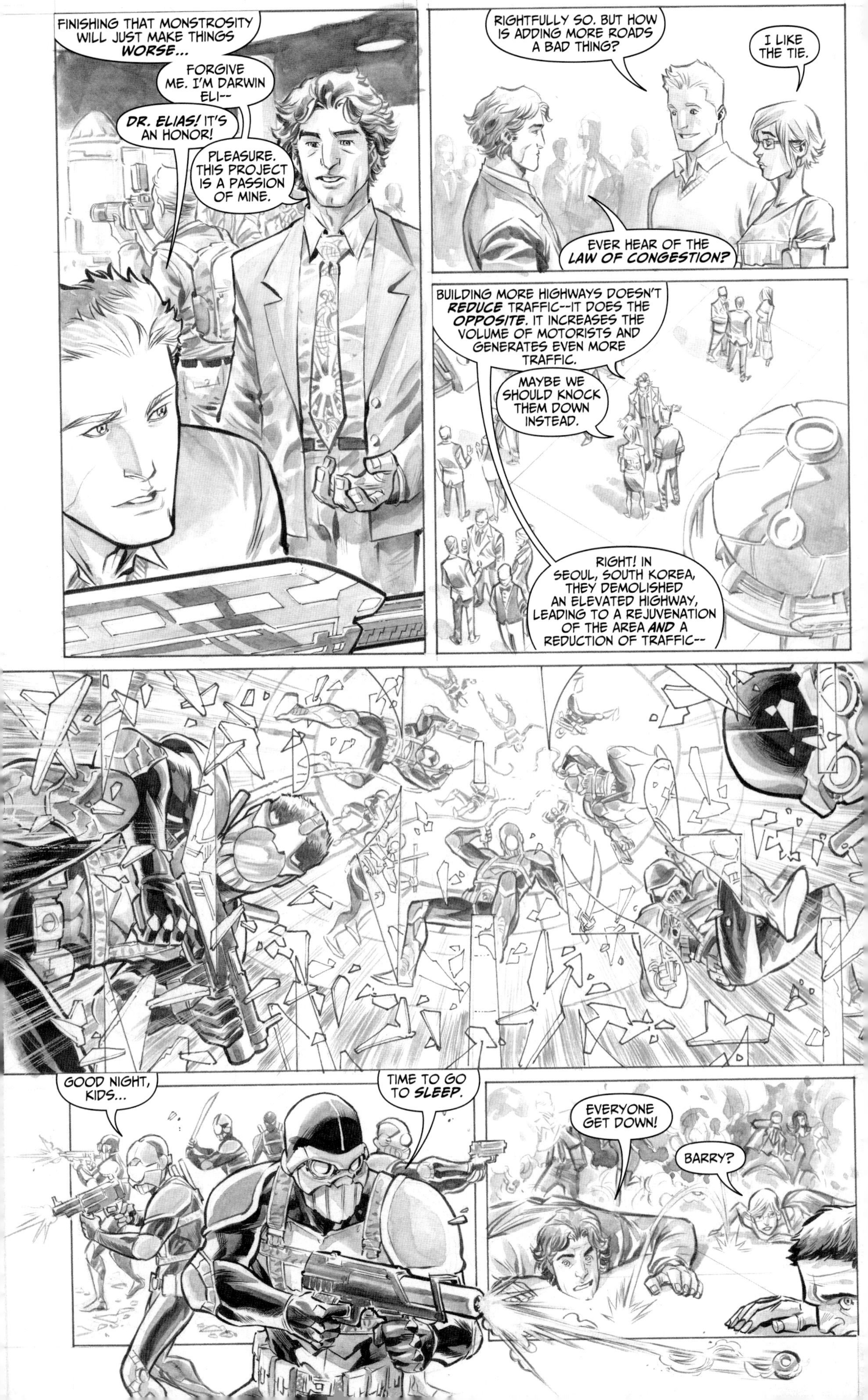
FINISHING THAT MONSTROSITY WILL JUST MAKE THINGS WORSE...
FORGIVE ME. I'M DARWIN ELI--
DR. ELIAS! IT'S AN HONOR!
PLEASURE. THIS PROJECT IS A PASSION OF MINE.
RIGHTFULLY SO. BUT HOW IS ADDING MORE ROADS A BAD THING?
I LIKE THE TIE.
EVER HEAR OF THE LAW OF CONGESTION?
BUILDING MORE HIGHWAYS DOESN'T REDUCE TRAFFIC--IT DOES THE OPPOSITE. IT INCREASES THE VOLUME OF MOTORISTS AND GENERATES EVEN MORE TRAFFIC.
MAYBE WE SHOULD KNOCK THEM DOWN INSTEAD.
RIGHT! IN SEOUL, SOUTH KOREA, THEY DEMOLISHED AN ELEVATED HIGHWAY, LEADING TO A REJUVENATION OF THE AREA AND A REDUCTION OF TRAFFIC--
GOOD NIGHT, KIDS...
TIME TO GO TO SLEEP.
EVERYONE GET DOWN!
BARRY?

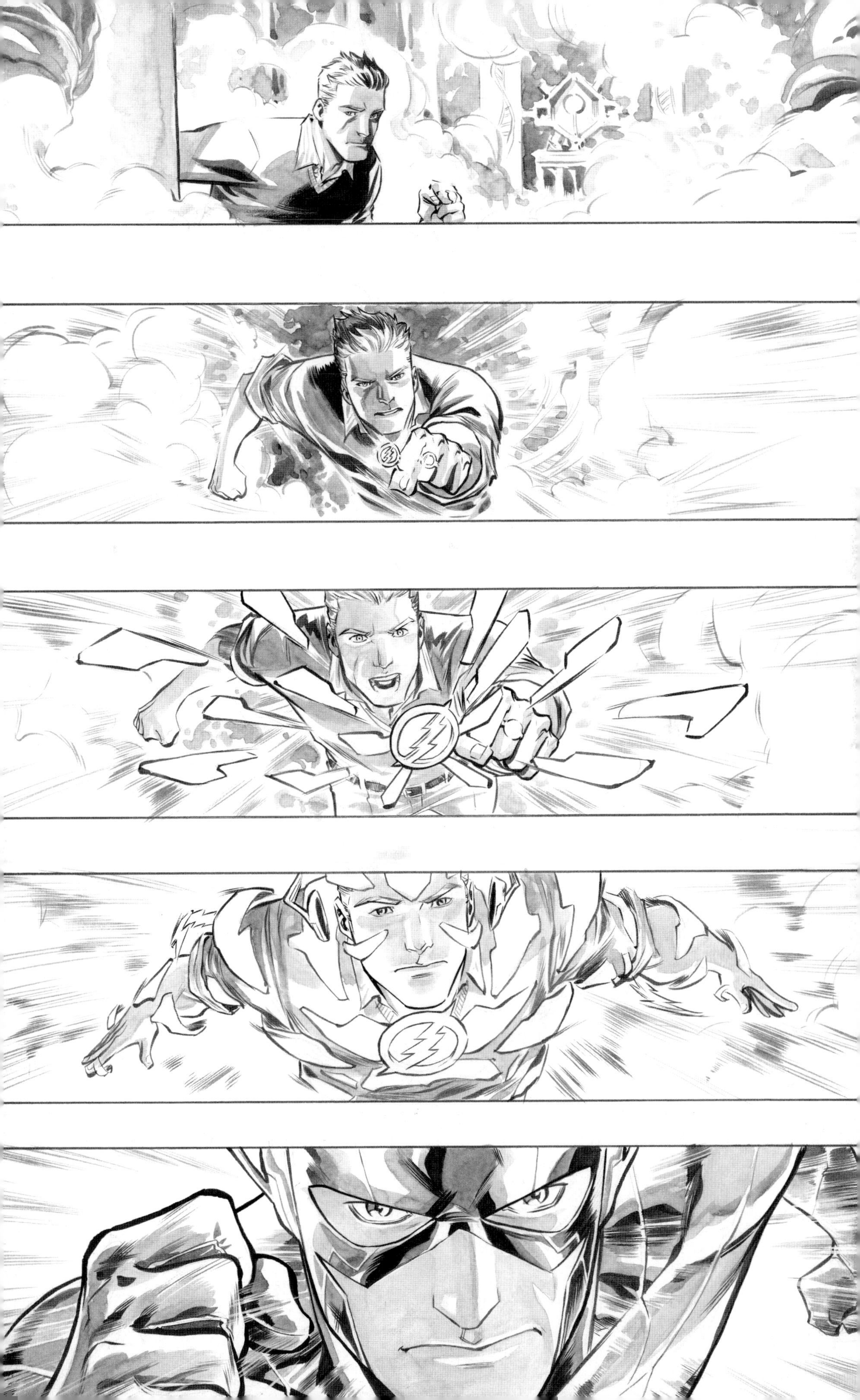

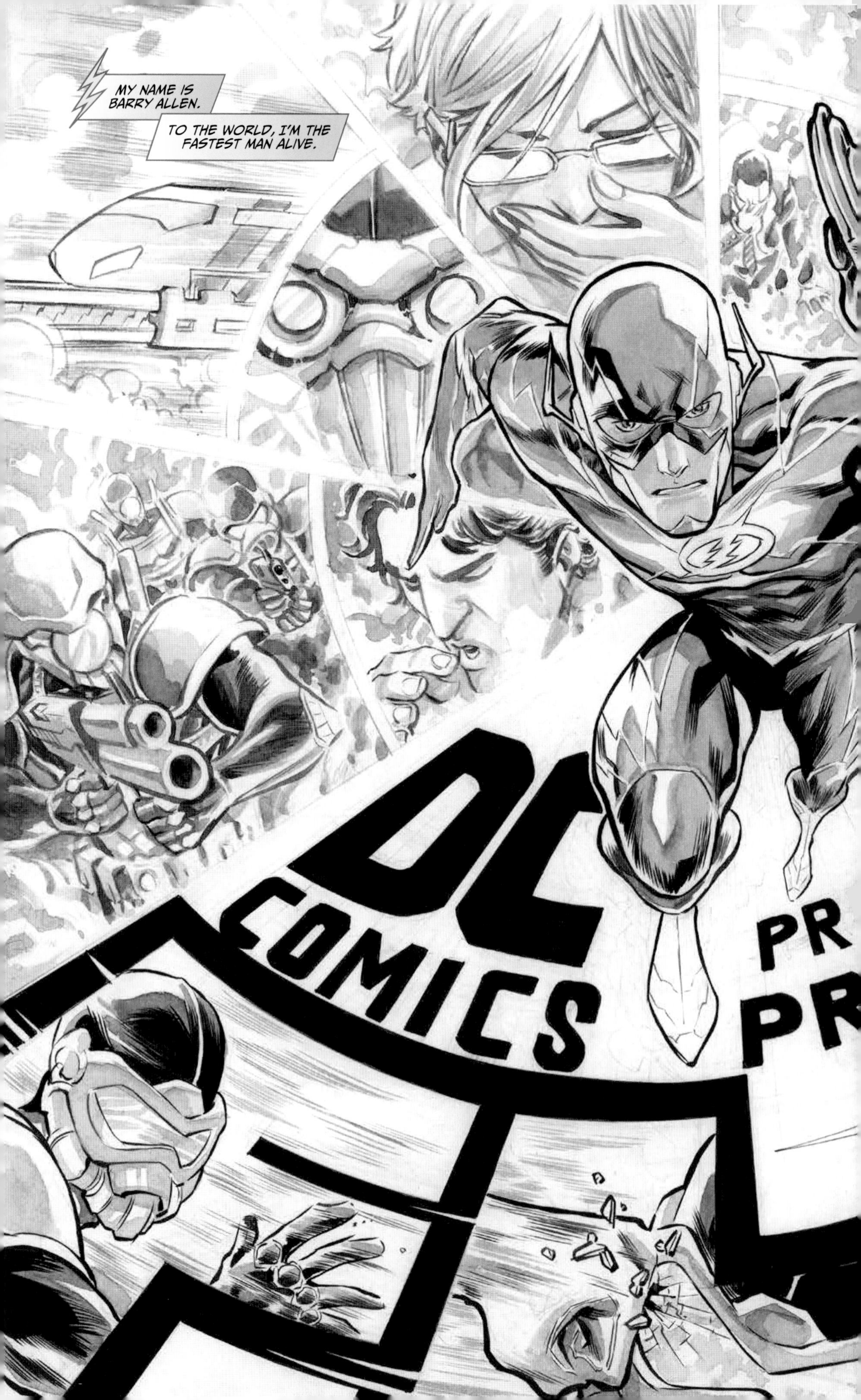
MY NAME IS BARRY ALLEN.
TO THE WORLD, I'M THE FASTEST MAN ALIVE.
DC COMICS
PR
PR

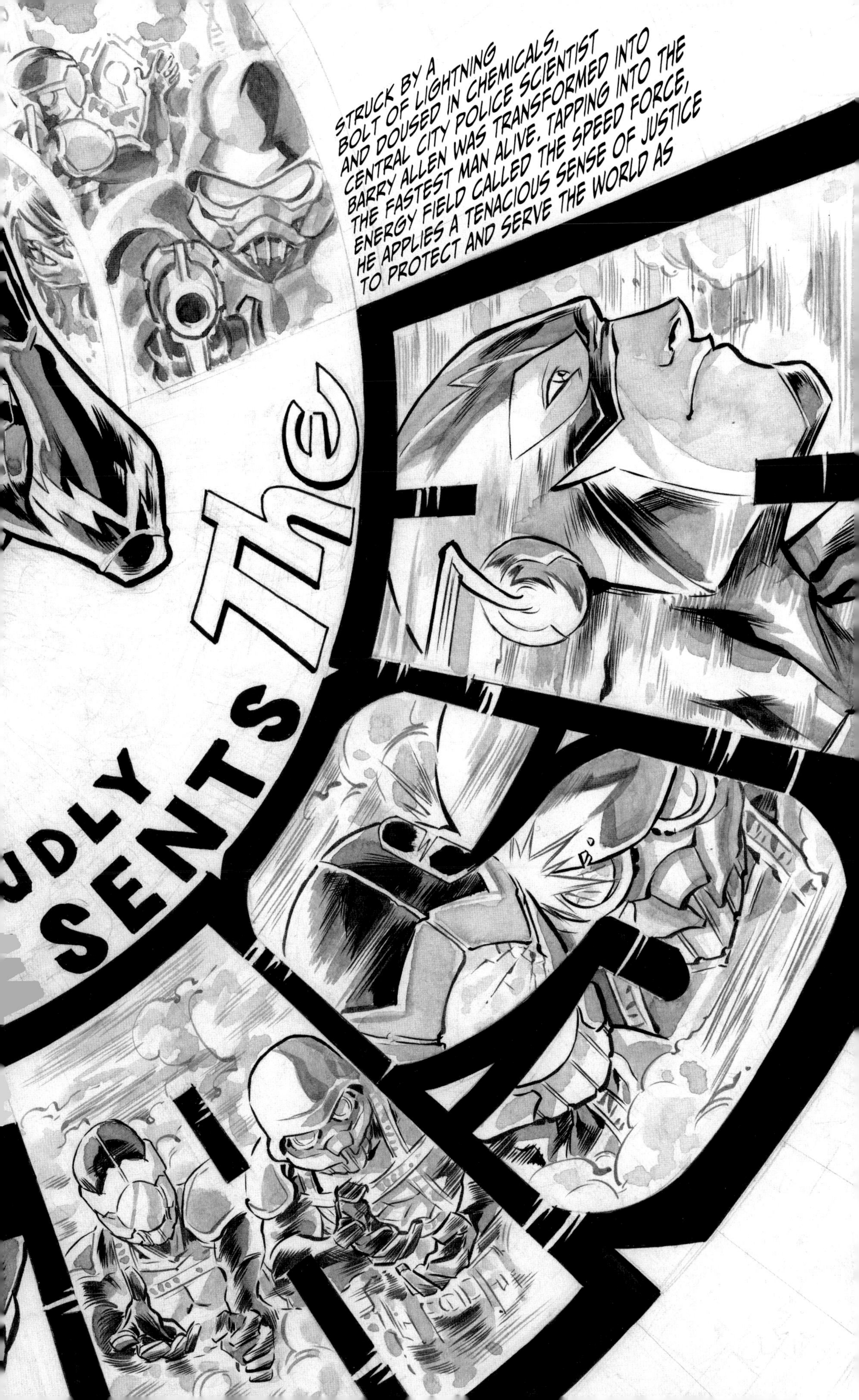
STRUCK BY A BOLT OF LIGHTNING AND DOUSED IN CHEMICALS, CENTRAL CITY POLICE SCIENTIST BARRY ALLEN WAS TRANSFORMED INTO THE FASTEST MAN ALIVE. TAPPING INTO THE ENERGY FIELD CALLED THE SPEED FORCE, HE APPLIES A TENACIOUS SENSE OF JUSTICE TO PROTECT AND SERVE THE WORLD AS
UDLY
SENTS
the

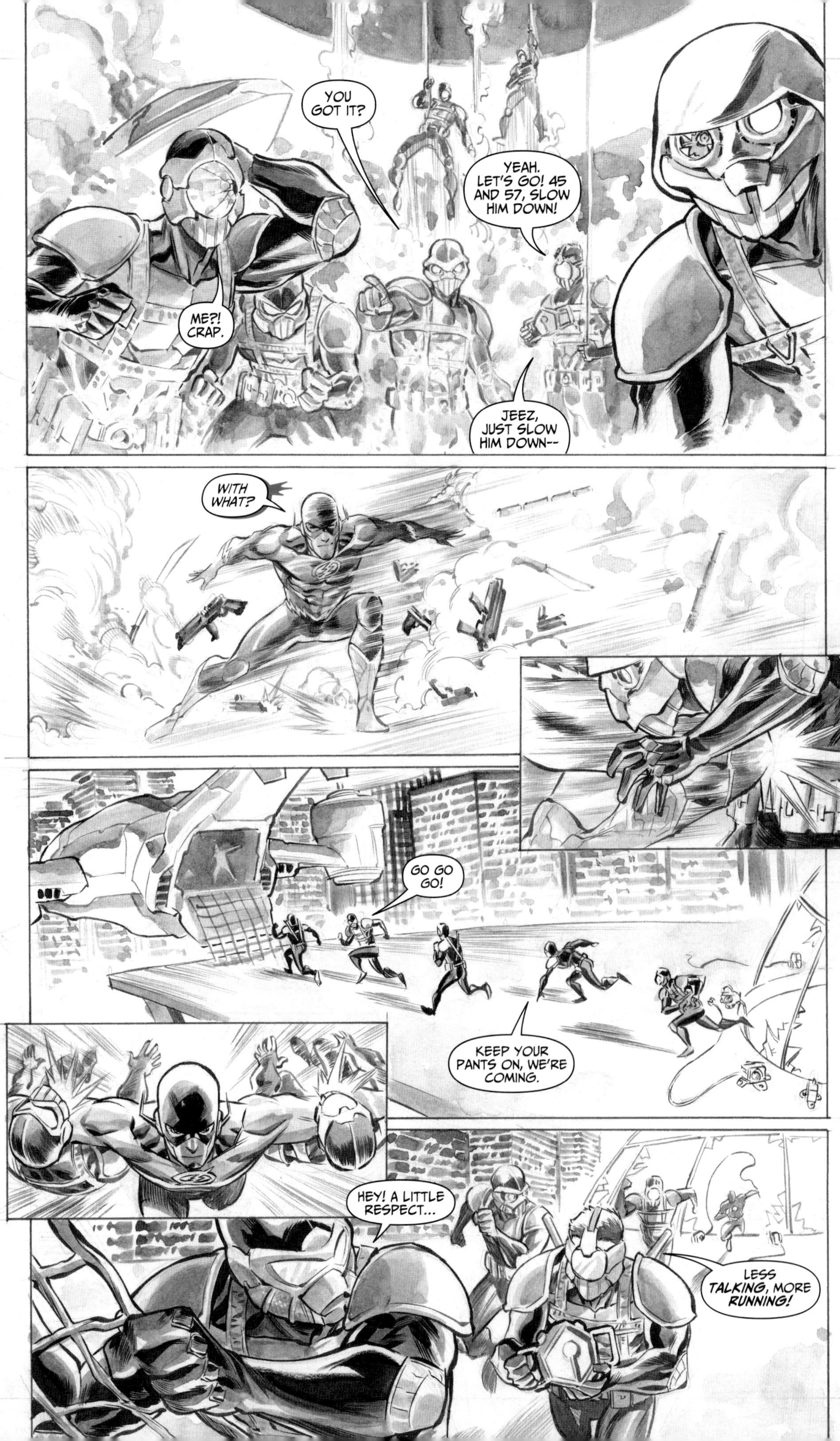
YOU GOT IT?
YEAH. LET'S GO! 45 AND 57, SLOW HIM DOWN!
ME?! CRAP.
JEEZ, JUST SLOW HIM DOWN--
WITH WHAT?
GO GO GO!
KEEP YOUR PANTS ON, WE'RE COMING.
HEY! A LITTLE RESPECT...
LESS *TALKING*, MORE *RUNNING*!

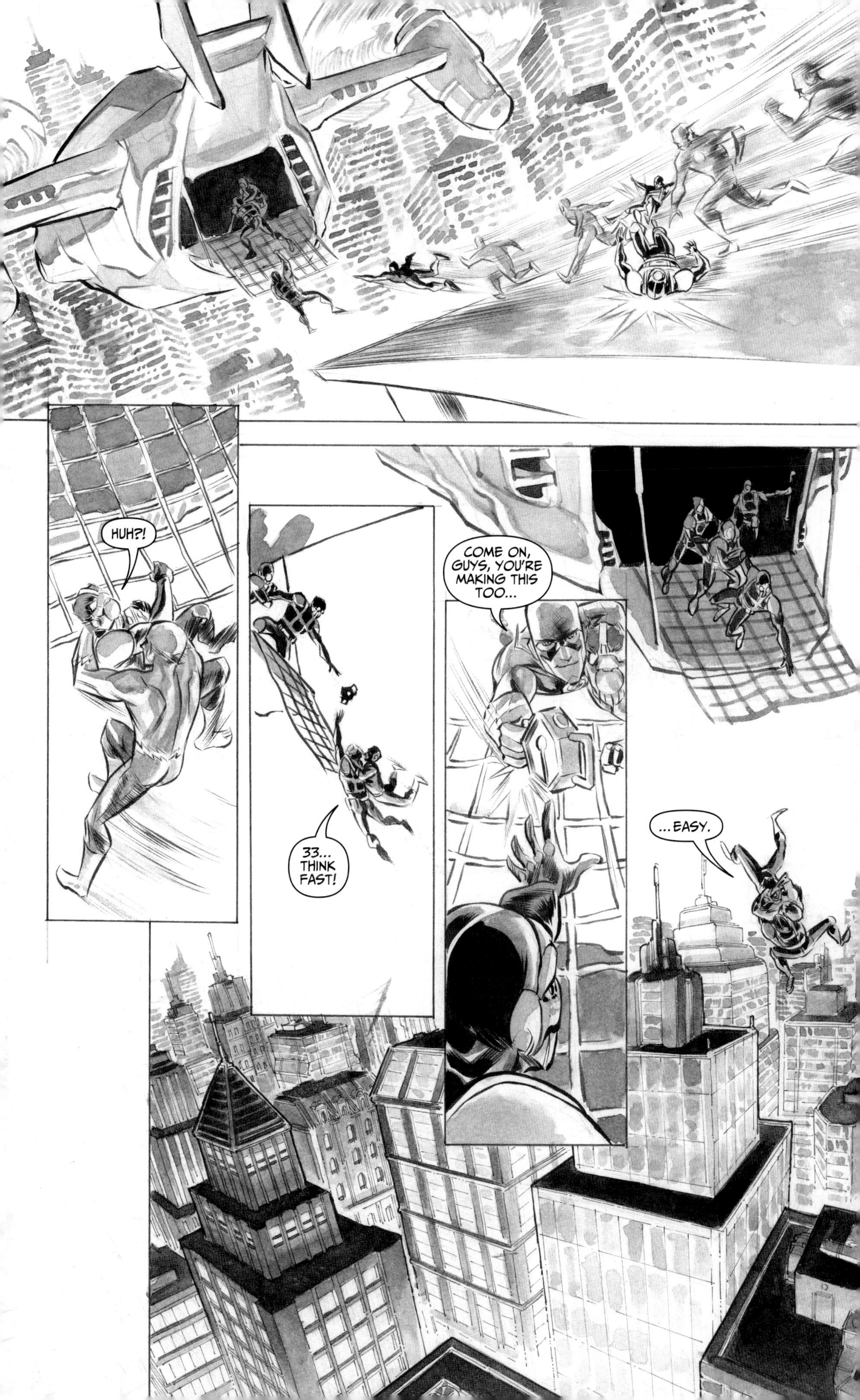
HUH?!
33... THINK FAST!
COME ON, GUYS, YOU'RE MAKING THIS TOO...
...EASY.

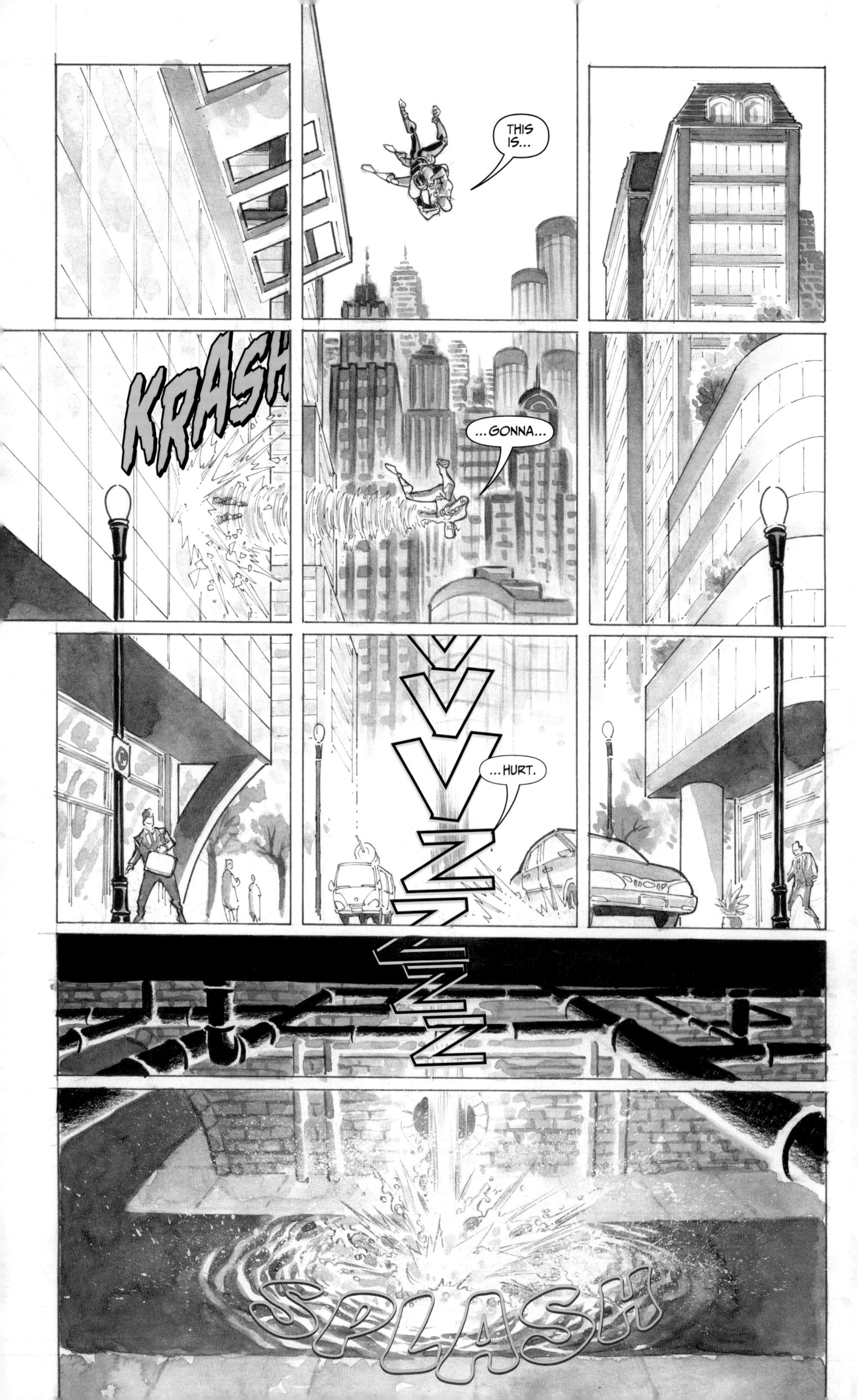
THIS IS...
KRASH
...GONNA...
...HURT.
SPLASH

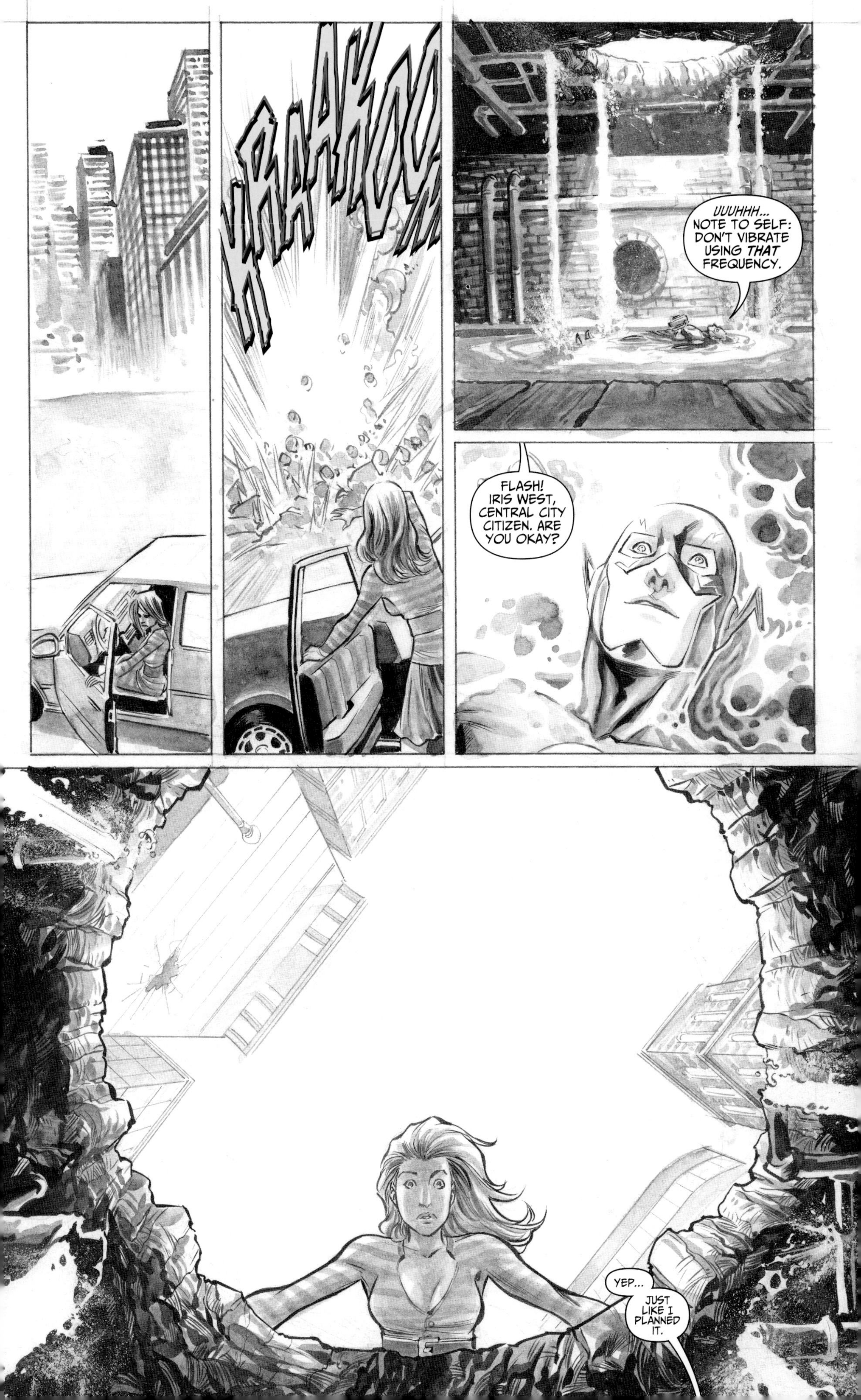
KRAKOO
UUUHHH... NOTE TO SELF: DON'T VIBRATE USING THAT FREQUENCY.
FLASH! IRIS WEST, CENTRAL CITY CITIZEN. ARE YOU OKAY?
YEP...
JUST LIKE I PLANNED IT.

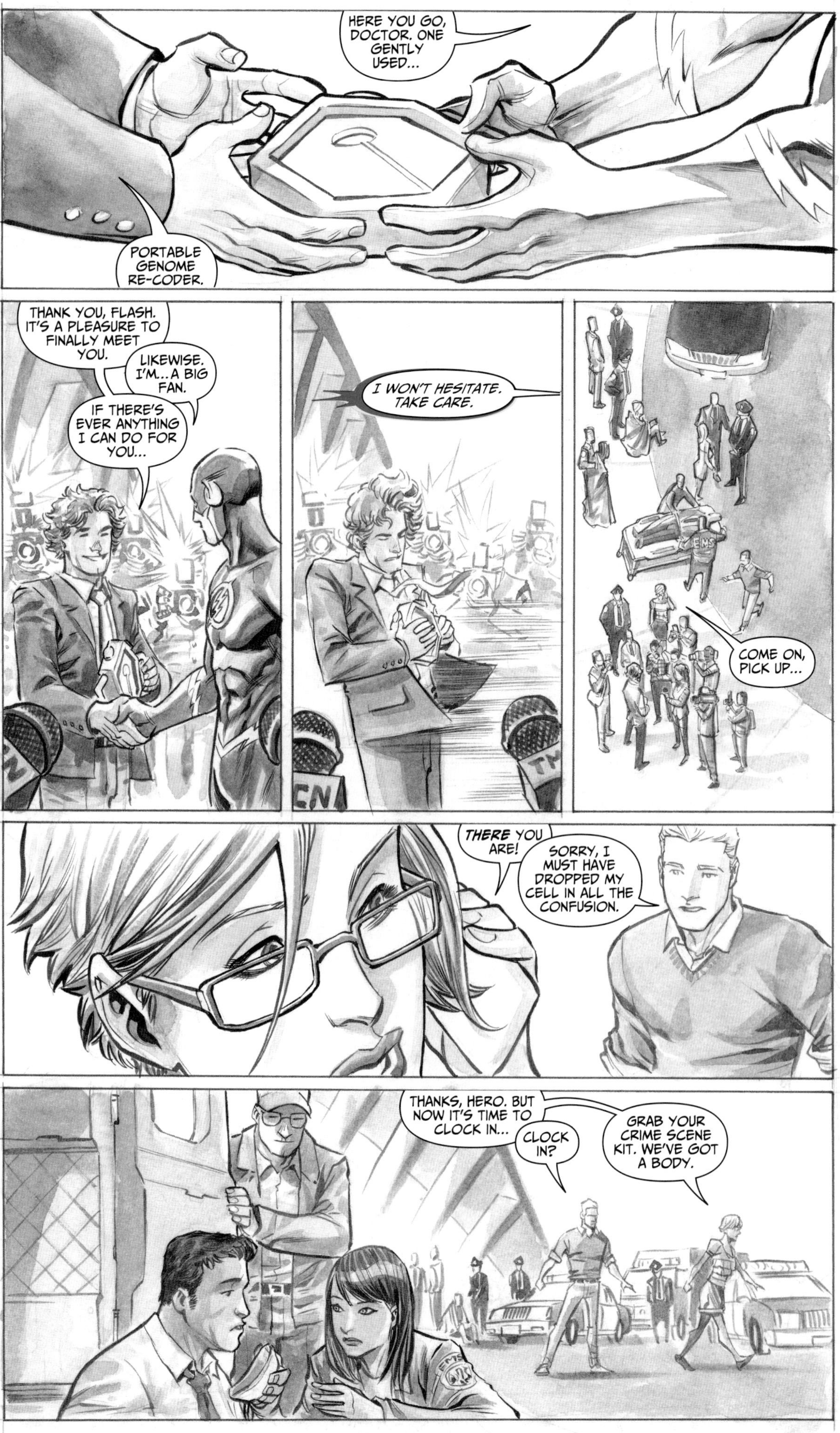
HERE YOU GO, DOCTOR. ONE GENTLY USED...
PORTABLE GENOME RE-CODER.
THANK YOU, FLASH. IT'S A PLEASURE TO FINALLY MEET YOU.
LIKEWISE. I'M...A BIG FAN.
IF THERE'S EVER ANYTHING I CAN DO FOR YOU...
I WON'T HESITATE. TAKE CARE.
COME ON, PICK UP...
THERE YOU ARE!
SORRY, I MUST HAVE DROPPED MY CELL IN ALL THE CONFUSION.
THANKS, HERO. BUT NOW IT'S TIME TO CLOCK IN...
CLOCK IN?
GRAB YOUR CRIME SCENE KIT. WE'VE GOT A BODY.

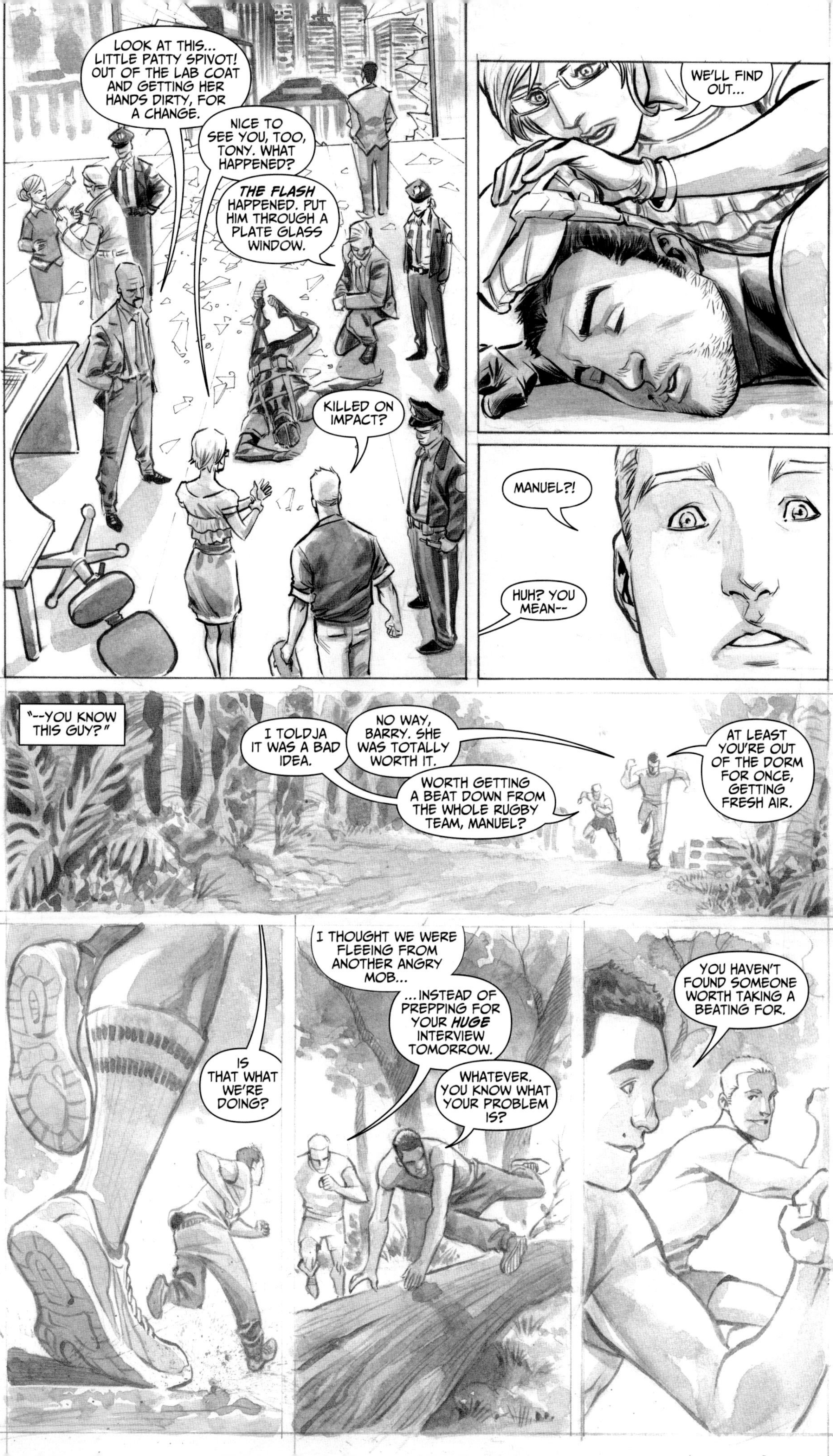

LOOK AT THIS... LITTLE PATTY SPIVOT! OUT OF THE LAB COAT AND GETTING HER HANDS DIRTY, FOR A CHANGE.
NICE TO SEE YOU, TOO, TONY. WHAT HAPPENED?
THE FLASH HAPPENED. PUT HIM THROUGH A PLATE GLASS WINDOW.
KILLED ON IMPACT?
WE'LL FIND OUT...
MANUEL?!
HUH? YOU MEAN--
"--YOU KNOW THIS GUY?"
I TOLDJA IT WAS A BAD IDEA.
NO WAY, BARRY. SHE WAS TOTALLY WORTH IT.
WORTH GETTING A BEAT DOWN FROM THE WHOLE RUGBY TEAM, MANUEL?
AT LEAST YOU'RE OUT OF THE DORM FOR ONCE, GETTING FRESH AIR.
IS THAT WHAT WE'RE DOING?
I THOUGHT WE WERE FLEEING FROM ANOTHER ANGRY MOB...
...INSTEAD OF PREPPING FOR YOUR HUGE INTERVIEW TOMORROW.
WHATEVER. YOU KNOW WHAT YOUR PROBLEM IS?
YOU HAVEN'T FOUND SOMEONE WORTH TAKING A BEATING FOR.

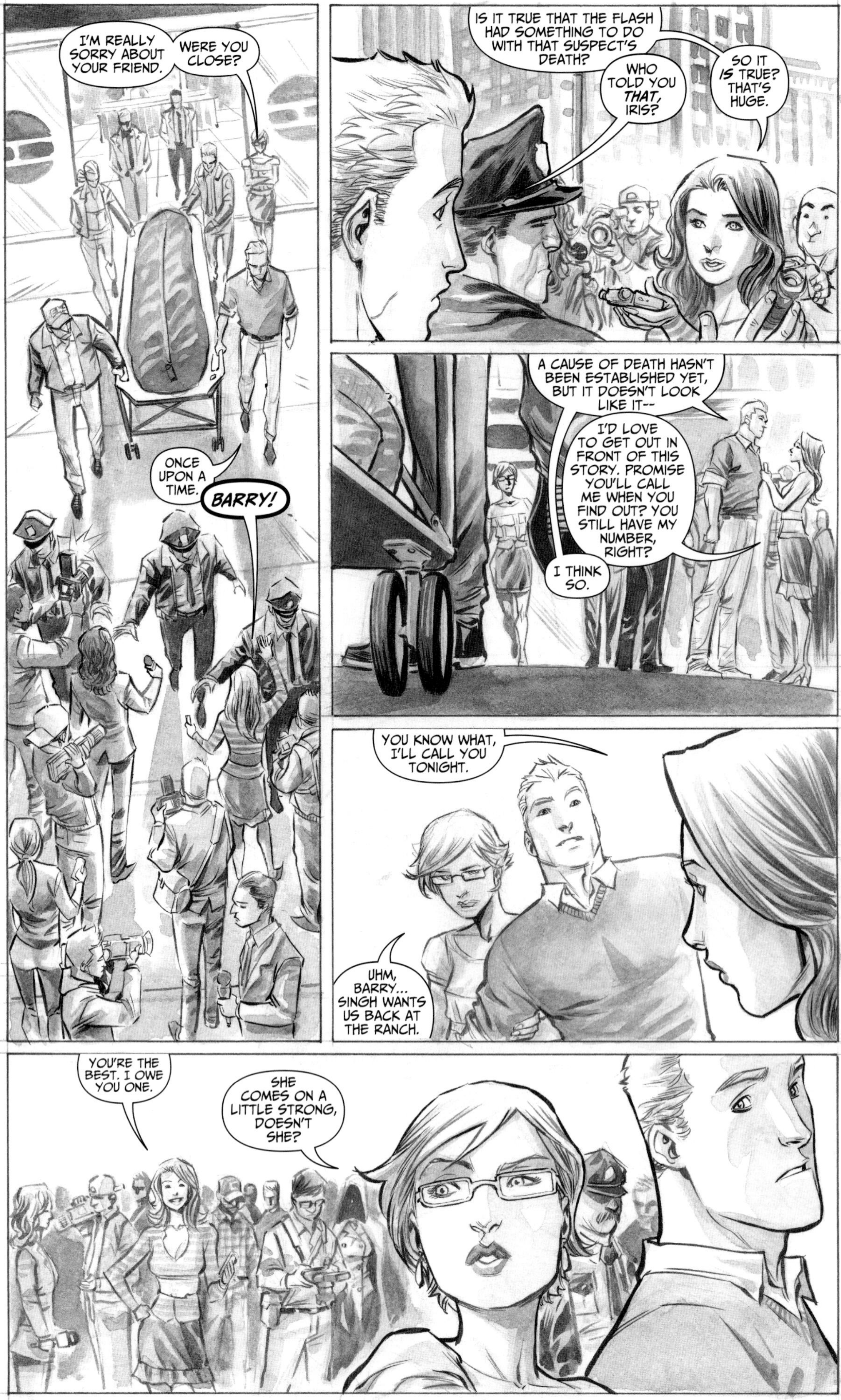
I'M REALLY SORRY ABOUT YOUR FRIEND.
WERE YOU CLOSE?
ONCE UPON A TIME.
BARRY!
IS IT TRUE THAT THE FLASH HAD SOMETHING TO DO WITH THAT SUSPECT'S DEATH?
WHO TOLD YOU THAT, IRIS?
SO IT IS TRUE? THAT'S HUGE.
A CAUSE OF DEATH HASN'T BEEN ESTABLISHED YET, BUT IT DOESN'T LOOK LIKE IT--
I'D LOVE TO GET OUT IN FRONT OF THIS STORY. PROMISE YOU'LL CALL ME WHEN YOU FIND OUT? YOU STILL HAVE MY NUMBER, RIGHT?
I THINK SO.
YOU KNOW WHAT, I'LL CALL YOU TONIGHT.
UHM, BARRY... SINGH WANTS US BACK AT THE RANCH.
YOU'RE THE BEST. I OWE YOU ONE.
SHE COMES ON A LITTLE STRONG, DOESN'T SHE?

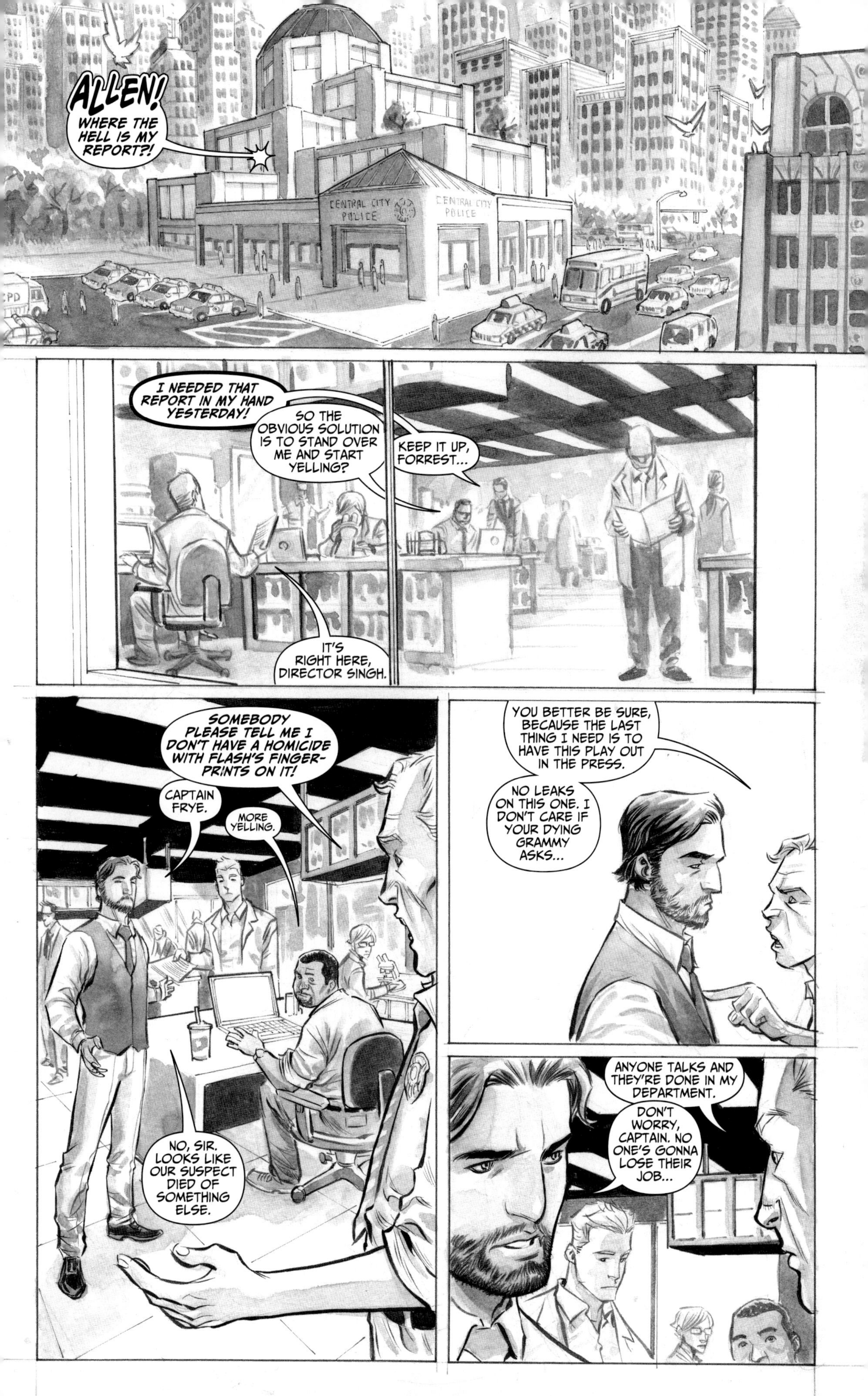
ALLEN!
WHERE THE HELL IS MY REPORT?!
CENTRAL CITY POLICE
CENTRAL CITY POLICE
I NEEDED THAT REPORT IN MY HAND YESTERDAY!
SO THE OBVIOUS SOLUTION IS TO STAND OVER ME AND START YELLING?
KEEP IT UP, FORREST...
IT'S RIGHT HERE, DIRECTOR SINGH.
SOMEBODY PLEASE TELL ME I DON'T HAVE A HOMICIDE WITH FLASH'S FINGER-PRINTS ON IT!
CAPTAIN FRYE.
MORE YELLING.
NO, SIR. LOOKS LIKE OUR SUSPECT DIED OF SOMETHING ELSE.
YOU BETTER BE SURE, BECAUSE THE LAST THING I NEED IS TO HAVE THIS PLAY OUT IN THE PRESS.
NO LEAKS ON THIS ONE. I DON'T CARE IF YOUR DYING GRAMMY ASKS...
ANYONE TALKS AND THEY'RE DONE IN MY DEPARTMENT.
DON'T WORRY, CAPTAIN. NO ONE'S GONNA LOSE THEIR JOB...

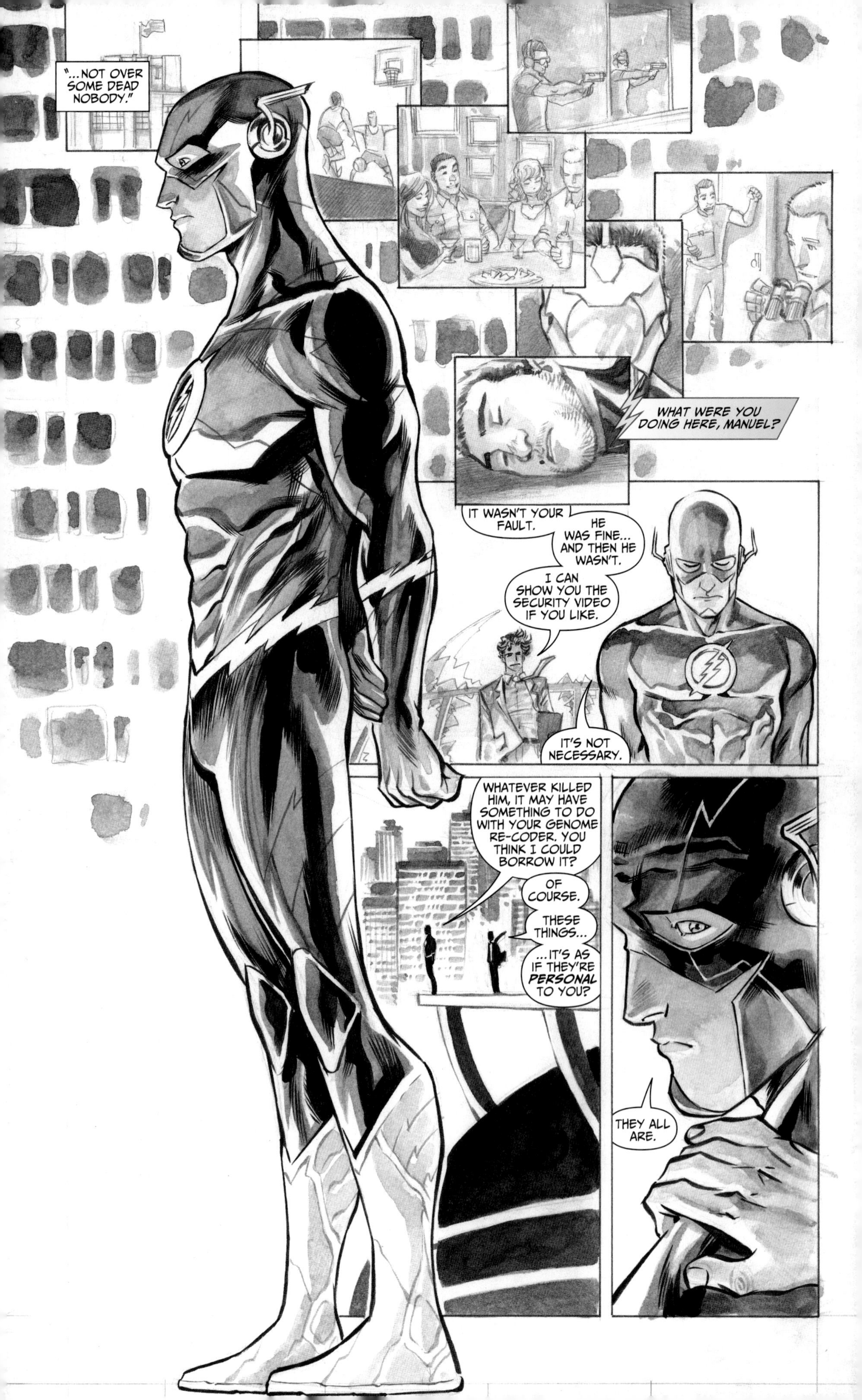
"...NOT OVER SOME DEAD NOBODY."
WHAT WERE YOU DOING HERE, MANUEL?
IT WASN'T YOUR FAULT.
HE WAS FINE... AND THEN HE WASN'T.
I CAN SHOW YOU THE SECURITY VIDEO IF YOU LIKE.
IT'S NOT NECESSARY.
WHATEVER KILLED HIM, IT MAY HAVE SOMETHING TO DO WITH YOUR GENOME RE-CODER. YOU THINK I COULD BORROW IT?
OF COURSE.
THESE THINGS...
...IT'S AS IF THEY'RE PERSONAL TO YOU?
THEY ALL ARE.

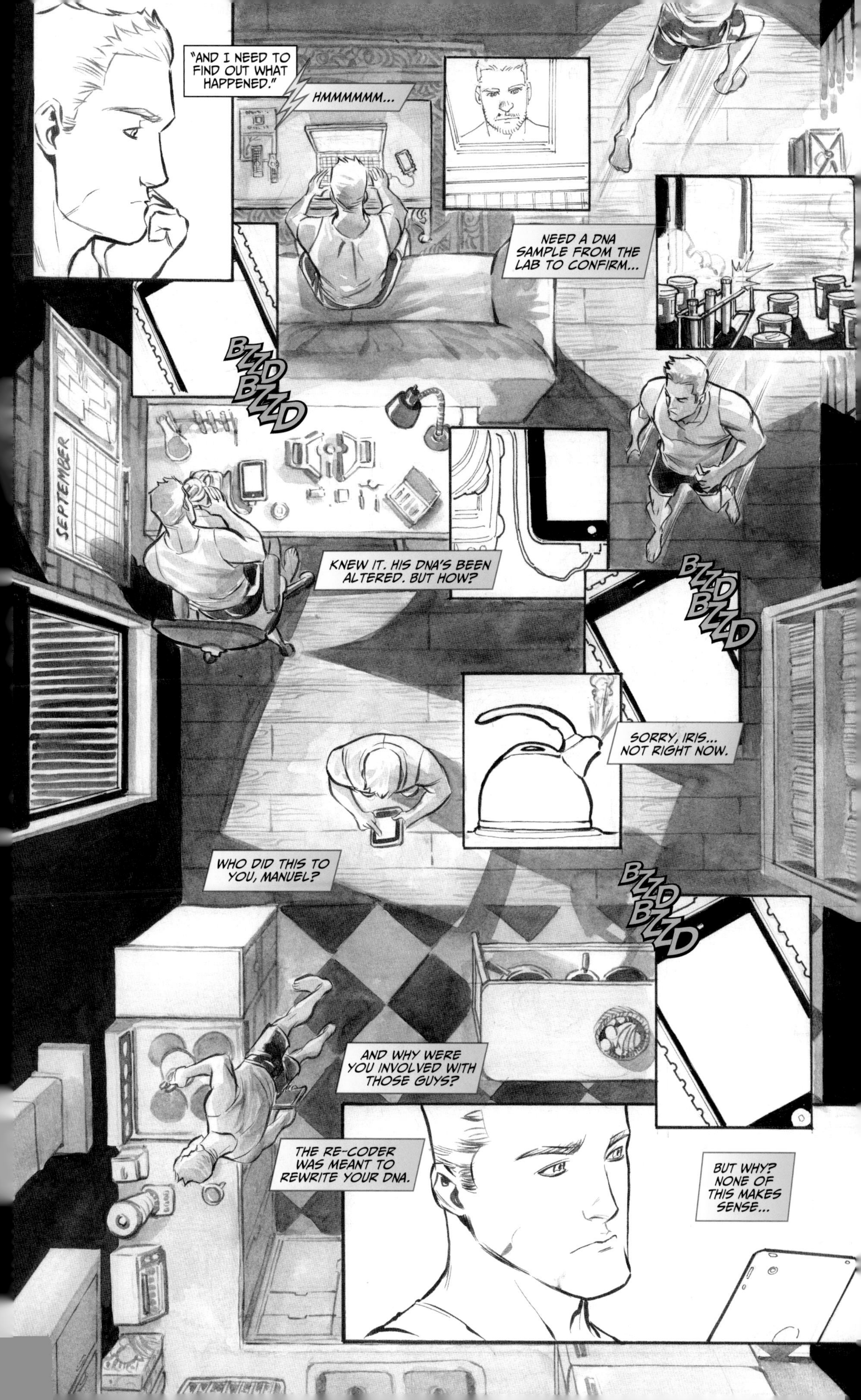
"AND I NEED TO FIND OUT WHAT HAPPENED."
HMMMMMM...
NEED A DNA SAMPLE FROM THE LAB TO CONFIRM...
BZZD BZZD
KNEW IT. HIS DNA'S BEEN ALTERED. BUT HOW?
SEPTEMBER
BZZD BZZD
SORRY, IRIS... NOT RIGHT NOW.
WHO DID THIS TO YOU, MANUEL?
BZZD BZZD
AND WHY WERE YOU INVOLVED WITH THOSE GUYS?
THE RE-CODER WAS MEANT TO REWRITE YOUR DNA.
BUT WHY? NONE OF THIS MAKES SENSE...

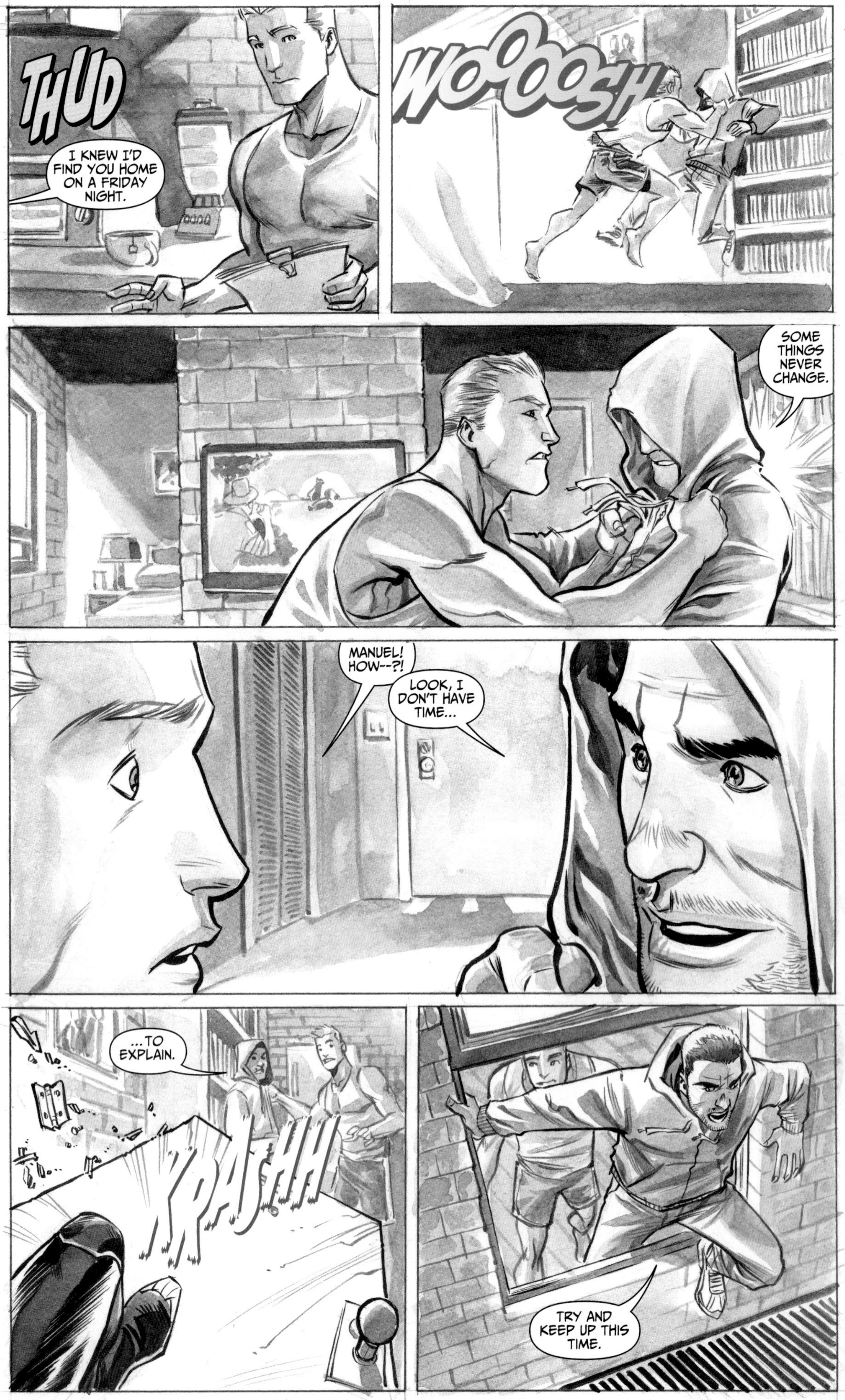
THUD
I KNEW I'D FIND YOU HOME ON A FRIDAY NIGHT.
WOOOOSH
SOME THINGS NEVER CHANGE.
MANUEL! HOW--?!
LOOK, I DON'T HAVE TIME...
...TO EXPLAIN.
KRASHH
TRY AND KEEP UP THIS TIME.

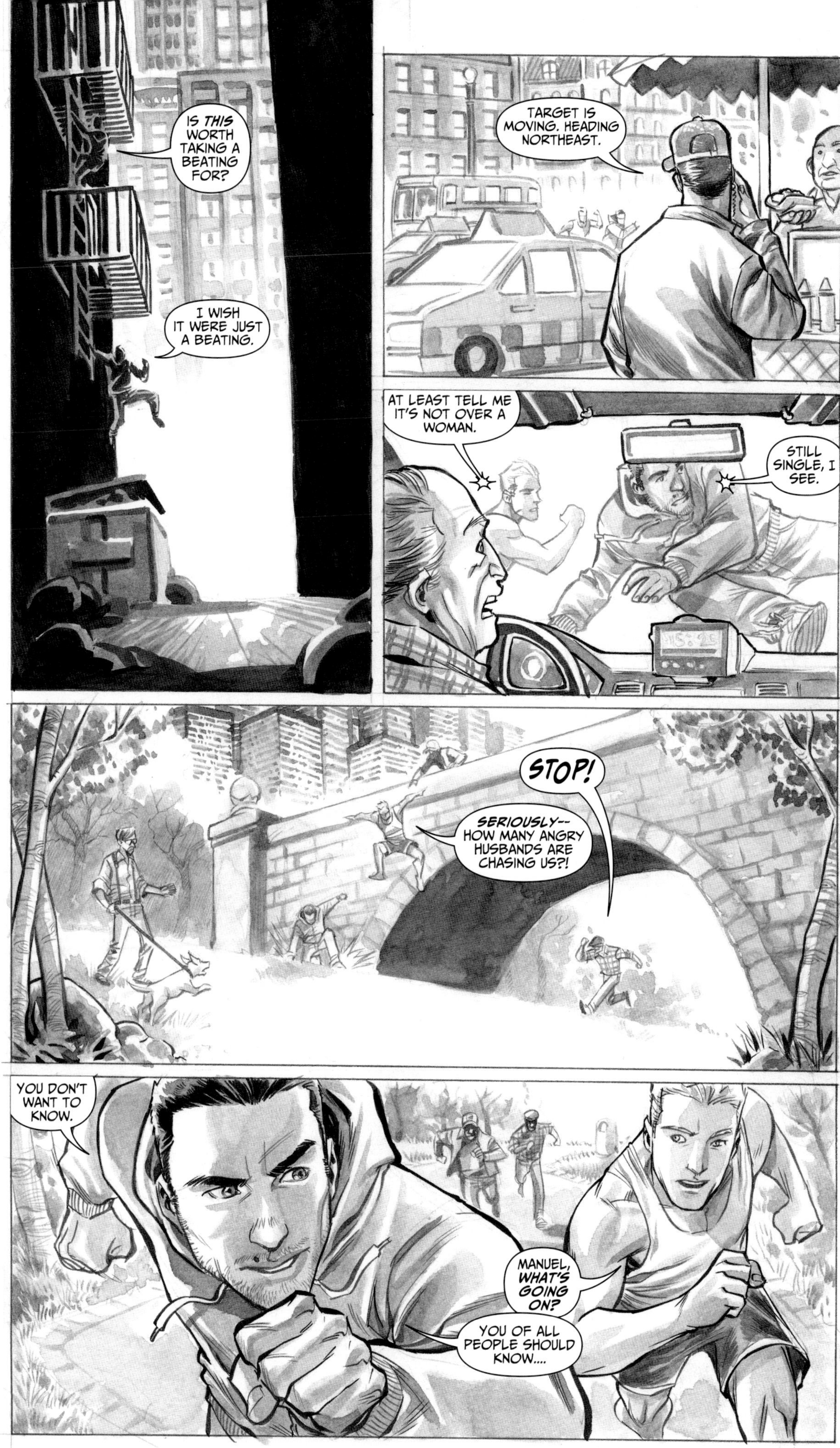
IS *THIS* WORTH TAKING A BEATING FOR?
I WISH IT WERE JUST A BEATING.
TARGET IS MOVING. HEADING NORTHEAST.
AT LEAST TELL ME IT'S NOT OVER A WOMAN.
STILL SINGLE, I SEE.
STOP!
SERIOUSLY-- HOW MANY ANGRY HUSBANDS ARE CHASING US?!
YOU DON'T WANT TO KNOW.
MANUEL, *WHAT'S GOING ON?*
YOU OF ALL PEOPLE SHOULD KNOW....

...WE'RE ALWAYS RUNNING FROM SOMETHING.

HE'S HALF RIGHT.

MY MOM ONCE TOLD ME THAT "LIFE IS LOCOMOTION..."

"IF YOU'RE NOT MOVING, YOU'RE NOT LIVING.

"BUT THERE COMES A TIME WHEN YOU'VE GOT TO STOP RUNNING *AWAY* FROM THINGS...

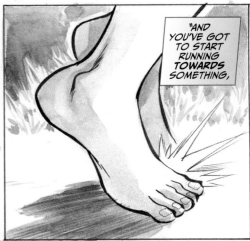

"AND YOU'VE GOT TO START RUNNING *TOWARDS* SOMETHING,

"YOU'VE GOT TO FORGE AHEAD.

BARRY?!

"KEEP MOVING."

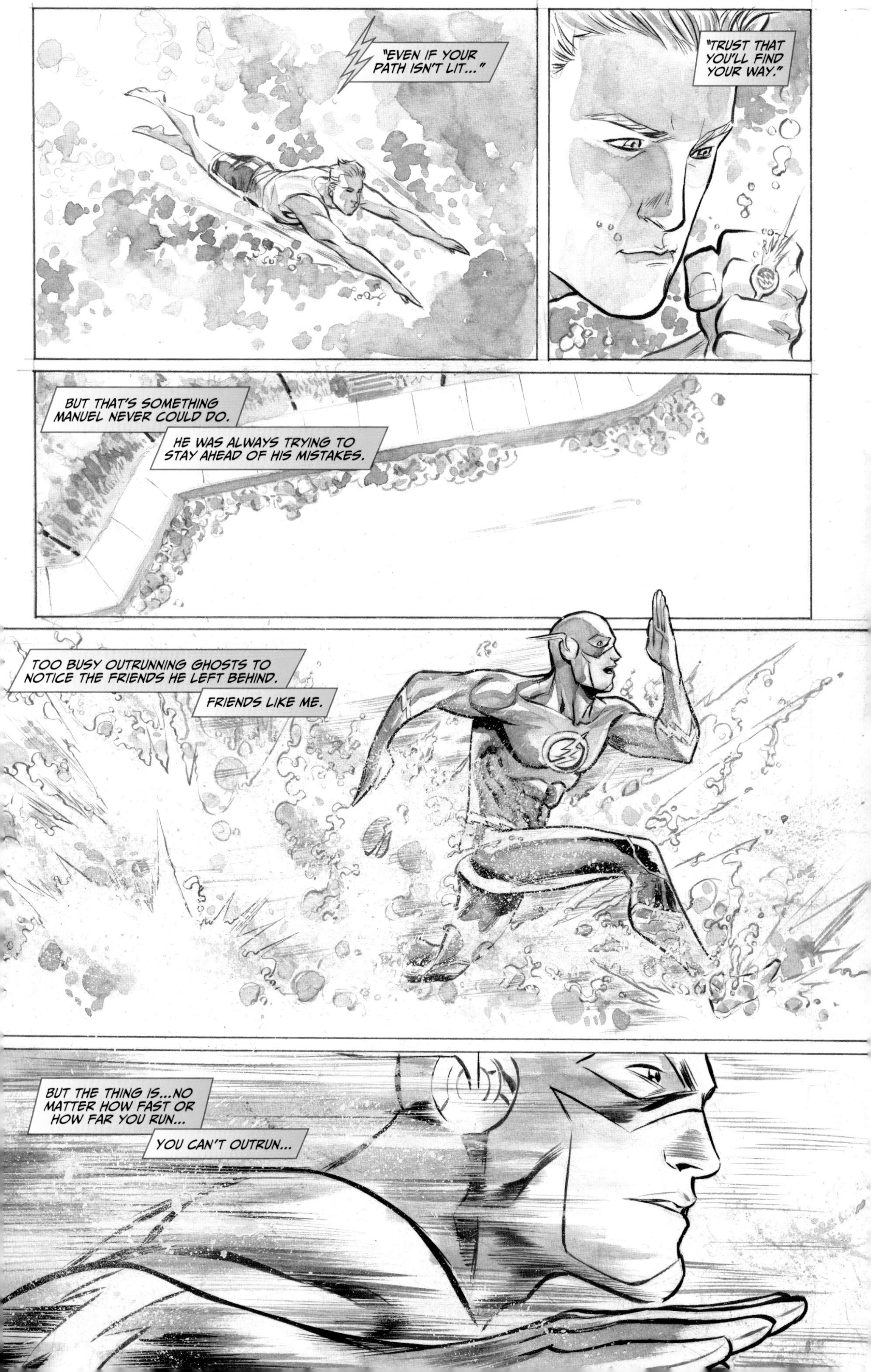
"EVEN IF YOUR PATH ISN'T LIT..."
"TRUST THAT YOU'LL FIND YOUR WAY."
BUT THAT'S SOMETHING MANUEL NEVER COULD DO.
HE WAS ALWAYS TRYING TO STAY AHEAD OF HIS MISTAKES.
TOO BUSY OUTRUNNING GHOSTS TO NOTICE THE FRIENDS HE LEFT BEHIND.
FRIENDS LIKE ME.
BUT THE THING IS...NO MATTER HOW FAST OR HOW FAR YOU RUN...
YOU CAN'T OUTRUN...

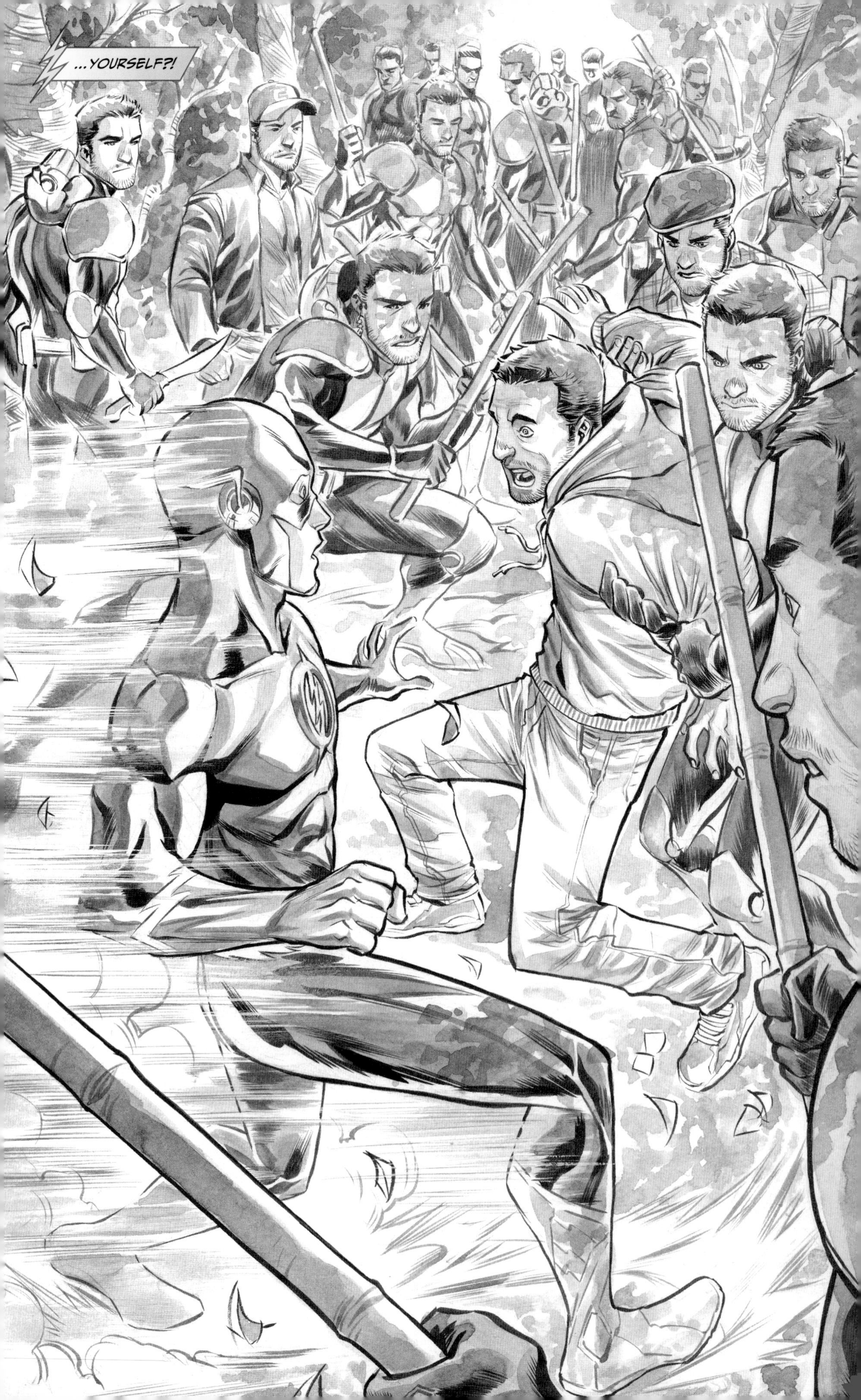
...YOURSELF?!

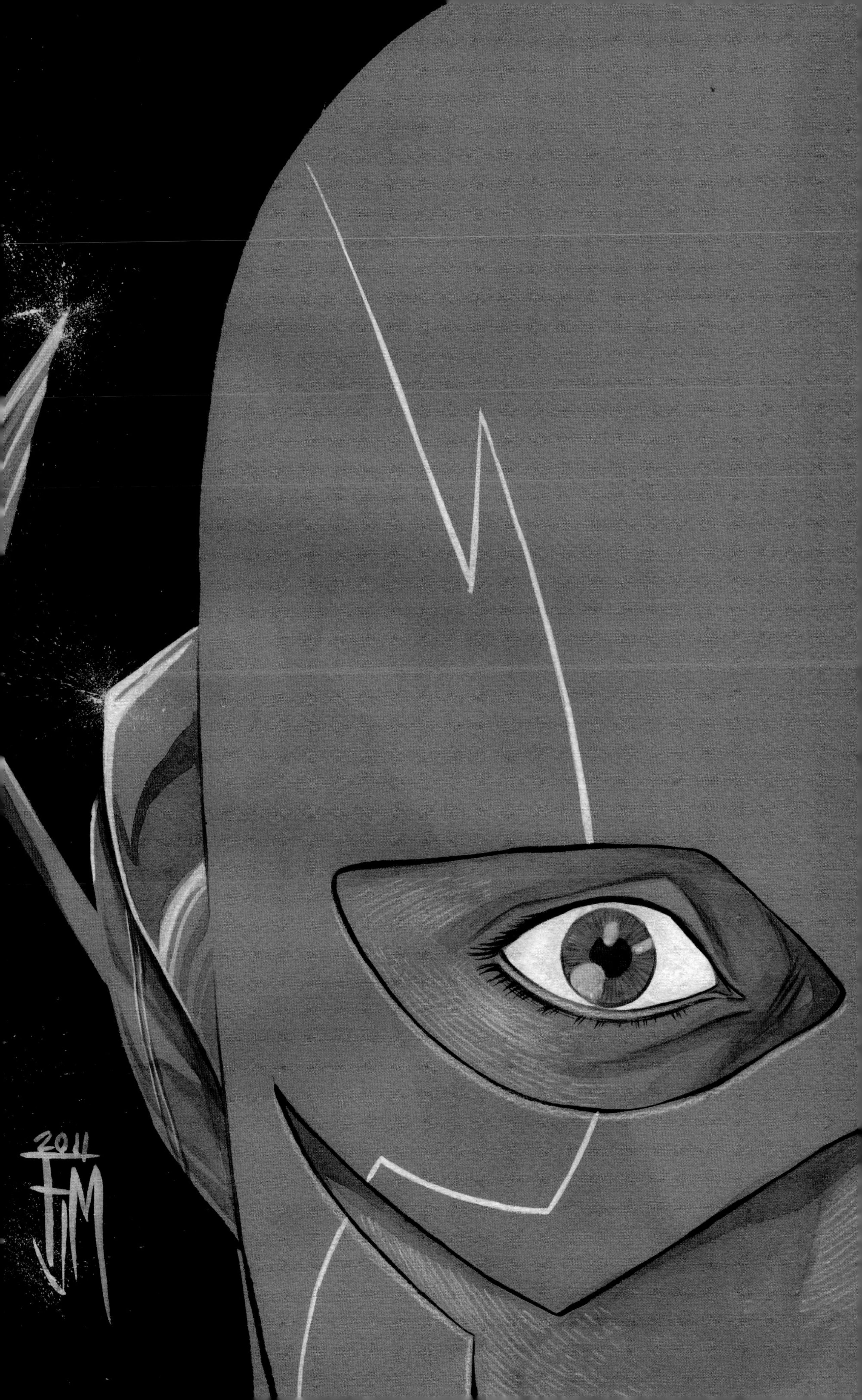
2011

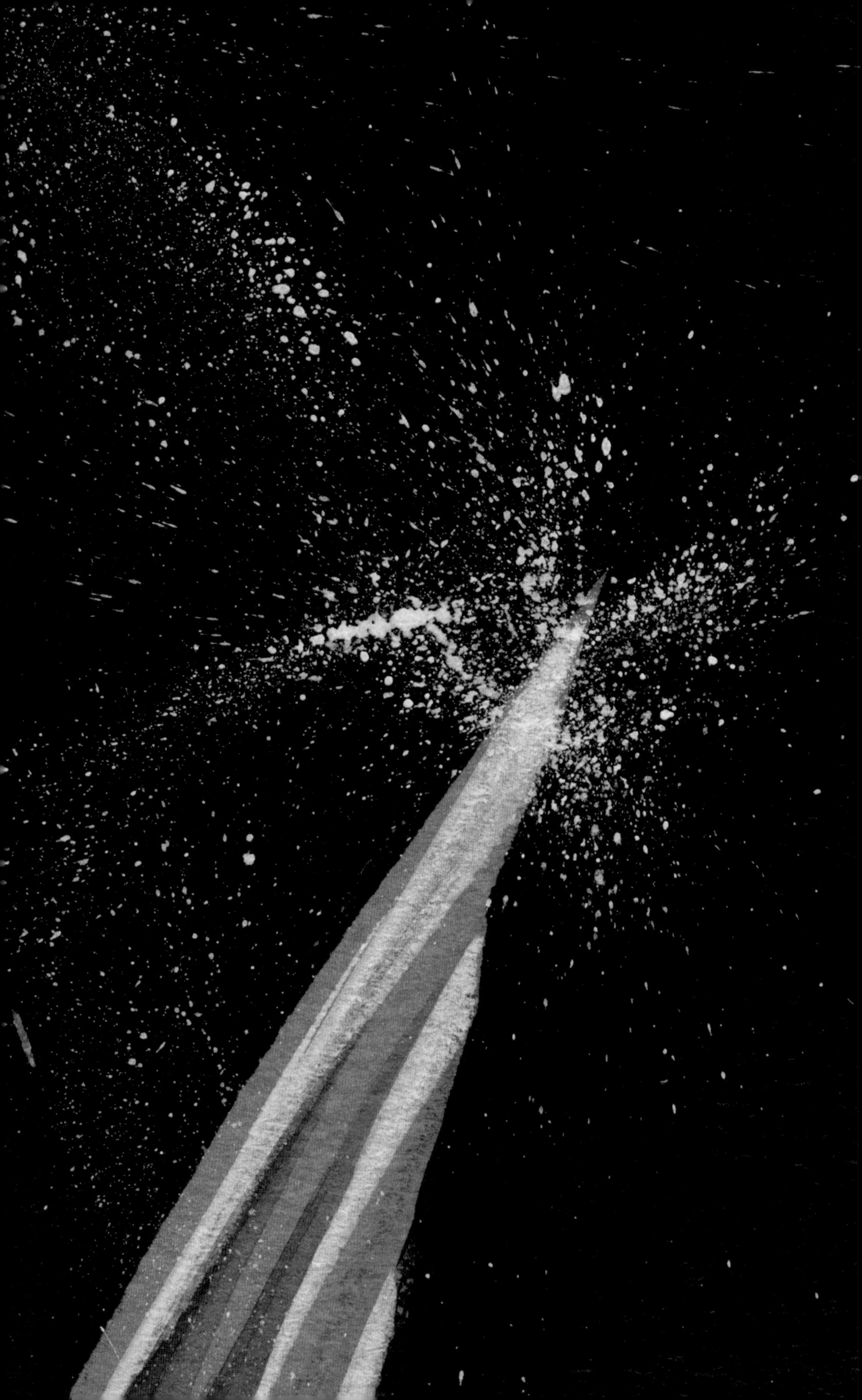

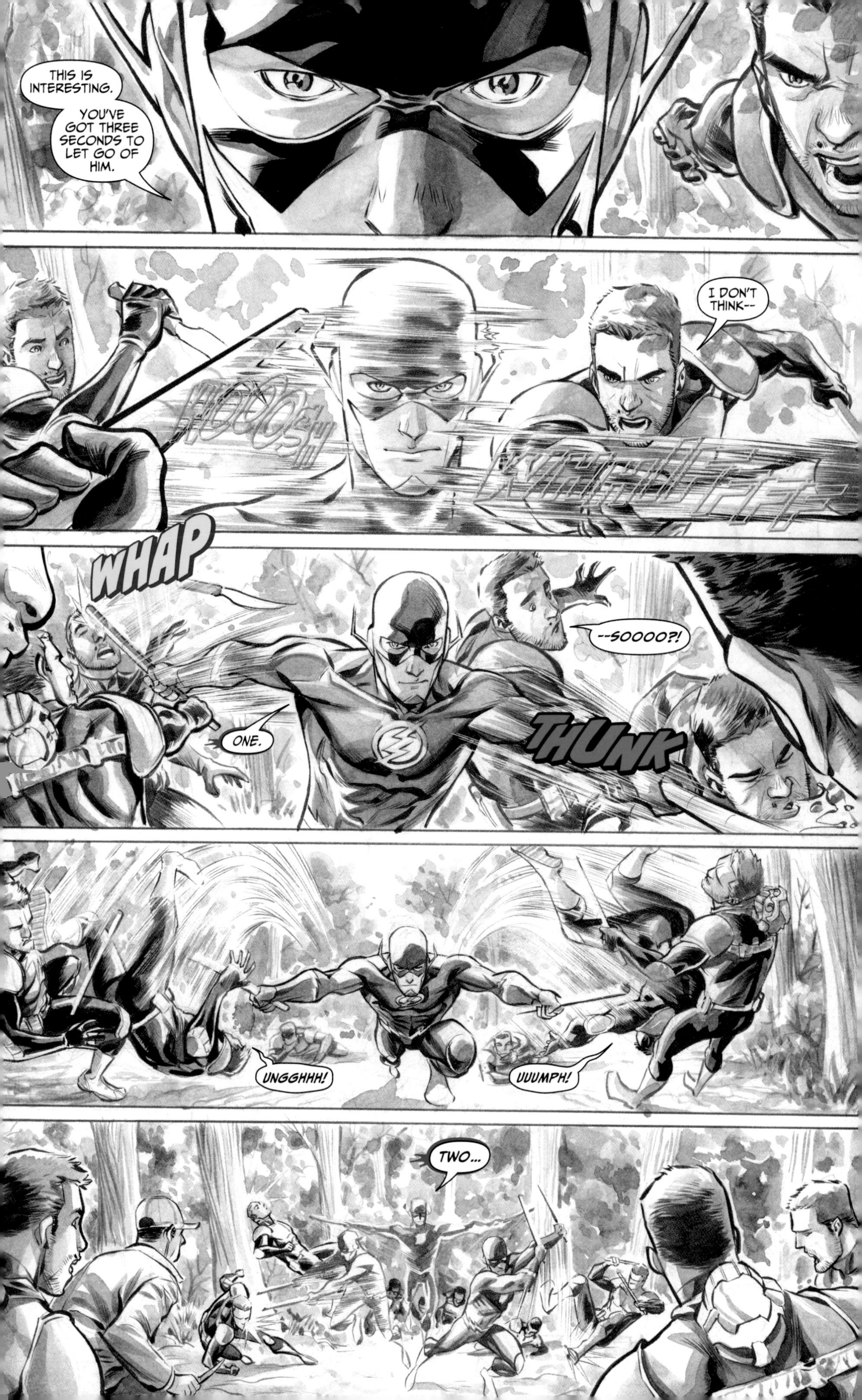
THIS IS INTERESTING.
YOU'VE GOT THREE SECONDS TO LET GO OF HIM.
I DON'T THINK--
WHAP
--SOOOO?!
ONE.
THUNK
UNGGHHH!
UUUMPH!
TWO...

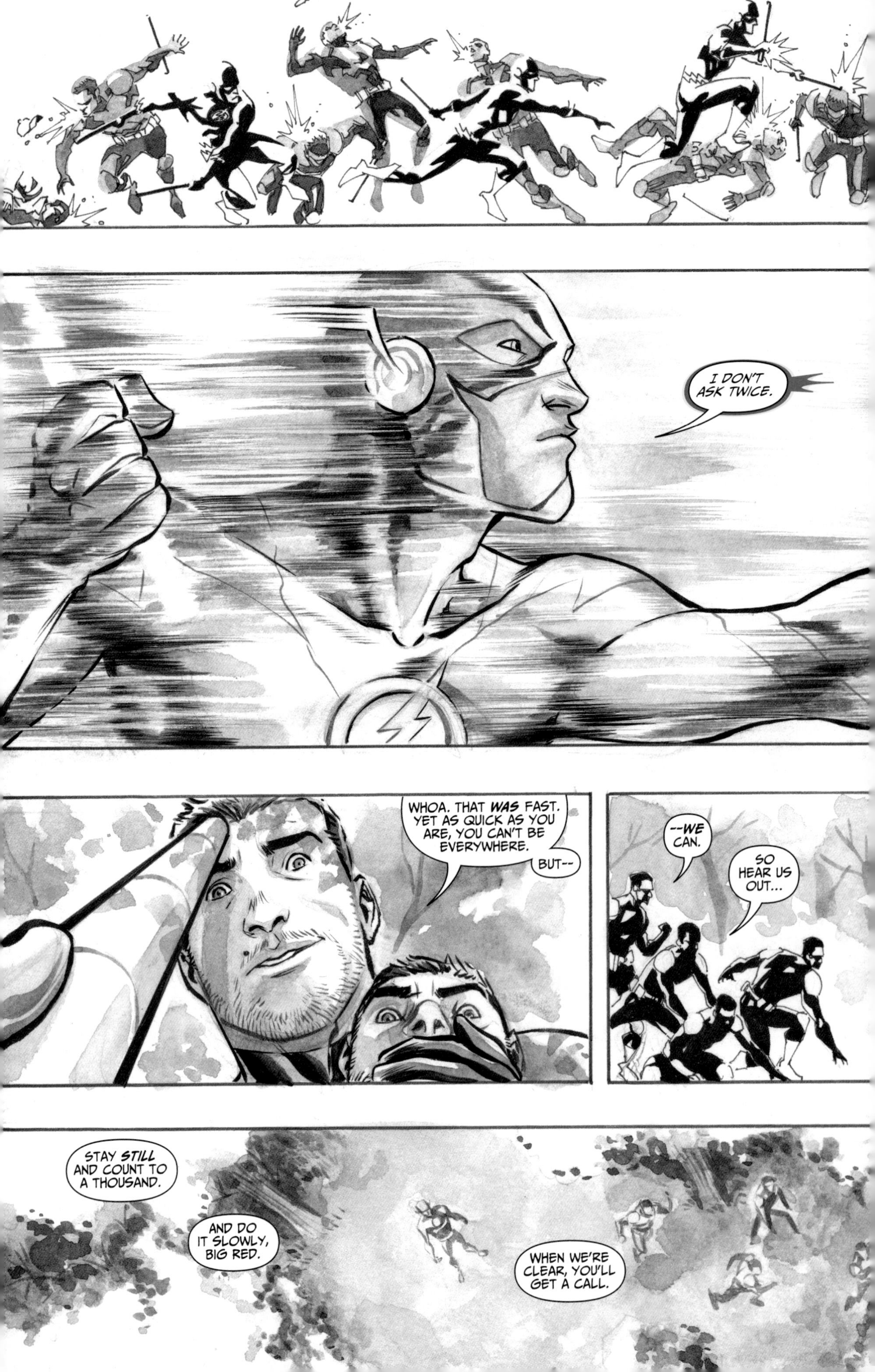
I DON'T ASK TWICE.
WHOA. THAT WAS FAST. YET AS QUICK AS YOU ARE, YOU CAN'T BE EVERYWHERE.
BUT--
--WE CAN.
SO HEAR US OUT...
STAY STILL AND COUNT TO A THOUSAND.
AND DO IT SLOWLY, BIG RED.
WHEN WE'RE CLEAR, YOU'LL GET A CALL.

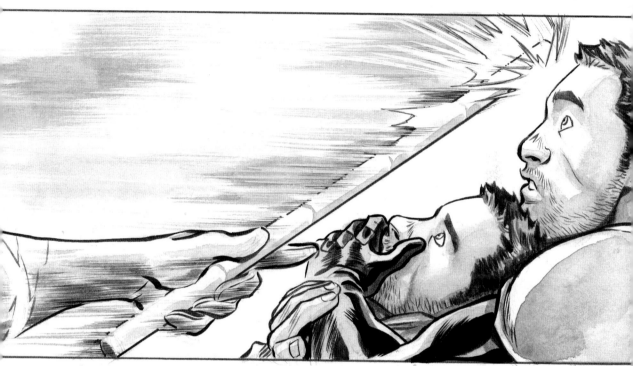

YOU KNOW THE IDIOT THAT DROWNED...?

WE GOT HIS LADY FRIEND.

IRIS WEST?

RIGHT. AND SINCE YOU LIKE COUNTING SO MUCH...

AND CUTIE-PIE GETS TO LIVE.

ONE MORE THING. FORGET ABOUT US. MANUEL LAGO IS NOT WORTH YOUR TROUBLE.

LEAVE HIM TO MOB RULE.

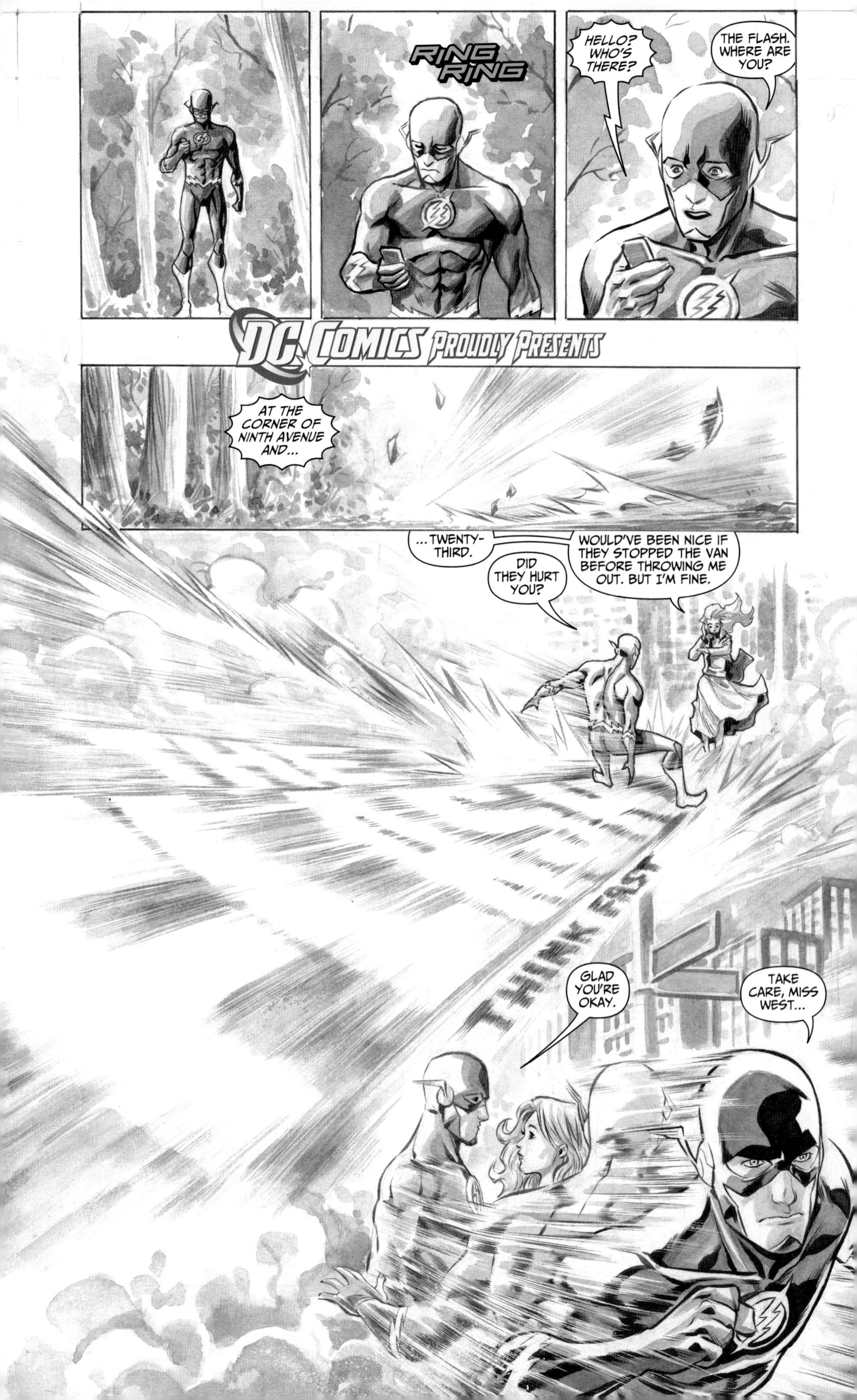
RING RING
HELLO? WHO'S THERE?
THE FLASH. WHERE ARE YOU?
DC COMICS PROUDLY PRESENTS
AT THE CORNER OF NINTH AVENUE AND...
...TWENTY-THIRD.
WOULD'VE BEEN NICE IF THEY STOPPED THE VAN BEFORE THROWING ME OUT. BUT I'M FINE.
DID THEY HURT YOU?
THINK FAST
GLAD YOU'RE OKAY.
TAKE CARE, MISS WEST...

"...I'VE GOTTA SEE A FRIEND."

NO, I'M NOT KIDDING.

I WANT YOU TO RUN ON IT.

I APPRECIATE YOUR HELP, DR. ELIAS. BUT THIS IS PRETTY SILLY.

PROGRESSIVE SCIENCE IS *ALWAYS* SKATING THE LINE OF ABSURDITY.

SO IS BEING IN TWO PLACES AT ONCE.

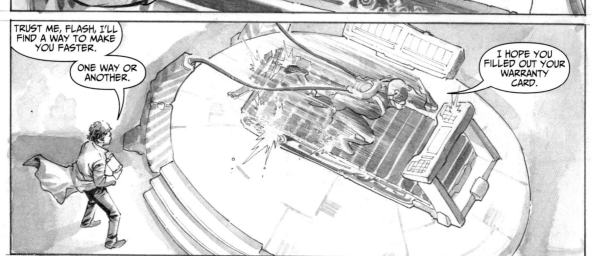

TRUST ME, FLASH, I'LL FIND A WAY TO MAKE YOU FASTER.

ONE WAY OR ANOTHER.

I HOPE YOU FILLED OUT YOUR WARRANTY CARD.

'CAUSE UNLESS THIS IS SOME SORTA "COSMIC" TREAD-MILL...

...ALL YOU'RE GONNA END UP WITH IS...

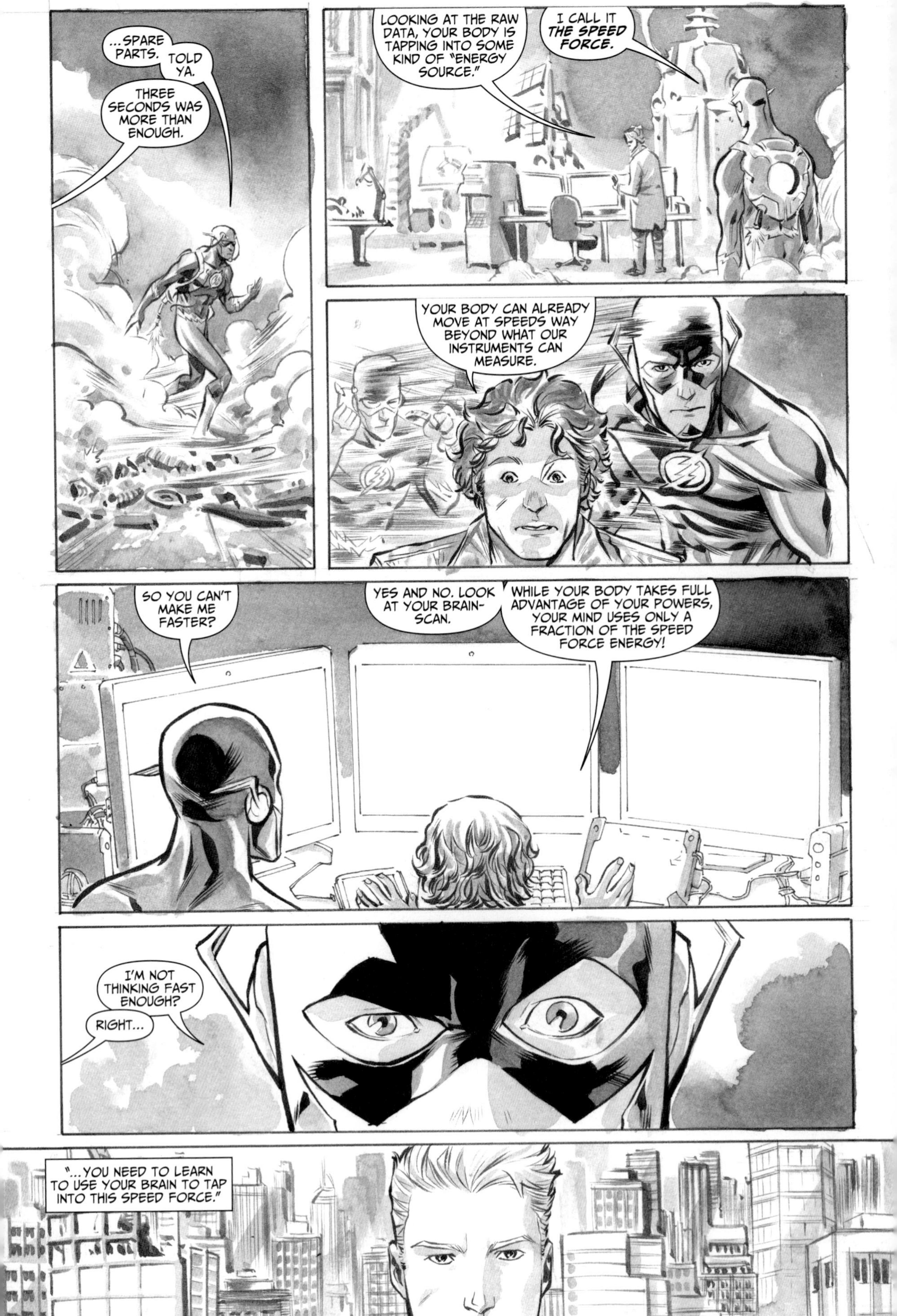
...SPARE PARTS.
TOLD YA.
THREE SECONDS WAS MORE THAN ENOUGH.
LOOKING AT THE RAW DATA, YOUR BODY IS TAPPING INTO SOME KIND OF "ENERGY SOURCE."
I CALL IT *THE SPEED FORCE.*
YOUR BODY CAN ALREADY MOVE AT SPEEDS WAY BEYOND WHAT OUR INSTRUMENTS CAN MEASURE.
SO YOU CAN'T MAKE ME FASTER?
YES AND NO. LOOK AT YOUR BRAIN-SCAN.
WHILE YOUR BODY TAKES FULL ADVANTAGE OF YOUR POWERS, YOUR MIND USES ONLY A FRACTION OF THE SPEED FORCE ENERGY!
I'M NOT THINKING FAST ENOUGH?
RIGHT...
"...YOU NEED TO LEARN TO USE YOUR BRAIN TO TAP INTO THIS SPEED FORCE."

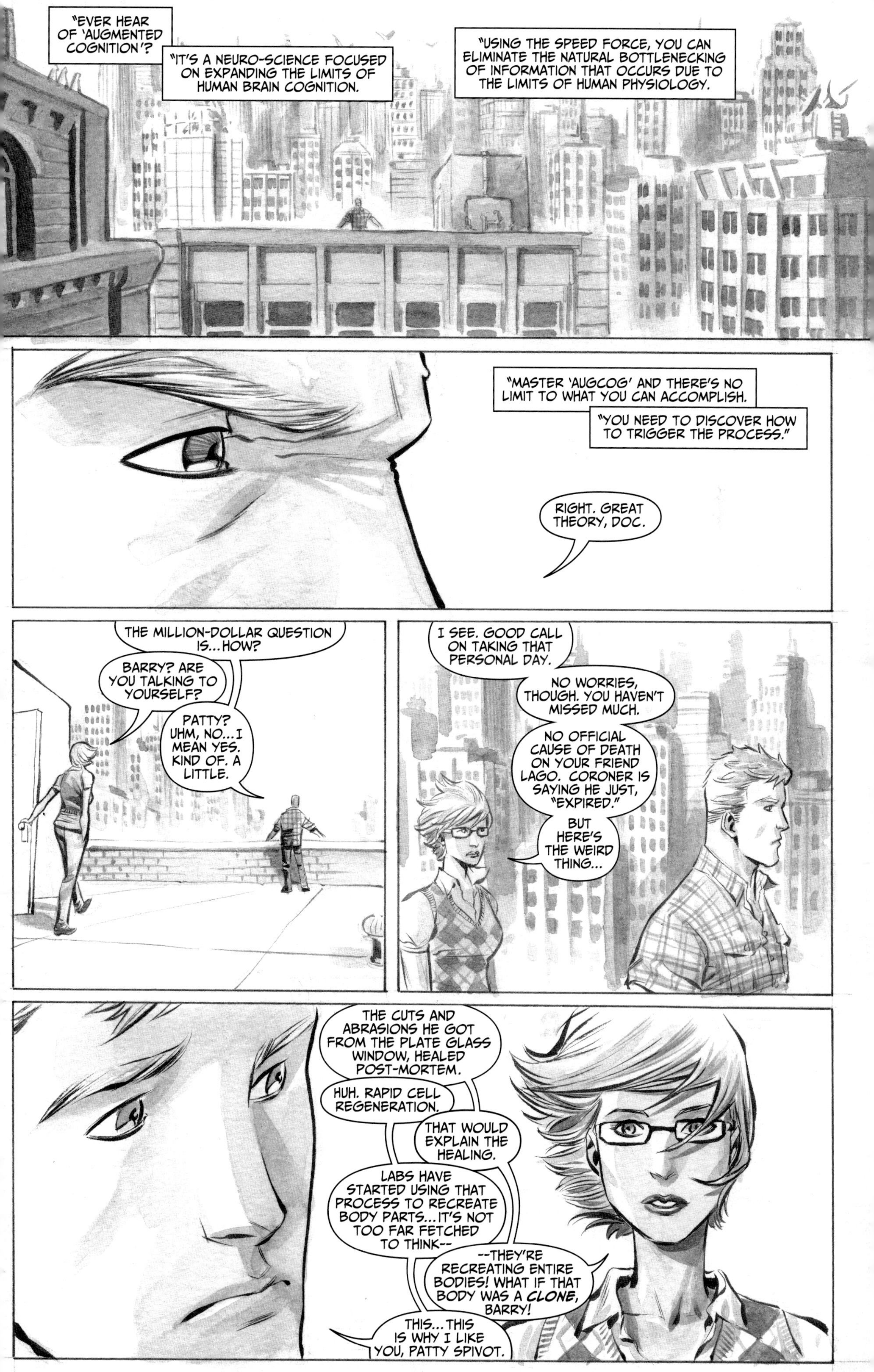
"EVER HEAR OF 'AUGMENTED COGNITION'?
"IT'S A NEURO-SCIENCE FOCUSED ON EXPANDING THE LIMITS OF HUMAN BRAIN COGNITION.
"USING THE SPEED FORCE, YOU CAN ELIMINATE THE NATURAL BOTTLENECKING OF INFORMATION THAT OCCURS DUE TO THE LIMITS OF HUMAN PHYSIOLOGY.
"MASTER 'AUGCOG' AND THERE'S NO LIMIT TO WHAT YOU CAN ACCOMPLISH.
"YOU NEED TO DISCOVER HOW TO TRIGGER THE PROCESS."
RIGHT. GREAT THEORY, DOC.
THE MILLION-DOLLAR QUESTION IS...HOW?
BARRY? ARE YOU TALKING TO YOURSELF?
PATTY? UHM, NO...I MEAN YES. KIND OF. A LITTLE.
I SEE. GOOD CALL ON TAKING THAT PERSONAL DAY.
NO WORRIES, THOUGH. YOU HAVEN'T MISSED MUCH.
NO OFFICIAL CAUSE OF DEATH ON YOUR FRIEND LAGO. CORONER IS SAYING HE JUST, "EXPIRED."
BUT HERE'S THE WEIRD THING...
THE CUTS AND ABRASIONS HE GOT FROM THE PLATE GLASS WINDOW, HEALED POST-MORTEM.
HUH. RAPID CELL REGENERATION.
THAT WOULD EXPLAIN THE HEALING.
LABS HAVE STARTED USING THAT PROCESS TO RECREATE BODY PARTS...IT'S NOT TOO FAR FETCHED TO THINK--
--THEY'RE RECREATING ENTIRE BODIES! WHAT IF THAT BODY WAS A *CLONE*, BARRY!
THIS...THIS IS WHY I LIKE YOU, PATTY SPIVOT.

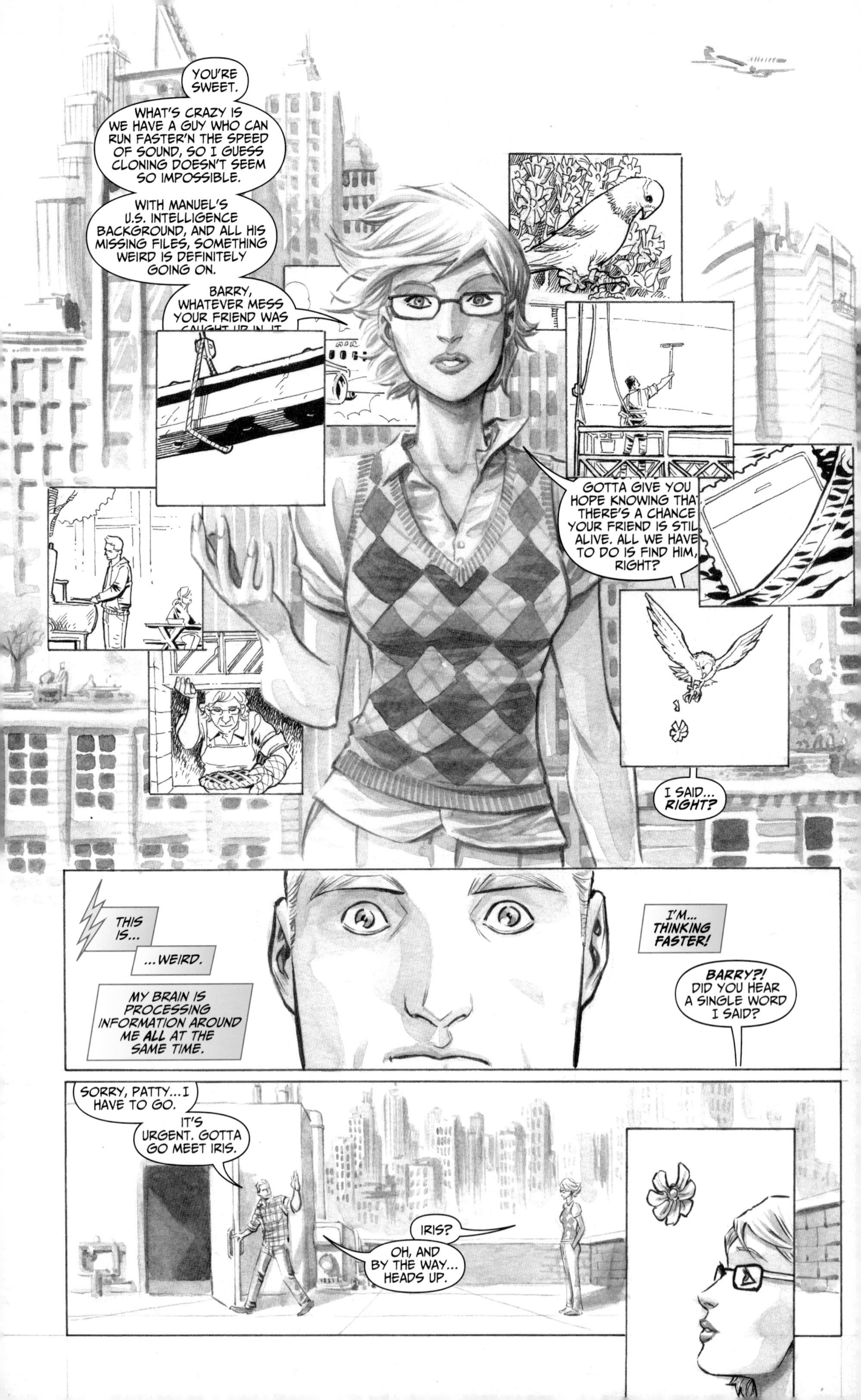
YOU'RE SWEET.
WHAT'S CRAZY IS WE HAVE A GUY WHO CAN RUN FASTER'N THE SPEED OF SOUND, SO I GUESS CLONING DOESN'T SEEM SO IMPOSSIBLE.
WITH MANUEL'S U.S. INTELLIGENCE BACKGROUND, AND ALL HIS MISSING FILES, SOMETHING WEIRD IS DEFINITELY GOING ON.
BARRY, WHATEVER MESS YOUR FRIEND WAS
GOTTA GIVE YOU HOPE KNOWING THAT THERE'S A CHANCE YOUR FRIEND IS STILL ALIVE. ALL WE HAVE TO DO IS FIND HIM, RIGHT?
I SAID... *RIGHT?*
THIS IS...
...*WEIRD.*
*MY BRAIN IS PROCESSING INFORMATION AROUND ME **ALL** AT THE SAME TIME.*
*I'M... **THINKING FASTER!***
BARRY?! DID YOU HEAR A SINGLE WORD I SAID?
SORRY, PATTY... I HAVE TO GO.
IT'S URGENT. GOTTA GO MEET IRIS.
IRIS?
OH, AND BY THE WAY... HEADS UP.

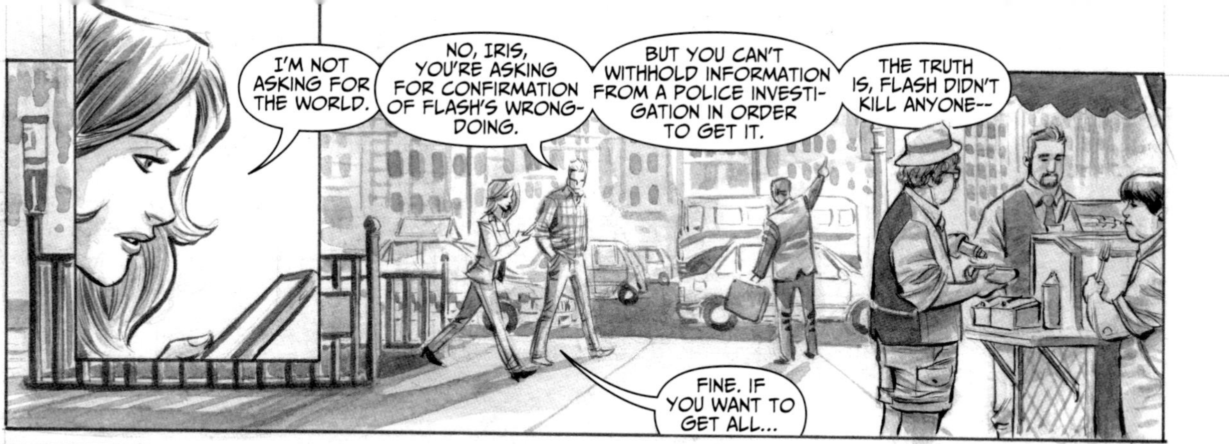
I'M NOT ASKING FOR THE WORLD.
NO, IRIS, YOU'RE ASKING FOR CONFIRMATION OF FLASH'S WRONG-DOING.
BUT YOU CAN'T WITHHOLD INFORMATION FROM A POLICE INVESTI-GATION IN ORDER TO GET IT.
THE TRUTH IS, FLASH DIDN'T KILL ANYONE--
FINE. IF YOU WANT TO GET ALL...

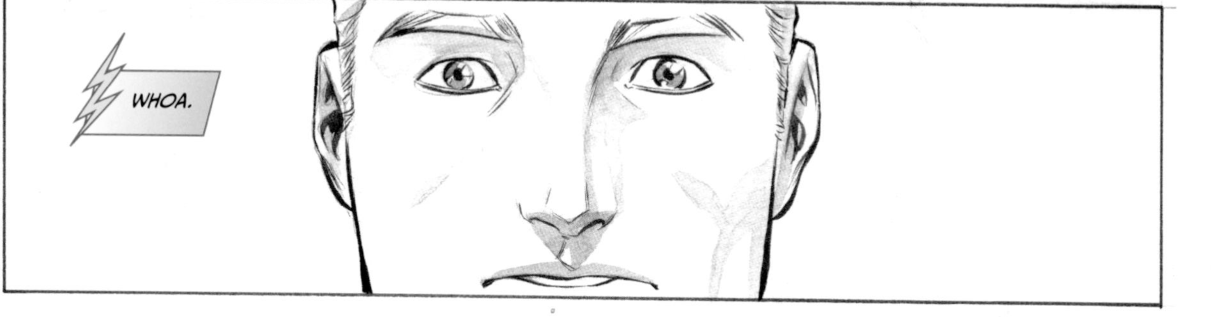
WHOA.

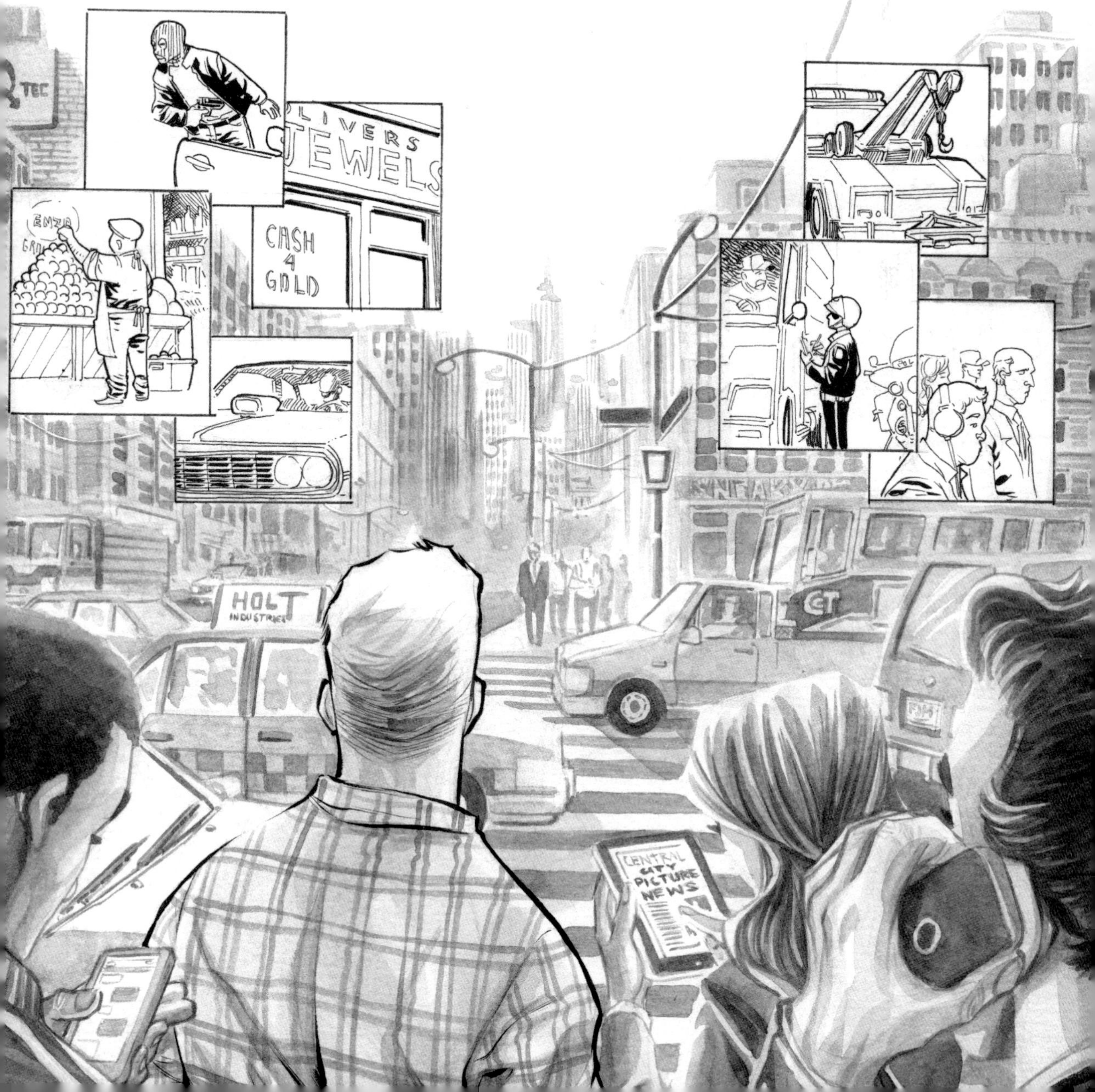
OLIVERS JEWELS
CASH 4 GOLD
HOLT
CENTRAL CITY PICTURE NEWS

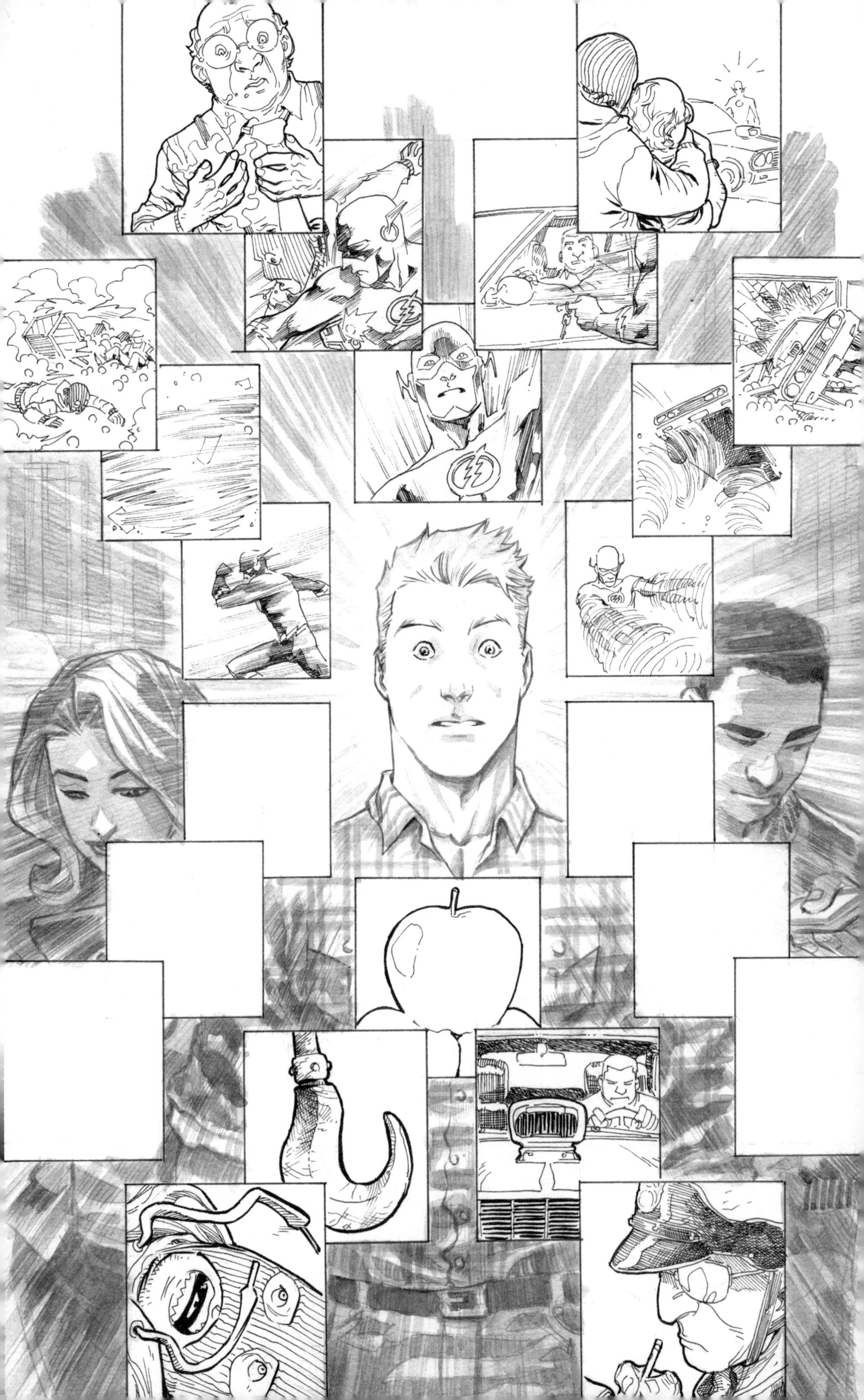

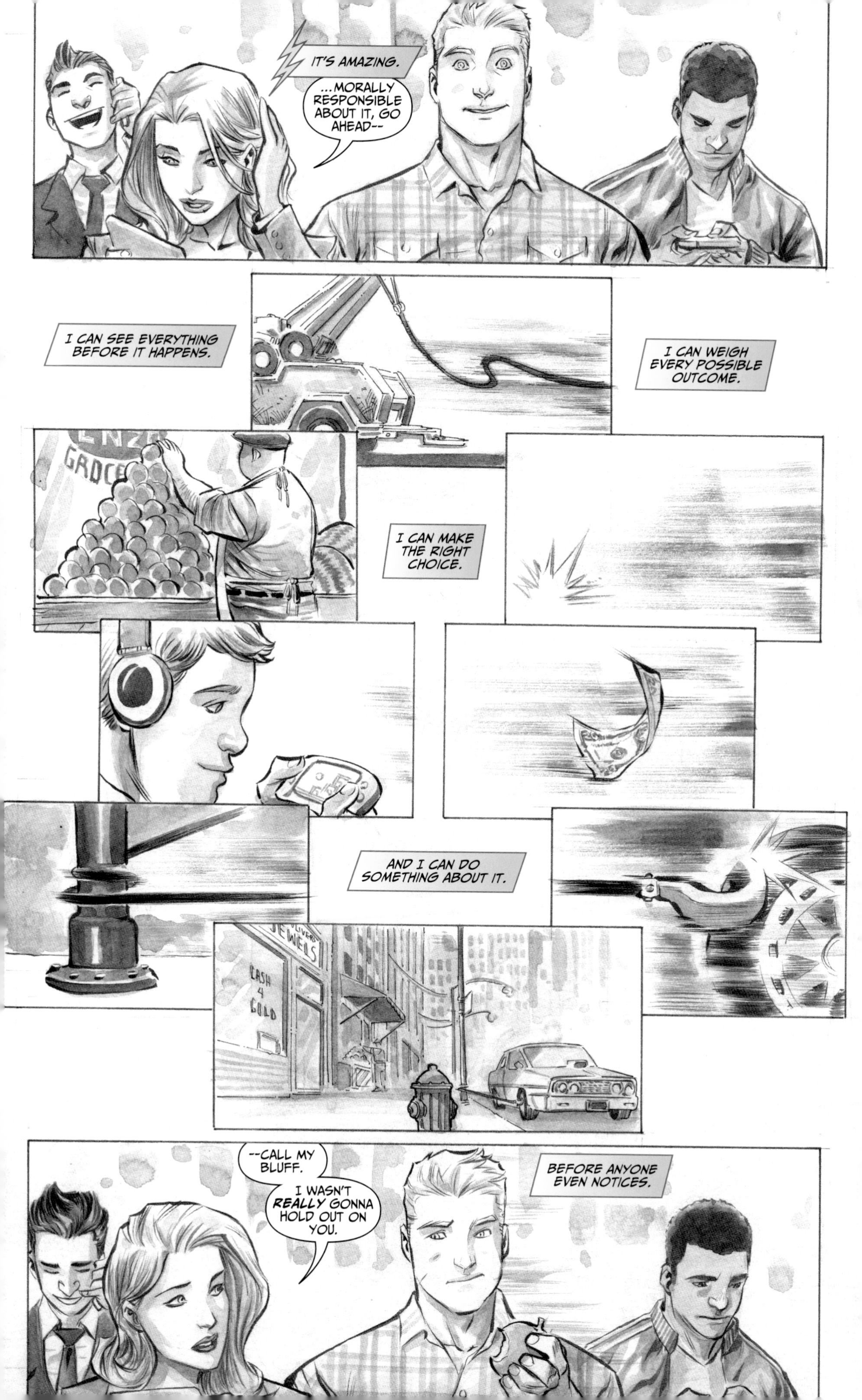
IT'S AMAZING.
...MORALLY RESPONSIBLE ABOUT IT, GO AHEAD--
I CAN SEE EVERYTHING BEFORE IT HAPPENS.
I CAN WEIGH EVERY POSSIBLE OUTCOME.
GROCE
I CAN MAKE THE RIGHT CHOICE.
AND I CAN DO SOMETHING ABOUT IT.
JEWELS
CASH 4 GOLD
--CALL MY BLUFF.
I WASN'T REALLY GONNA HOLD OUT ON YOU.
BEFORE ANYONE EVEN NOTICES.

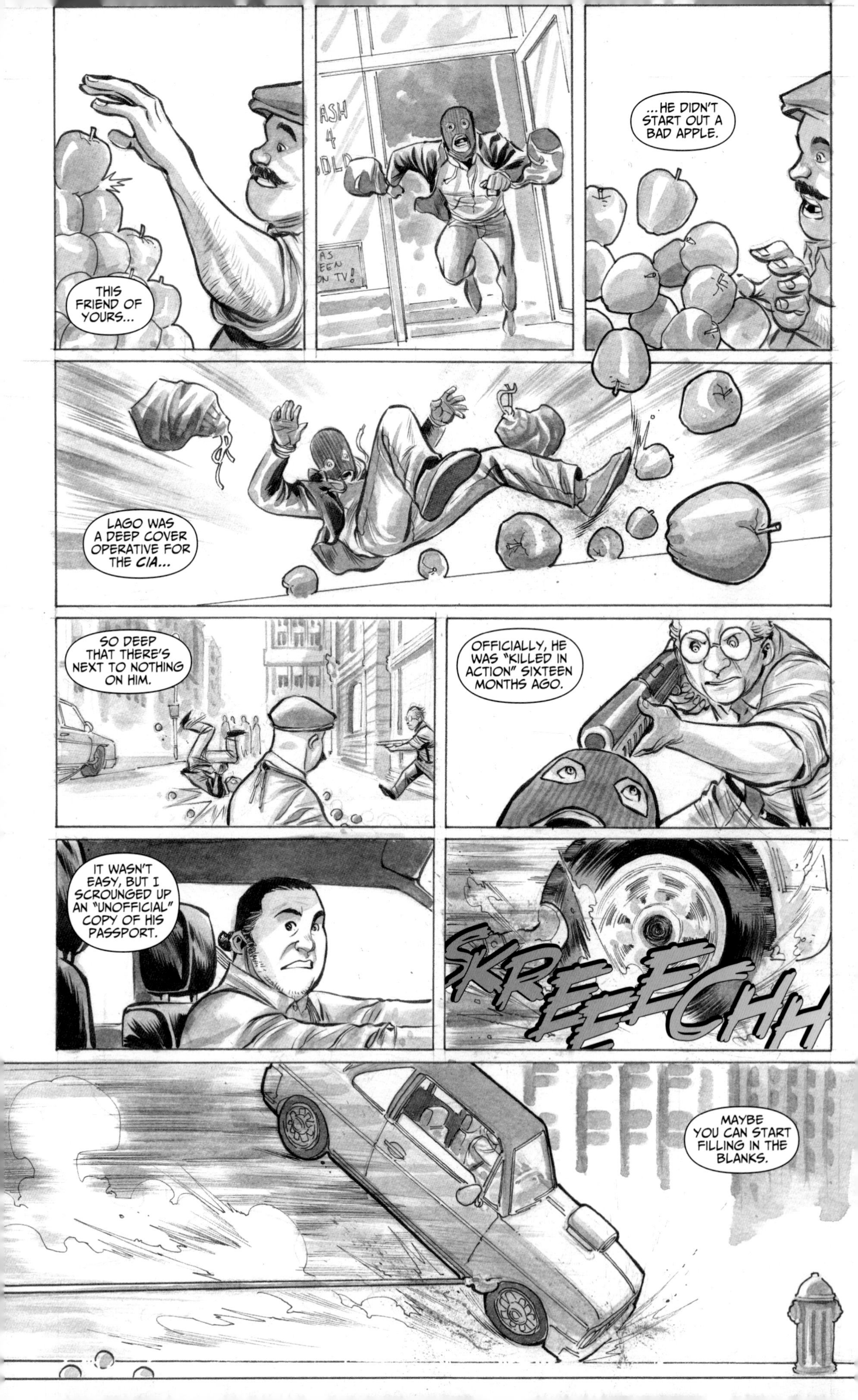
THIS FRIEND OF YOURS...
ASH 4 GOLD
AS SEEN ON TV!
...HE DIDN'T START OUT A BAD APPLE.
LAGO WAS A DEEP COVER OPERATIVE FOR THE *CIA*...
SO DEEP THAT THERE'S NEXT TO NOTHING ON HIM.
OFFICIALLY, HE WAS "KILLED IN ACTION" SIXTEEN MONTHS AGO.
IT WASN'T EASY, BUT I SCROUNGED UP AN "UNOFFICIAL" COPY OF HIS PASSPORT.
SKREEECHH
MAYBE YOU CAN START FILLING IN THE BLANKS.

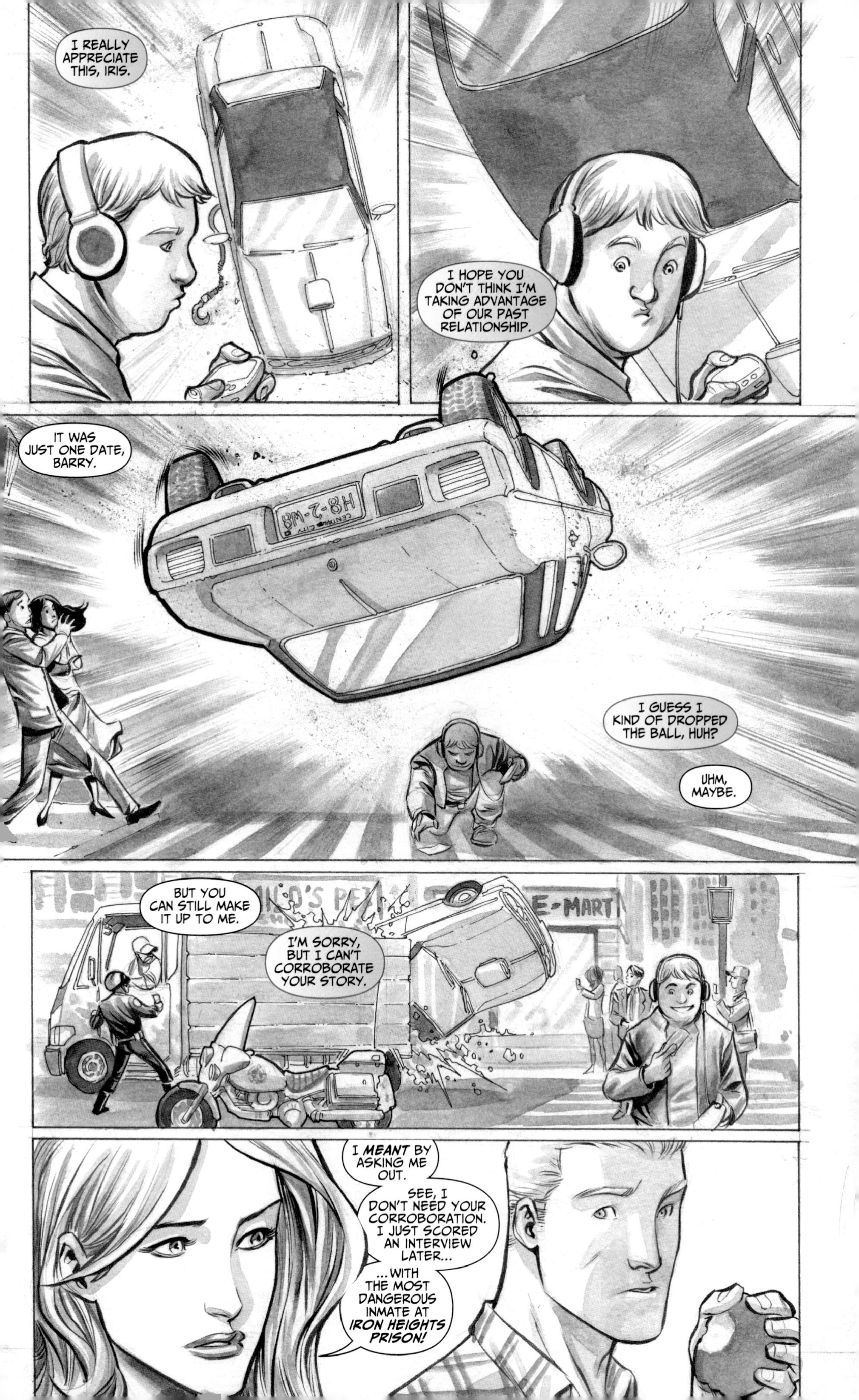
I REALLY APPRECIATE THIS, IRIS.
I HOPE YOU DON'T THINK I'M TAKING ADVANTAGE OF OUR PAST RELATIONSHIP.
IT WAS JUST ONE DATE, BARRY.
CENTRAL CITY
I GUESS I KIND OF DROPPED THE BALL, HUH?
UHM, MAYBE.
BUT YOU CAN STILL MAKE IT UP TO ME.
I'M SORRY, BUT I CAN'T CORROBORATE YOUR STORY.
E-MART
I *MEANT* BY ASKING ME OUT.
SEE, I DON'T NEED YOUR CORROBORATION. I JUST SCORED AN INTERVIEW LATER...
...WITH THE MOST DANGEROUS INMATE AT *IRON HEIGHTS PRISON!*

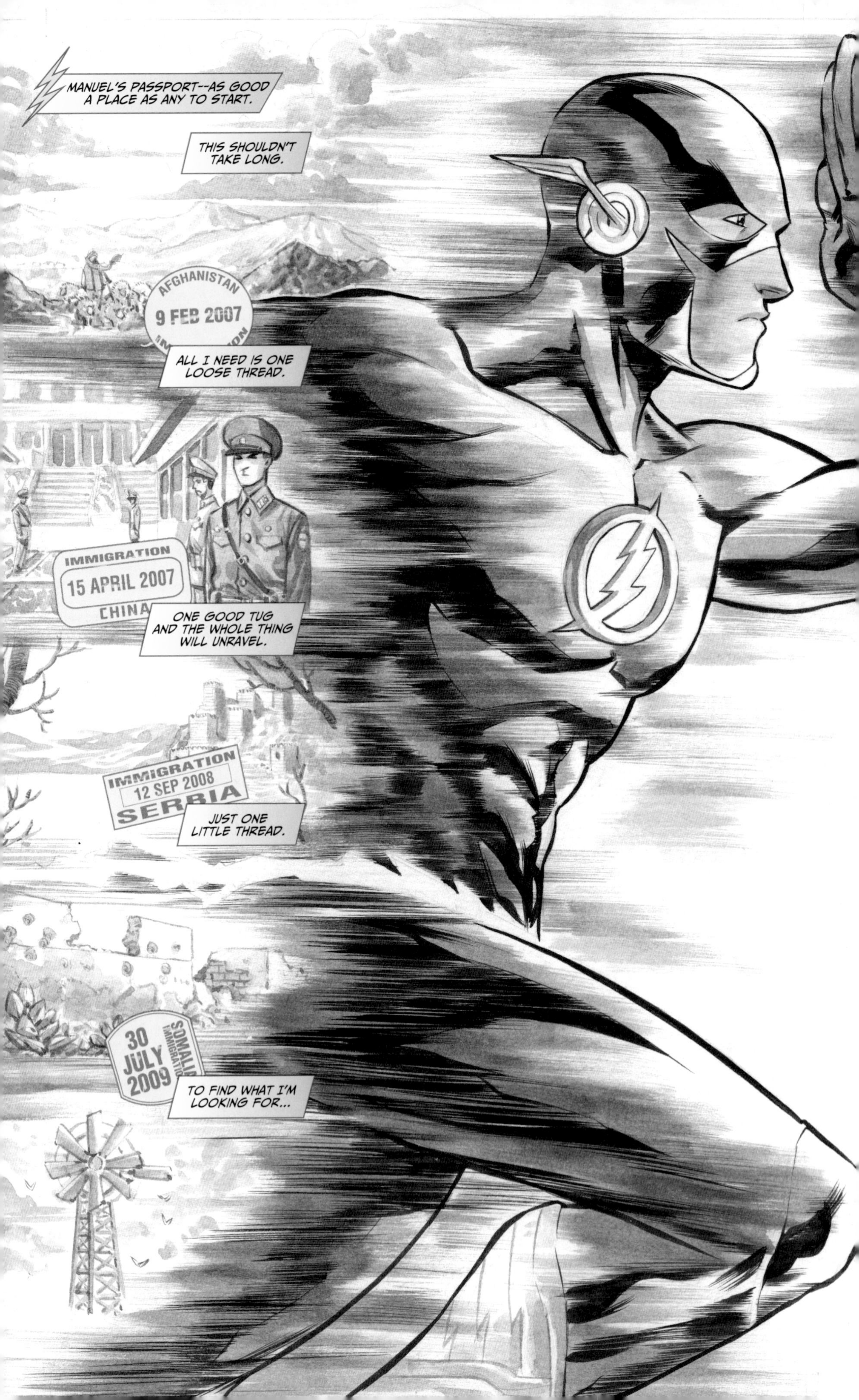
MANUEL'S PASSPORT--AS GOOD A PLACE AS ANY TO START.
THIS SHOULDN'T TAKE LONG.
AFGHANISTAN
9 FEB 2007
ALL I NEED IS ONE LOOSE THREAD.
IMMIGRATION
15 APRIL 2007
CHINA
ONE GOOD TUG AND THE WHOLE THING WILL UNRAVEL.
IMMIGRATION
12 SEP 2008
SERBIA
JUST ONE LITTLE THREAD.
30 JULY 2009
SOMALIA
IMMIGRATION
TO FIND WHAT I'M LOOKING FOR...

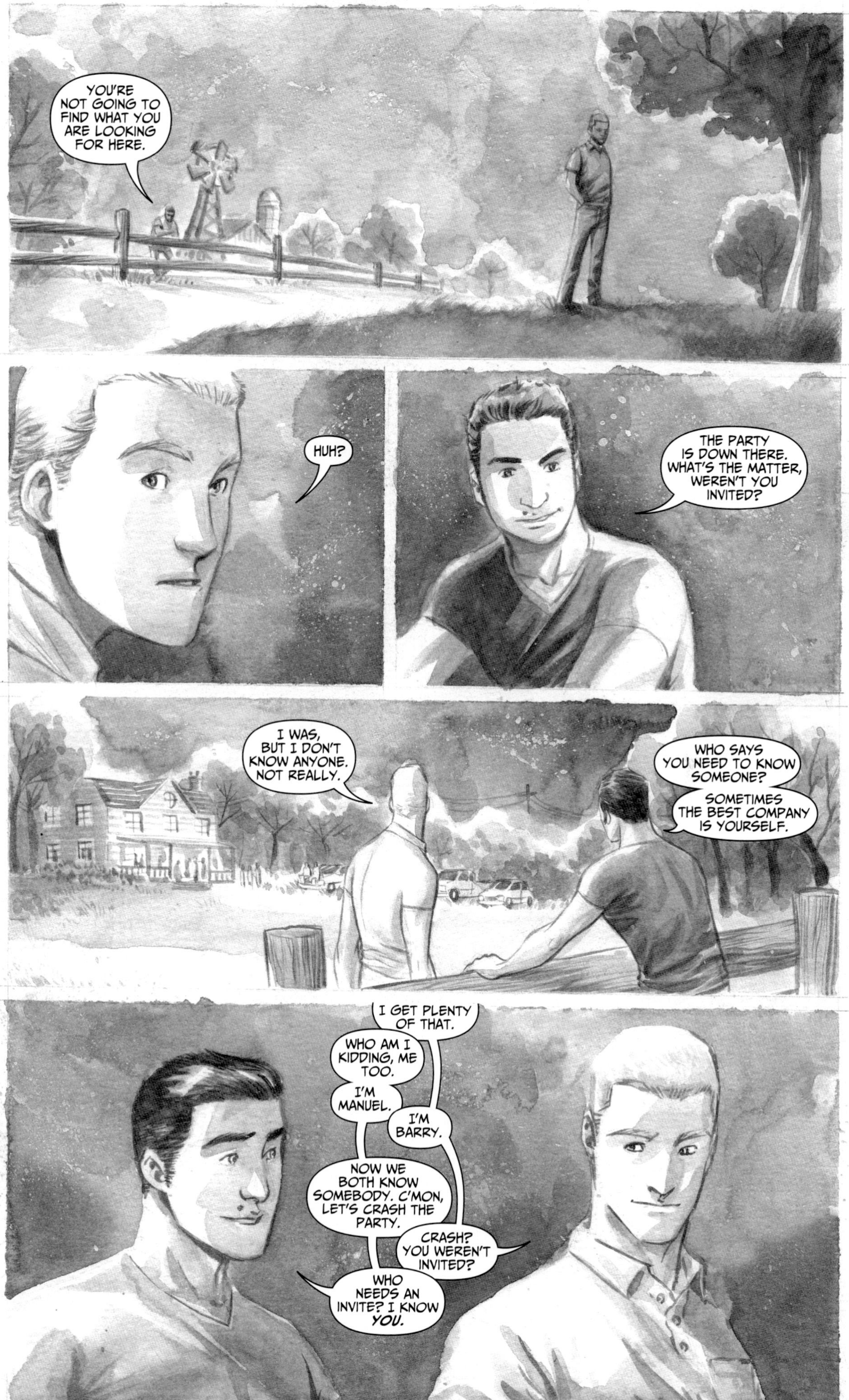
YOU'RE NOT GOING TO FIND WHAT YOU ARE LOOKING FOR HERE.
HUH?
THE PARTY IS DOWN THERE. WHAT'S THE MATTER, WEREN'T YOU INVITED?
I WAS, BUT I DON'T KNOW ANYONE. NOT REALLY.
WHO SAYS YOU NEED TO KNOW SOMEONE?
SOMETIMES THE BEST COMPANY IS YOURSELF.
I GET PLENTY OF THAT.
WHO AM I KIDDING, ME TOO.
I'M MANUEL.
I'M BARRY.
NOW WE BOTH KNOW SOMEBODY. C'MON, LET'S CRASH THE PARTY.
CRASH? YOU WEREN'T INVITED?
WHO NEEDS AN INVITE? I KNOW YOU.

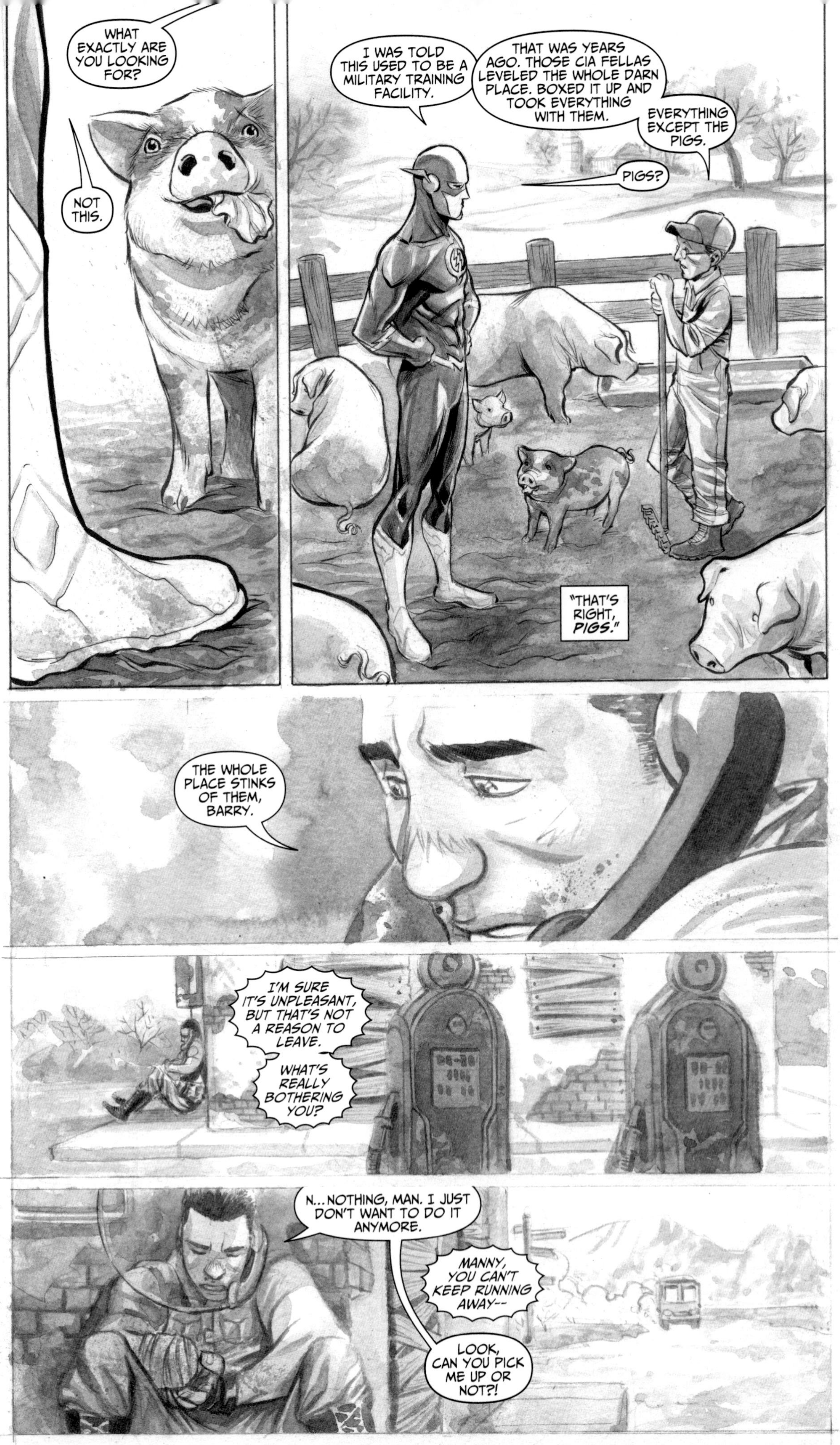
WHAT EXACTLY ARE YOU LOOKING FOR?
NOT THIS.
I WAS TOLD THIS USED TO BE A MILITARY TRAINING FACILITY.
THAT WAS YEARS AGO. THOSE CIA FELLAS LEVELED THE WHOLE DARN PLACE. BOXED IT UP AND TOOK EVERYTHING WITH THEM.
EVERYTHING EXCEPT THE PIGS.
PIGS?
"THAT'S RIGHT, *PIGS.*"
THE WHOLE PLACE STINKS OF THEM, BARRY.
I'M SURE IT'S UNPLEASANT, BUT THAT'S NOT A REASON TO LEAVE.
WHAT'S REALLY BOTHERING YOU?
N...NOTHING, MAN. I JUST DON'T WANT TO DO IT ANYMORE.
MANNY, YOU CAN'T KEEP RUNNING AWAY--
LOOK, CAN YOU PICK ME UP OR NOT?!

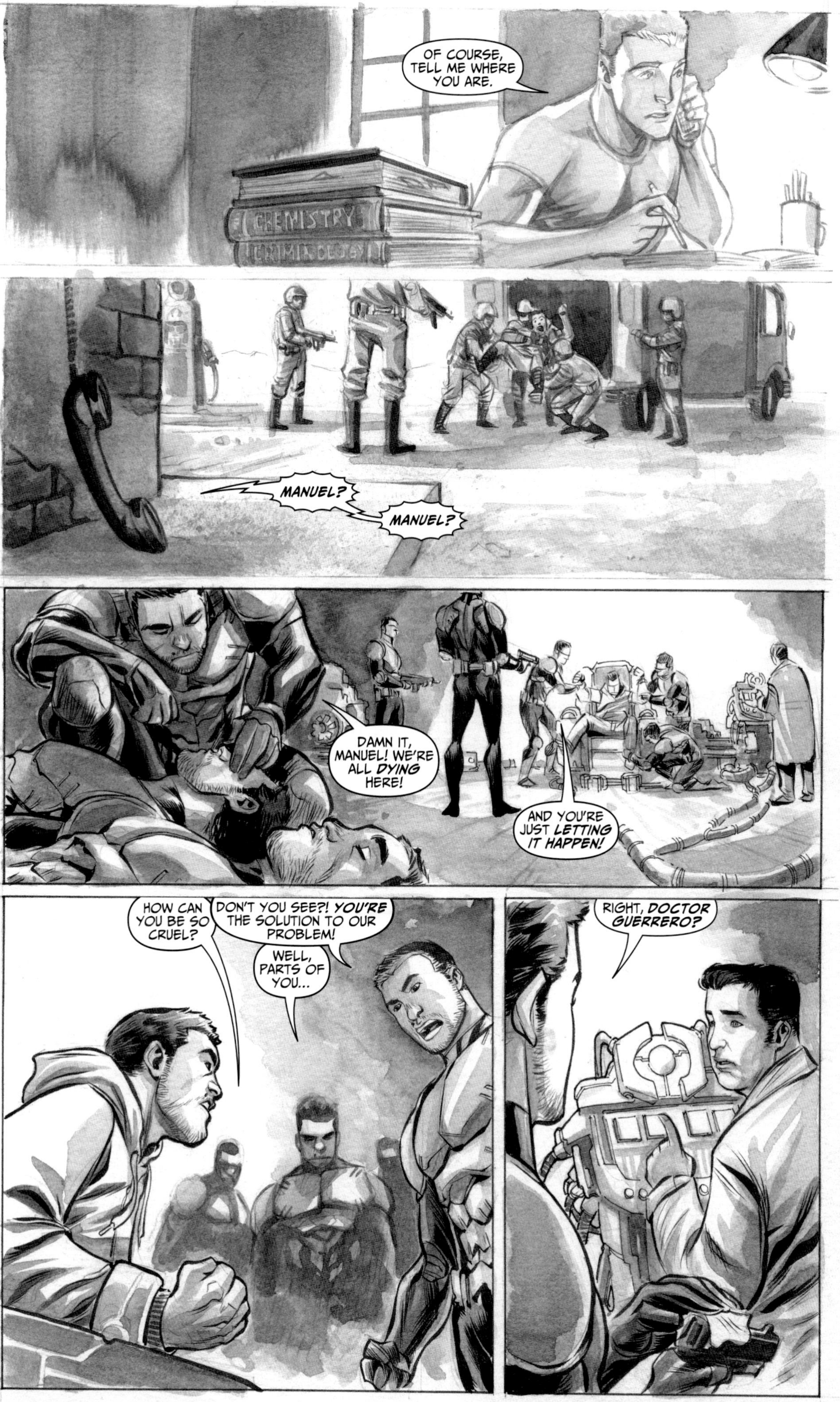
OF COURSE, TELL ME WHERE YOU ARE.
CHEMISTRY
CRIMINOLOGY
MANUEL?
MANUEL?
DAMN IT, MANUEL! WE'RE ALL DYING HERE!
AND YOU'RE JUST LETTING IT HAPPEN!
HOW CAN YOU BE SO CRUEL?
DON'T YOU SEE?! YOU'RE THE SOLUTION TO OUR PROBLEM!
WELL, PARTS OF YOU...
RIGHT, DOCTOR GUERRERO?

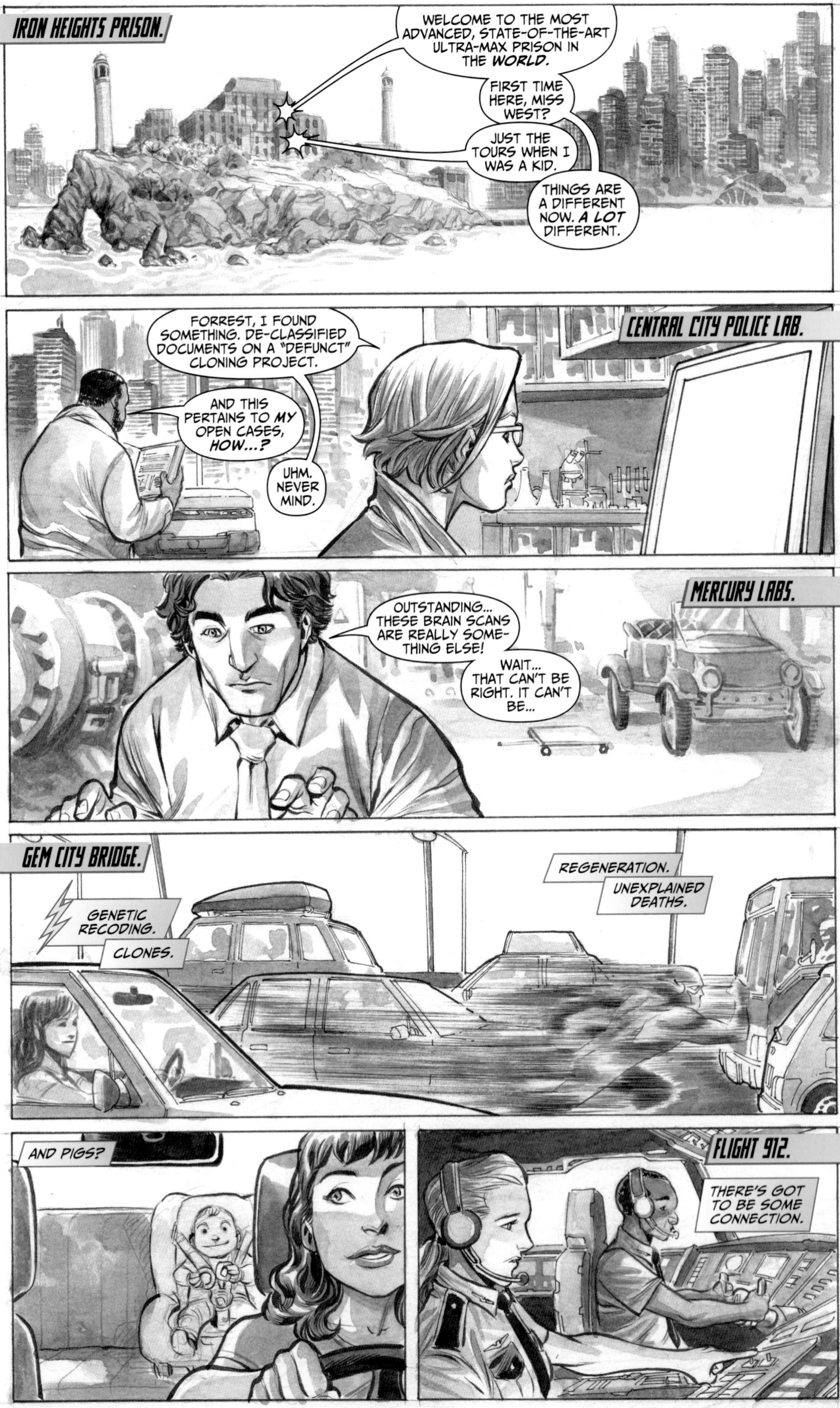

IRON HEIGHTS PRISON.
WELCOME TO THE MOST ADVANCED, STATE-OF-THE-ART ULTRA-MAX PRISON IN THE WORLD.
FIRST TIME HERE, MISS WEST?
JUST THE TOURS WHEN I WAS A KID.
THINGS ARE A DIFFERENT NOW. A LOT DIFFERENT.
CENTRAL CITY POLICE LAB.
FORREST, I FOUND SOMETHING. DE-CLASSIFIED DOCUMENTS ON A "DEFUNCT" CLONING PROJECT.
AND THIS PERTAINS TO MY OPEN CASES, HOW...?
UHM. NEVER MIND.
MERCURY LABS.
OUTSTANDING... THESE BRAIN SCANS ARE REALLY SOME-THING ELSE!
WAIT... THAT CAN'T BE RIGHT. IT CAN'T BE...
GEM CITY BRIDGE.
GENETIC RECODING.
CLONES.
REGENERATION.
UNEXPLAINED DEATHS.
AND PIGS?
FLIGHT 912.
THERE'S GOT TO BE SOME CONNECTION.

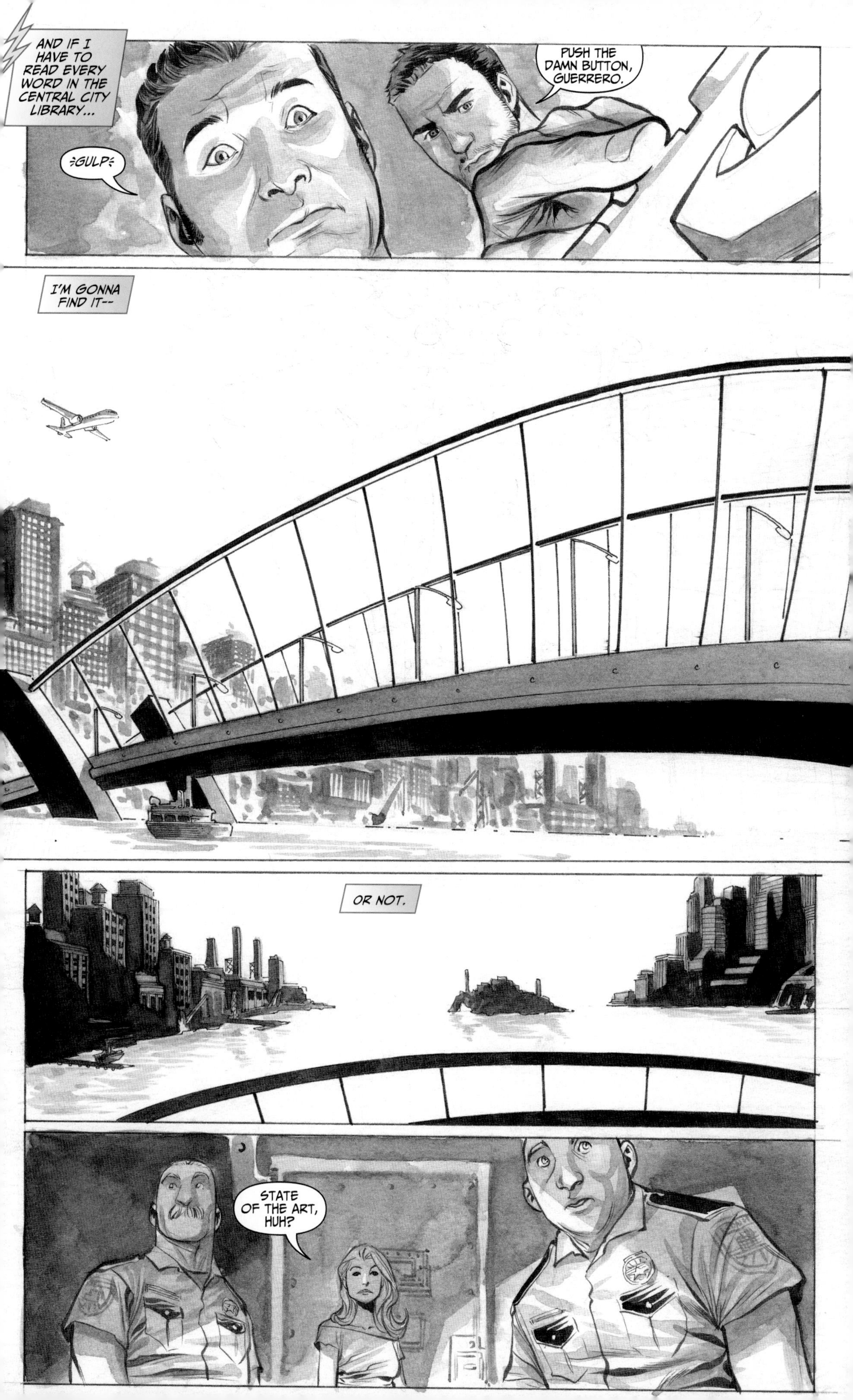
AND IF I HAVE TO READ EVERY WORD IN THE CENTRAL CITY LIBRARY...
PUSH THE DAMN BUTTON, GUERRERO.
GULP
I'M GONNA FIND IT--
OR NOT.
STATE OF THE ART, HUH?

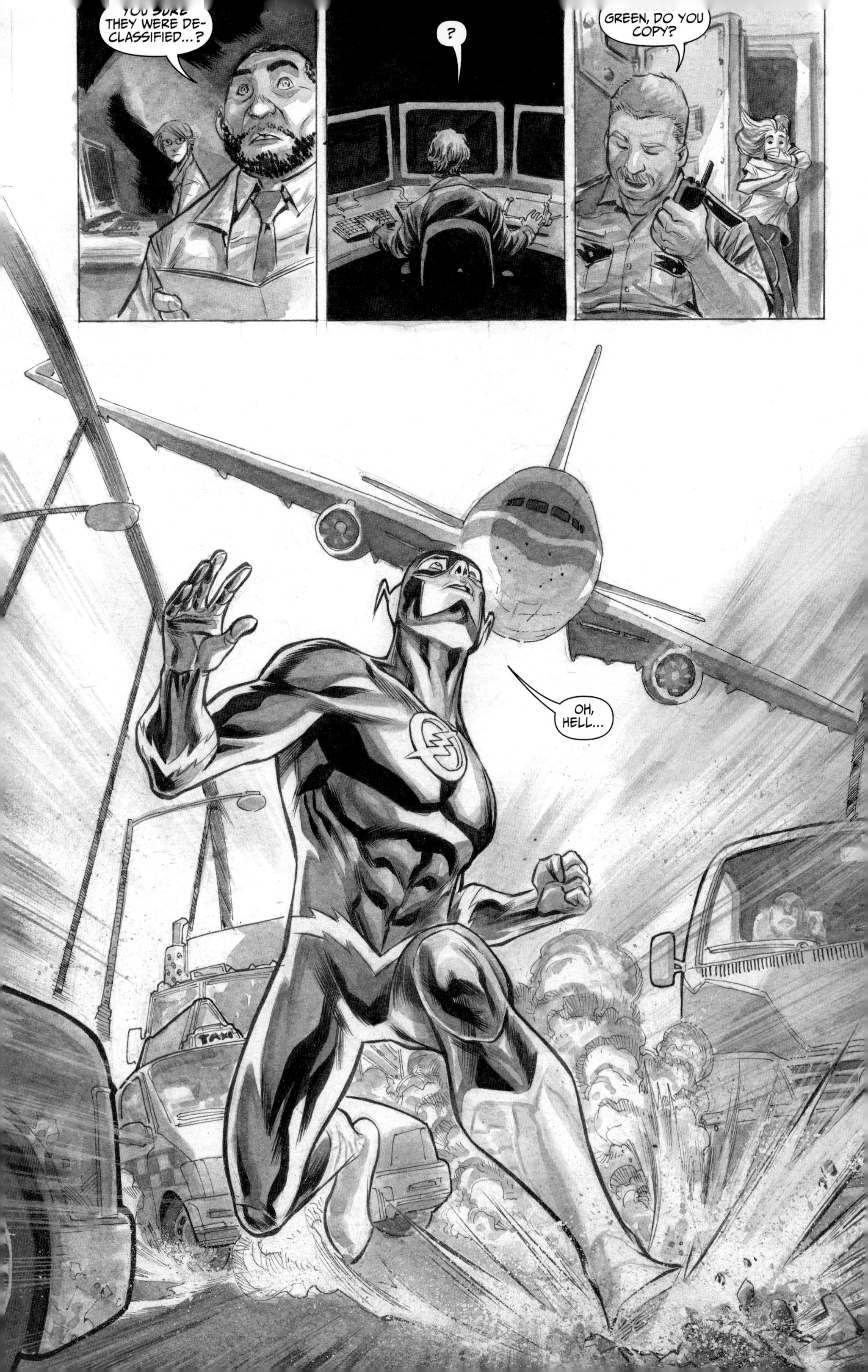
YOU SURE THEY WERE DE-CLASSIFIED...?
?
GREEN, DO YOU COPY?
OH, HELL...
TAXI

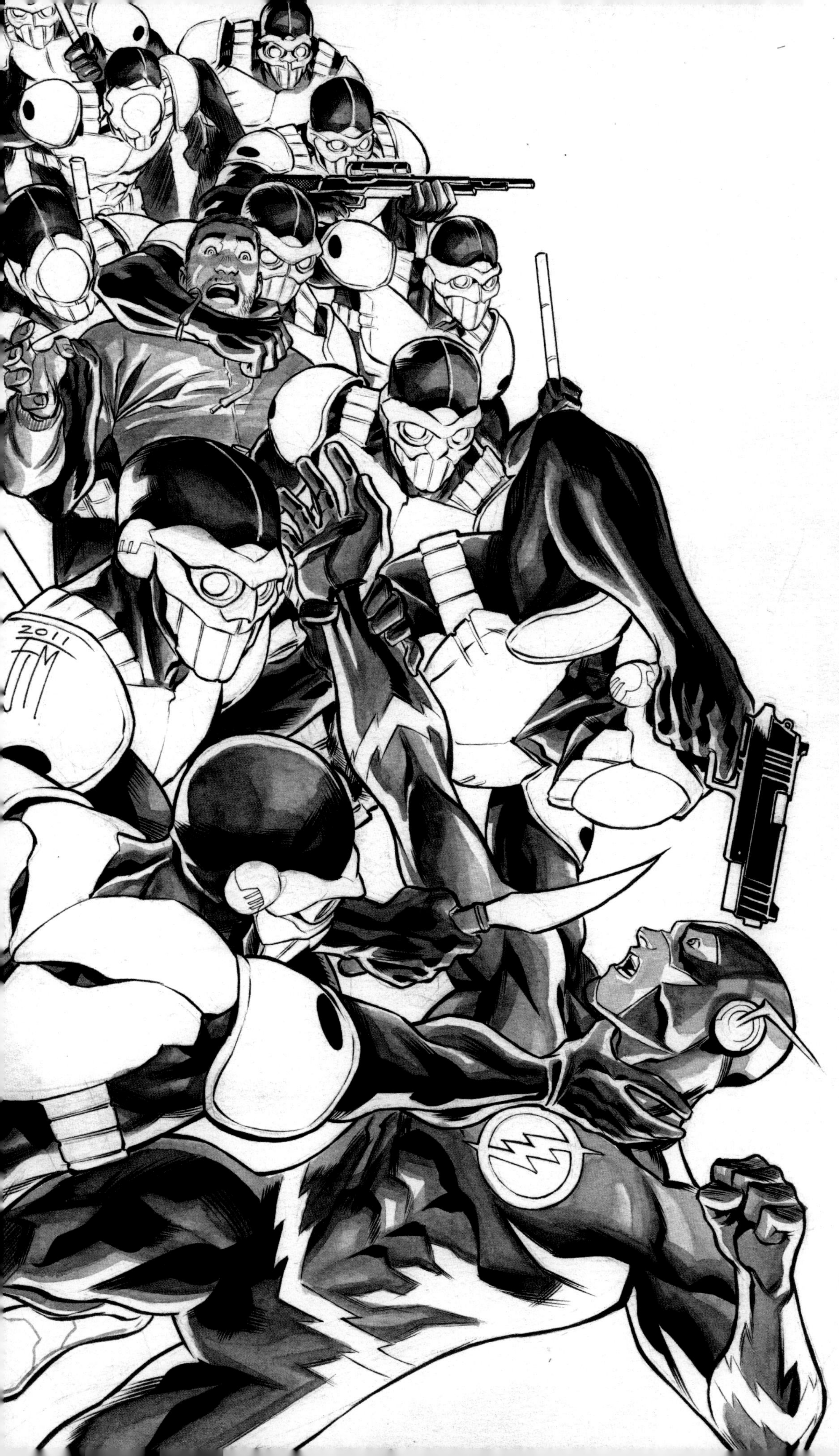
2011

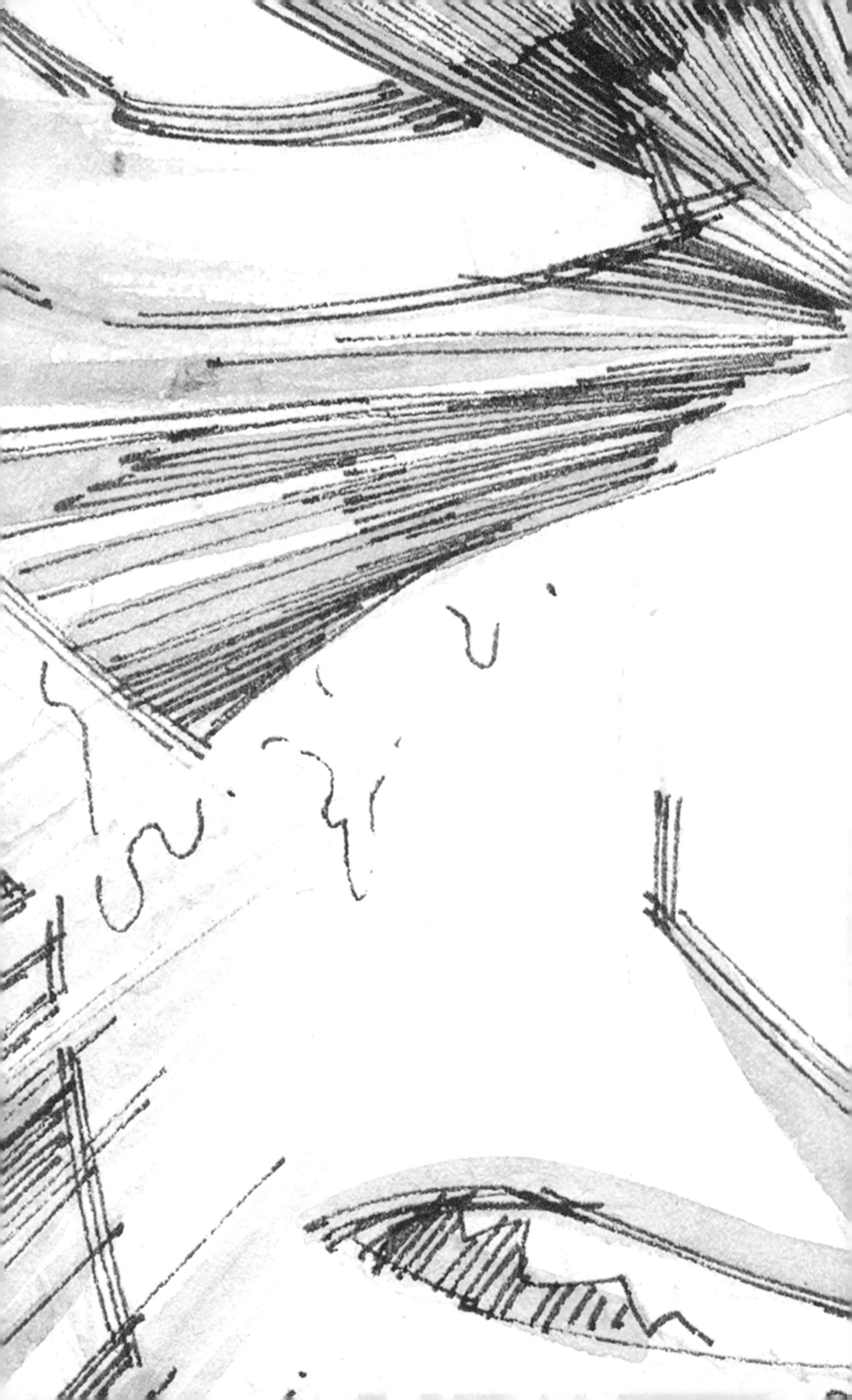

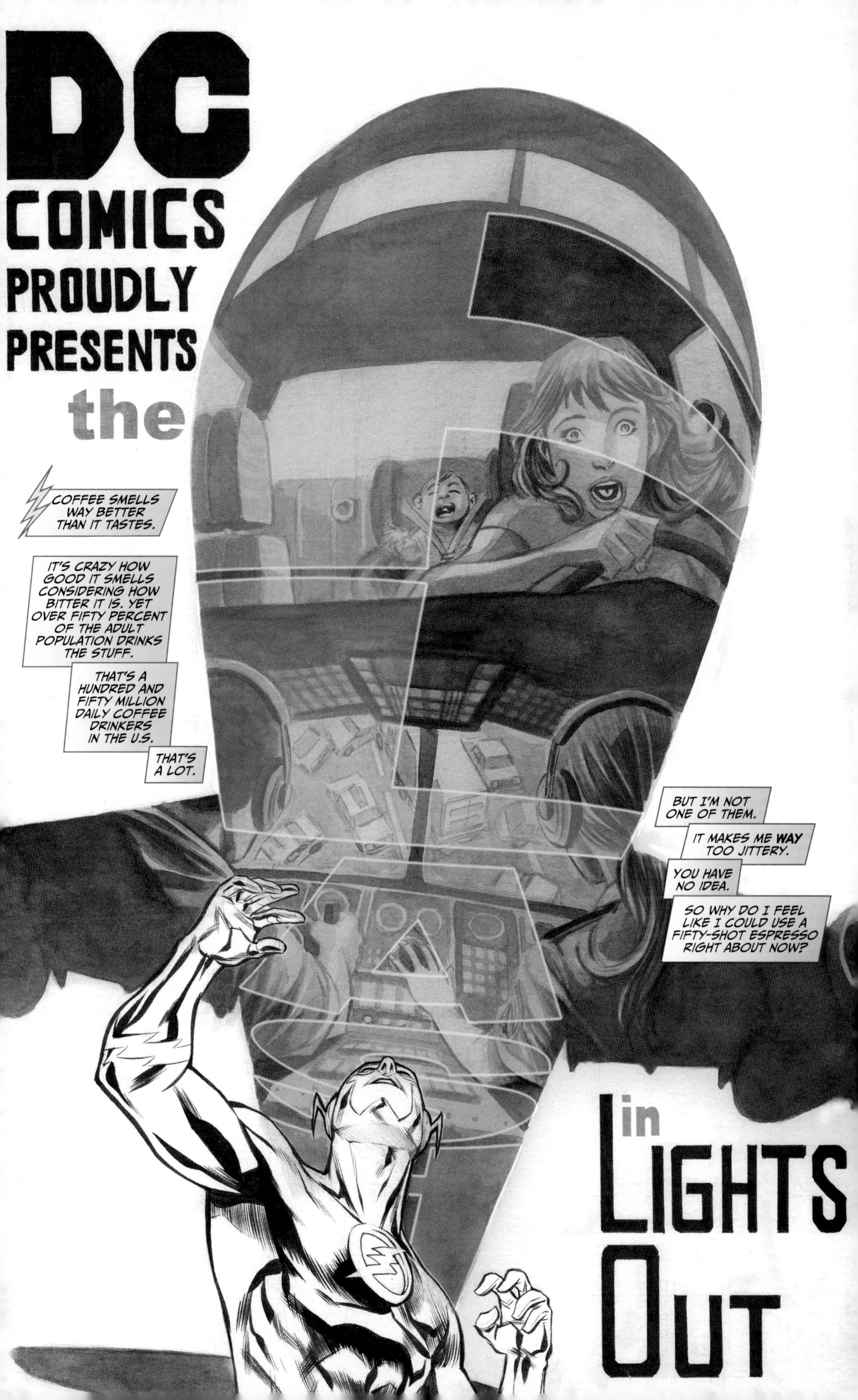

DC COMICS PROUDLY PRESENTS
the
COFFEE SMELLS WAY BETTER THAN IT TASTES.
IT'S CRAZY HOW GOOD IT SMELLS CONSIDERING HOW BITTER IT IS. YET OVER FIFTY PERCENT OF THE ADULT POPULATION DRINKS THE STUFF.
THAT'S A HUNDRED AND FIFTY MILLION DAILY COFFEE DRINKERS IN THE U.S.
THAT'S A LOT.
BUT I'M NOT ONE OF THEM.
IT MAKES ME WAY TOO JITTERY.
YOU HAVE NO IDEA.
SO WHY DO I FEEL LIKE I COULD USE A FIFTY-SHOT ESPRESSO RIGHT ABOUT NOW?
in
LIGHTS OUT

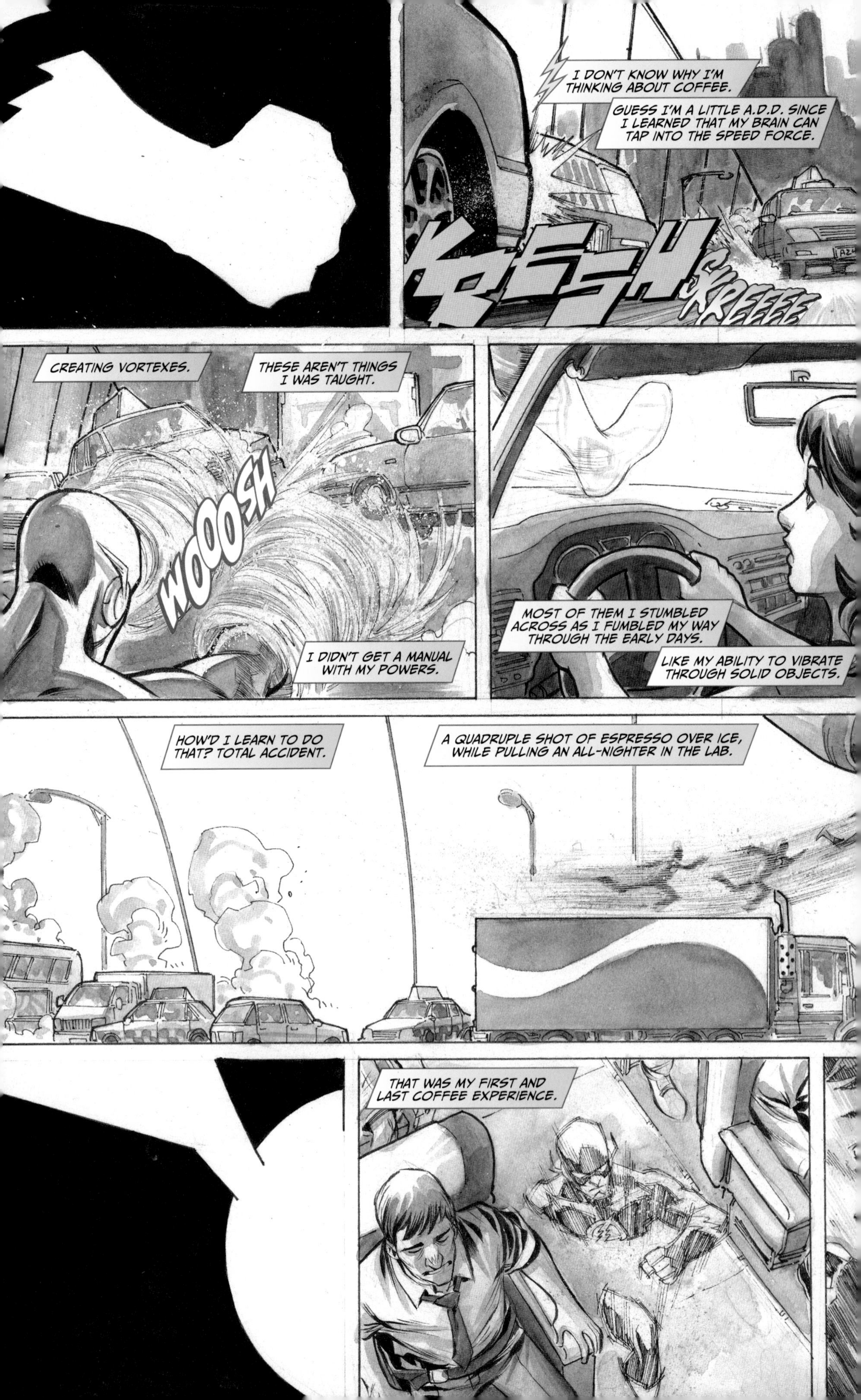
I DON'T KNOW WHY I'M THINKING ABOUT COFFEE.
GUESS I'M A LITTLE A.D.D. SINCE I LEARNED THAT MY BRAIN CAN TAP INTO THE SPEED FORCE.
KRESH
SKREEEE
CREATING VORTEXES.
THESE AREN'T THINGS I WAS TAUGHT.
WOOOSH
I DIDN'T GET A MANUAL WITH MY POWERS.
MOST OF THEM I STUMBLED ACROSS AS I FUMBLED MY WAY THROUGH THE EARLY DAYS.
LIKE MY ABILITY TO VIBRATE THROUGH SOLID OBJECTS.
HOW'D I LEARN TO DO THAT? TOTAL ACCIDENT.
A QUADRUPLE SHOT OF ESPRESSO OVER ICE, WHILE PULLING AN ALL-NIGHTER IN THE LAB.
THAT WAS MY FIRST AND LAST COFFEE EXPERIENCE.

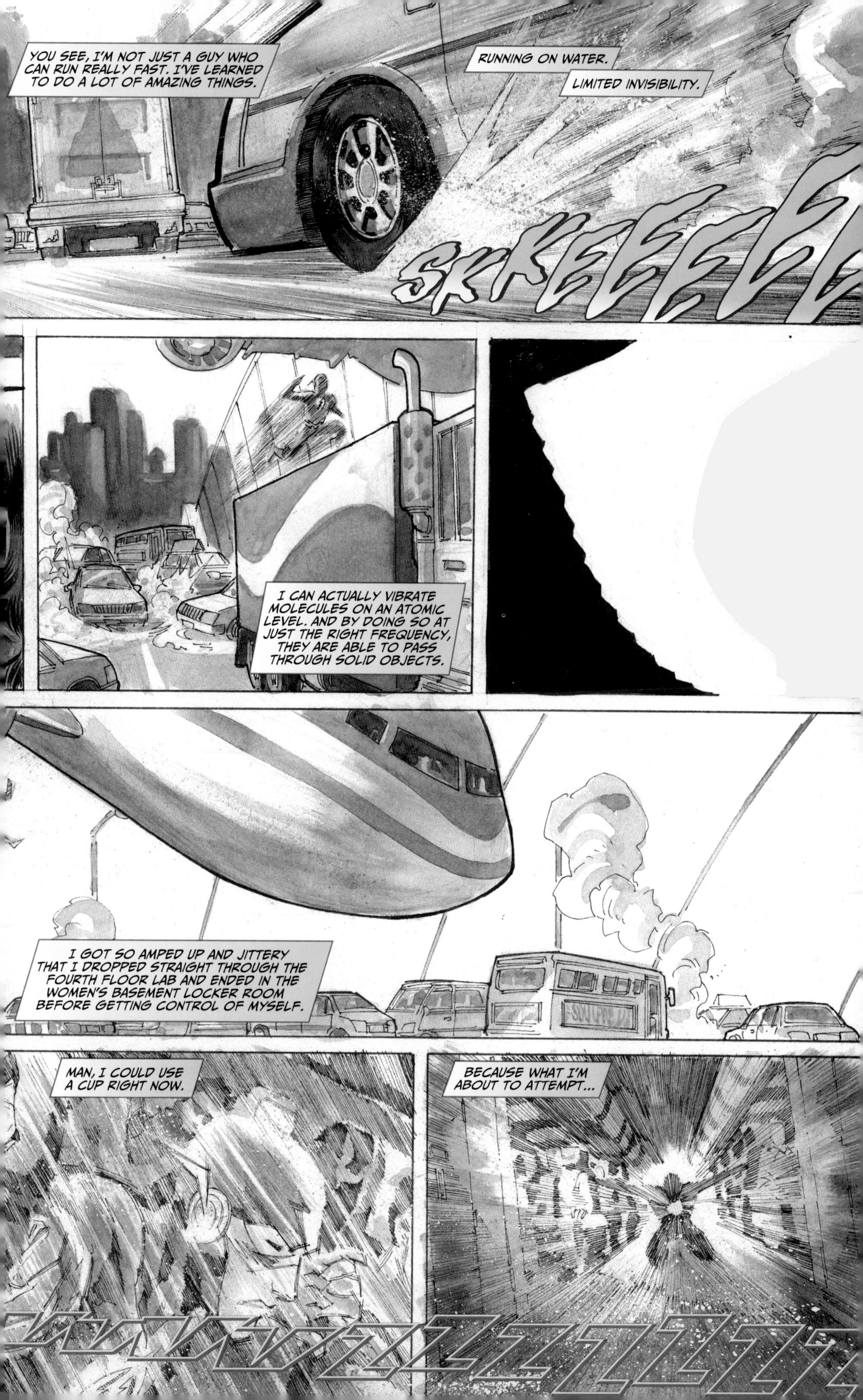

YOU SEE, I'M NOT JUST A GUY WHO CAN RUN REALLY FAST. I'VE LEARNED TO DO A LOT OF AMAZING THINGS.
RUNNING ON WATER.
LIMITED INVISIBILITY.
SKREEEEE
I CAN ACTUALLY VIBRATE MOLECULES ON AN ATOMIC LEVEL. AND BY DOING SO AT JUST THE RIGHT FREQUENCY, THEY ARE ABLE TO PASS THROUGH SOLID OBJECTS.
I GOT SO AMPED UP AND JITTERY THAT I DROPPED STRAIGHT THROUGH THE FOURTH FLOOR LAB AND ENDED IN THE WOMEN'S BASEMENT LOCKER ROOM BEFORE GETTING CONTROL OF MYSELF.
MAN, I COULD USE A CUP RIGHT NOW.
BECAUSE WHAT I'M ABOUT TO ATTEMPT...

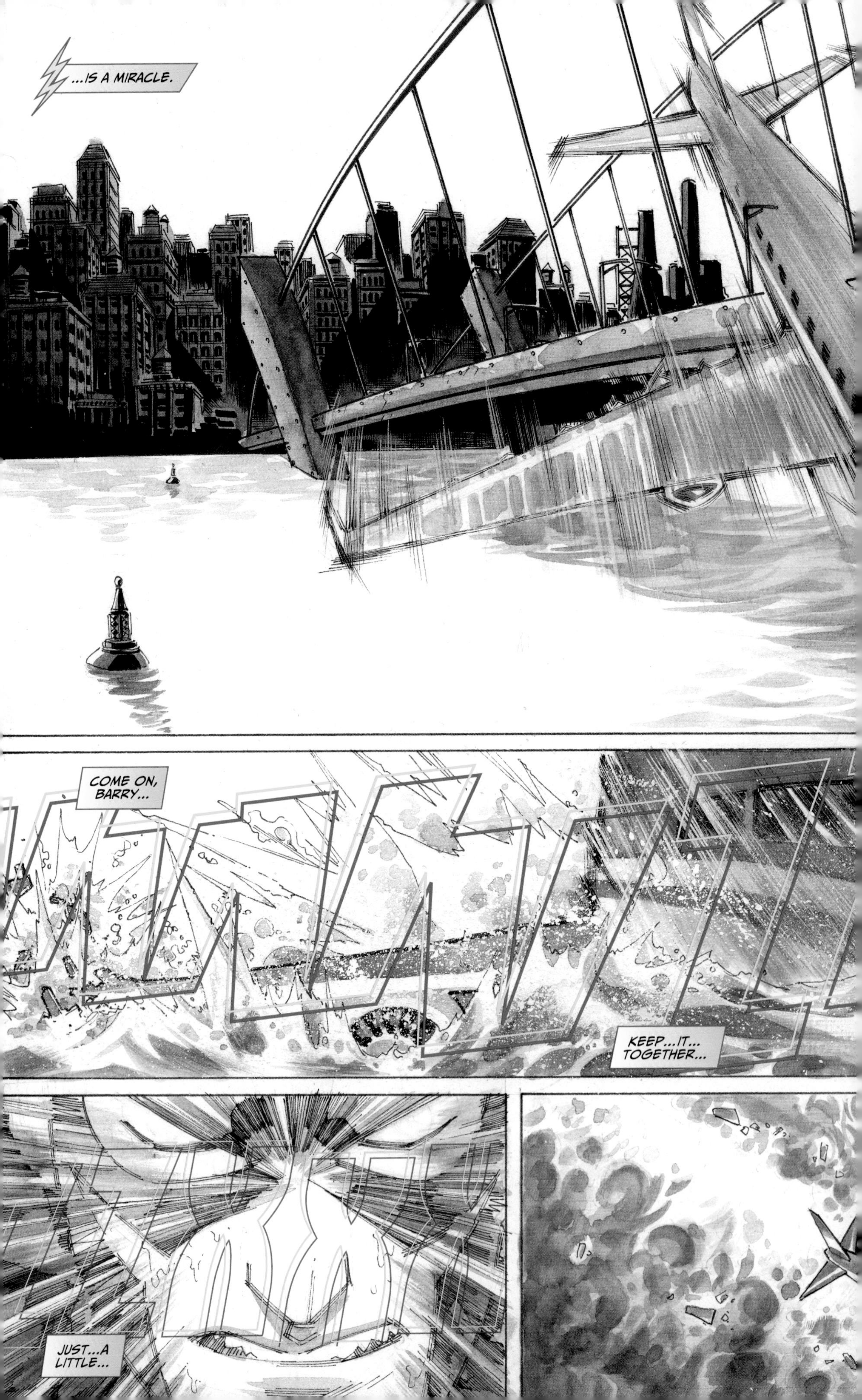
...IS A MIRACLE.
COME ON, BARRY...
KEEP...IT... TOGETHER...
JUST...A LITTLE...

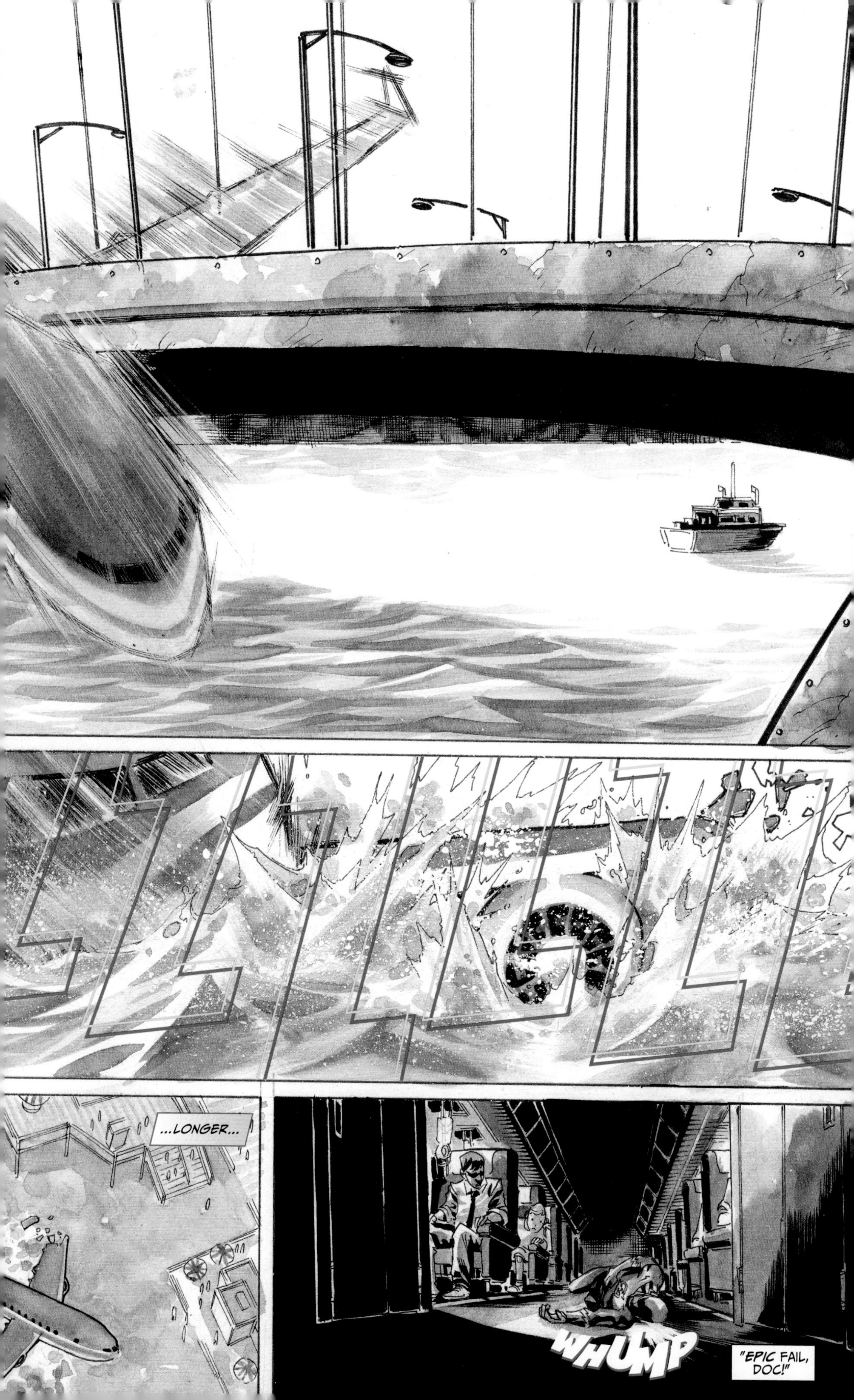
...LONGER...
WHUMP
"EPIC FAIL, DOC!"

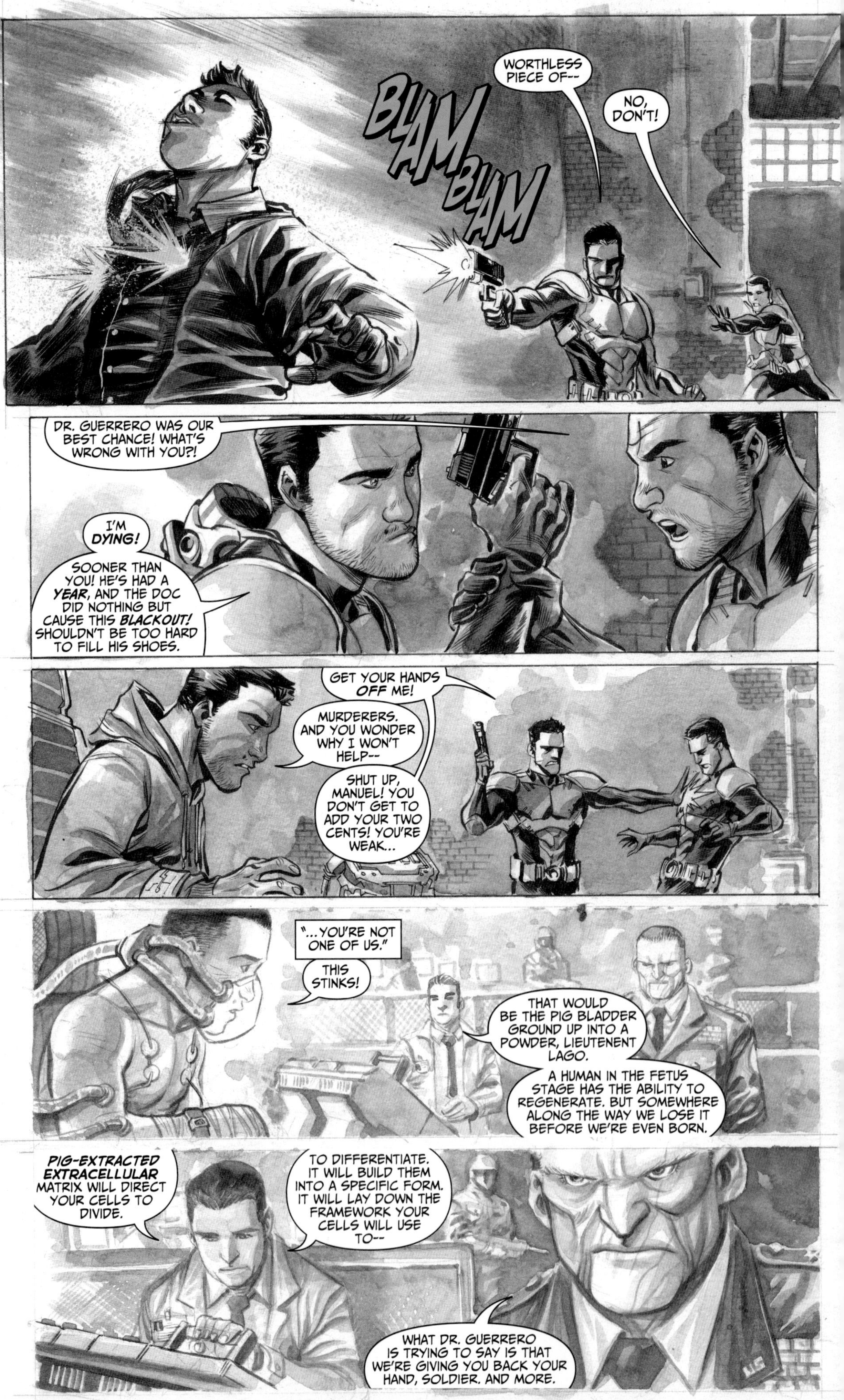

BLAM
BLAM
WORTHLESS PIECE OF--
NO, DON'T!
DR. GUERRERO WAS OUR BEST CHANCE! WHAT'S WRONG WITH YOU?!
I'M *DYING!*
SOONER THAN YOU! HE'S HAD A *YEAR,* AND THE DOC DID NOTHING BUT CAUSE THIS *BLACKOUT!* SHOULDN'T BE TOO HARD TO FILL HIS SHOES.
GET YOUR HANDS *OFF* ME!
MURDERERS. AND YOU WONDER WHY I WON'T HELP--
SHUT UP, MANUEL! YOU DON'T GET TO ADD YOUR TWO CENTS! YOU'RE WEAK...
"...YOU'RE NOT ONE OF US."
THIS STINKS!
THAT WOULD BE THE PIG BLADDER GROUND UP INTO A POWDER, LIEUTENENT LAGO.
A HUMAN IN THE FETUS STAGE HAS THE ABILITY TO REGENERATE. BUT SOMEWHERE ALONG THE WAY WE LOSE IT BEFORE WE'RE EVEN BORN.
PIG-EXTRACTED EXTRACELLULAR MATRIX WILL DIRECT YOUR CELLS TO DIVIDE.
TO DIFFERENTIATE. IT WILL BUILD THEM INTO A SPECIFIC FORM. IT WILL LAY DOWN THE FRAMEWORK YOUR CELLS WILL USE TO--
WHAT DR. GUERRERO IS TRYING TO SAY IS THAT WE'RE GIVING YOU BACK YOUR HAND, SOLDIER. AND MORE.

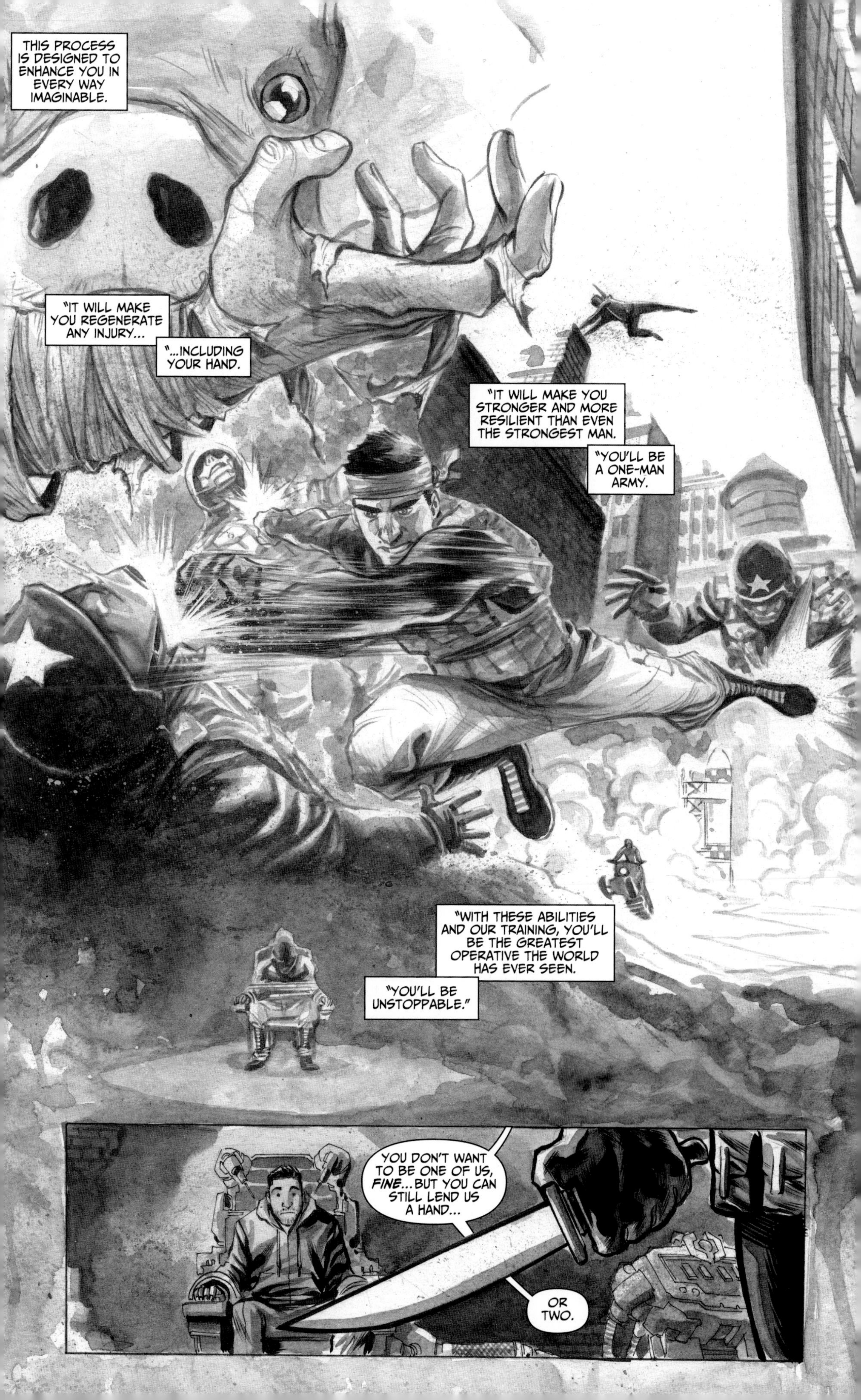
THIS PROCESS IS DESIGNED TO ENHANCE YOU IN EVERY WAY IMAGINABLE.
"IT WILL MAKE YOU REGENERATE ANY INJURY...
"...INCLUDING YOUR HAND.
"IT WILL MAKE YOU STRONGER AND MORE RESILIENT THAN EVEN THE STRONGEST MAN.
"YOU'LL BE A ONE-MAN ARMY.
"WITH THESE ABILITIES AND OUR TRAINING, YOU'LL BE THE GREATEST OPERATIVE THE WORLD HAS EVER SEEN.
"YOU'LL BE UNSTOPPABLE."
YOU DON'T WANT TO BE ONE OF US, *FINE*...BUT YOU CAN STILL LEND US A HAND...
OR TWO.

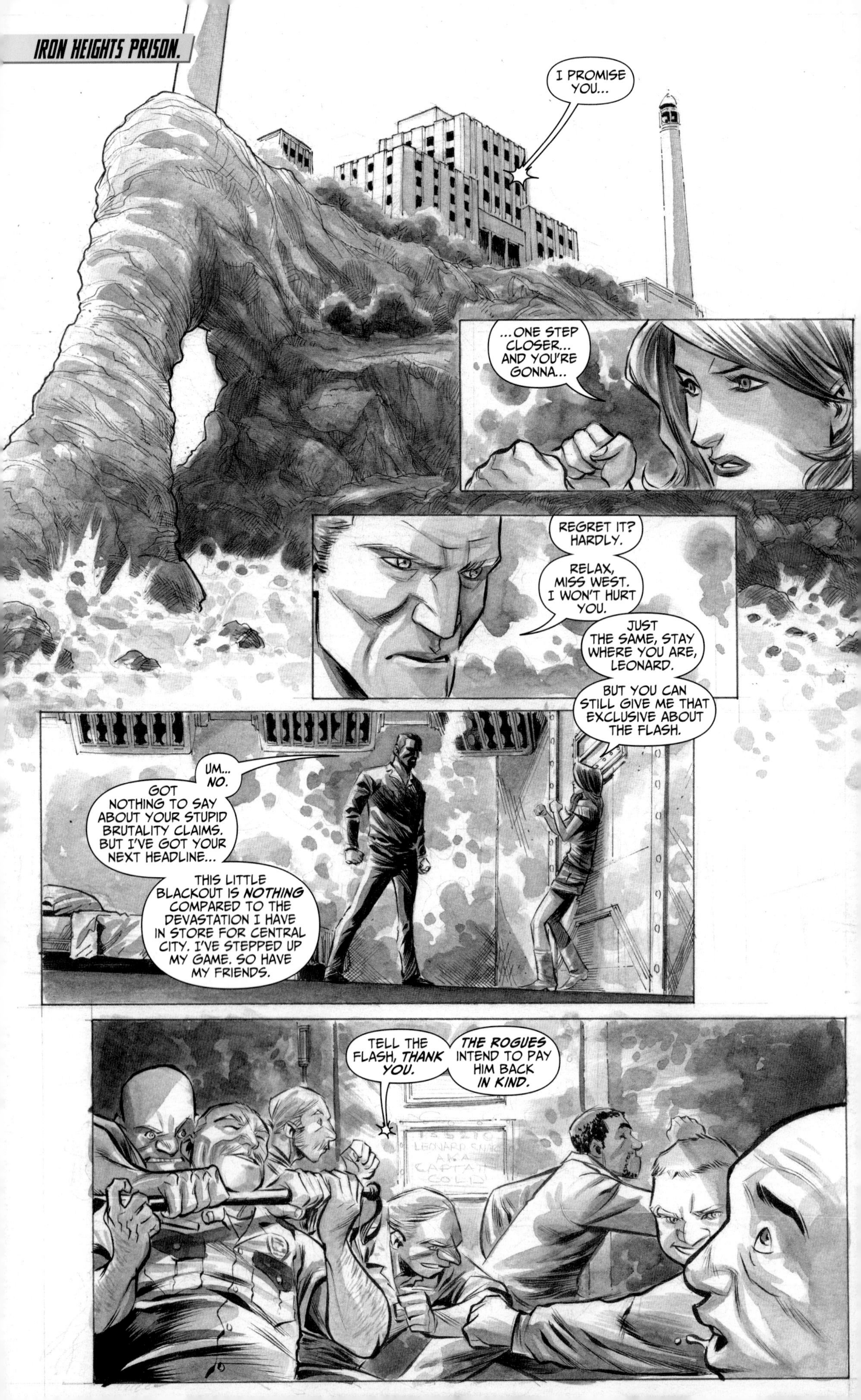
IRON HEIGHTS PRISON.
I PROMISE YOU...
...ONE STEP CLOSER... AND YOU'RE GONNA...
REGRET IT? HARDLY.
RELAX, MISS WEST. I WON'T HURT YOU.
JUST THE SAME, STAY WHERE YOU ARE, LEONARD.
BUT YOU CAN STILL GIVE ME THAT EXCLUSIVE ABOUT THE FLASH.
UM... NO.
GOT NOTHING TO SAY ABOUT YOUR STUPID BRUTALITY CLAIMS. BUT I'VE GOT YOUR NEXT HEADLINE...
THIS LITTLE BLACKOUT IS NOTHING COMPARED TO THE DEVASTATION I HAVE IN STORE FOR CENTRAL CITY. I'VE STEPPED UP MY GAME. SO HAVE MY FRIENDS.
TELL THE FLASH, THANK YOU.
THE ROGUES INTEND TO PAY HIM BACK IN KIND.

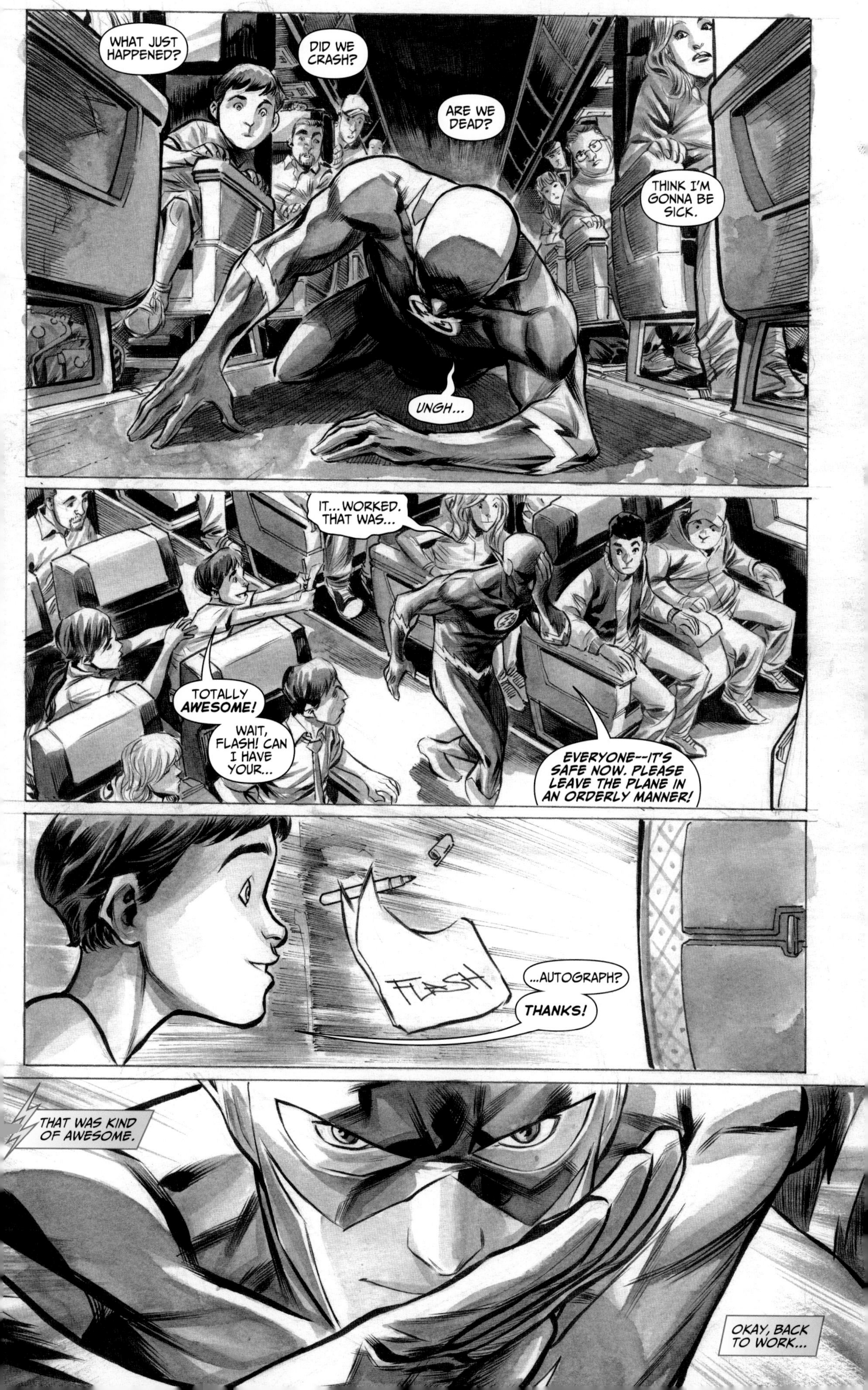
WHAT JUST HAPPENED?
DID WE CRASH?
ARE WE DEAD?
THINK I'M GONNA BE SICK.
UNGH...
IT... WORKED. THAT WAS...
TOTALLY AWESOME!
WAIT, FLASH! CAN I HAVE YOUR...
EVERYONE--IT'S SAFE NOW. PLEASE LEAVE THE PLANE IN AN ORDERLY MANNER!
FLASH
...AUTOGRAPH?
THANKS!
THAT WAS KIND OF AWESOME.
OKAY, BACK TO WORK...

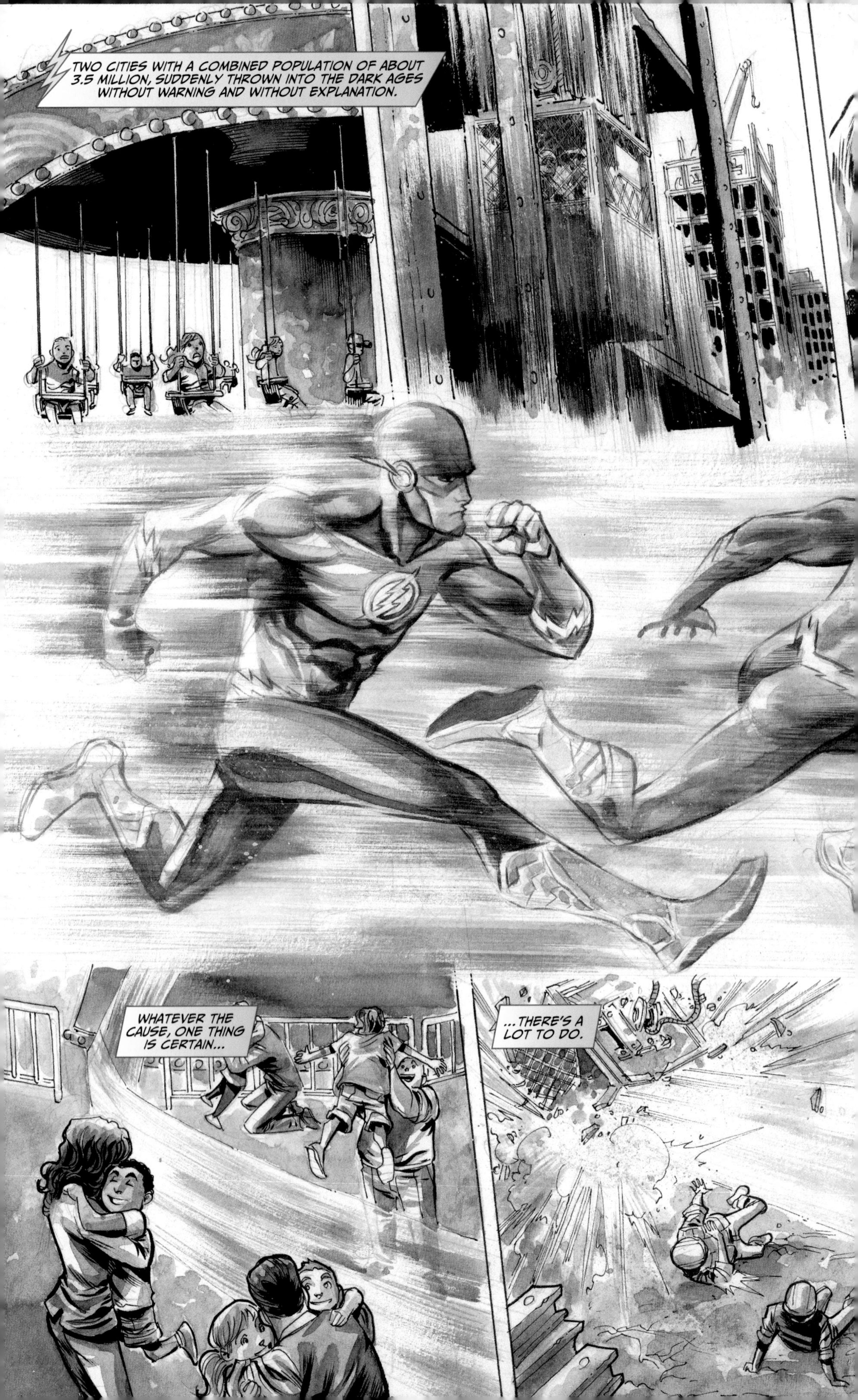
TWO CITIES WITH A COMBINED POPULATION OF ABOUT 3.5 MILLION, SUDDENLY THROWN INTO THE DARK AGES WITHOUT WARNING AND WITHOUT EXPLANATION.
WHATEVER THE CAUSE, ONE THING IS CERTAIN...
...THERE'S A LOT TO DO.

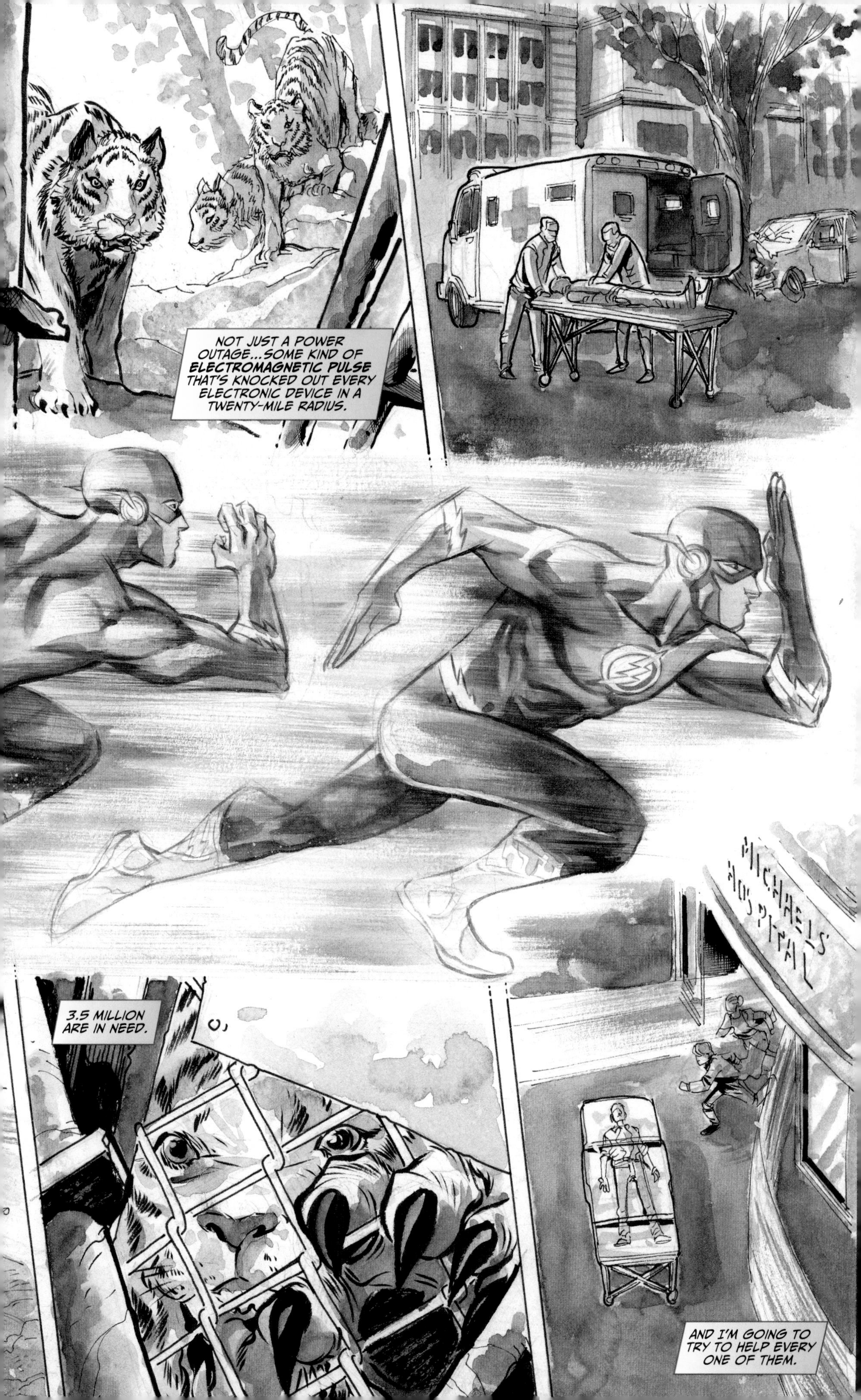
NOT JUST A POWER OUTAGE...SOME KIND OF **ELECTROMAGNETIC PULSE** THAT'S KNOCKED OUT EVERY ELECTRONIC DEVICE IN A TWENTY-MILE RADIUS.
3.5 MILLION ARE IN NEED.
AND I'M GOING TO TRY TO HELP EVERY ONE OF THEM.

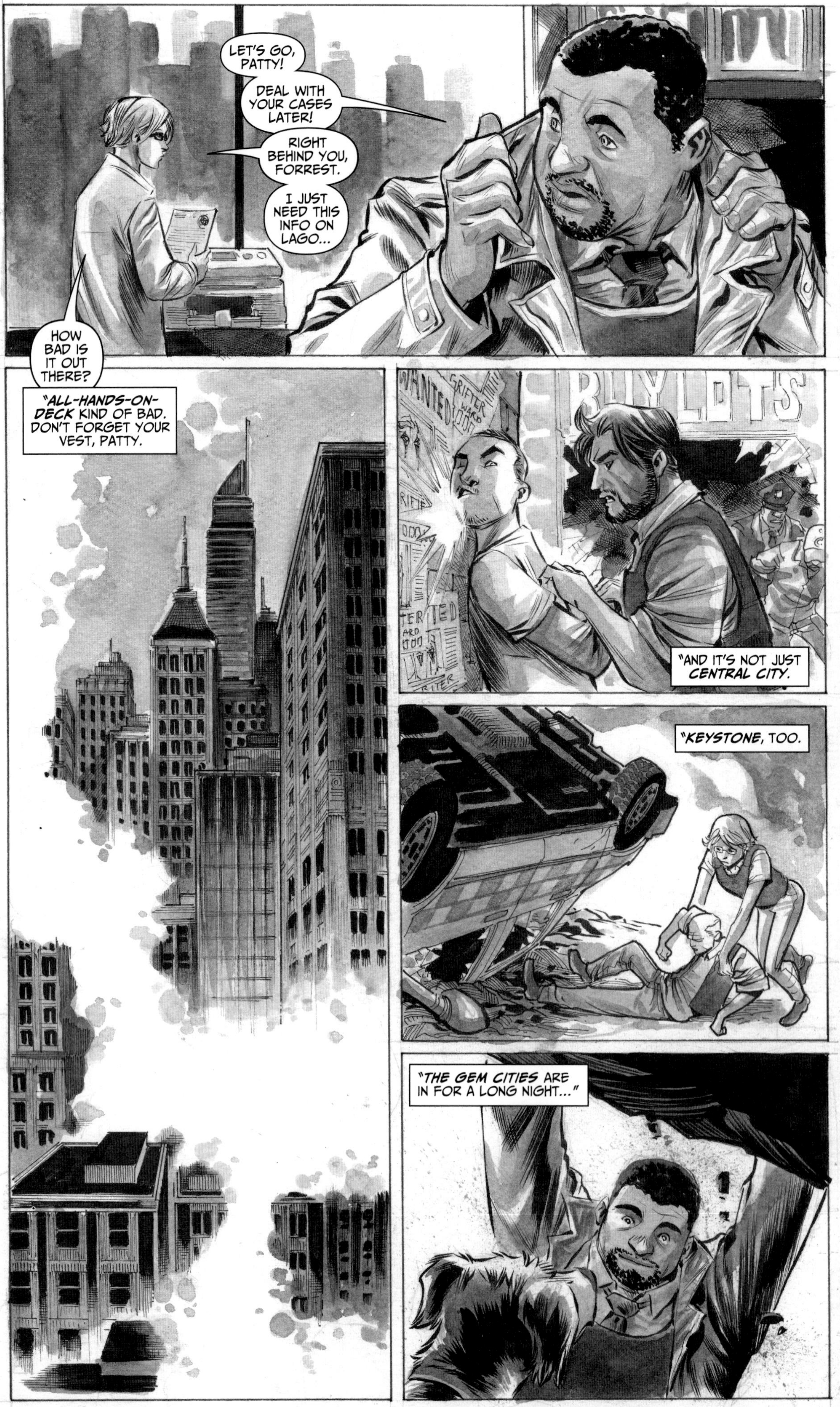
LET'S GO, PATTY!
DEAL WITH YOUR CASES LATER!
RIGHT BEHIND YOU, FORREST.
I JUST NEED THIS INFO ON LAGO...
HOW BAD IS IT OUT THERE?
"ALL-HANDS-ON-DECK KIND OF BAD. DON'T FORGET YOUR VEST, PATTY.
WANTED
GRIFTER
BUYLOTS
"AND IT'S NOT JUST CENTRAL CITY.
"KEYSTONE, TOO.
"THE GEM CITIES ARE IN FOR A LONG NIGHT..."

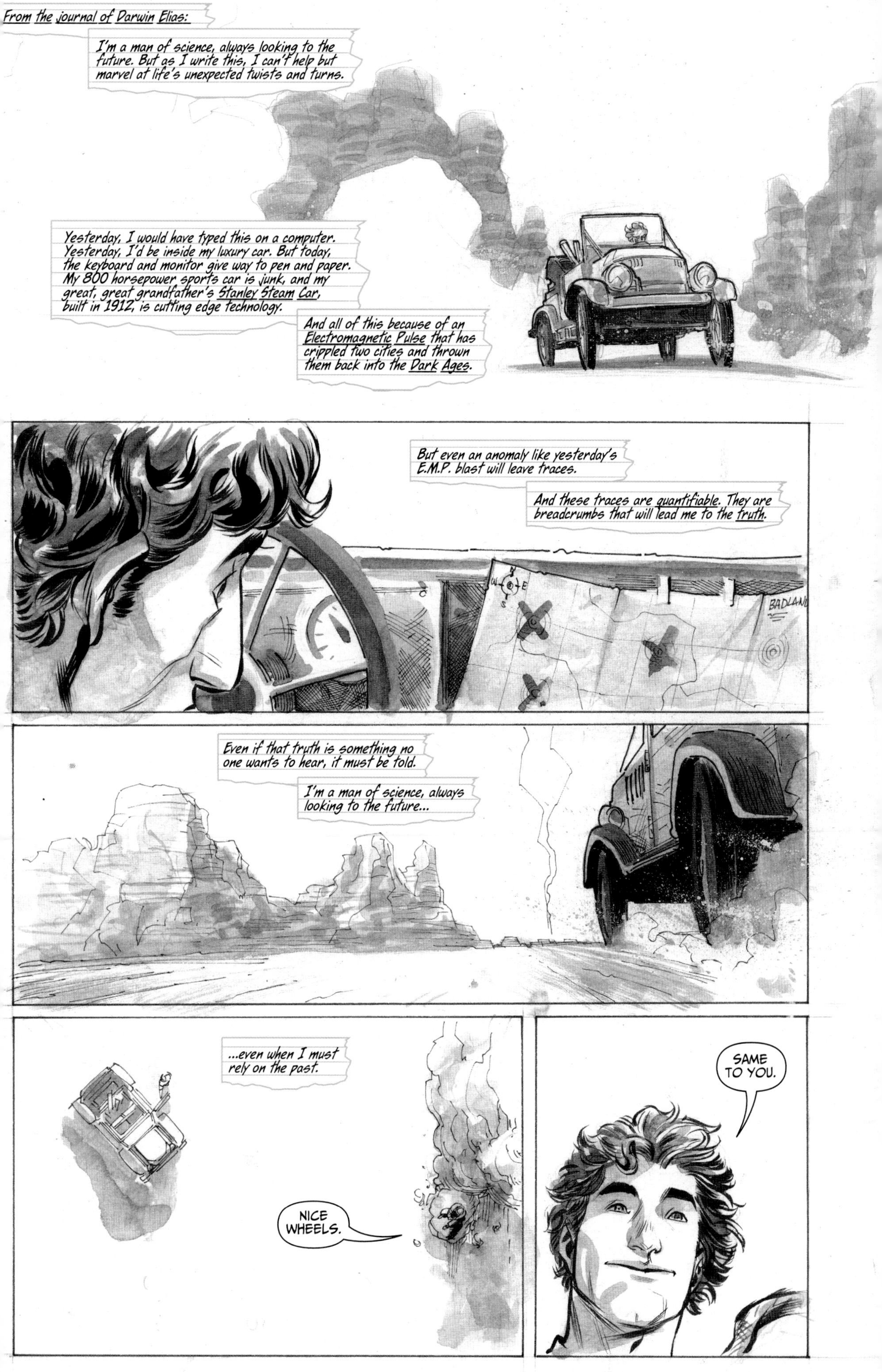
From the journal of Darwin Elias:
I'm a man of science, always looking to the future. But as I write this, I can't help but marvel at life's unexpected twists and turns.
Yesterday, I would have typed this on a computer. Yesterday, I'd be inside my luxury car. But today, the keyboard and monitor give way to pen and paper. My 800 horsepower sports car is junk, and my great, great grandfather's Stanley Steam Car, built in 1912, is cutting edge technology.
And all of this because of an Electromagnetic Pulse that has crippled two cities and thrown them back into the Dark Ages.
But even an anomaly like yesterday's E.M.P. blast will leave traces.
And these traces are quantifiable. They are breadcrumbs that will lead me to the truth.
Even if that truth is something no one wants to hear, it must be told.
I'm a man of science, always looking to the future...
...even when I must rely on the past.
NICE WHEELS.
SAME TO YOU.

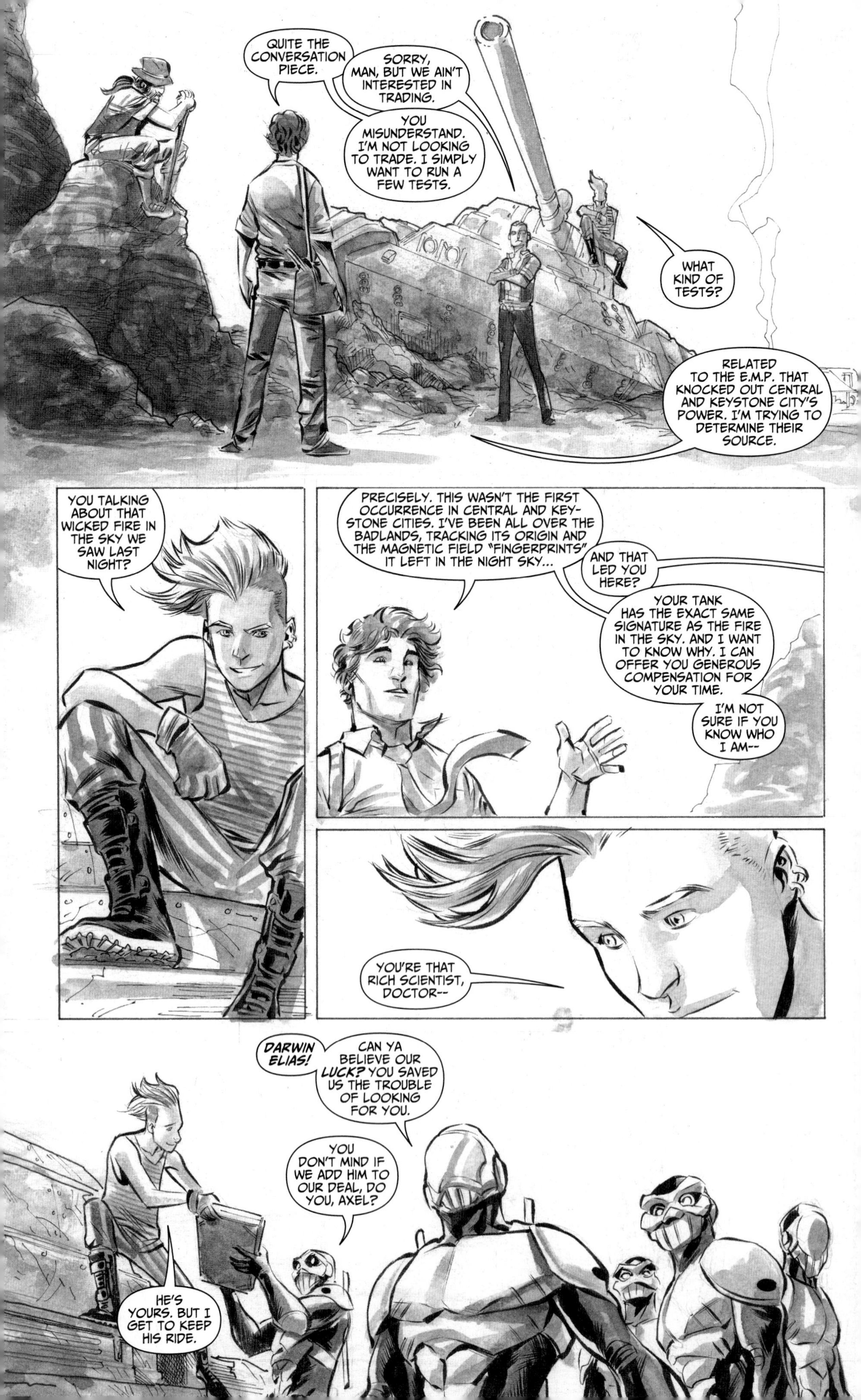

QUITE THE CONVERSATION PIECE.
SORRY, MAN, BUT WE AIN'T INTERESTED IN TRADING.
YOU MISUNDERSTAND. I'M NOT LOOKING TO TRADE. I SIMPLY WANT TO RUN A FEW TESTS.
WHAT KIND OF TESTS?
RELATED TO THE E.M.P. THAT KNOCKED OUT CENTRAL AND KEYSTONE CITY'S POWER. I'M TRYING TO DETERMINE THEIR SOURCE.
YOU TALKING ABOUT THAT WICKED FIRE IN THE SKY WE SAW LAST NIGHT?
PRECISELY. THIS WASN'T THE FIRST OCCURRENCE IN CENTRAL AND KEYSTONE CITIES. I'VE BEEN ALL OVER THE BADLANDS, TRACKING ITS ORIGIN AND THE MAGNETIC FIELD "FINGERPRINTS" IT LEFT IN THE NIGHT SKY...
AND THAT LED YOU HERE?
YOUR TANK HAS THE EXACT SAME SIGNATURE AS THE FIRE IN THE SKY. AND I WANT TO KNOW WHY. I CAN OFFER YOU GENEROUS COMPENSATION FOR YOUR TIME.
I'M NOT SURE IF YOU KNOW WHO I AM--
YOU'RE THAT RICH SCIENTIST, DOCTOR--
DARWIN ELIAS!
CAN YA BELIEVE OUR LUCK? YOU SAVED US THE TROUBLE OF LOOKING FOR YOU.
YOU DON'T MIND IF WE ADD HIM TO OUR DEAL, DO YOU, AXEL?
HE'S YOURS. BUT I GET TO KEEP HIS RIDE.

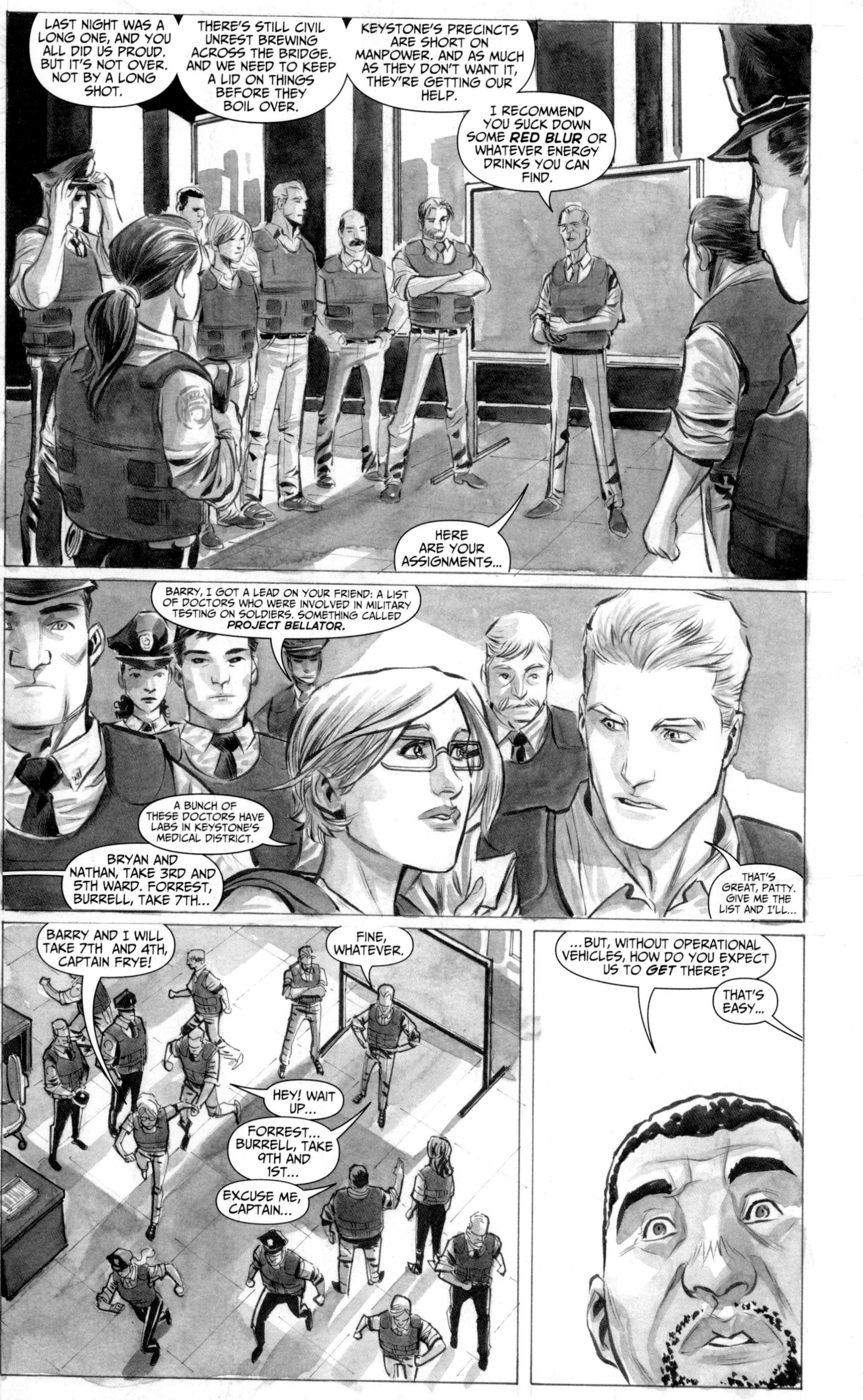
LAST NIGHT WAS A LONG ONE, AND YOU ALL DID US PROUD. BUT IT'S NOT OVER. NOT BY A LONG SHOT.
THERE'S STILL CIVIL UNREST BREWING ACROSS THE BRIDGE. AND WE NEED TO KEEP A LID ON THINGS BEFORE THEY BOIL OVER.
KEYSTONE'S PRECINCTS ARE SHORT ON MANPOWER. AND AS MUCH AS THEY DON'T WANT IT, THEY'RE GETTING OUR HELP.
I RECOMMEND YOU SUCK DOWN SOME RED BLUR OR WHATEVER ENERGY DRINKS YOU CAN FIND.
HERE ARE YOUR ASSIGNMENTS...
BARRY, I GOT A LEAD ON YOUR FRIEND: A LIST OF DOCTORS WHO WERE INVOLVED IN MILITARY TESTING ON SOLDIERS. SOMETHING CALLED PROJECT BELLATOR.
A BUNCH OF THESE DOCTORS HAVE LABS IN KEYSTONE'S MEDICAL DISTRICT.
BRYAN AND NATHAN, TAKE 3RD AND 5TH WARD. FORREST, BURRELL, TAKE 7TH...
THAT'S GREAT, PATTY. GIVE ME THE LIST AND I'LL...
BARRY AND I WILL TAKE 7TH AND 4TH, CAPTAIN FRYE!
FINE, WHATEVER.
HEY! WAIT UP...
FORREST... BURRELL, TAKE 9TH AND 1ST...
EXCUSE ME, CAPTAIN...
...BUT, WITHOUT OPERATIONAL VEHICLES, HOW DO YOU EXPECT US TO GET THERE?
THAT'S EASY...

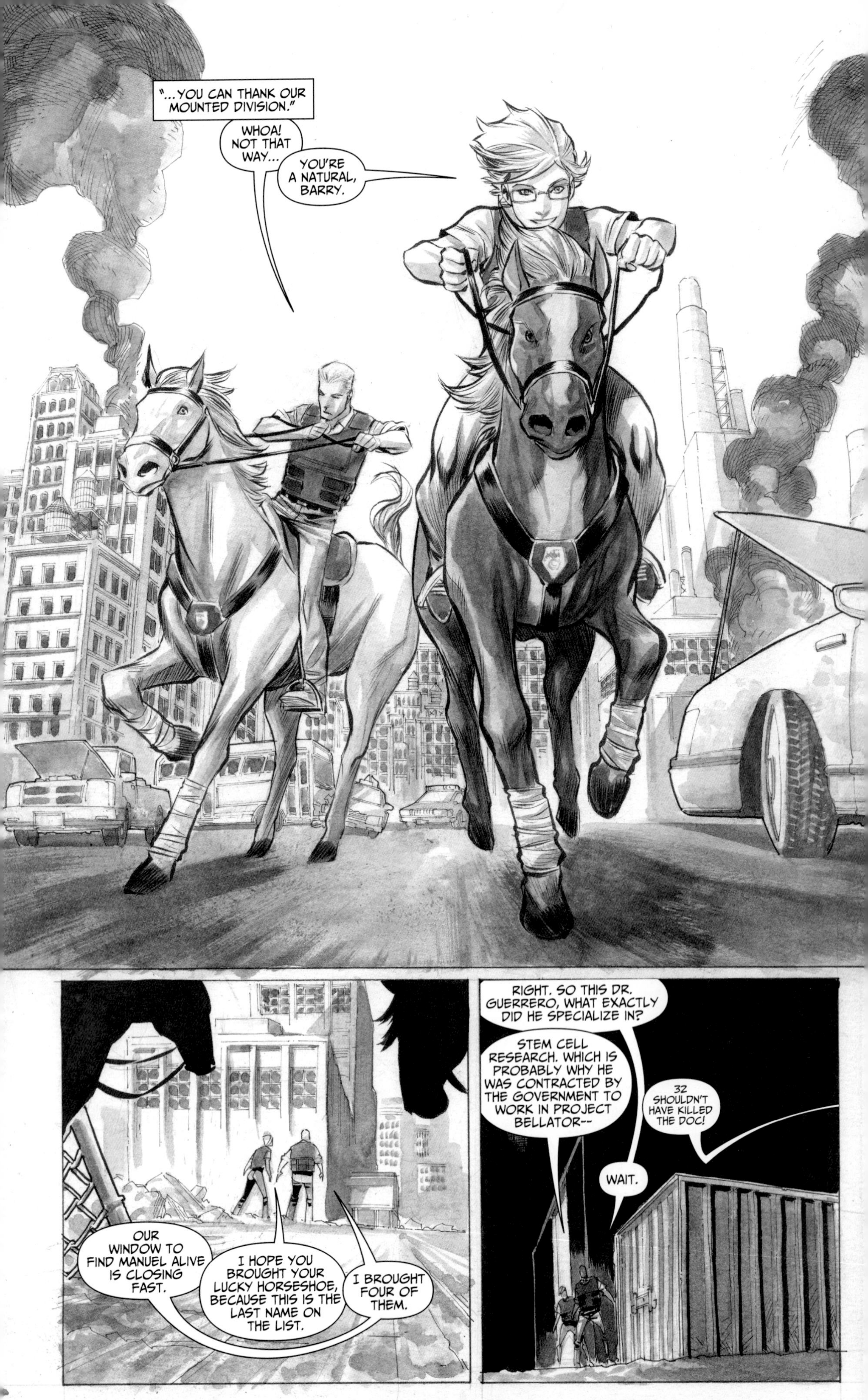
"...YOU CAN THANK OUR MOUNTED DIVISION."
WHOA! NOT THAT WAY...
YOU'RE A NATURAL, BARRY.
OUR WINDOW TO FIND MANUEL ALIVE IS CLOSING FAST.
I HOPE YOU BROUGHT YOUR LUCKY HORSESHOE, BECAUSE THIS IS THE LAST NAME ON THE LIST.
I BROUGHT FOUR OF THEM.
RIGHT. SO THIS DR. GUERRERO, WHAT EXACTLY DID HE SPECIALIZE IN?
STEM CELL RESEARCH. WHICH IS PROBABLY WHY HE WAS CONTRACTED BY THE GOVERNMENT TO WORK IN PROJECT BELLATOR--
32 SHOULDN'T HAVE KILLED THE DOC!
WAIT.

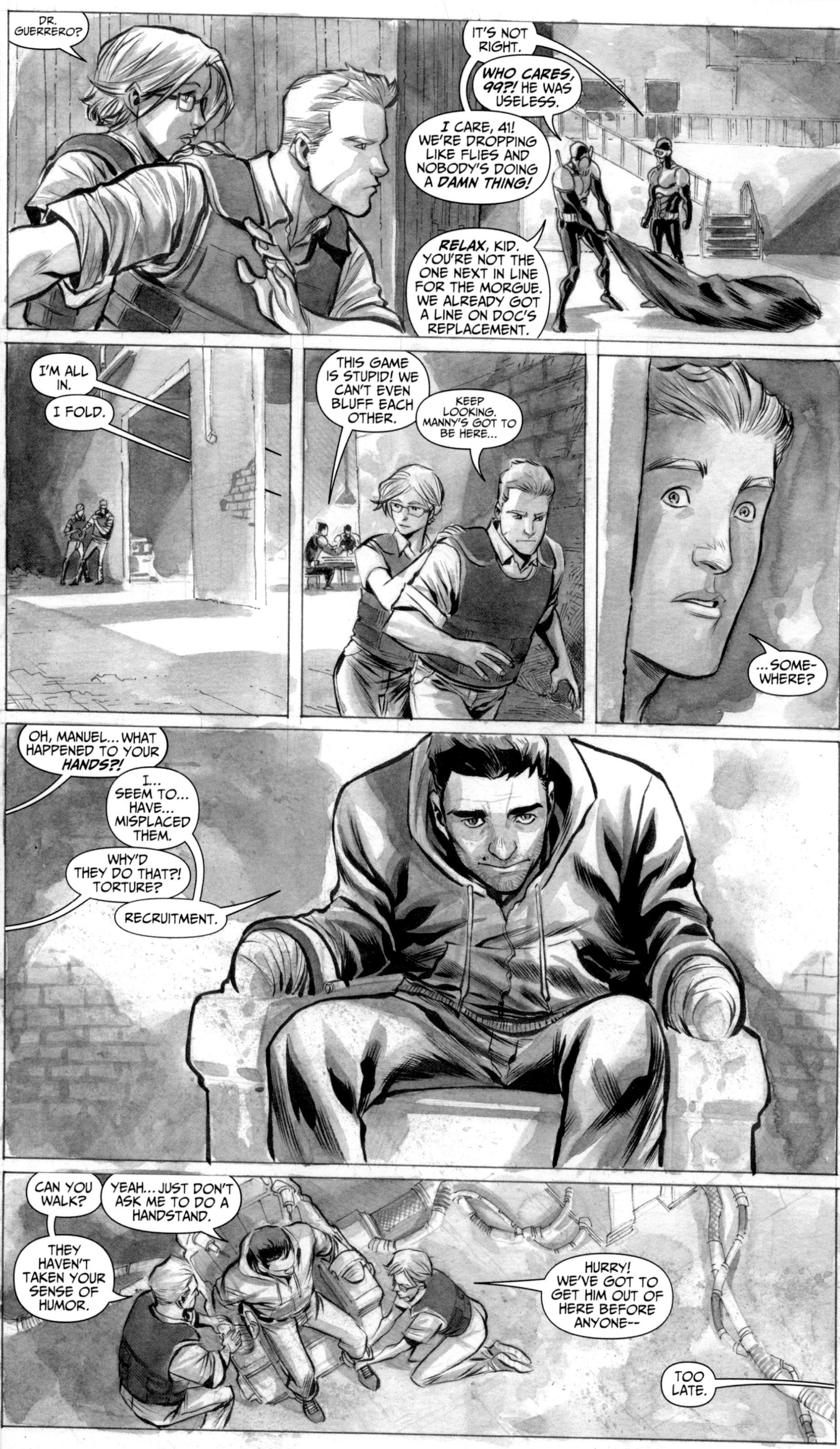
DR. GUERRERO?
IT'S NOT RIGHT.
WHO CARES, 99?! HE WAS USELESS.
I CARE, 41! WE'RE DROPPING LIKE FLIES AND NOBODY'S DOING A DAMN THING!
RELAX, KID. YOU'RE NOT THE ONE NEXT IN LINE FOR THE MORGUE. WE ALREADY GOT A LINE ON DOC'S REPLACEMENT.
I'M ALL IN.
I FOLD.
THIS GAME IS STUPID! WE CAN'T EVEN BLUFF EACH OTHER.
KEEP LOOKING. MANNY'S GOT TO BE HERE...
...SOME-WHERE?
OH, MANUEL... WHAT HAPPENED TO YOUR HANDS?!
I... SEEM TO... HAVE... MISPLACED THEM.
WHY'D THEY DO THAT?! TORTURE?
RECRUITMENT.
CAN YOU WALK?
YEAH... JUST DON'T ASK ME TO DO A HANDSTAND.
THEY HAVEN'T TAKEN YOUR SENSE OF HUMOR.
HURRY! WE'VE GOT TO GET HIM OUT OF HERE BEFORE ANYONE--
TOO LATE.

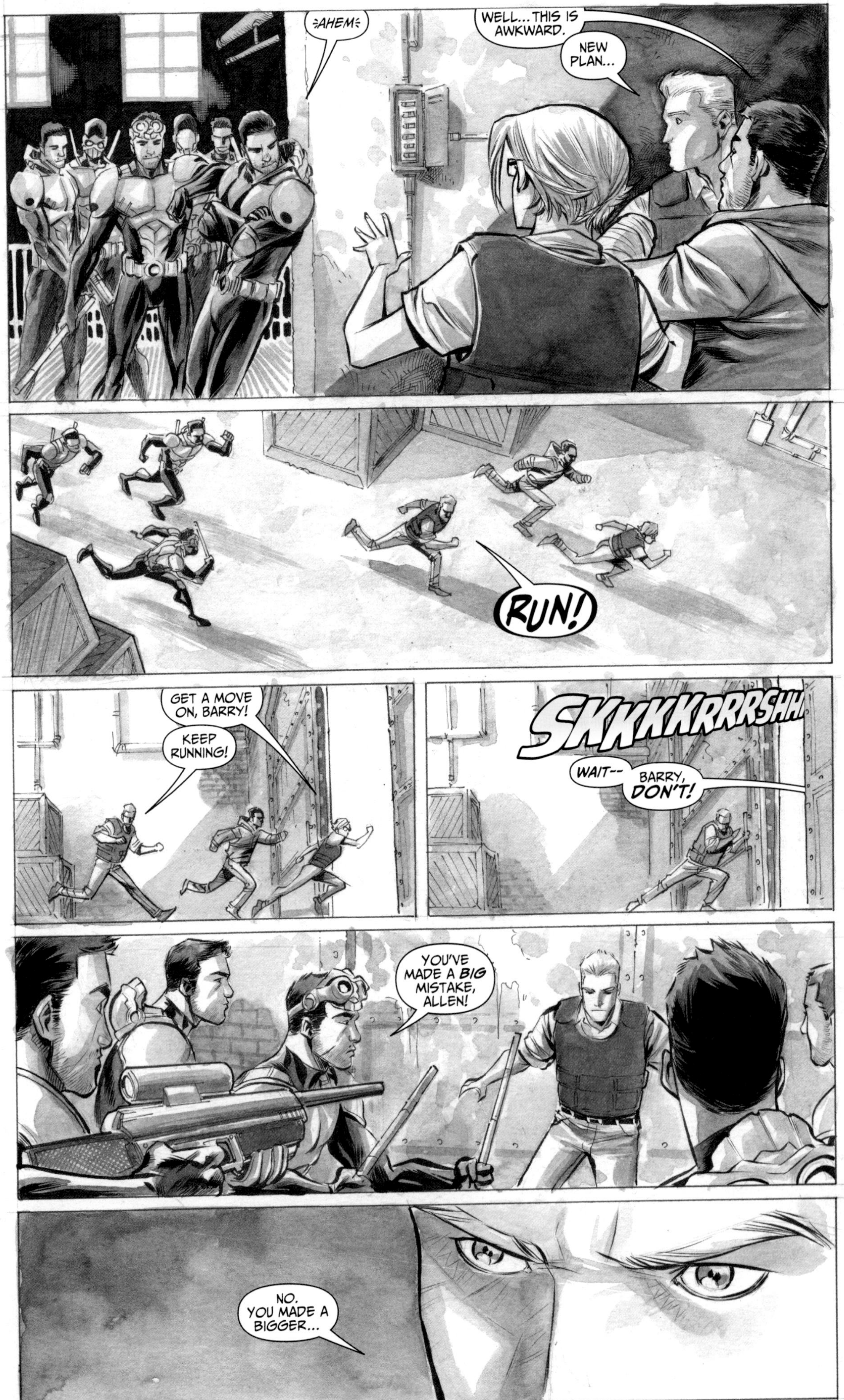
AHEM
WELL...THIS IS AWKWARD.
NEW PLAN...
RUN!
GET A MOVE ON, BARRY!
KEEP RUNNING!
SKKKKRRRSHH
WAIT--
BARRY, DON'T!
YOU'VE MADE A BIG MISTAKE, ALLEN!
NO. YOU MADE A BIGGER...

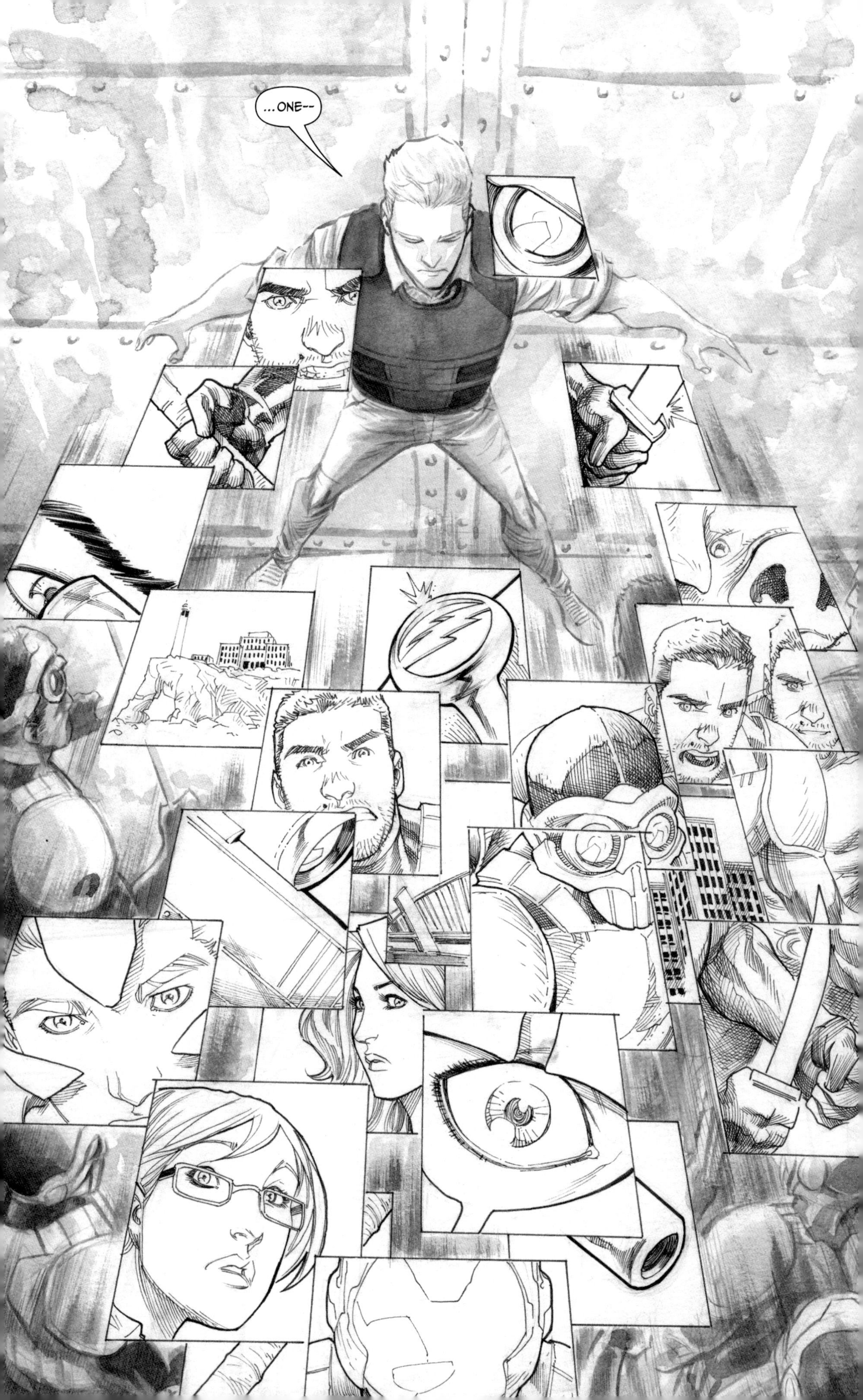
...ONE--

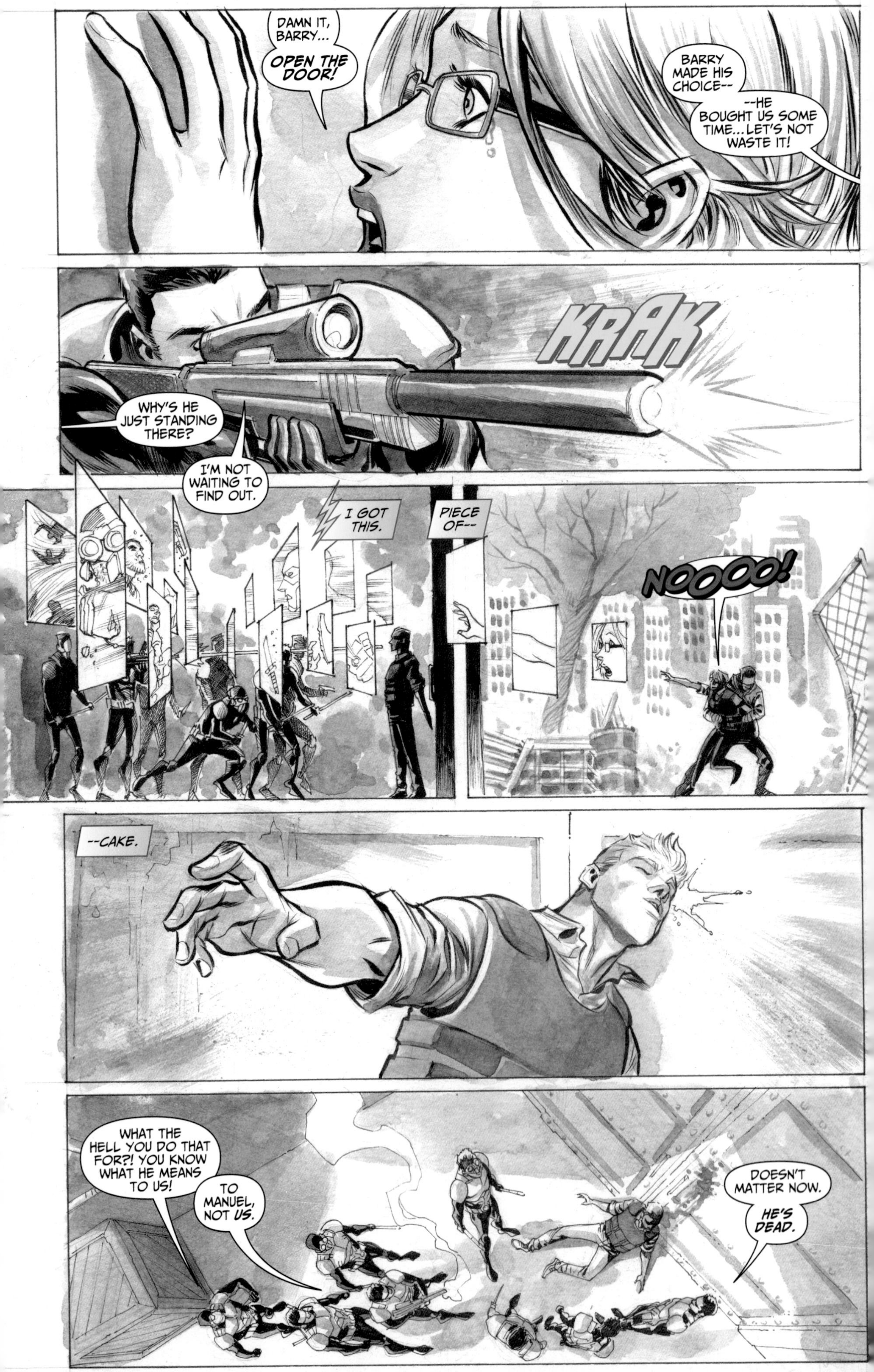
DAMN IT, BARRY... OPEN THE DOOR!
BARRY MADE HIS CHOICE--
--HE BOUGHT US SOME TIME...LET'S NOT WASTE IT!
KRAK
WHY'S HE JUST STANDING THERE?
I'M NOT WAITING TO FIND OUT.
I GOT THIS.
PIECE OF--
NOOOOO!
--CAKE.
WHAT THE HELL YOU DO THAT FOR?! YOU KNOW WHAT HE MEANS TO US!
TO MANUEL, NOT US.
DOESN'T MATTER NOW.
HE'S DEAD.

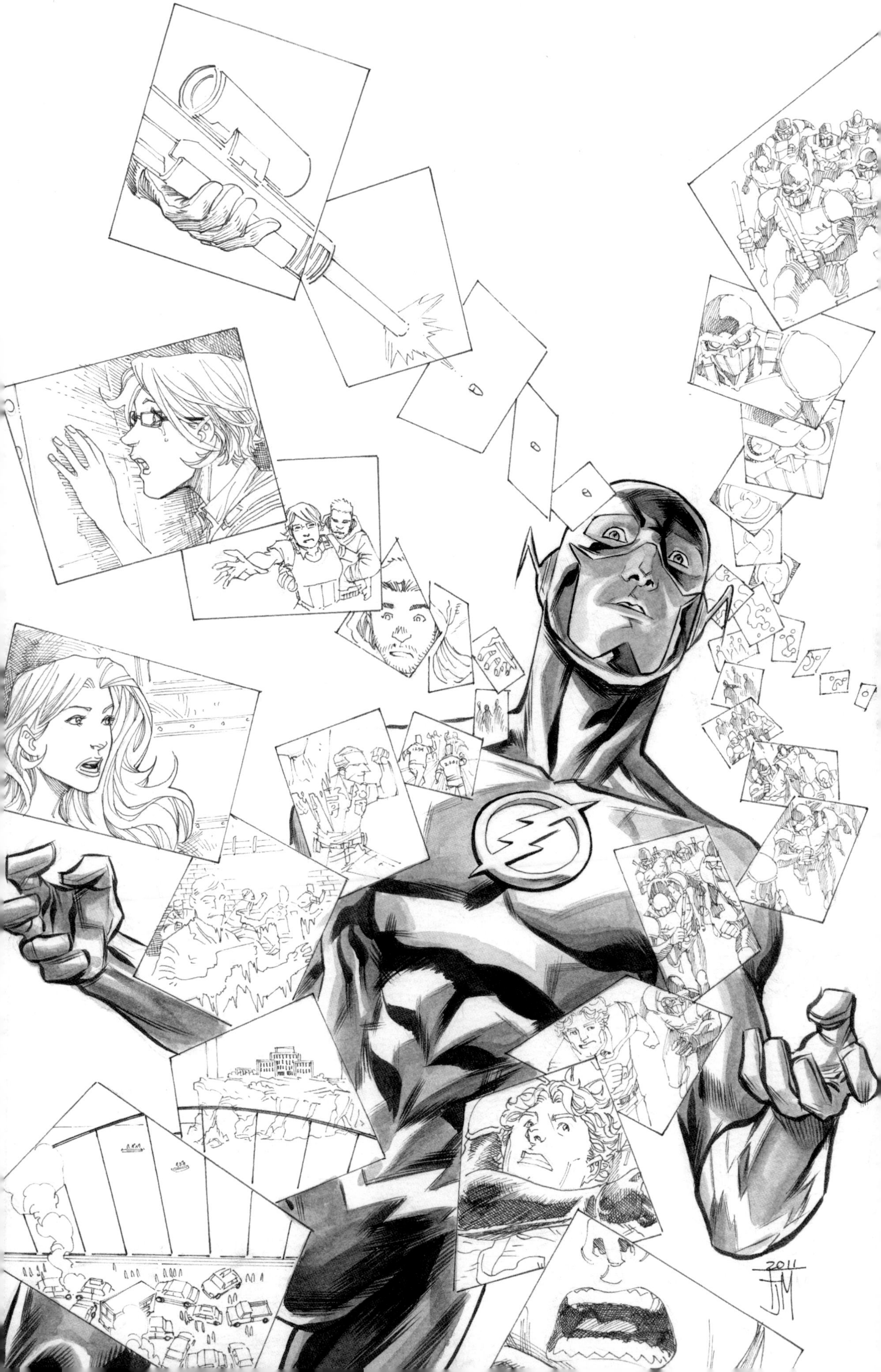
2011

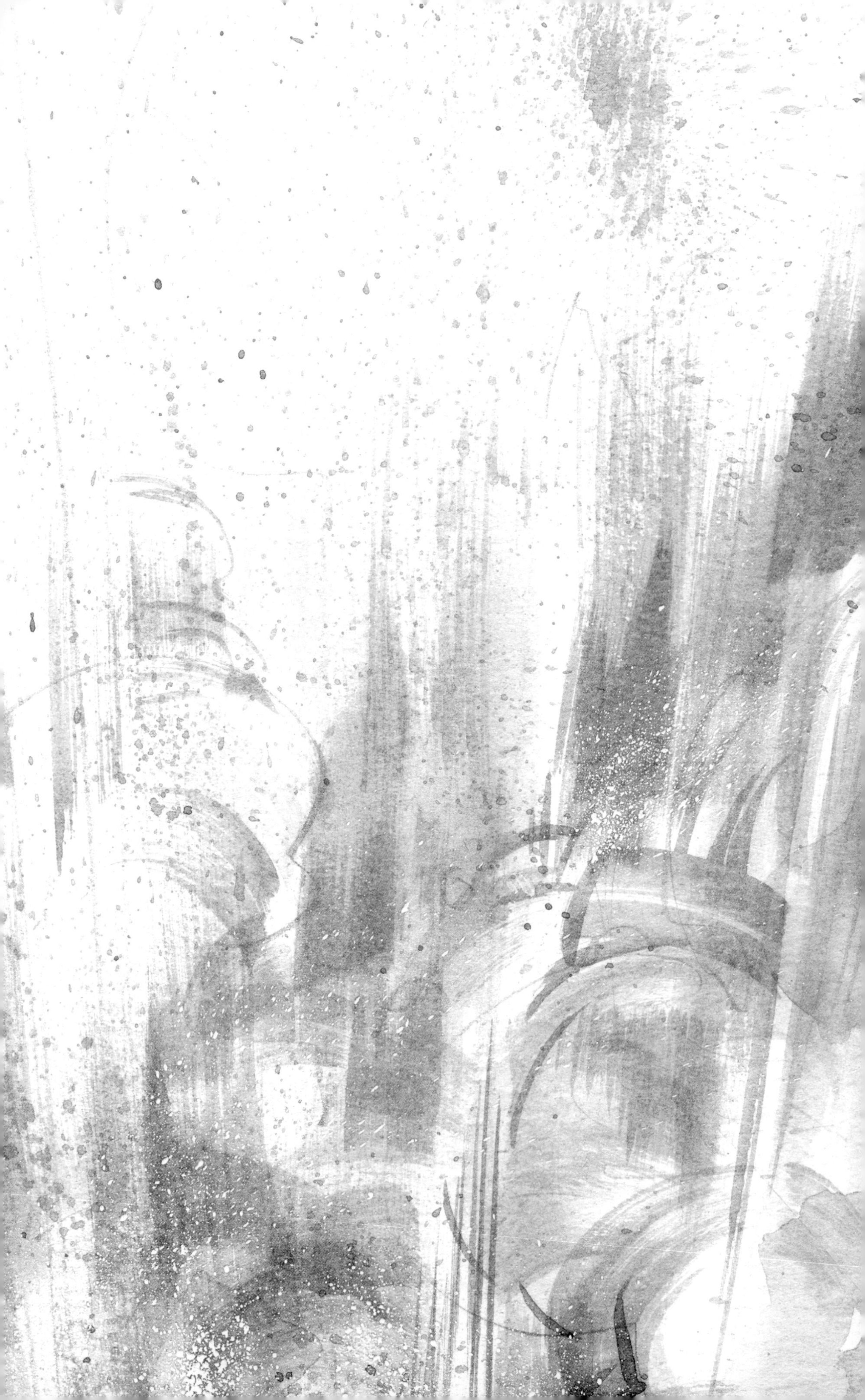

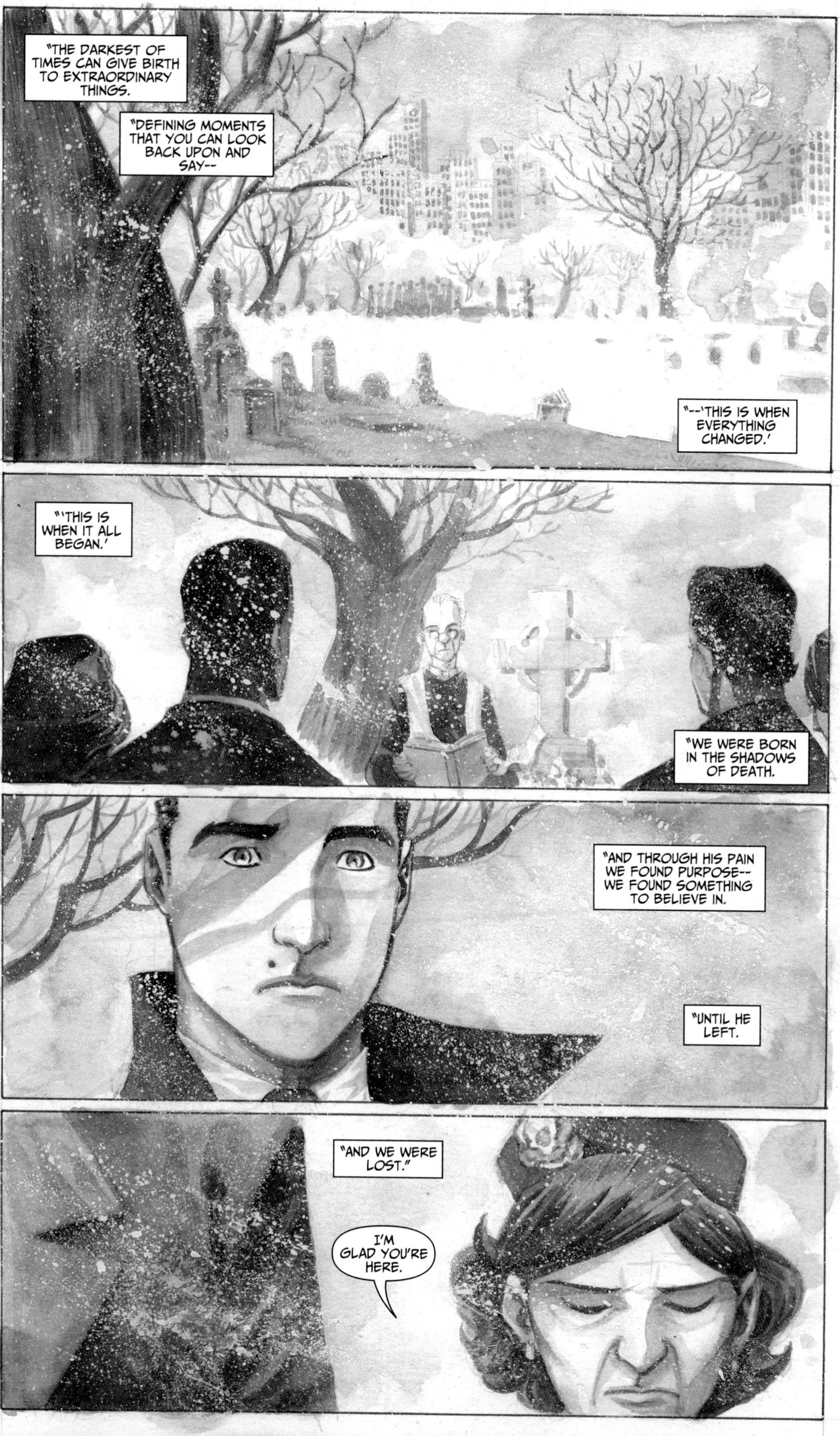
"THE DARKEST OF TIMES CAN GIVE BIRTH TO EXTRAORDINARY THINGS.
"DEFINING MOMENTS THAT YOU CAN LOOK BACK UPON AND SAY--
"--'THIS IS WHEN EVERYTHING CHANGED.'
"'THIS IS WHEN IT ALL BEGAN.'
"WE WERE BORN IN THE SHADOWS OF DEATH.
"AND THROUGH HIS PAIN WE FOUND PURPOSE-- WE FOUND SOMETHING TO BELIEVE IN.
"UNTIL HE LEFT.
"AND WE WERE LOST."
I'M GLAD YOU'RE HERE.

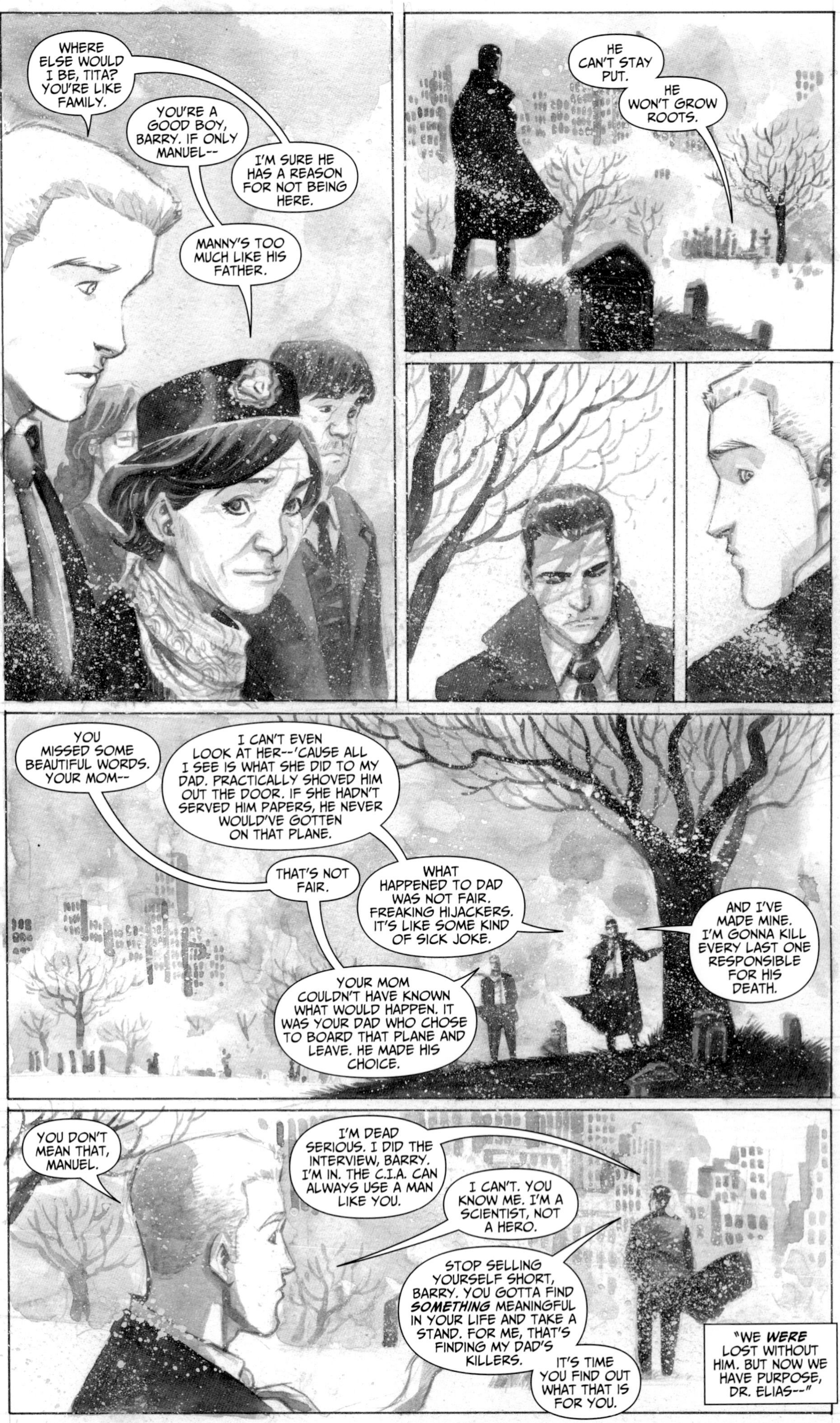
WHERE ELSE WOULD I BE, TITA? YOU'RE LIKE FAMILY.
YOU'RE A GOOD BOY, BARRY. IF ONLY MANUEL--
I'M SURE HE HAS A REASON FOR NOT BEING HERE.
MANNY'S TOO MUCH LIKE HIS FATHER.
HE CAN'T STAY PUT.
HE WON'T GROW ROOTS.
YOU MISSED SOME BEAUTIFUL WORDS. YOUR MOM--
I CAN'T EVEN LOOK AT HER--'CAUSE ALL I SEE IS WHAT SHE DID TO MY DAD. PRACTICALLY SHOVED HIM OUT THE DOOR. IF SHE HADN'T SERVED HIM PAPERS, HE NEVER WOULD'VE GOTTEN ON THAT PLANE.
THAT'S NOT FAIR.
WHAT HAPPENED TO DAD WAS NOT FAIR. FREAKING HIJACKERS. IT'S LIKE SOME KIND OF SICK JOKE.
YOUR MOM COULDN'T HAVE KNOWN WHAT WOULD HAPPEN. IT WAS YOUR DAD WHO CHOSE TO BOARD THAT PLANE AND LEAVE. HE MADE HIS CHOICE.
AND I'VE MADE MINE. I'M GONNA KILL EVERY LAST ONE RESPONSIBLE FOR HIS DEATH.
YOU DON'T MEAN THAT, MANUEL.
I'M DEAD SERIOUS. I DID THE INTERVIEW, BARRY. I'M IN. THE C.I.A. CAN ALWAYS USE A MAN LIKE YOU.
I CAN'T. YOU KNOW ME. I'M A SCIENTIST, NOT A HERO.
STOP SELLING YOURSELF SHORT, BARRY. YOU GOTTA FIND *SOMETHING* MEANINGFUL IN YOUR LIFE AND TAKE A STAND. FOR ME, THAT'S FINDING MY DAD'S KILLERS.
IT'S TIME YOU FIND OUT WHAT THAT IS FOR YOU.
"WE *WERE* LOST WITHOUT HIM. BUT NOW WE HAVE PURPOSE, DR. ELIAS--"

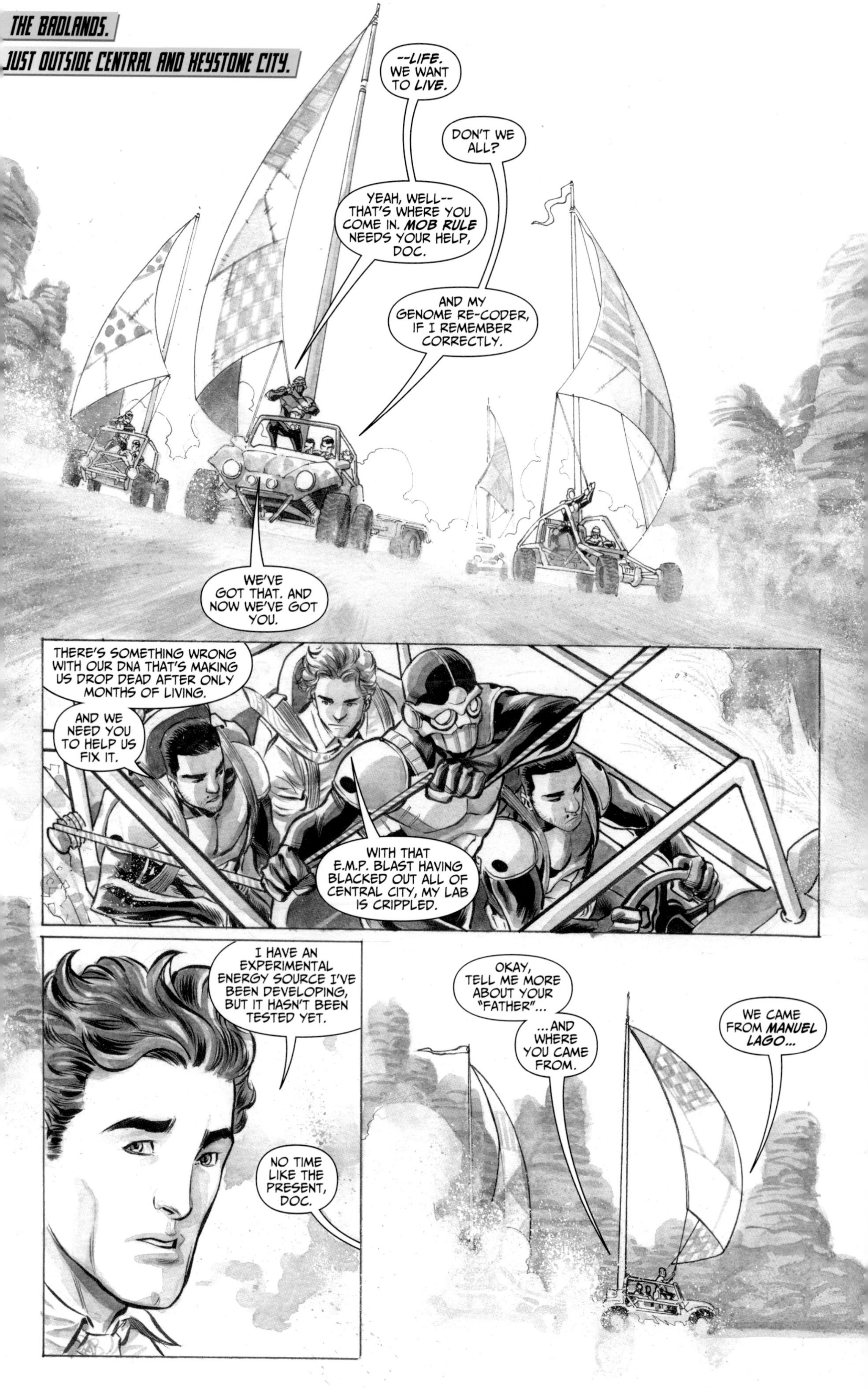
THE BADLANDS.
JUST OUTSIDE CENTRAL AND KEYSTONE CITY.
--LIFE. WE WANT TO LIVE.
DON'T WE ALL?
YEAH, WELL-- THAT'S WHERE YOU COME IN. MOB RULE NEEDS YOUR HELP, DOC.
AND MY GENOME RE-CODER, IF I REMEMBER CORRECTLY.
WE'VE GOT THAT. AND NOW WE'VE GOT YOU.
THERE'S SOMETHING WRONG WITH OUR DNA THAT'S MAKING US DROP DEAD AFTER ONLY MONTHS OF LIVING.
AND WE NEED YOU TO HELP US FIX IT.
WITH THAT E.M.P. BLAST HAVING BLACKED OUT ALL OF CENTRAL CITY, MY LAB IS CRIPPLED.
I HAVE AN EXPERIMENTAL ENERGY SOURCE I'VE BEEN DEVELOPING, BUT IT HASN'T BEEN TESTED YET.
NO TIME LIKE THE PRESENT, DOC.
OKAY, TELL ME MORE ABOUT YOUR "FATHER"...
...AND WHERE YOU CAME FROM.
WE CAME FROM MANUEL LAGO...

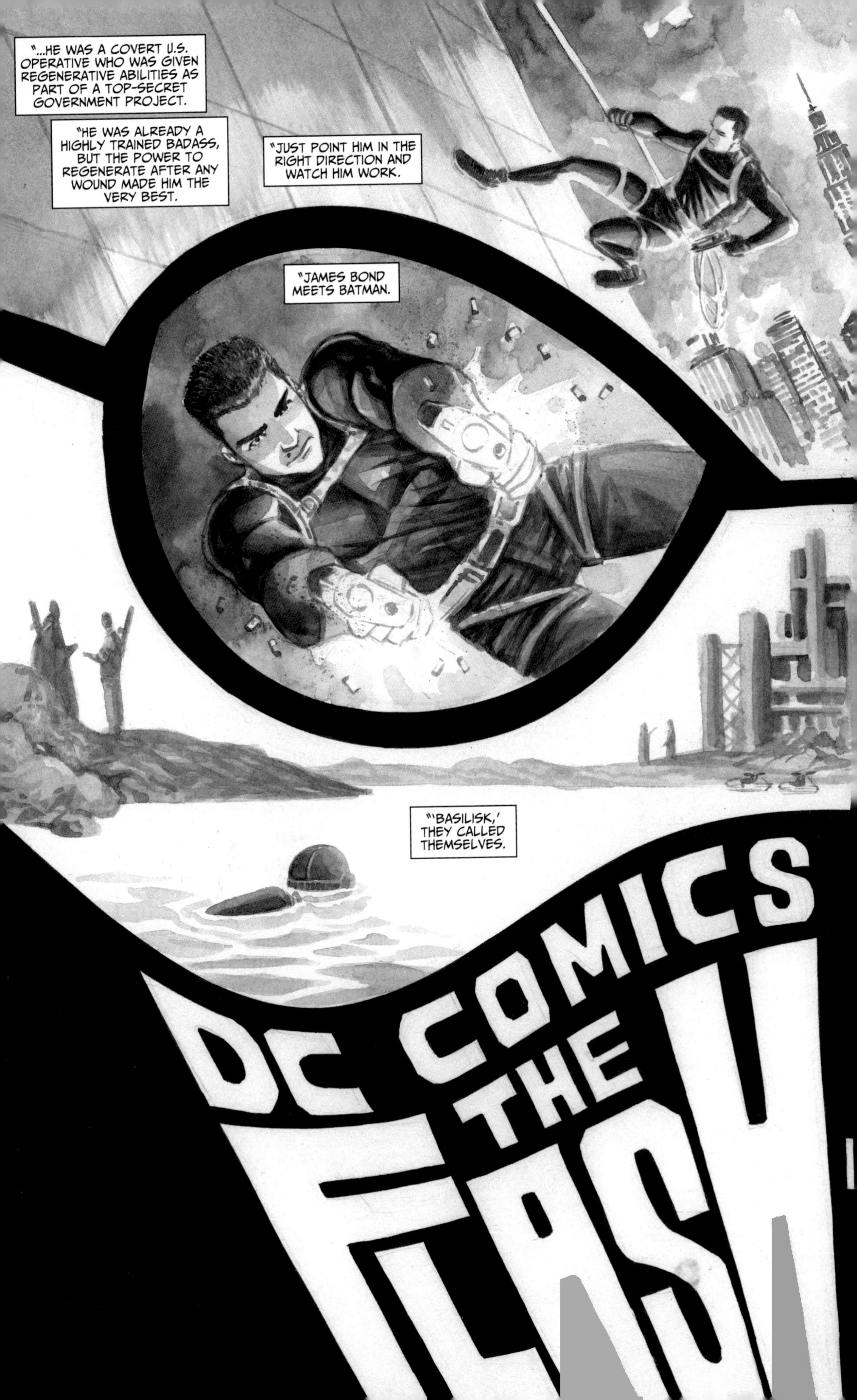
"...HE WAS A COVERT U.S. OPERATIVE WHO WAS GIVEN REGENERATIVE ABILITIES AS PART OF A TOP-SECRET GOVERNMENT PROJECT.
"HE WAS ALREADY A HIGHLY TRAINED BADASS, BUT THE POWER TO REGENERATE AFTER ANY WOUND MADE HIM THE VERY BEST.
"JUST POINT HIM IN THE RIGHT DIRECTION AND WATCH HIM WORK.
"JAMES BOND MEETS BATMAN.
"'BASILISK,' THEY CALLED THEMSELVES.
DC COMICS
THE
FLASH

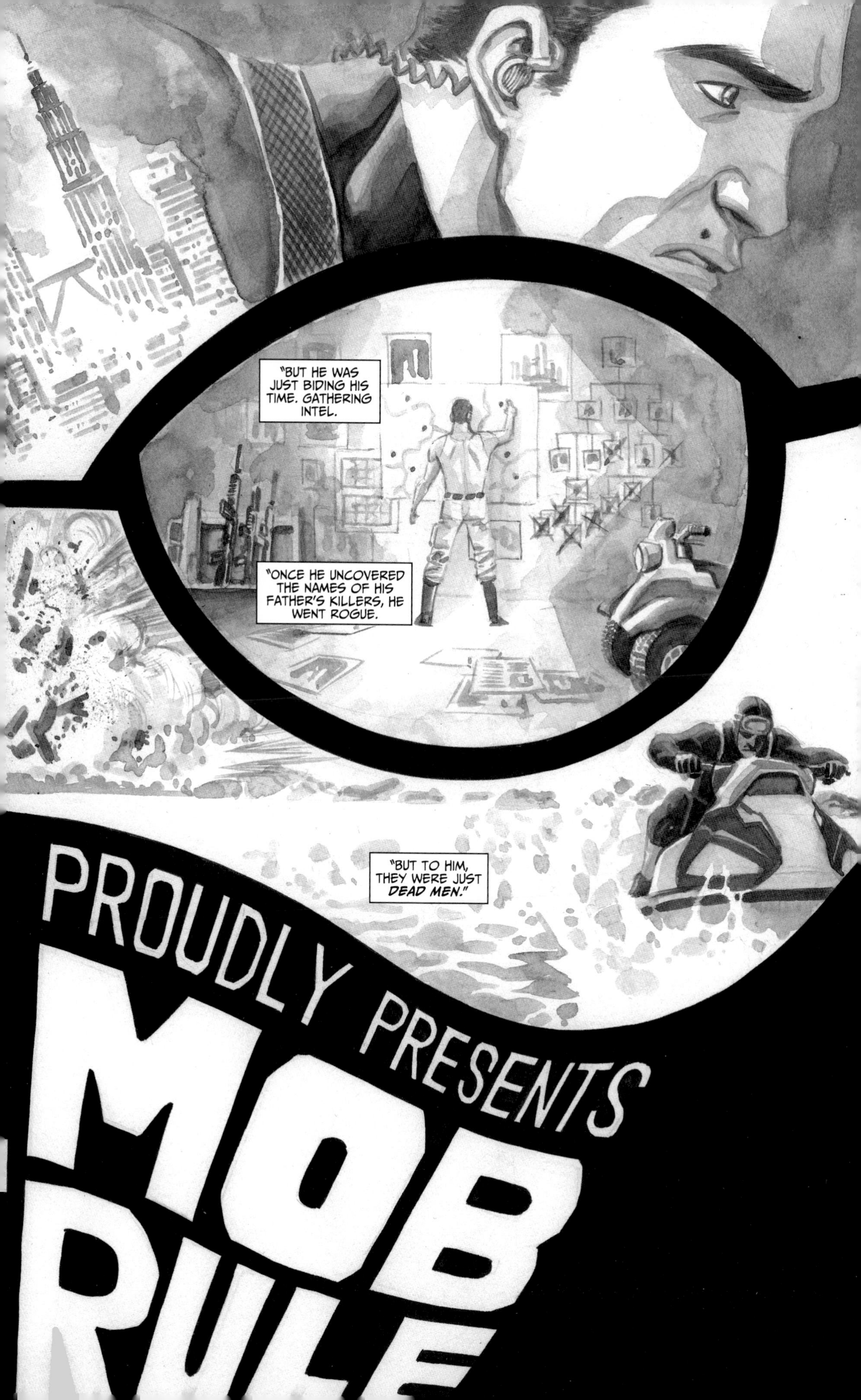
"BUT HE WAS JUST BIDING HIS TIME. GATHERING INTEL.
"ONCE HE UNCOVERED THE NAMES OF HIS FATHER'S KILLERS, HE WENT ROGUE.
"BUT TO HIM, THEY WERE JUST *DEAD MEN.*"
PROUDLY PRESENTS
MOB RULE

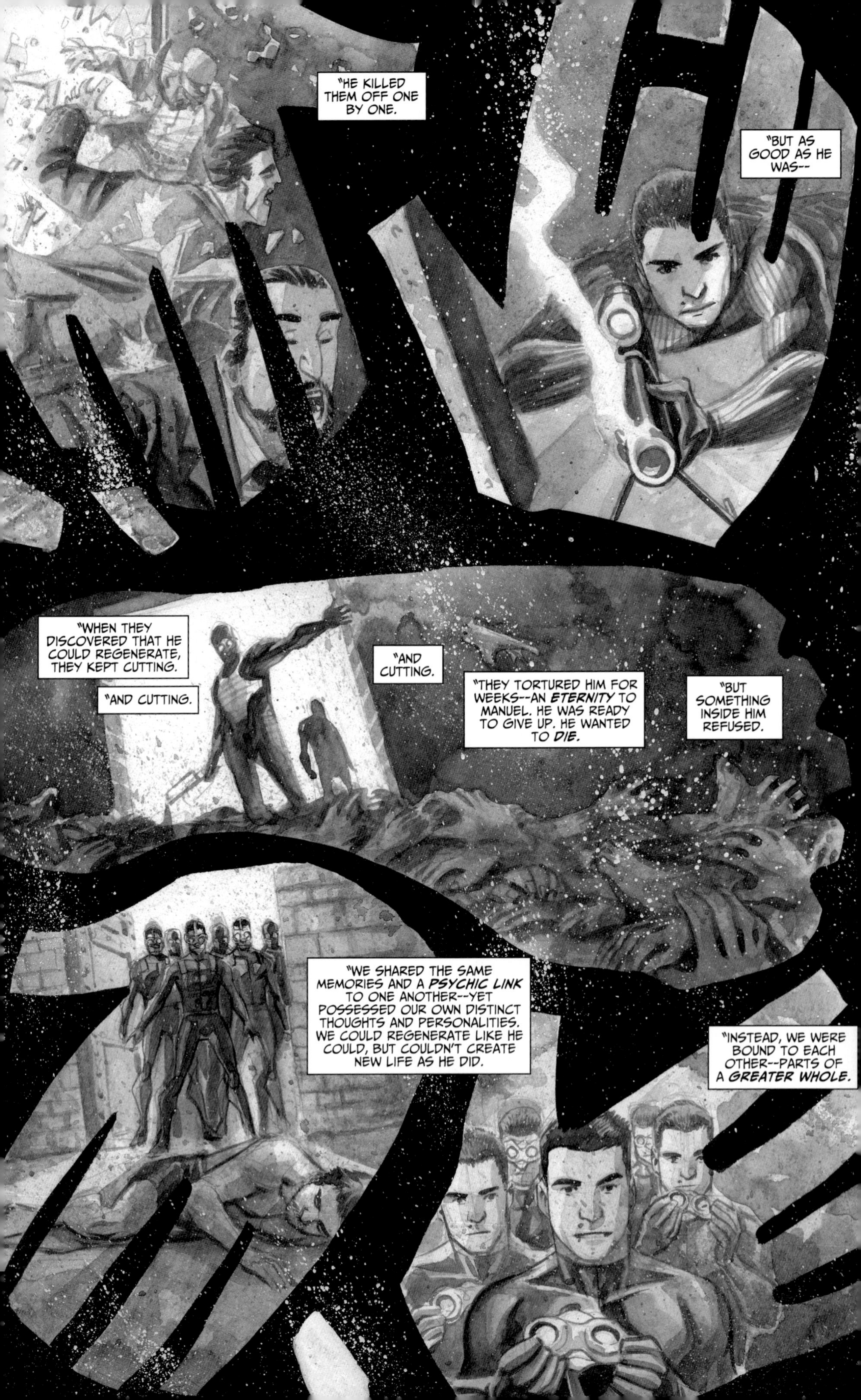
"HE KILLED THEM OFF ONE BY ONE.
"BUT AS GOOD AS HE WAS--
"WHEN THEY DISCOVERED THAT HE COULD REGENERATE, THEY KEPT CUTTING.
"AND CUTTING.
"AND CUTTING.
"THEY TORTURED HIM FOR WEEKS--AN *ETERNITY* TO MANUEL. HE WAS READY TO GIVE UP. HE WANTED TO *DIE.*
"BUT SOMETHING INSIDE HIM REFUSED.
"WE SHARED THE SAME MEMORIES AND A *PSYCHIC LINK* TO ONE ANOTHER--YET POSSESSED OUR OWN DISTINCT THOUGHTS AND PERSONALITIES. WE COULD REGENERATE LIKE HE COULD, BUT COULDN'T CREATE NEW LIFE AS HE DID.
"INSTEAD, WE WERE BOUND TO EACH OTHER--PARTS OF A *GREATER WHOLE.*

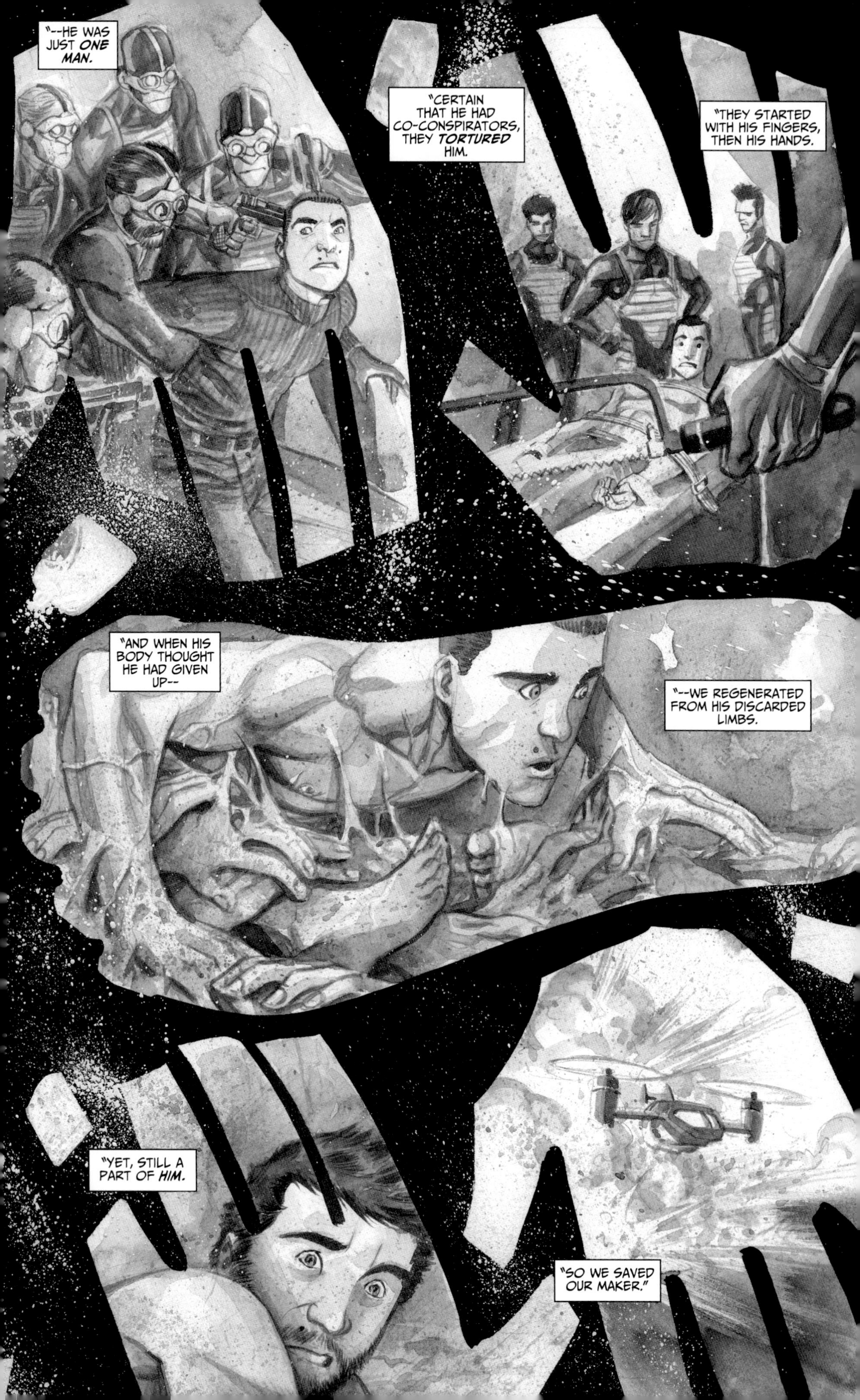
"--HE WAS JUST ONE MAN.
"CERTAIN THAT HE HAD CO-CONSPIRATORS, THEY TORTURED HIM.
"THEY STARTED WITH HIS FINGERS, THEN HIS HANDS.
"AND WHEN HIS BODY THOUGHT HE HAD GIVEN UP--
"--WE REGENERATED FROM HIS DISCARDED LIMBS.
"YET, STILL A PART OF HIM.
"SO WE SAVED OUR MAKER."

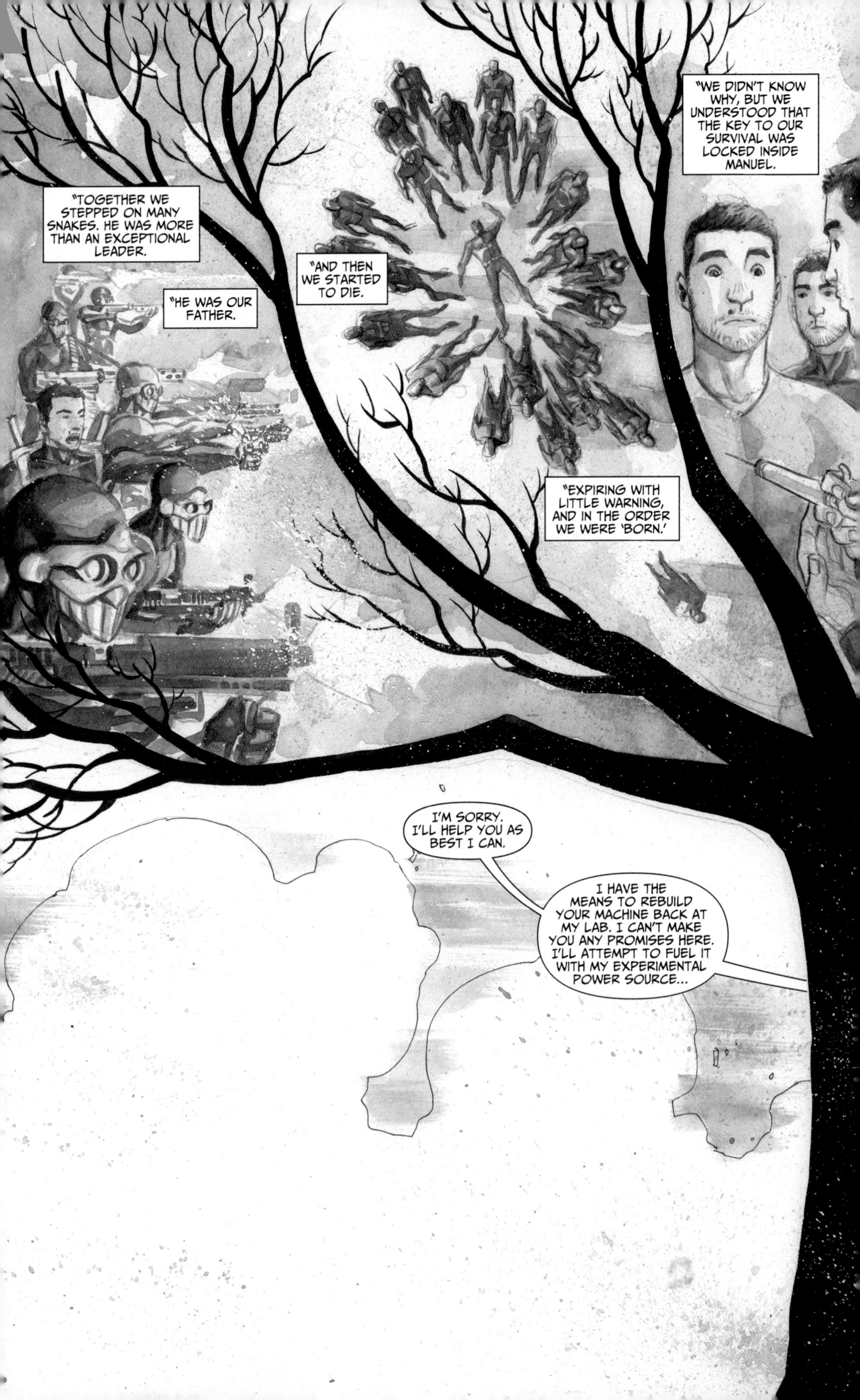
"TOGETHER WE STEPPED ON MANY SNAKES. HE WAS MORE THAN AN EXCEPTIONAL LEADER.
"HE WAS OUR FATHER.
"AND THEN WE STARTED TO DIE.
"WE DIDN'T KNOW WHY, BUT WE UNDERSTOOD THAT THE KEY TO OUR SURVIVAL WAS LOCKED INSIDE MANUEL.
"EXPIRING WITH LITTLE WARNING, AND IN THE ORDER WE WERE 'BORN.'
I'M SORRY. I'LL HELP YOU AS BEST I CAN.
I HAVE THE MEANS TO REBUILD YOUR MACHINE BACK AT MY LAB. I CAN'T MAKE YOU ANY PROMISES HERE. I'LL ATTEMPT TO FUEL IT WITH MY EXPERIMENTAL POWER SOURCE...

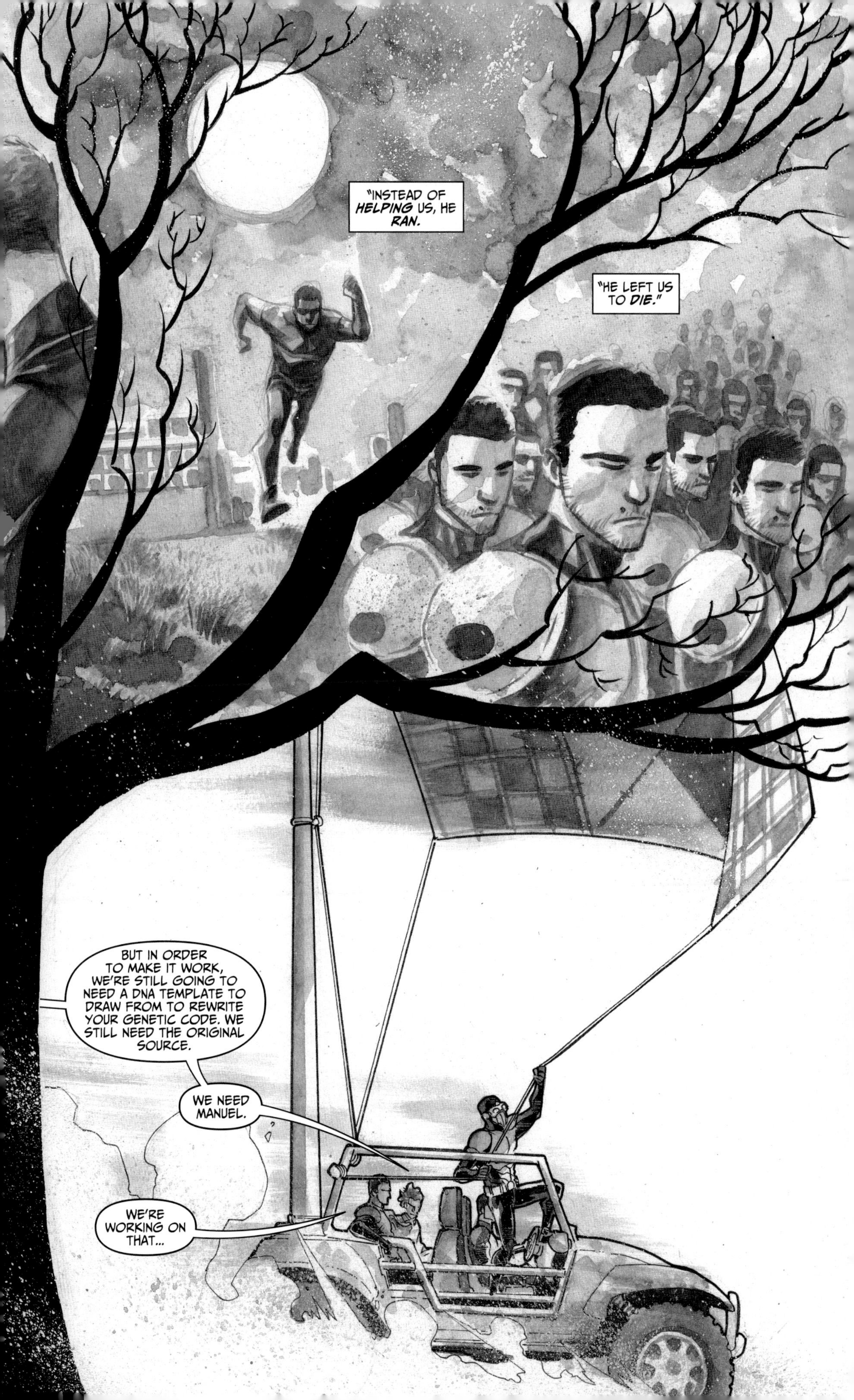
"INSTEAD OF HELPING US, HE RAN.
"HE LEFT US TO DIE."
BUT IN ORDER TO MAKE IT WORK, WE'RE STILL GOING TO NEED A DNA TEMPLATE TO DRAW FROM TO REWRITE YOUR GENETIC CODE. WE STILL NEED THE ORIGINAL SOURCE.
WE NEED MANUEL.
WE'RE WORKING ON THAT...

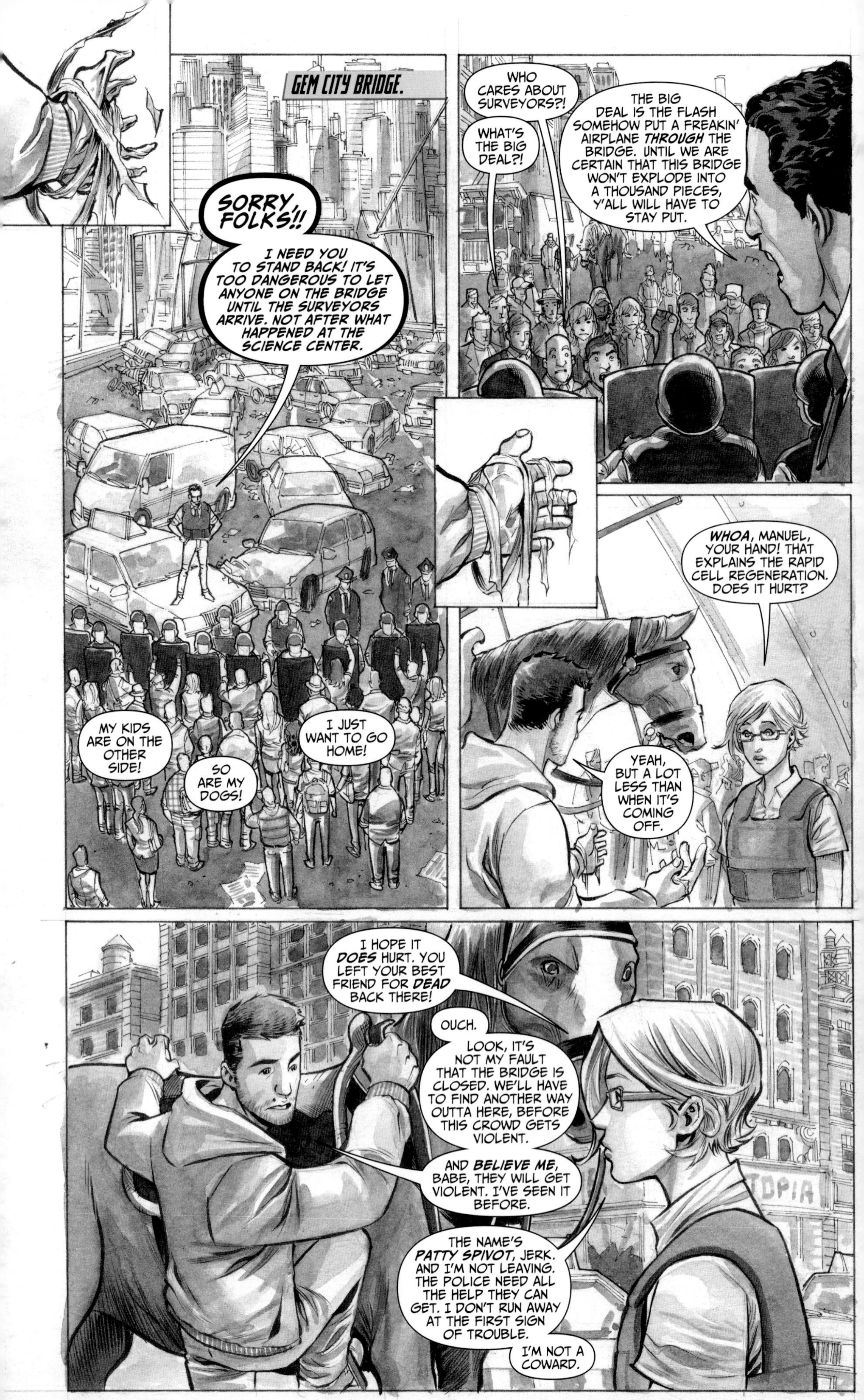
GEM CITY BRIDGE.
SORRY, FOLKS!!
I NEED YOU TO STAND BACK! IT'S TOO DANGEROUS TO LET ANYONE ON THE BRIDGE UNTIL THE SURVEYORS ARRIVE. NOT AFTER WHAT HAPPENED AT THE SCIENCE CENTER.
MY KIDS ARE ON THE OTHER SIDE!
SO ARE MY DOGS!
I JUST WANT TO GO HOME!
WHAT'S THE BIG DEAL?!
WHO CARES ABOUT SURVEYORS?!
THE BIG DEAL IS THE FLASH SOMEHOW PUT A FREAKIN' AIRPLANE THROUGH THE BRIDGE. UNTIL WE ARE CERTAIN THAT THIS BRIDGE WON'T EXPLODE INTO A THOUSAND PIECES, Y'ALL WILL HAVE TO STAY PUT.
WHOA, MANUEL, YOUR HAND! THAT EXPLAINS THE RAPID CELL REGENERATION. DOES IT HURT?
YEAH, BUT A LOT LESS THAN WHEN IT'S COMING OFF.
I HOPE IT DOES HURT. YOU LEFT YOUR BEST FRIEND FOR DEAD BACK THERE!
OUCH.
LOOK, IT'S NOT MY FAULT THAT THE BRIDGE IS CLOSED. WE'LL HAVE TO FIND ANOTHER WAY OUTTA HERE, BEFORE THIS CROWD GETS VIOLENT.
AND BELIEVE ME, BABE, THEY WILL GET VIOLENT. I'VE SEEN IT BEFORE.
THE NAME'S PATTY SPIVOT, JERK. AND I'M NOT LEAVING. THE POLICE NEED ALL THE HELP THEY CAN GET. I DON'T RUN AWAY AT THE FIRST SIGN OF TROUBLE.
I'M NOT A COWARD.

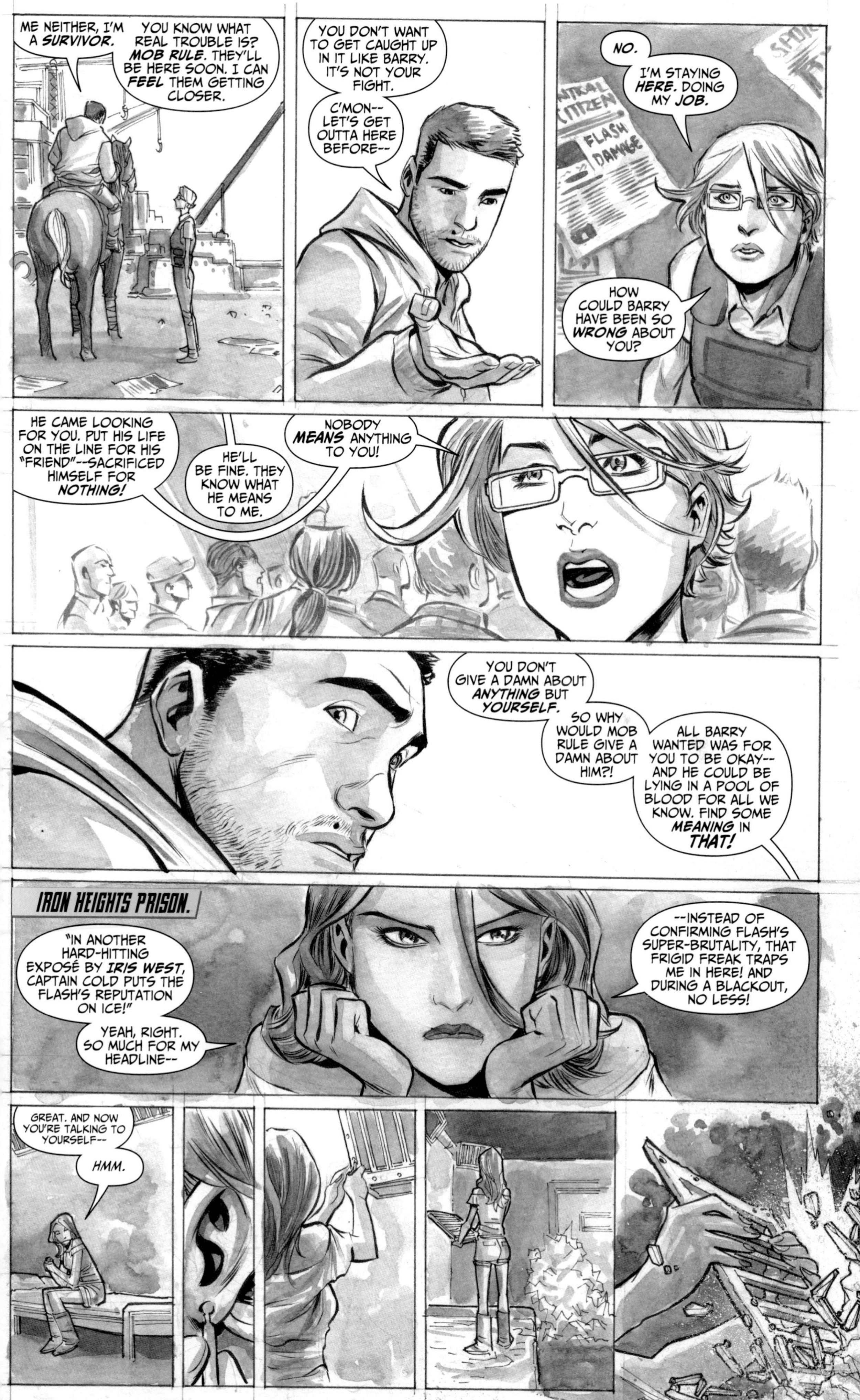
ME NEITHER, I'M A SURVIVOR.
YOU KNOW WHAT REAL TROUBLE IS? MOB RULE. THEY'LL BE HERE SOON. I CAN FEEL THEM GETTING CLOSER.
YOU DON'T WANT TO GET CAUGHT UP IN IT LIKE BARRY. IT'S NOT YOUR FIGHT.
C'MON-- LET'S GET OUTTA HERE BEFORE--
NO.
I'M STAYING HERE. DOING MY JOB.
FLASH DAMAGE
HOW COULD BARRY HAVE BEEN SO WRONG ABOUT YOU?
HE CAME LOOKING FOR YOU. PUT HIS LIFE ON THE LINE FOR HIS "FRIEND"--SACRIFICED HIMSELF FOR NOTHING!
HE'LL BE FINE. THEY KNOW WHAT HE MEANS TO ME.
NOBODY MEANS ANYTHING TO YOU!
YOU DON'T GIVE A DAMN ABOUT ANYTHING BUT YOURSELF.
SO WHY WOULD MOB RULE GIVE A DAMN ABOUT HIM?!
ALL BARRY WANTED WAS FOR YOU TO BE OKAY-- AND HE COULD BE LYING IN A POOL OF BLOOD FOR ALL WE KNOW. FIND SOME MEANING IN THAT!
IRON HEIGHTS PRISON.
"IN ANOTHER HARD-HITTING EXPOSÉ BY IRIS WEST, CAPTAIN COLD PUTS THE FLASH'S REPUTATION ON ICE!"
YEAH, RIGHT. SO MUCH FOR MY HEADLINE--
--INSTEAD OF CONFIRMING FLASH'S SUPER-BRUTALITY, THAT FRIGID FREAK TRAPS ME IN HERE! AND DURING A BLACKOUT, NO LESS!
GREAT. AND NOW YOU'RE TALKING TO YOURSELF--
HMM.

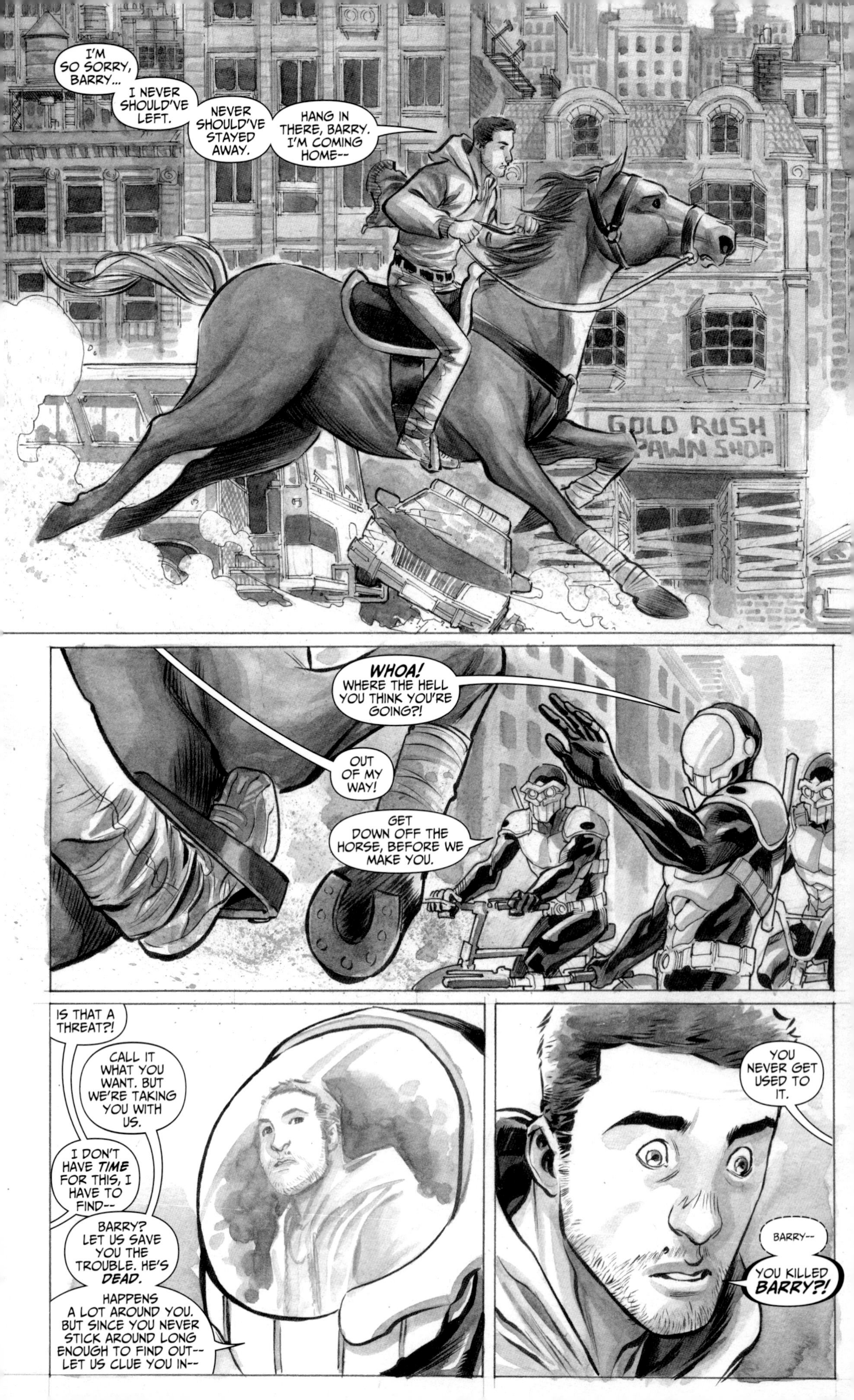
I'M SO SORRY, BARRY...
I NEVER SHOULD'VE LEFT.
NEVER SHOULD'VE STAYED AWAY.
HANG IN THERE, BARRY. I'M COMING HOME--
GOLD RUSH PAWN SHOP
WHOA! WHERE THE HELL YOU THINK YOU'RE GOING?!
OUT OF MY WAY!
GET DOWN OFF THE HORSE, BEFORE WE MAKE YOU.
IS THAT A THREAT?!
CALL IT WHAT YOU WANT. BUT WE'RE TAKING YOU WITH US.
I DON'T HAVE TIME FOR THIS, I HAVE TO FIND--
BARRY? LET US SAVE YOU THE TROUBLE. HE'S DEAD.
HAPPENS A LOT AROUND YOU. BUT SINCE YOU NEVER STICK AROUND LONG ENOUGH TO FIND OUT-- LET US CLUE YOU IN--
YOU NEVER GET USED TO IT.
BARRY--
YOU KILLED BARRY?!

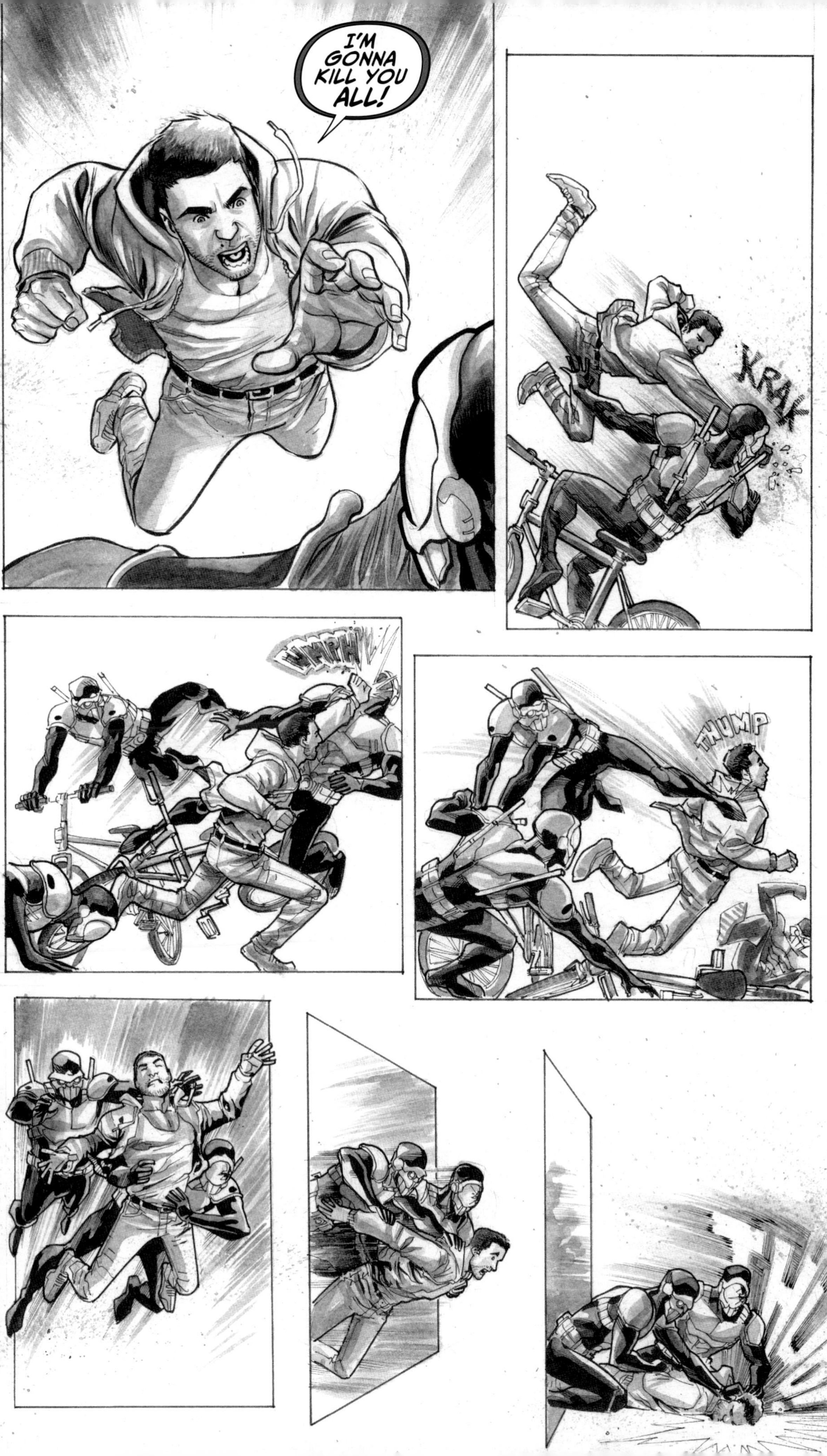
I'M GONNA KILL YOU ALL!
XRAK
THUMP

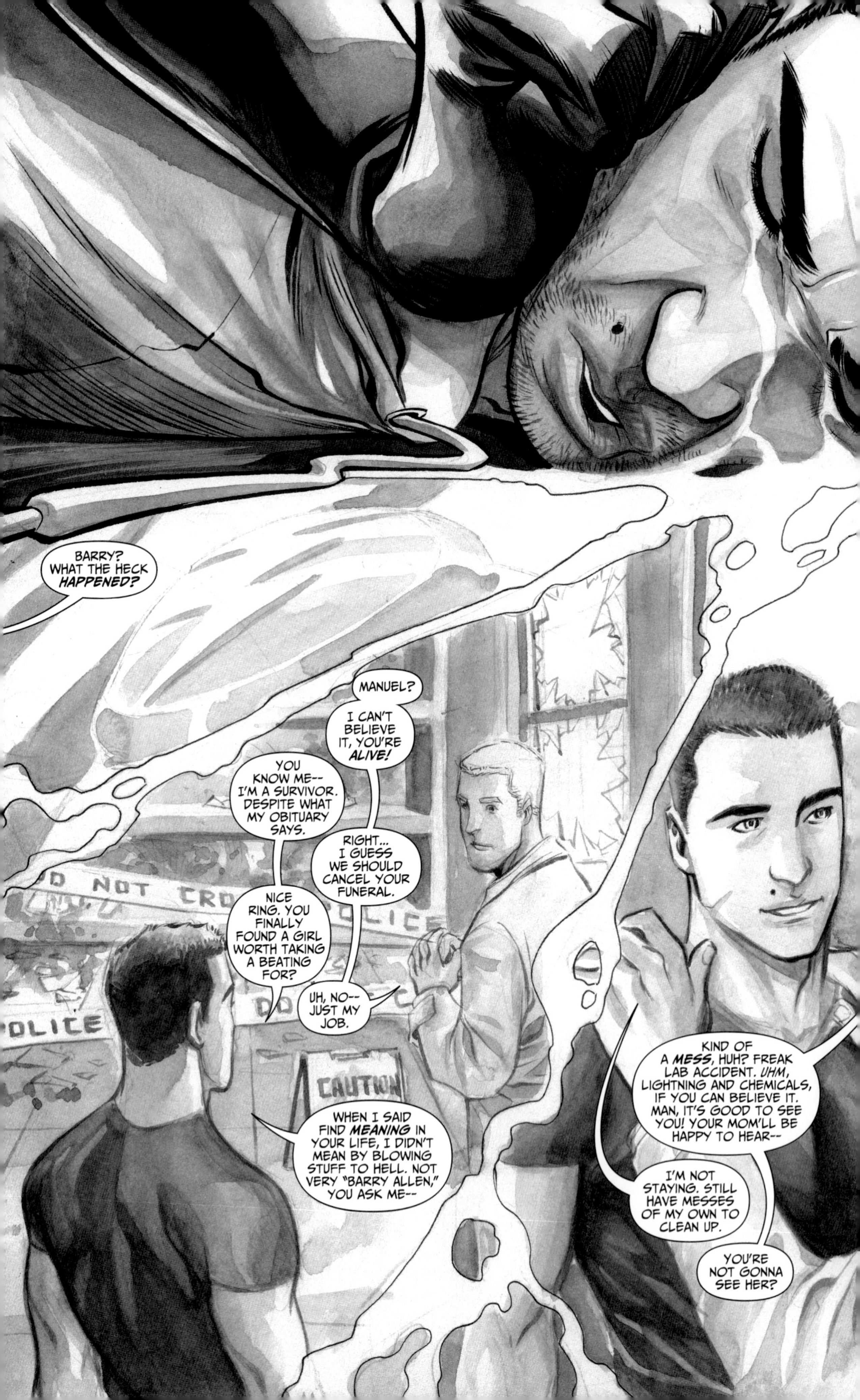
BARRY? WHAT THE HECK *HAPPENED?*
MANUEL?
I CAN'T BELIEVE IT, YOU'RE *ALIVE!*
YOU KNOW ME-- I'M A SURVIVOR. DESPITE WHAT MY OBITUARY SAYS.
RIGHT... I GUESS WE SHOULD CANCEL YOUR FUNERAL.
NICE RING. YOU FINALLY FOUND A GIRL WORTH TAKING A BEATING FOR?
UH, NO-- JUST MY JOB.
DO NOT CROSS
POLICE
CAUTION
KIND OF A *MESS*, HUH? FREAK LAB ACCIDENT. *UHM*, LIGHTNING AND CHEMICALS, IF YOU CAN BELIEVE IT. MAN, IT'S GOOD TO SEE YOU! YOUR MOM'LL BE HAPPY TO HEAR--
WHEN I SAID FIND *MEANING* IN YOUR LIFE, I DIDN'T MEAN BY BLOWING STUFF TO HELL. NOT VERY "BARRY ALLEN," YOU ASK ME--
I'M NOT STAYING. STILL HAVE MESSES OF MY OWN TO CLEAN UP.
YOU'RE NOT GONNA SEE HER?

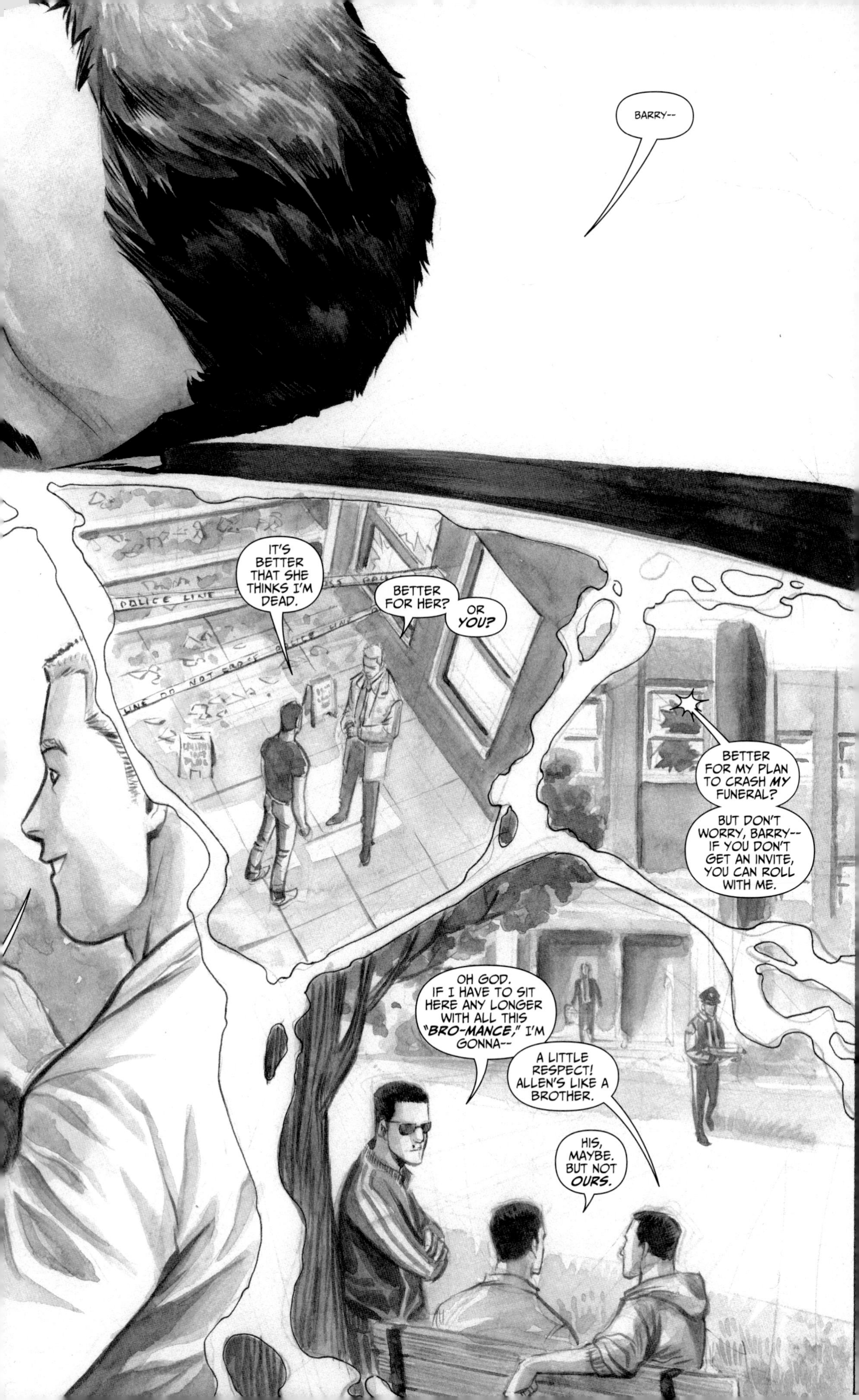
BARRY--
IT'S BETTER THAT SHE THINKS I'M DEAD.
BETTER FOR HER?
OR *YOU?*
BETTER FOR MY PLAN TO CRASH *MY* FUNERAL?
BUT DON'T WORRY, BARRY-- IF YOU DON'T GET AN INVITE, YOU CAN ROLL WITH ME.
OH GOD. IF I HAVE TO SIT HERE ANY LONGER WITH ALL THIS "*BRO-MANCE,*" I'M GONNA--
A LITTLE RESPECT! ALLEN'S LIKE A BROTHER.
HIS, MAYBE. BUT NOT *OURS.*

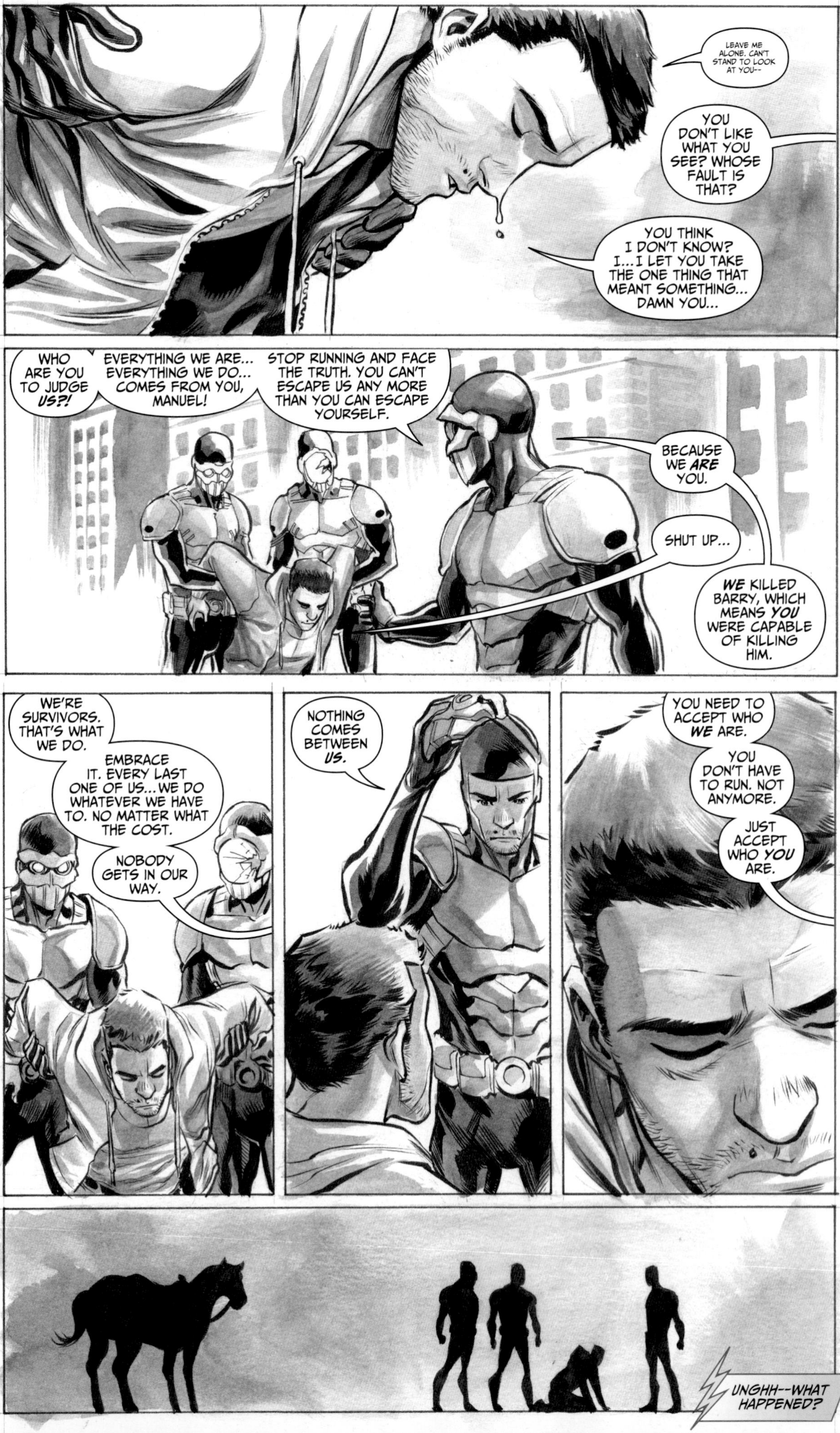
LEAVE ME ALONE. CAN'T STAND TO LOOK AT YOU--
YOU DON'T LIKE WHAT YOU SEE? WHOSE FAULT IS THAT?
YOU THINK I DON'T KNOW? I...I LET YOU TAKE THE ONE THING THAT MEANT SOMETHING... DAMN YOU...
WHO ARE YOU TO JUDGE US?!
EVERYTHING WE ARE... EVERYTHING WE DO... COMES FROM YOU, MANUEL!
STOP RUNNING AND FACE THE TRUTH. YOU CAN'T ESCAPE US ANY MORE THAN YOU CAN ESCAPE YOURSELF.
BECAUSE WE ARE YOU.
SHUT UP...
WE KILLED BARRY, WHICH MEANS YOU WERE CAPABLE OF KILLING HIM.
WE'RE SURVIVORS. THAT'S WHAT WE DO.
EMBRACE IT. EVERY LAST ONE OF US...WE DO WHATEVER WE HAVE TO. NO MATTER WHAT THE COST.
NOBODY GETS IN OUR WAY.
NOTHING COMES BETWEEN US.
YOU NEED TO ACCEPT WHO WE ARE.
YOU DON'T HAVE TO RUN. NOT ANYMORE.
JUST ACCEPT WHO YOU ARE.
UNGHH--WHAT HAPPENED?

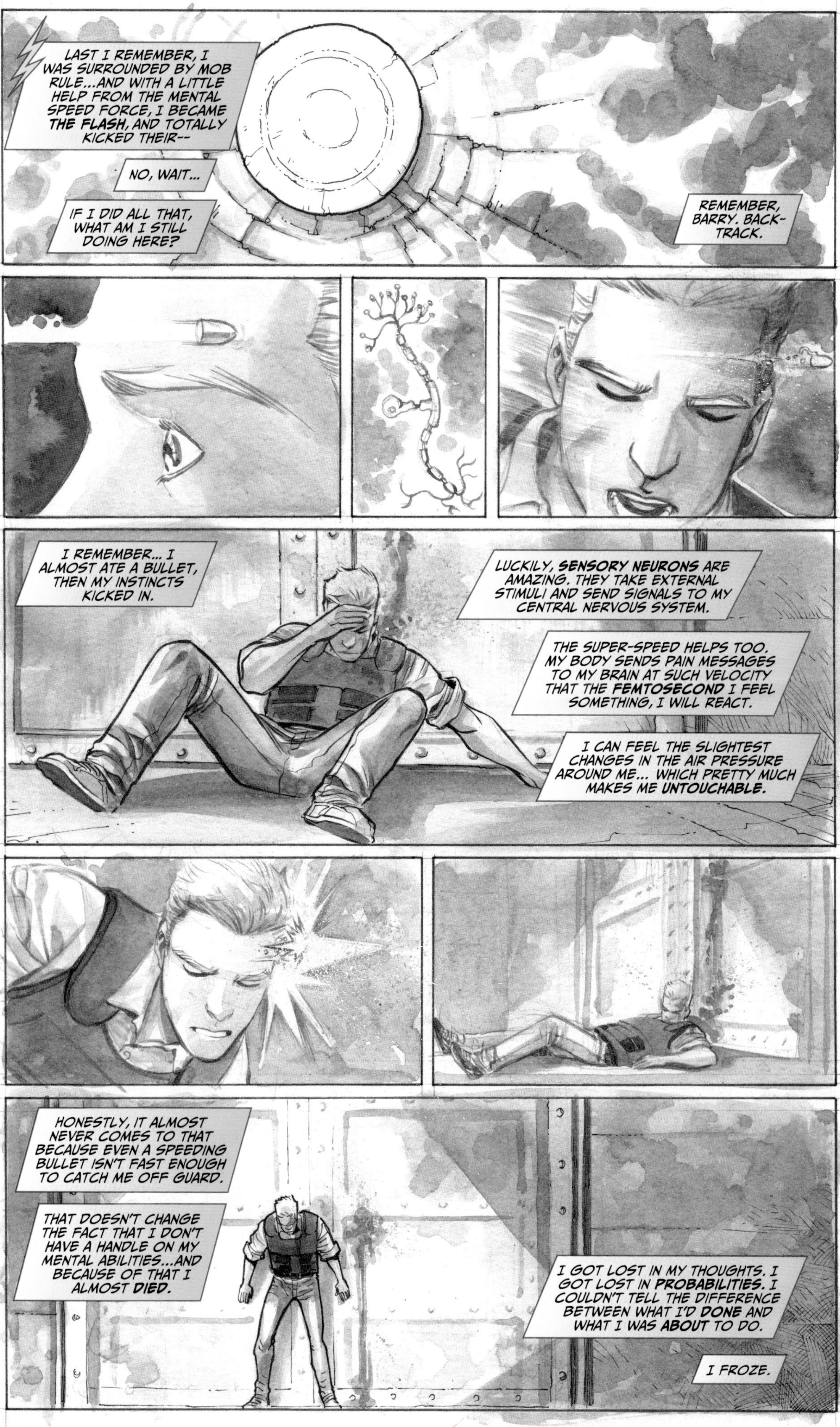
LAST I REMEMBER, I WAS SURROUNDED BY MOB RULE...AND WITH A LITTLE HELP FROM THE MENTAL SPEED FORCE, I BECAME **THE FLASH**, AND TOTALLY KICKED THEIR--
NO, WAIT...
IF I DID ALL THAT, WHAT AM I STILL DOING HERE?
REMEMBER, BARRY. BACK-TRACK.
I REMEMBER... I ALMOST ATE A BULLET, THEN MY INSTINCTS KICKED IN.
LUCKILY, **SENSORY NEURONS** ARE AMAZING. THEY TAKE EXTERNAL STIMULI AND SEND SIGNALS TO MY CENTRAL NERVOUS SYSTEM.
THE SUPER-SPEED HELPS TOO. MY BODY SENDS PAIN MESSAGES TO MY BRAIN AT SUCH VELOCITY THAT THE **FEMTOSECOND** I FEEL SOMETHING, I WILL REACT.
I CAN FEEL THE SLIGHTEST CHANGES IN THE AIR PRESSURE AROUND ME... WHICH PRETTY MUCH MAKES ME **UNTOUCHABLE.**
HONESTLY, IT ALMOST NEVER COMES TO THAT BECAUSE EVEN A SPEEDING BULLET ISN'T FAST ENOUGH TO CATCH ME OFF GUARD.
THAT DOESN'T CHANGE THE FACT THAT I DON'T HAVE A HANDLE ON MY MENTAL ABILITIES...AND BECAUSE OF THAT I ALMOST **DIED.**
I GOT LOST IN MY THOUGHTS. I GOT LOST IN **PROBABILITIES.** I COULDN'T TELL THE DIFFERENCE BETWEEN WHAT I'D **DONE** AND WHAT I WAS **ABOUT** TO DO.
I FROZE.

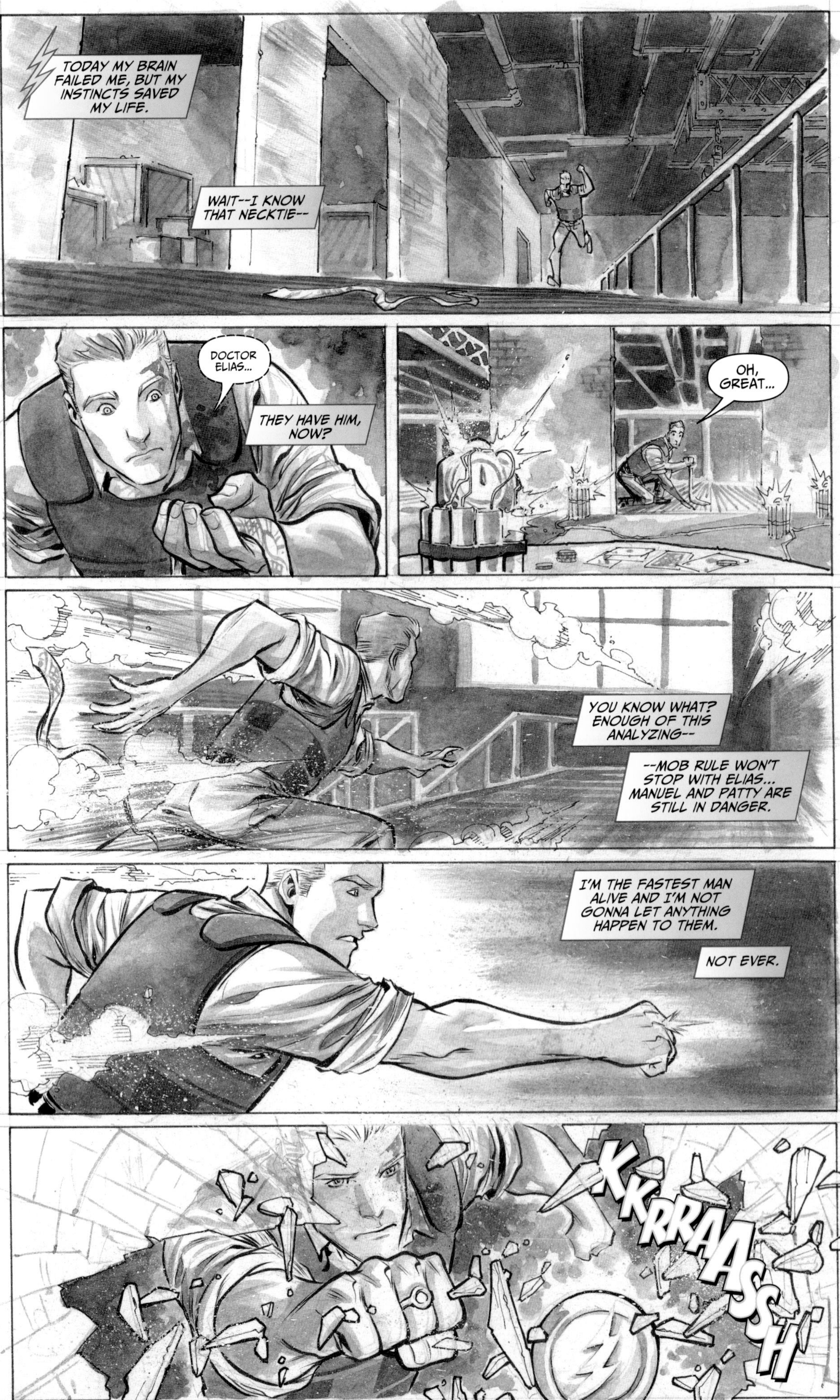
TODAY MY BRAIN FAILED ME, BUT MY INSTINCTS SAVED MY LIFE.
WAIT--I KNOW THAT NECKTIE--
DOCTOR ELIAS...
THEY HAVE HIM, NOW?
OH, GREAT...
YOU KNOW WHAT? ENOUGH OF THIS ANALYZING--
--MOB RULE WON'T STOP WITH ELIAS... MANUEL AND PATTY ARE STILL IN DANGER.
I'M THE FASTEST MAN ALIVE AND I'M NOT GONNA LET ANYTHING HAPPEN TO THEM.
NOT EVER.
KKRRAASSH

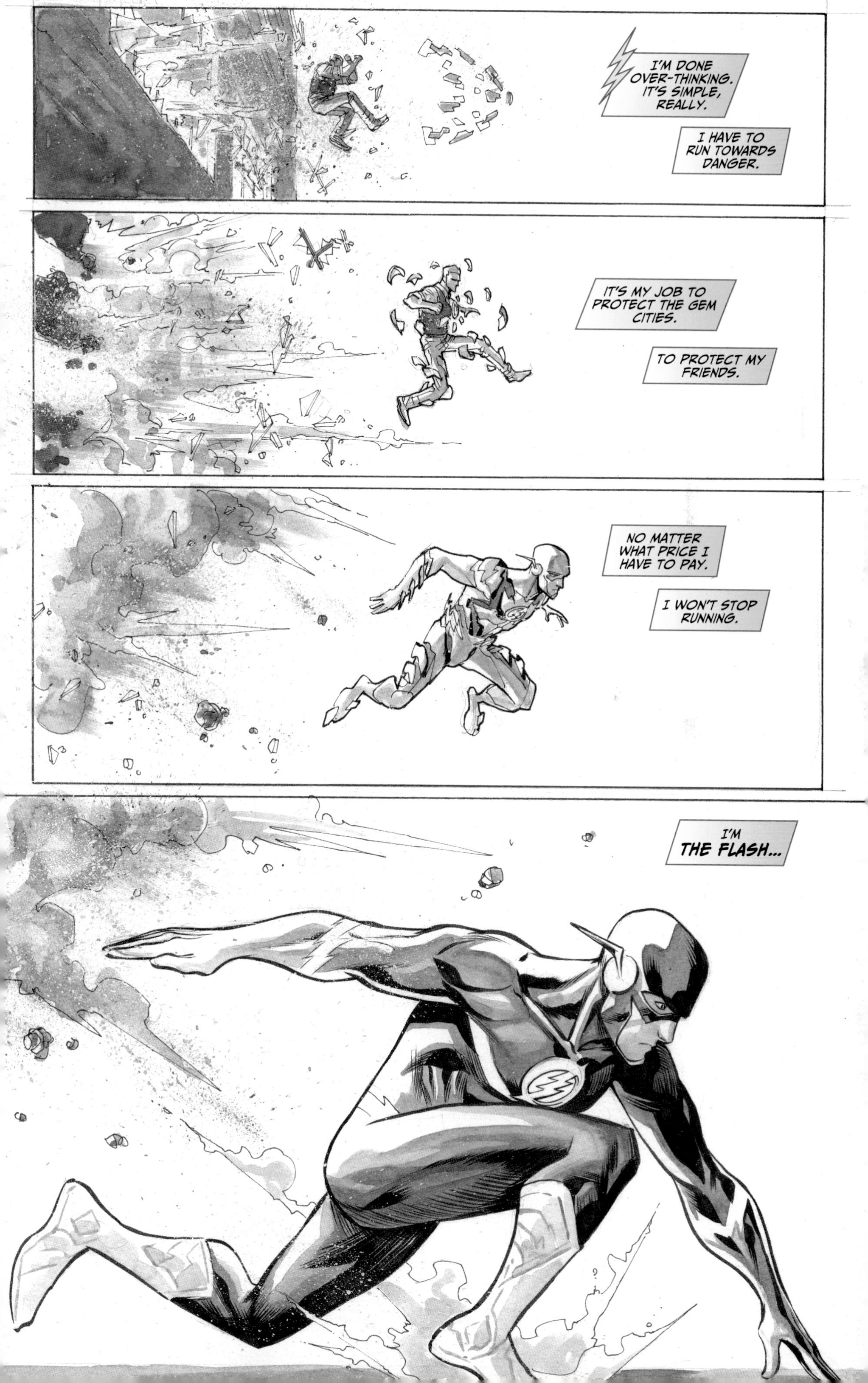
I'M DONE OVER-THINKING. IT'S SIMPLE, REALLY.
I HAVE TO RUN TOWARDS DANGER.
IT'S MY JOB TO PROTECT THE GEM CITIES.
TO PROTECT MY FRIENDS.
NO MATTER WHAT PRICE I HAVE TO PAY.
I WON'T STOP RUNNING.
I'M THE FLASH...

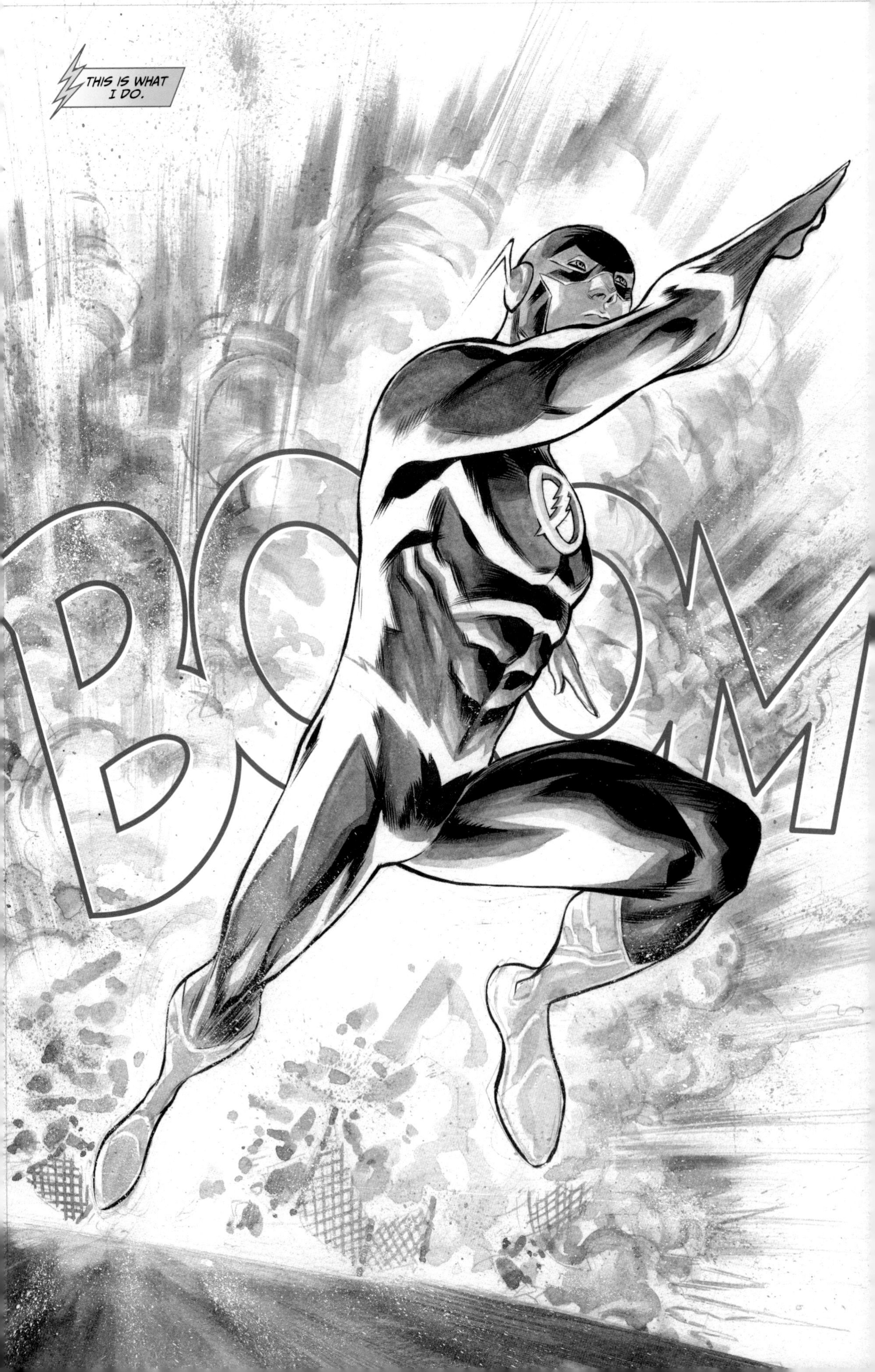
THIS IS WHAT I DO.
BOOM

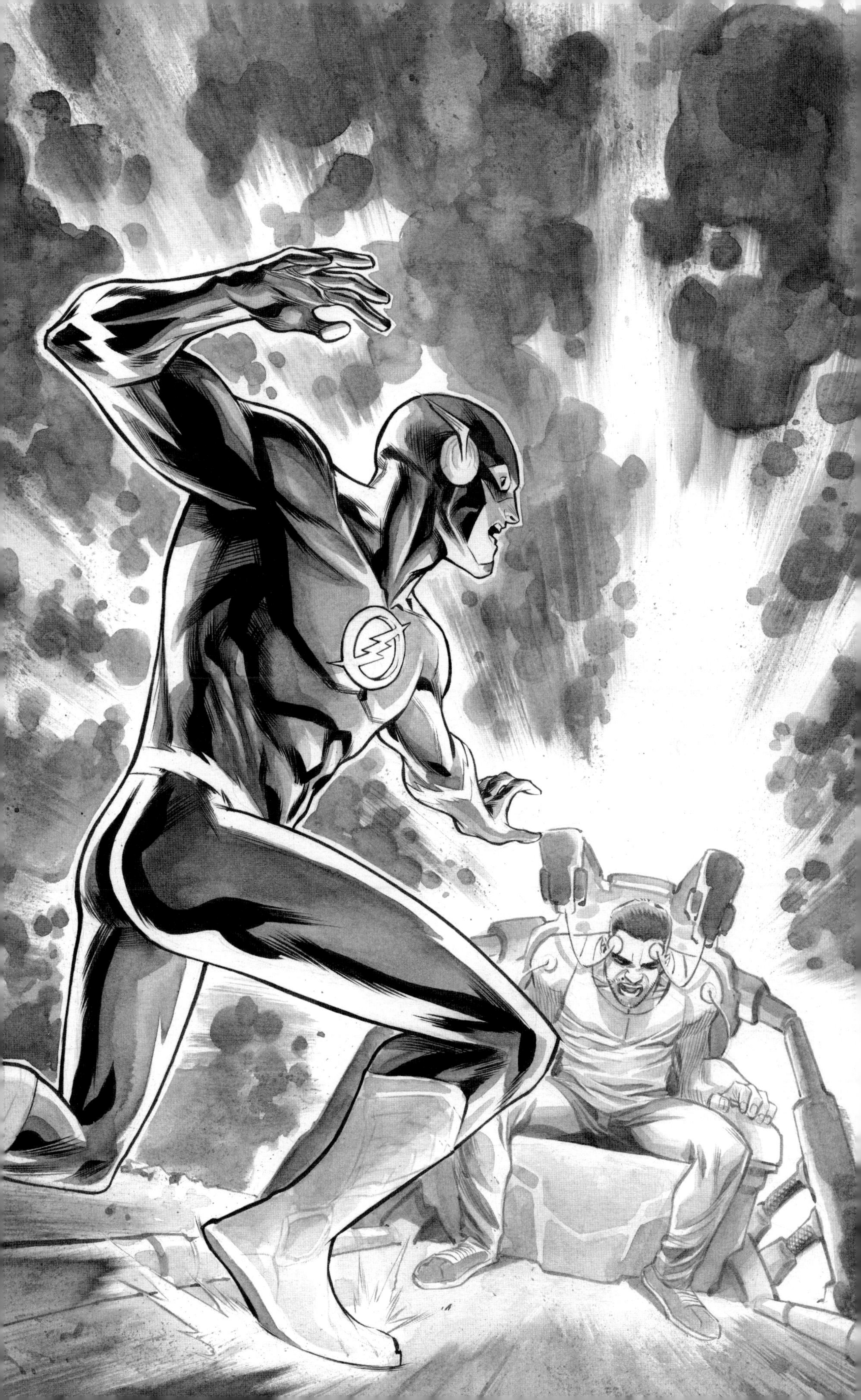

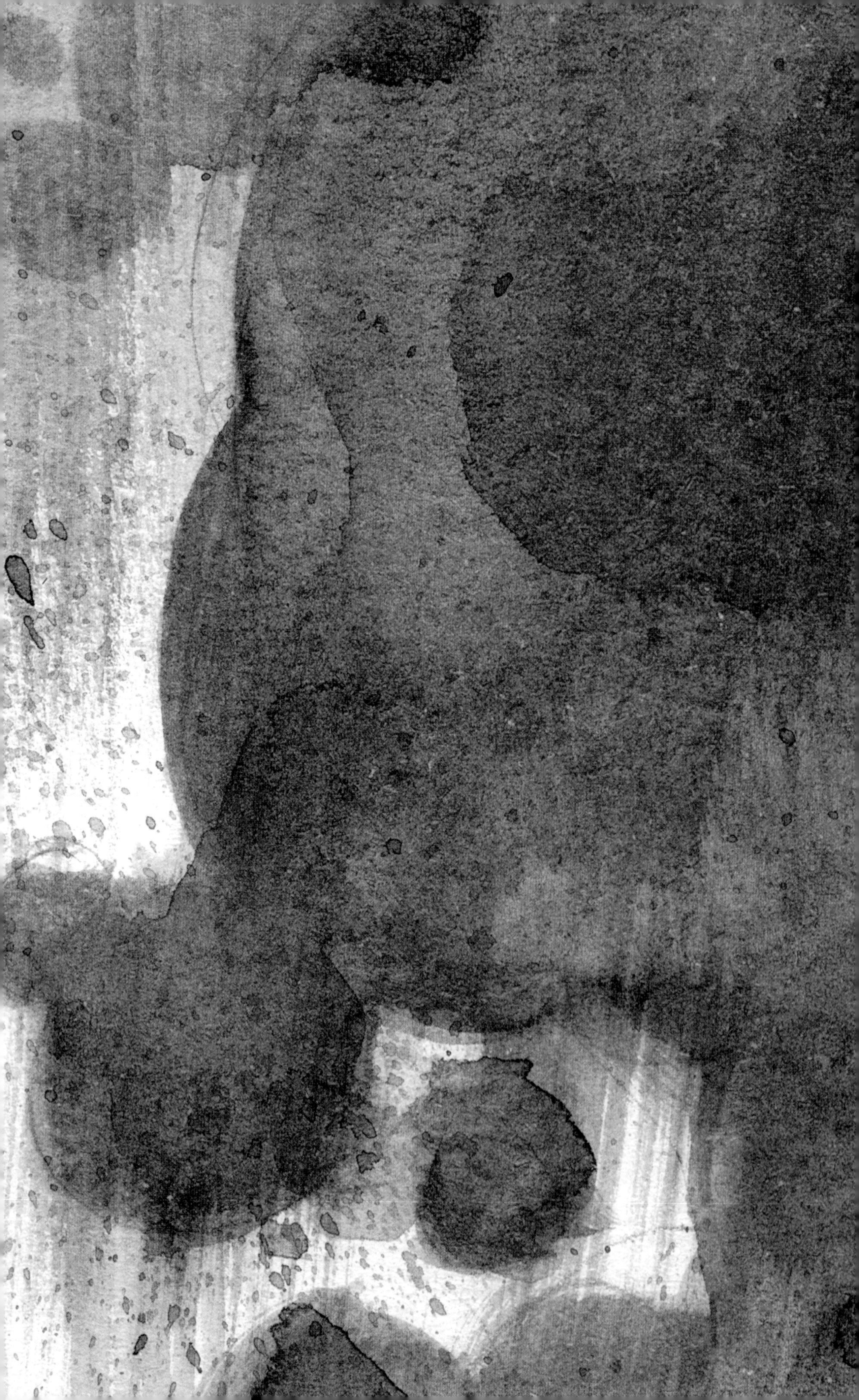

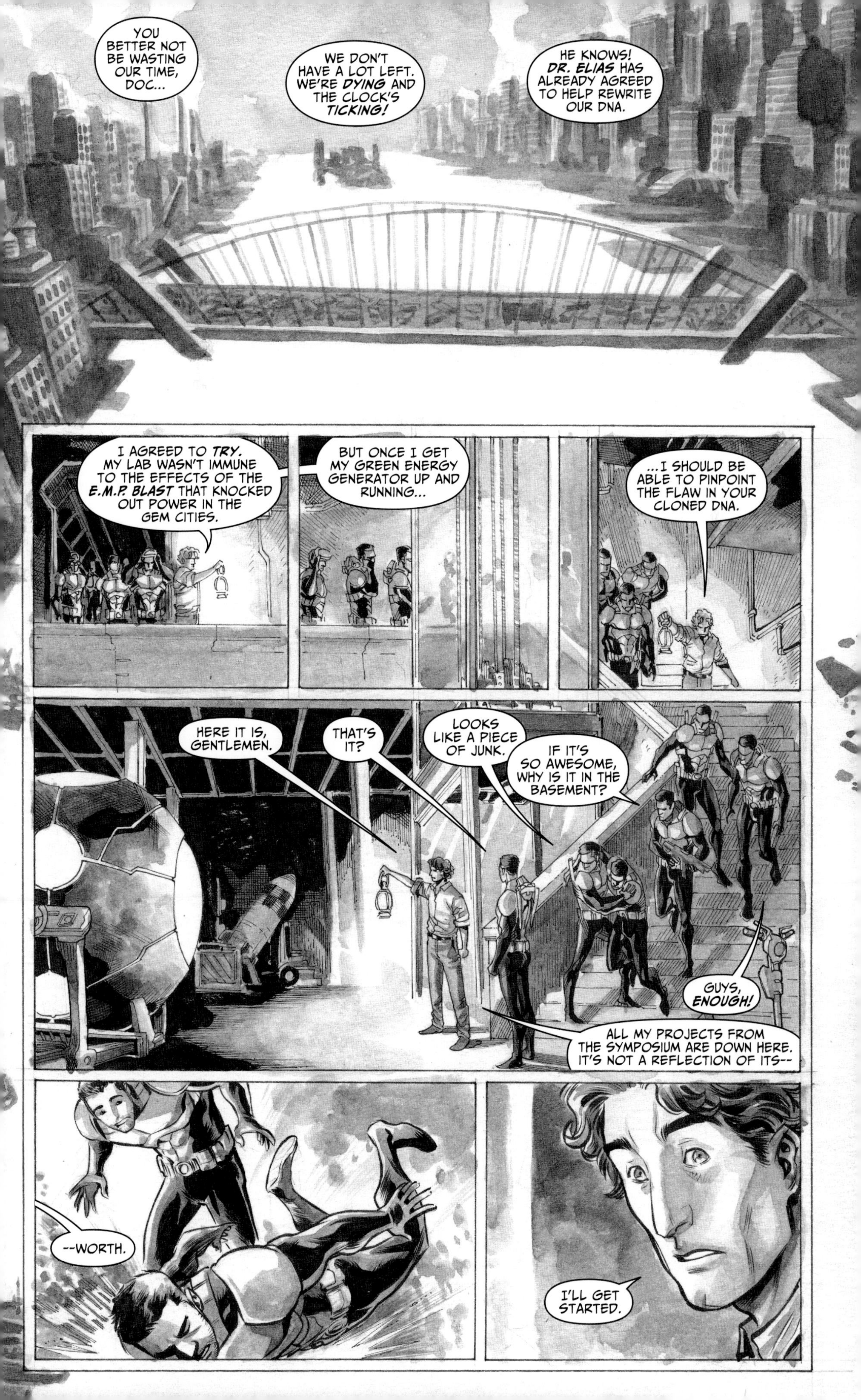
YOU BETTER NOT BE WASTING OUR TIME, DOC...
WE DON'T HAVE A LOT LEFT. WE'RE DYING AND THE CLOCK'S TICKING!
HE KNOWS! DR. ELIAS HAS ALREADY AGREED TO HELP REWRITE OUR DNA.
I AGREED TO TRY. MY LAB WASN'T IMMUNE TO THE EFFECTS OF THE E.M.P. BLAST THAT KNOCKED OUT POWER IN THE GEM CITIES.
BUT ONCE I GET MY GREEN ENERGY GENERATOR UP AND RUNNING...
...I SHOULD BE ABLE TO PINPOINT THE FLAW IN YOUR CLONED DNA.
HERE IT IS, GENTLEMEN.
THAT'S IT?
LOOKS LIKE A PIECE OF JUNK.
IF IT'S SO AWESOME, WHY IS IT IN THE BASEMENT?
GUYS, ENOUGH!
ALL MY PROJECTS FROM THE SYMPOSIUM ARE DOWN HERE. IT'S NOT A REFLECTION OF ITS--
--WORTH.
I'LL GET STARTED.

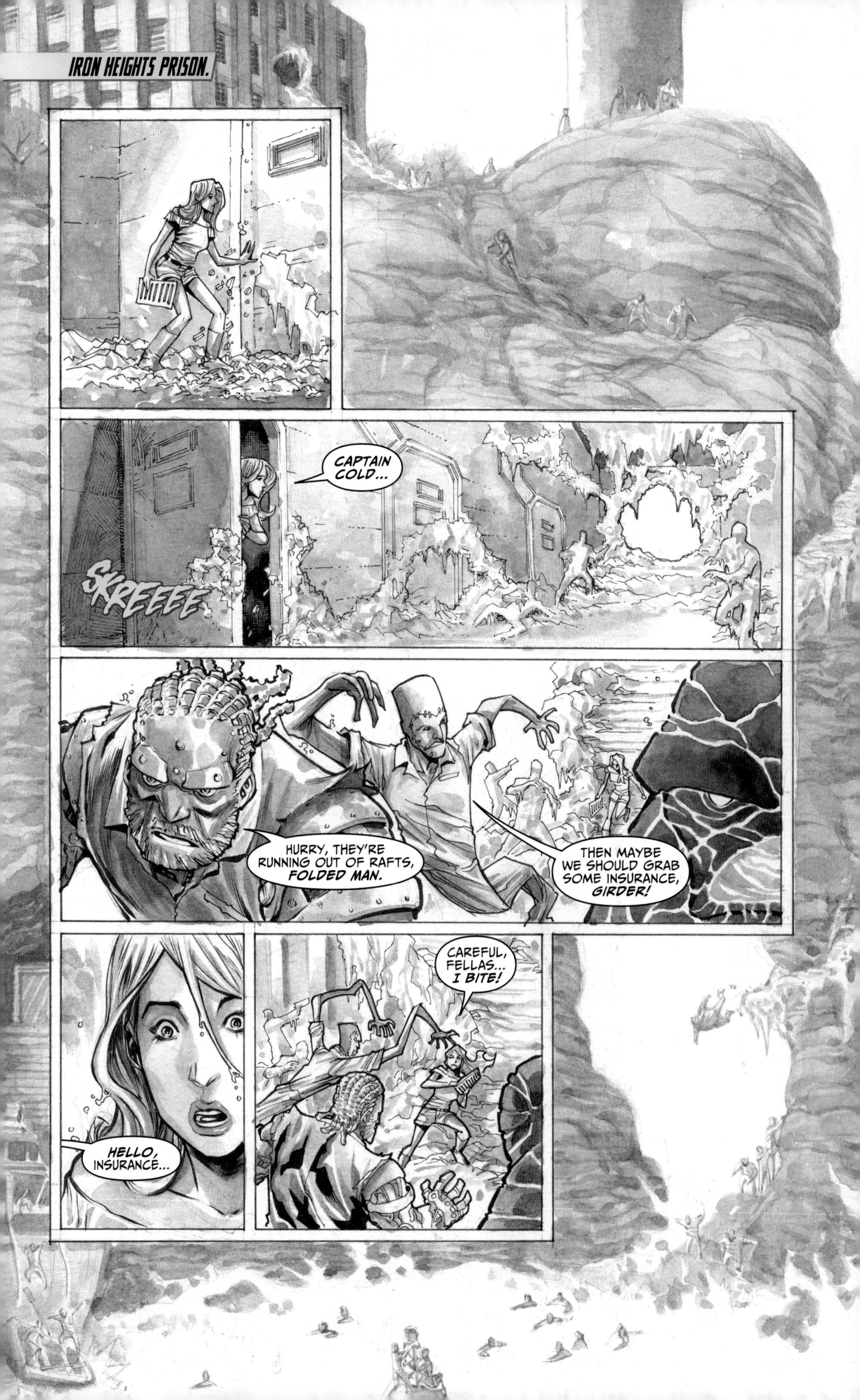
IRON HEIGHTS PRISON.
CAPTAIN COLD...
SKREEEEE
HURRY, THEY'RE RUNNING OUT OF RAFTS, FOLDED MAN.
THEN MAYBE WE SHOULD GRAB SOME INSURANCE, GIRDER!
HELLO, INSURANCE...
CAREFUL, FELLAS... I BITE!

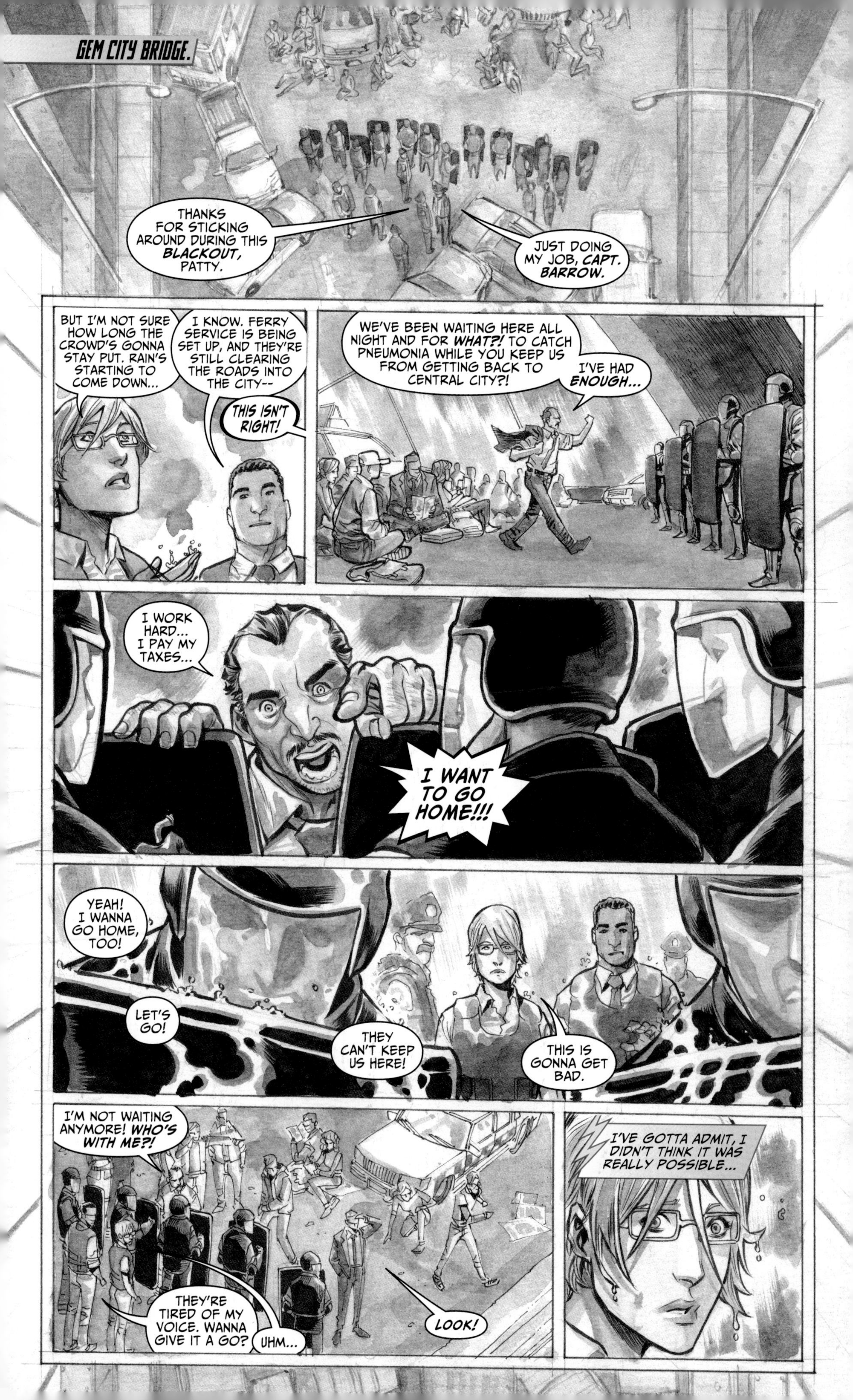
GEM CITY BRIDGE.
THANKS FOR STICKING AROUND DURING THIS BLACKOUT, PATTY.
JUST DOING MY JOB, CAPT. BARROW.
BUT I'M NOT SURE HOW LONG THE CROWD'S GONNA STAY PUT. RAIN'S STARTING TO COME DOWN...
I KNOW. FERRY SERVICE IS BEING SET UP, AND THEY'RE STILL CLEARING THE ROADS INTO THE CITY--
THIS ISN'T RIGHT!
WE'VE BEEN WAITING HERE ALL NIGHT AND FOR WHAT?! TO CATCH PNEUMONIA WHILE YOU KEEP US FROM GETTING BACK TO CENTRAL CITY?!
I'VE HAD ENOUGH...
I WORK HARD... I PAY MY TAXES...
I WANT TO GO HOME!!!
YEAH! I WANNA GO HOME, TOO!
LET'S GO!
THEY CAN'T KEEP US HERE!
THIS IS GONNA GET BAD.
I'M NOT WAITING ANYMORE! WHO'S WITH ME?!
THEY'RE TIRED OF MY VOICE. WANNA GIVE IT A GO?
UHM...
LOOK!
I'VE GOTTA ADMIT, I DIDN'T THINK IT WAS REALLY POSSIBLE...

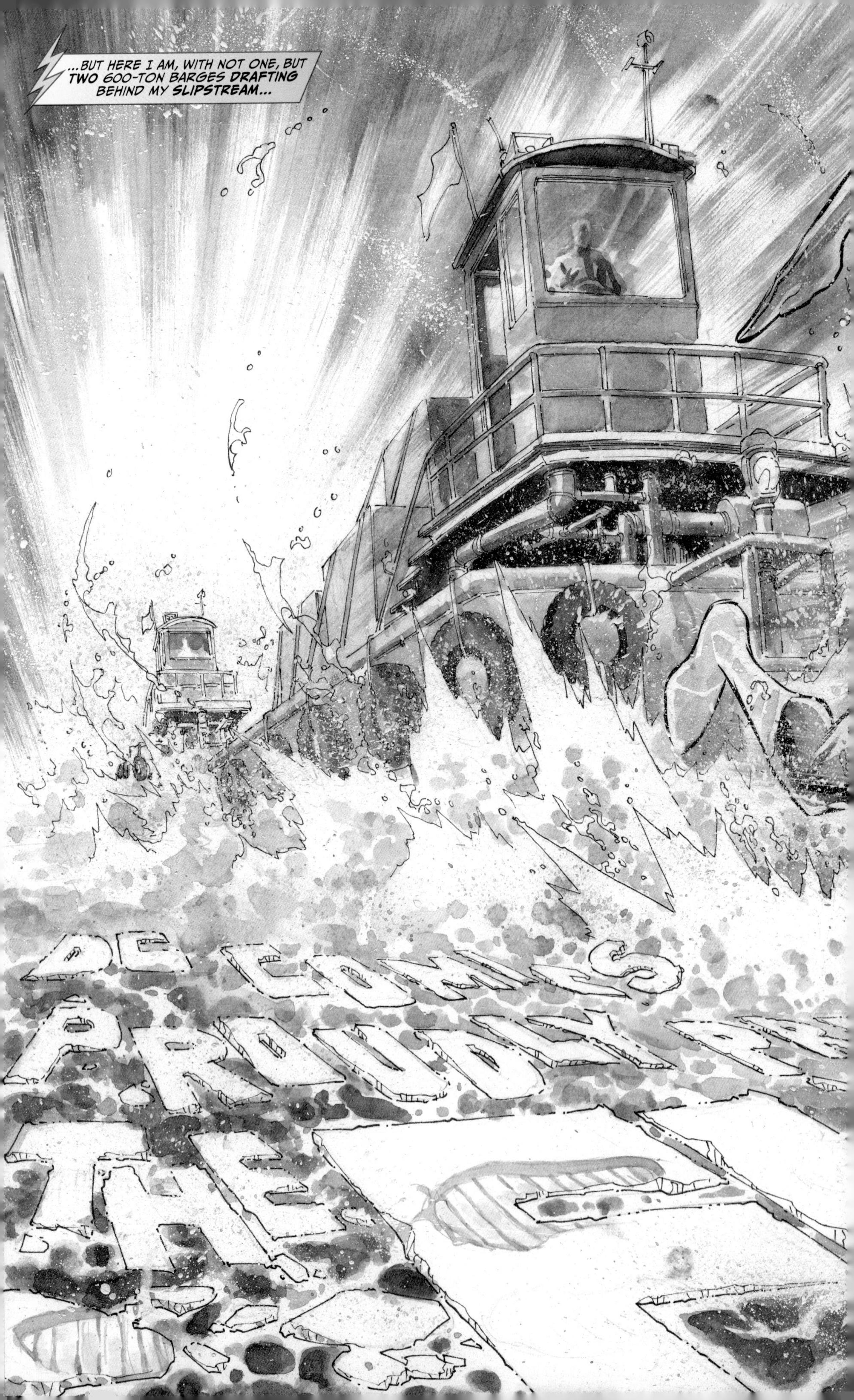
...BUT HERE I AM, WITH NOT ONE, BUT TWO 600-TON BARGES DRAFTING BEHIND MY SLIPSTREAM...
DC COMICS
PROUDLY
THE

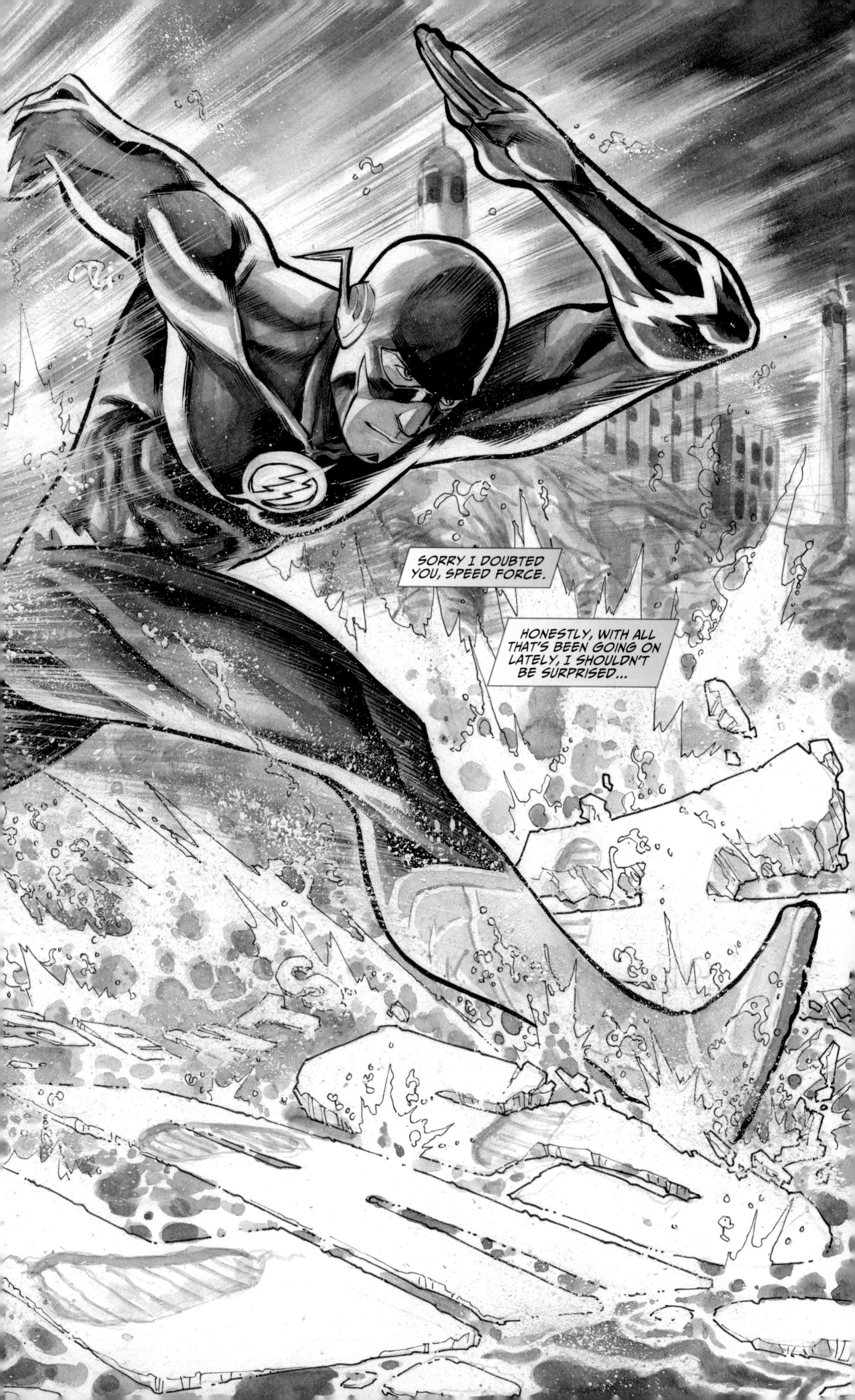
SORRY I DOUBTED YOU, SPEED FORCE.
HONESTLY, WITH ALL THAT'S BEEN GOING ON LATELY, I SHOULDN'T BE SURPRISED...

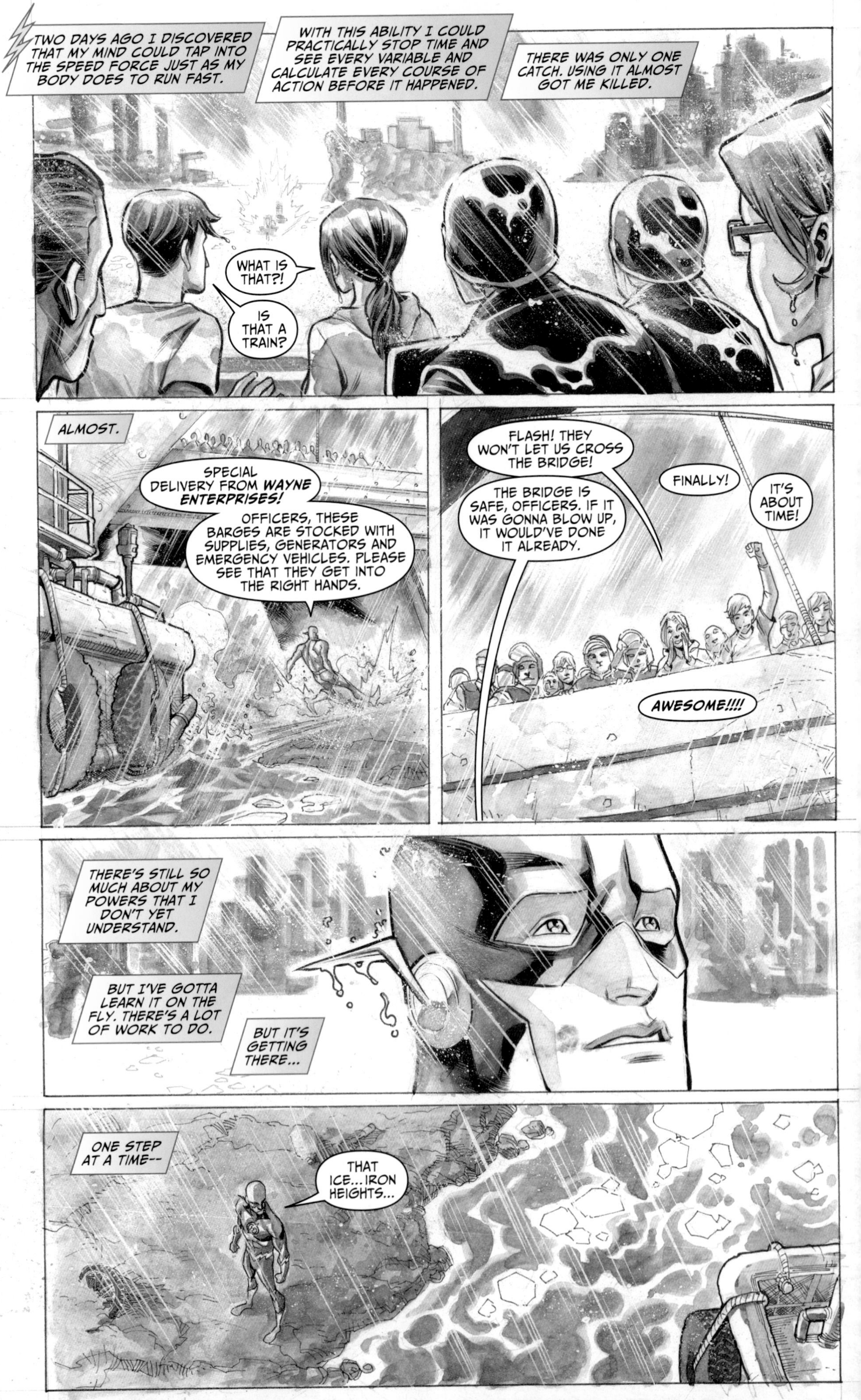
TWO DAYS AGO I DISCOVERED THAT MY MIND COULD TAP INTO THE SPEED FORCE JUST AS MY BODY DOES TO RUN FAST.
WITH THIS ABILITY I COULD PRACTICALLY STOP TIME AND SEE EVERY VARIABLE AND CALCULATE EVERY COURSE OF ACTION BEFORE IT HAPPENED.
THERE WAS ONLY ONE CATCH. USING IT ALMOST GOT ME KILLED.
WHAT IS THAT?!
IS THAT A TRAIN?
ALMOST.
SPECIAL DELIVERY FROM WAYNE ENTERPRISES!
OFFICERS, THESE BARGES ARE STOCKED WITH SUPPLIES, GENERATORS AND EMERGENCY VEHICLES. PLEASE SEE THAT THEY GET INTO THE RIGHT HANDS.
FLASH! THEY WON'T LET US CROSS THE BRIDGE!
THE BRIDGE IS SAFE, OFFICERS. IF IT WAS GONNA BLOW UP, IT WOULD'VE DONE IT ALREADY.
FINALLY!
IT'S ABOUT TIME!
AWESOME!!!!
THERE'S STILL SO MUCH ABOUT MY POWERS THAT I DON'T YET UNDERSTAND.
BUT I'VE GOTTA LEARN IT ON THE FLY. THERE'S A LOT OF WORK TO DO.
BUT IT'S GETTING THERE...
ONE STEP AT A TIME--
THAT ICE...IRON HEIGHTS...

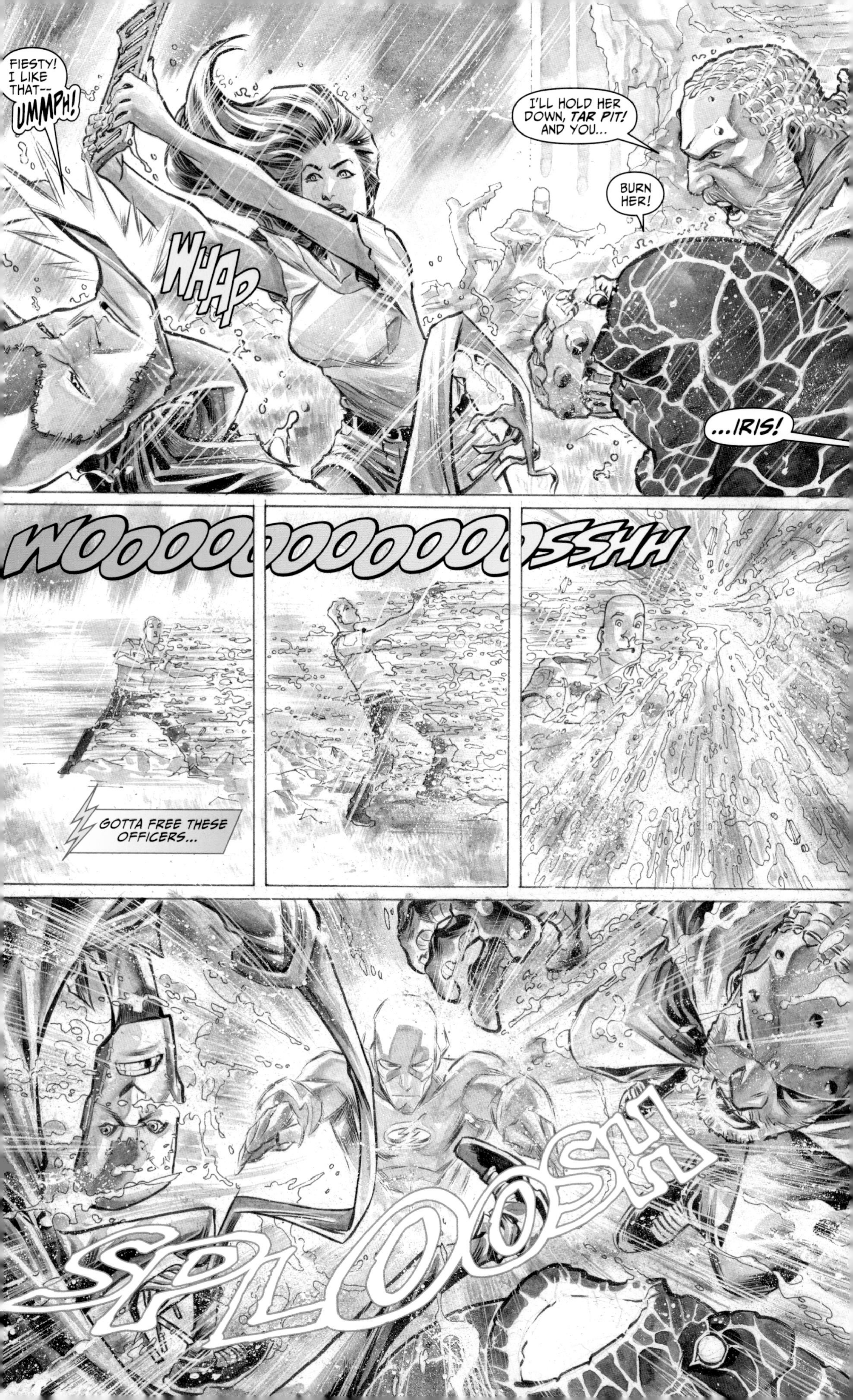
FIESTY! I LIKE THAT--
UMMPH!
WHAP
I'LL HOLD HER DOWN, TAR PIT! AND YOU...
BURN HER!
...IRIS!
WOOOOOOOOOOOOSSHH
GOTTA FREE THESE OFFICERS...
SPLOOOSH

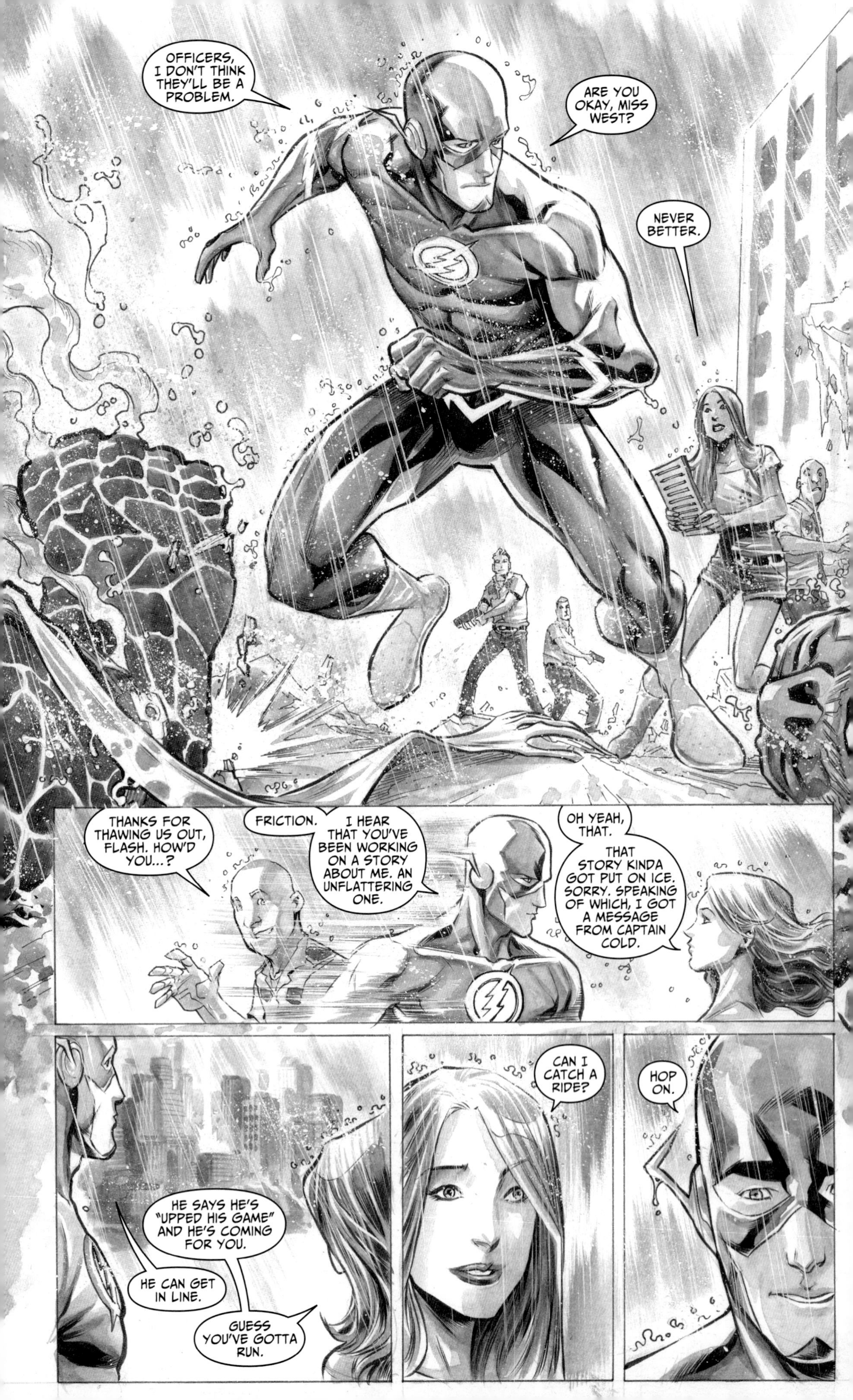
OFFICERS, I DON'T THINK THEY'LL BE A PROBLEM.
ARE YOU OKAY, MISS WEST?
NEVER BETTER.
THANKS FOR THAWING US OUT, FLASH. HOW'D YOU...?
FRICTION.
I HEAR THAT YOU'VE BEEN WORKING ON A STORY ABOUT ME. AN UNFLATTERING ONE.
OH YEAH, THAT.
THAT STORY KINDA GOT PUT ON ICE. SORRY. SPEAKING OF WHICH, I GOT A MESSAGE FROM CAPTAIN COLD.
HE SAYS HE'S "UPPED HIS GAME" AND HE'S COMING FOR YOU.
HE CAN GET IN LINE.
GUESS YOU'VE GOTTA RUN.
CAN I CATCH A RIDE?
HOP ON.

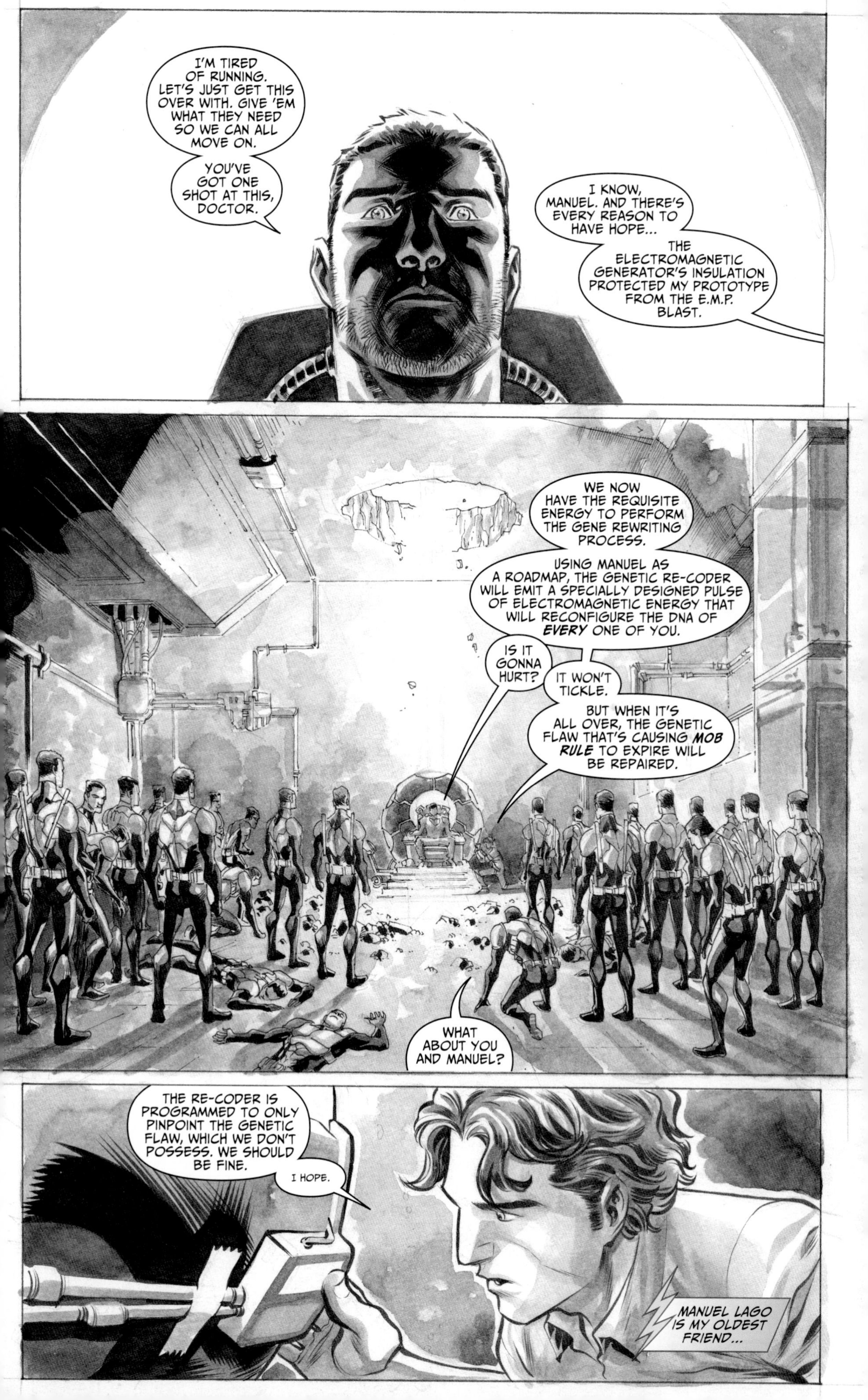
I'M TIRED OF RUNNING. LET'S JUST GET THIS OVER WITH. GIVE 'EM WHAT THEY NEED SO WE CAN ALL MOVE ON.
YOU'VE GOT ONE SHOT AT THIS, DOCTOR.
I KNOW, MANUEL. AND THERE'S EVERY REASON TO HAVE HOPE...
THE ELECTROMAGNETIC GENERATOR'S INSULATION PROTECTED MY PROTOTYPE FROM THE E.M.P. BLAST.
WE NOW HAVE THE REQUISITE ENERGY TO PERFORM THE GENE REWRITING PROCESS.
USING MANUEL AS A ROADMAP, THE GENETIC RE-CODER WILL EMIT A SPECIALLY DESIGNED PULSE OF ELECTROMAGNETIC ENERGY THAT WILL RECONFIGURE THE DNA OF *EVERY* ONE OF YOU.
IS IT GONNA HURT?
IT WON'T TICKLE.
BUT WHEN IT'S ALL OVER, THE GENETIC FLAW THAT'S CAUSING *MOB RULE* TO EXPIRE WILL BE REPAIRED.
WHAT ABOUT YOU AND MANUEL?
THE RE-CODER IS PROGRAMMED TO ONLY PINPOINT THE GENETIC FLAW, WHICH WE DON'T POSSESS. WE SHOULD BE FINE.
I HOPE.
MANUEL LAGO IS MY OLDEST FRIEND...

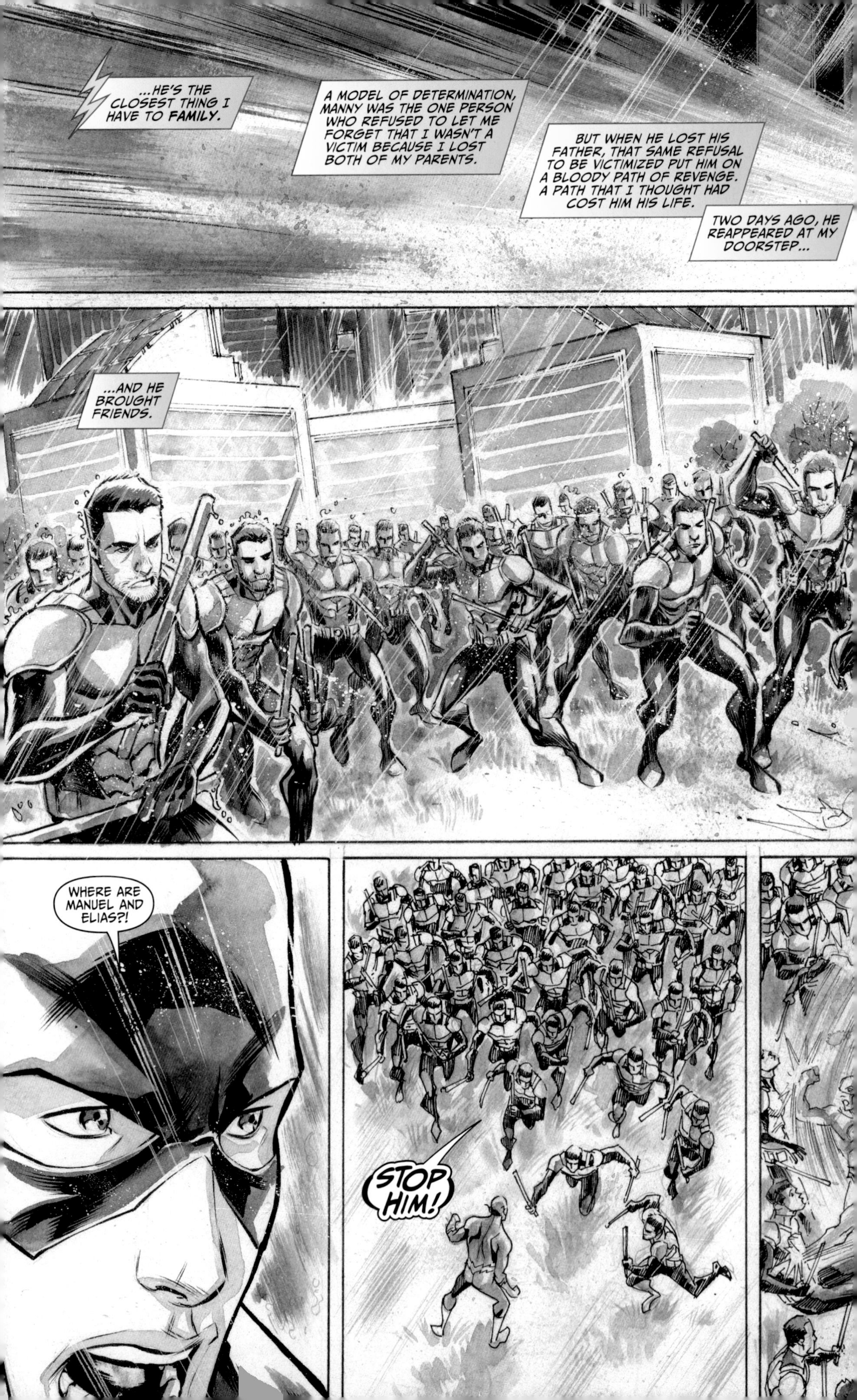
...HE'S THE CLOSEST THING I HAVE TO FAMILY.
A MODEL OF DETERMINATION, MANNY WAS THE ONE PERSON WHO REFUSED TO LET ME FORGET THAT I WASN'T A VICTIM BECAUSE I LOST BOTH OF MY PARENTS.
BUT WHEN HE LOST HIS FATHER, THAT SAME REFUSAL TO BE VICTIMIZED PUT HIM ON A BLOODY PATH OF REVENGE. A PATH THAT I THOUGHT HAD COST HIM HIS LIFE.
TWO DAYS AGO, HE REAPPEARED AT MY DOORSTEP...
...AND HE BROUGHT FRIENDS.
WHERE ARE MANUEL AND ELIAS?!
STOP HIM!

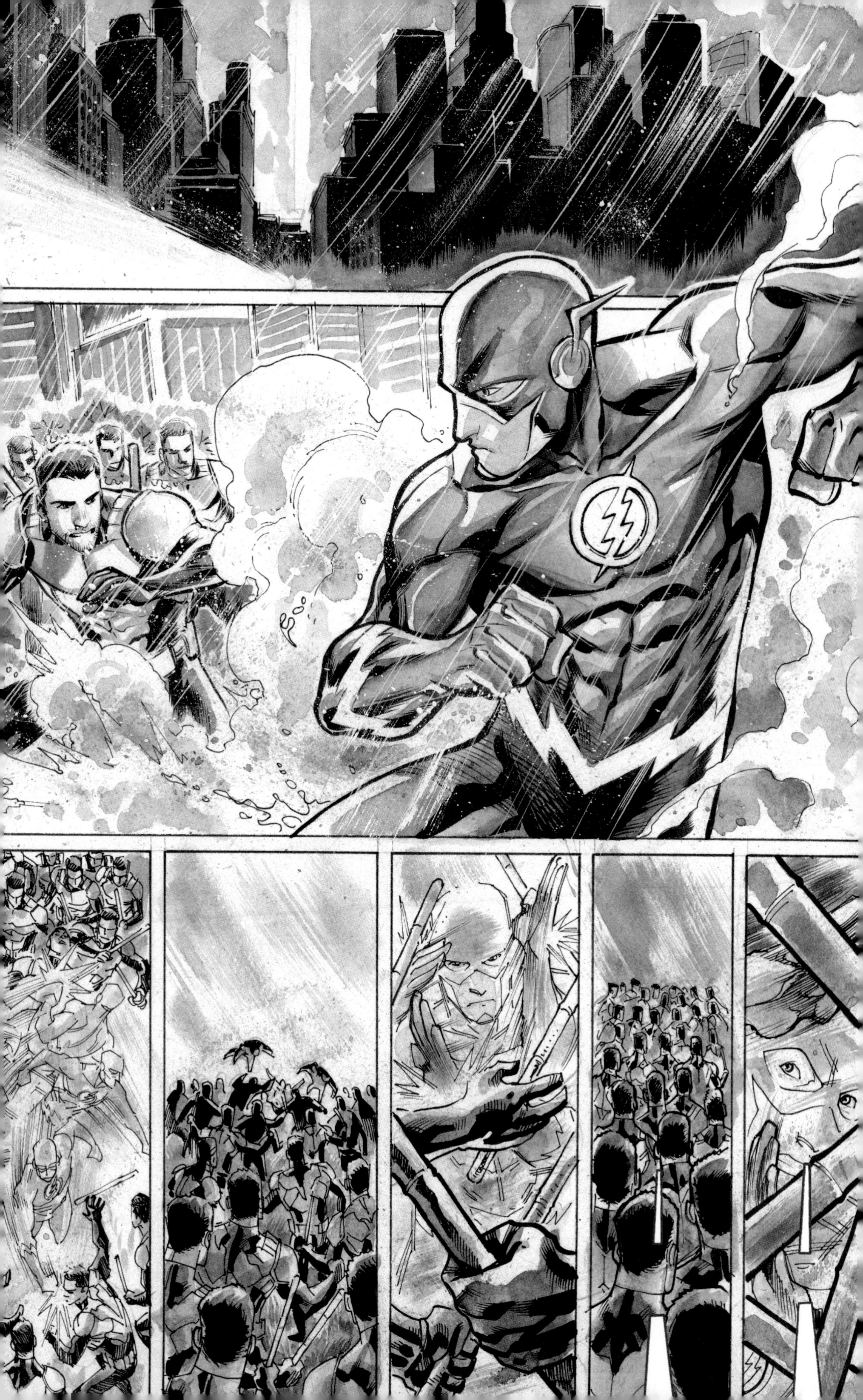

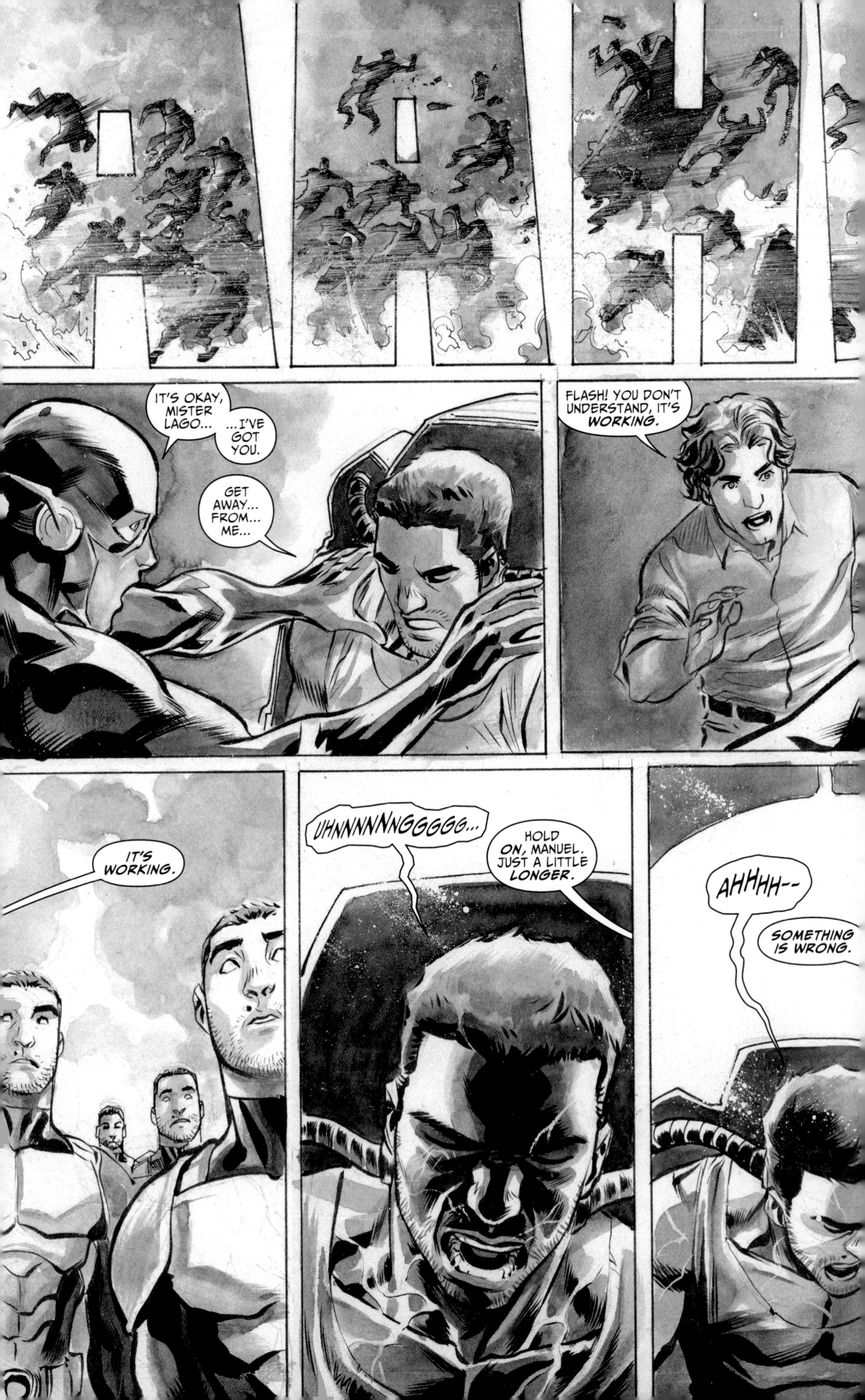
IT'S OKAY, MISTER LAGO...
...I'VE GOT YOU.
GET AWAY... FROM... ME...
FLASH! YOU DON'T UNDERSTAND, IT'S WORKING.
IT'S WORKING.
UHNNNNNNGGGGG...
HOLD ON, MANUEL. JUST A LITTLE LONGER.
AHHHH--
SOMETHING IS WRONG.

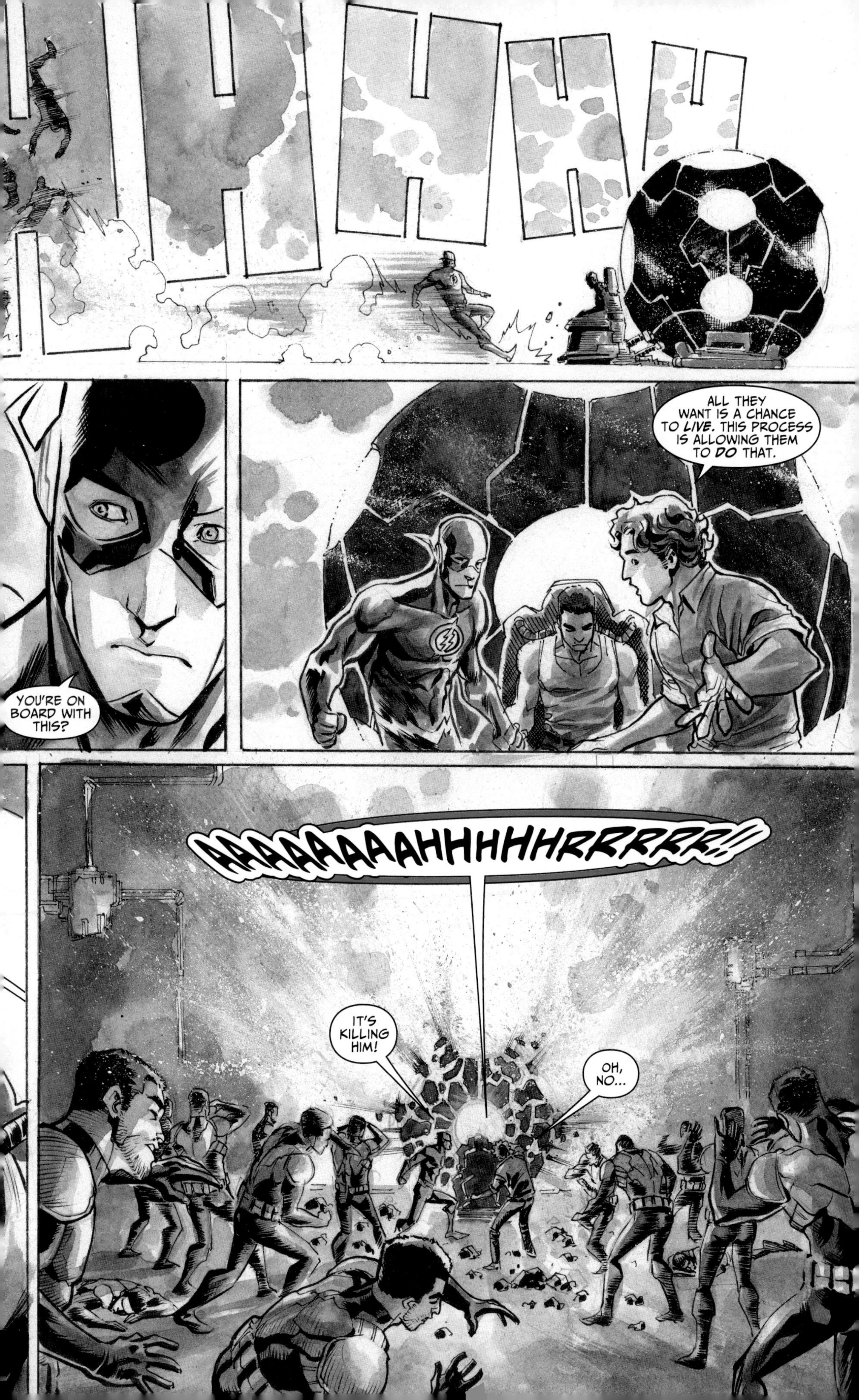
YOU'RE ON BOARD WITH THIS?
ALL THEY WANT IS A CHANCE TO LIVE. THIS PROCESS IS ALLOWING THEM TO DO THAT.
AAAAAAAAHHHHHRRRRRR!!
IT'S KILLING HIM!
OH, NO...

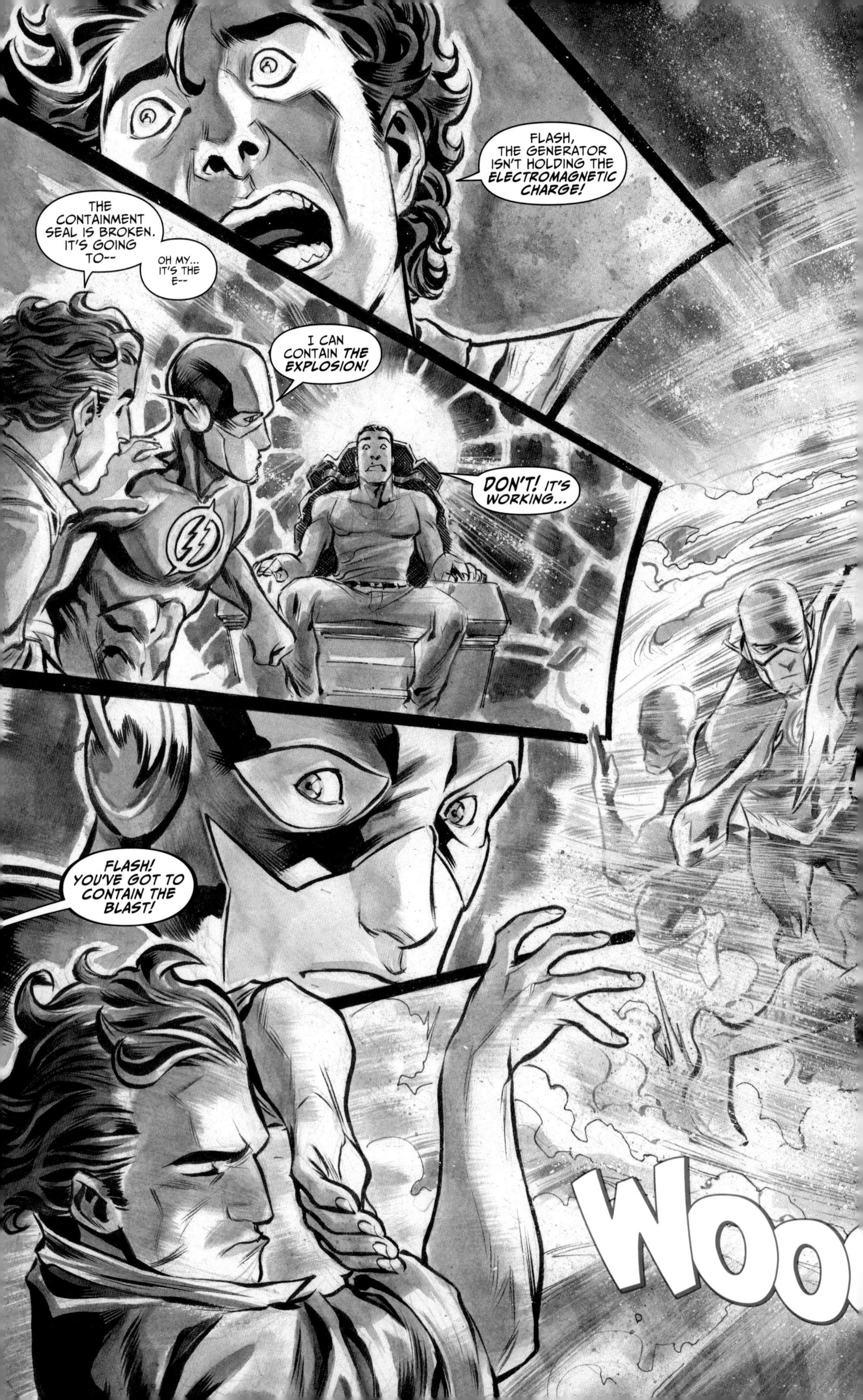
FLASH, THE GENERATOR ISN'T HOLDING THE ELECTROMAGNETIC CHARGE!
THE CONTAINMENT SEAL IS BROKEN. IT'S GOING TO--
OH MY... IT'S THE E--
I CAN CONTAIN THE EXPLOSION!
DON'T! IT'S WORKING...
FLASH! YOU'VE GOT TO CONTAIN THE BLAST!
WOO

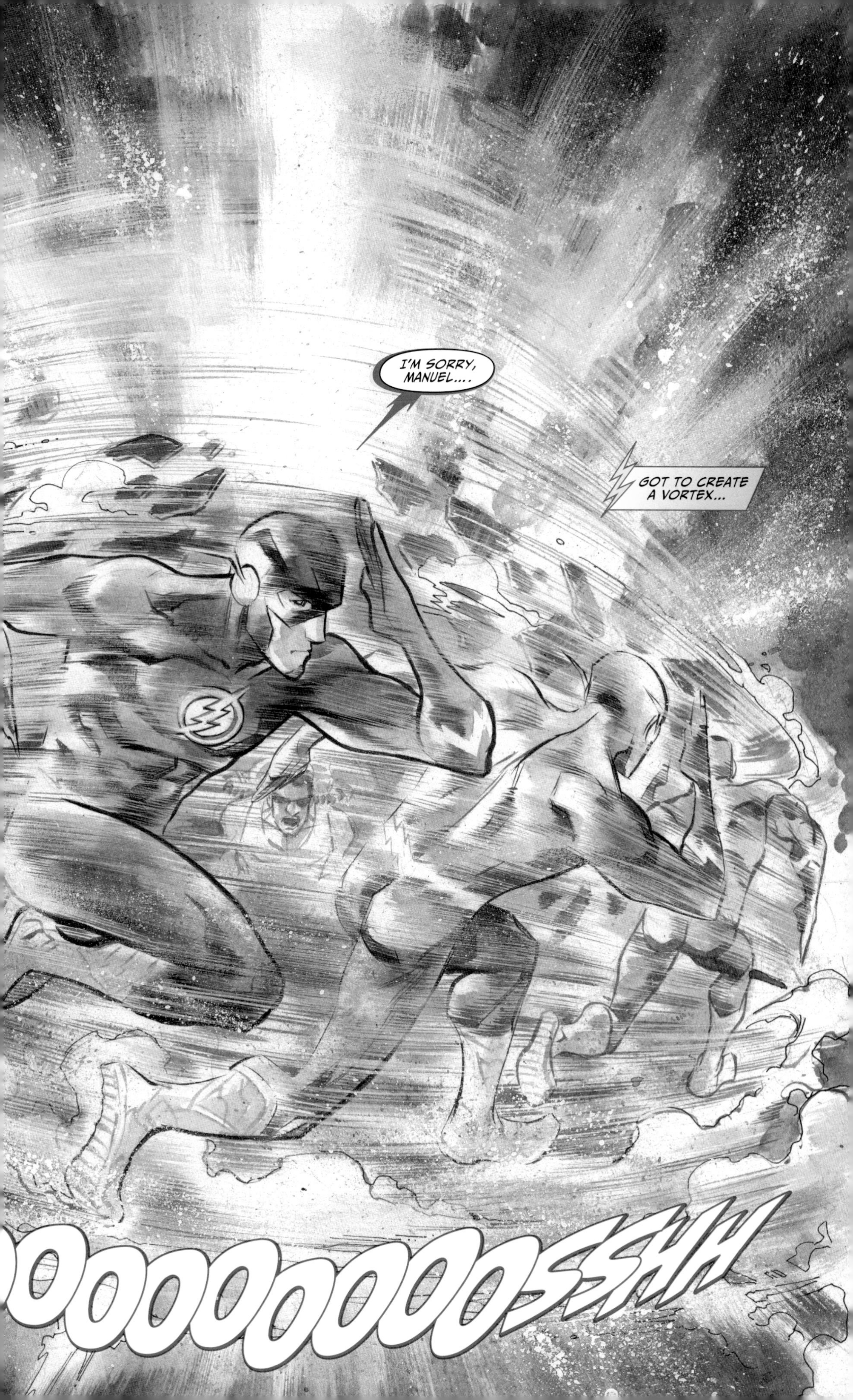
I'M SORRY, MANUEL....
GOT TO CREATE A VORTEX...
OOOOOOOOOSSHH

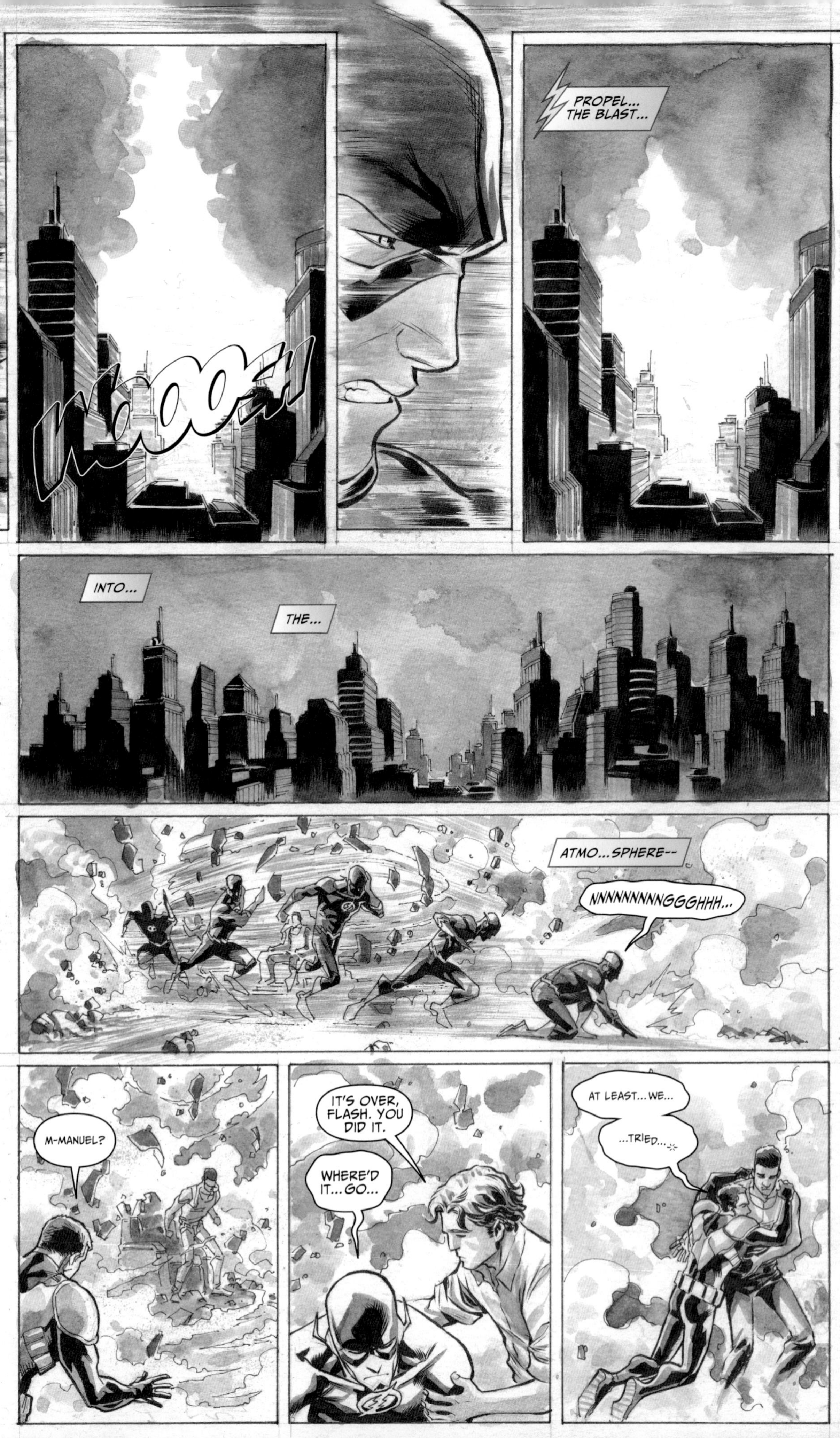

WHOOSH
PROPEL... THE BLAST...
INTO...
THE...
ATMO...SPHERE--
NNNNNNNNNGGHHH...
M-MANUEL?
IT'S OVER, FLASH. YOU DID IT.
WHERE'D IT...GO...
AT LEAST...WE...
...TRIED...

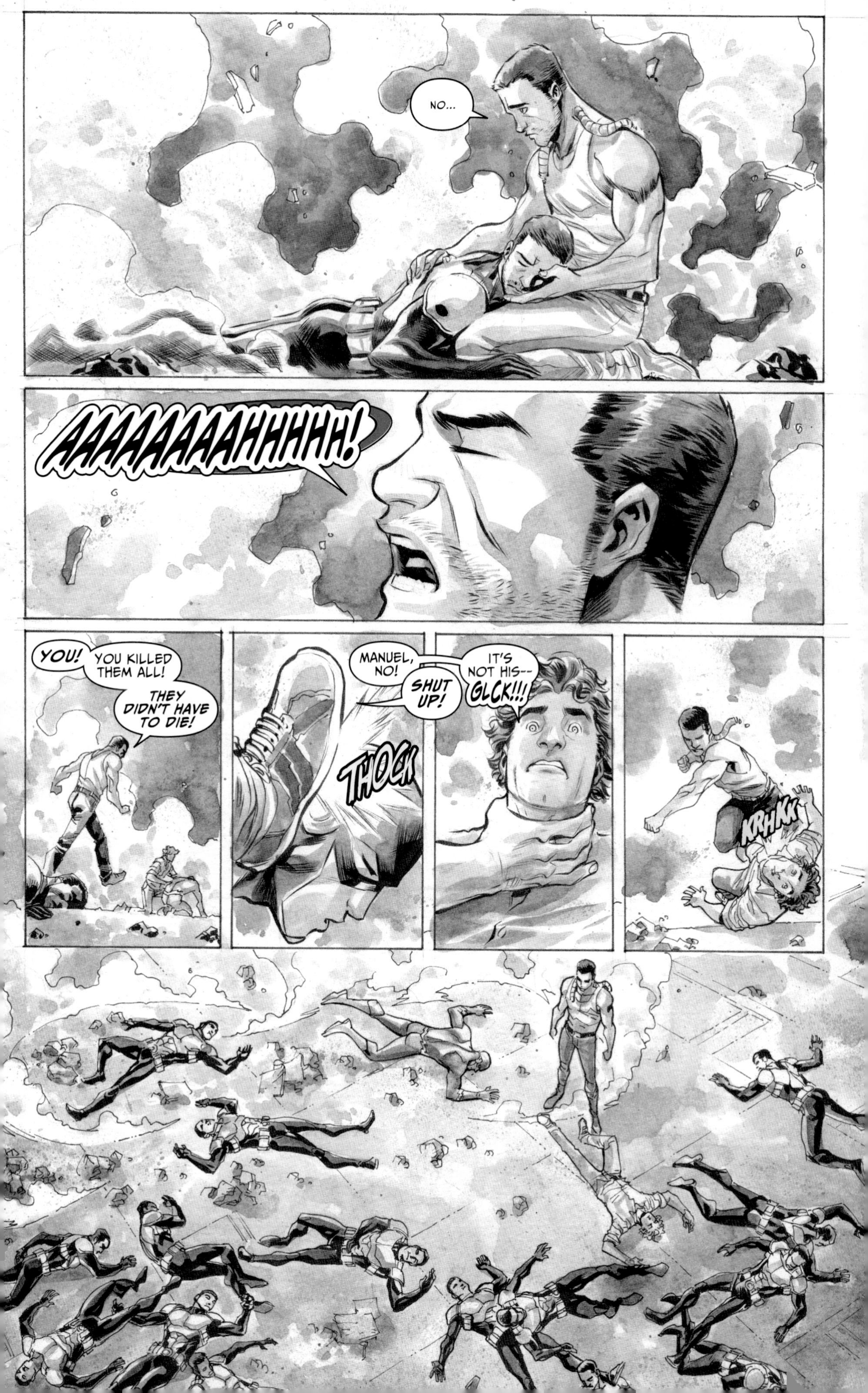
NO...
AAAAAAAAAHHHHH!
YOU!
YOU KILLED THEM ALL!
THEY DIDN'T HAVE TO DIE!
THOCK
MANUEL, NO!
SHUT UP!
IT'S NOT HIS--
GLCK!!!
KRHKK

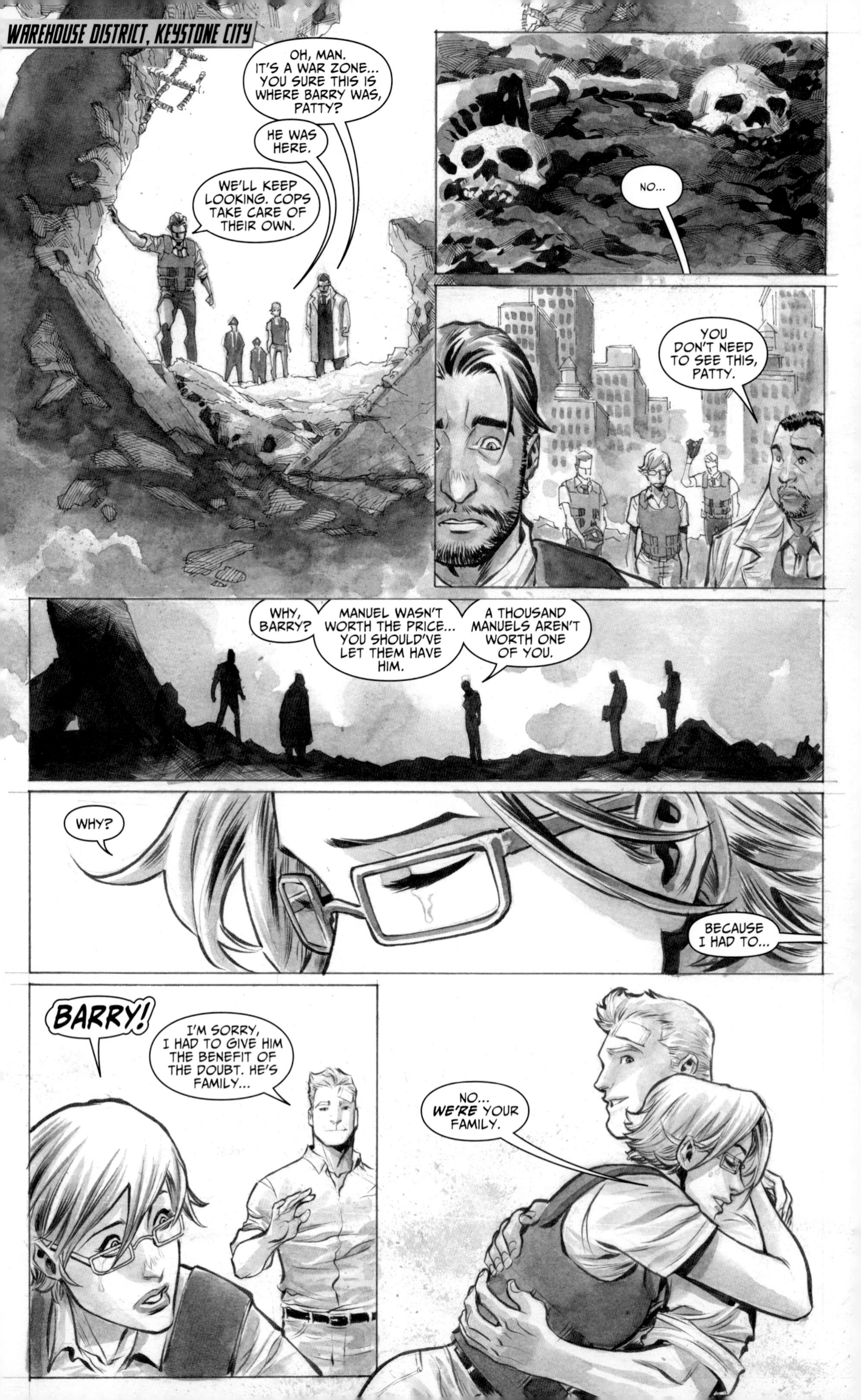
WAREHOUSE DISTRICT, KEYSTONE CITY
OH, MAN. IT'S A WAR ZONE... YOU SURE THIS IS WHERE BARRY WAS, PATTY?
HE WAS HERE.
WE'LL KEEP LOOKING. COPS TAKE CARE OF THEIR OWN.
NO...
YOU DON'T NEED TO SEE THIS, PATTY.
WHY, BARRY?
MANUEL WASN'T WORTH THE PRICE... YOU SHOULD'VE LET THEM HAVE HIM.
A THOUSAND MANUELS AREN'T WORTH ONE OF YOU.
WHY?
BECAUSE I HAD TO...
BARRY!
I'M SORRY, I HAD TO GIVE HIM THE BENEFIT OF THE DOUBT. HE'S FAMILY...
NO... WE'RE YOUR FAMILY.

YOU ARE THE CLOSEST THING I HAVE TO FAMILY...

NO MATTER HOW MANY OF US THEY KILL, NO MATTER WHO GETS IN OUR WAY...

ONE BY ONE...LIMB BY LIMB...

WE WILL FIND ANOTHER WAY.

WE ARE SURVIVORS...

WE ARE...

...MOB RULE.

I DON'T HAVE MUCH OF A BEDSIDE MANNER, FLASH... SO I'M GOING TO BE BLUNT. IT'S ALL OUR FAULT.

I KNOW YOU FEEL HORRIBLE ABOUT WHAT HAPPENED WITH MOB RULE, BUT DON'T BLAME--

YOU DON'T UNDERSTAND. LAST NIGHT...MOB RULE... THE E.M.P. BLACKOUT... IT'S ALL CONNECTED.

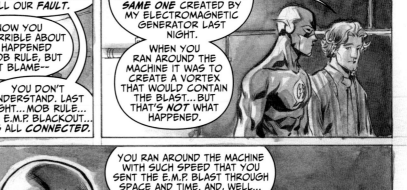

THE E.M.P. BLAST THAT DEVASTATED THE CITY THREE DAYS AGO WAS THE SAME ONE CREATED BY MY ELECTROMAGNETIC GENERATOR LAST NIGHT.

WHEN YOU RAN AROUND THE MACHINE IT WAS TO CREATE A VORTEX THAT WOULD CONTAIN THE BLAST...BUT THAT'S NOT WHAT HAPPENED.

WHAT ARE YOU SAYING?

YOU RAN AROUND THE MACHINE WITH SUCH SPEED THAT YOU SENT THE E.M.P. BLAST THROUGH SPACE AND TIME. AND, WELL... YOU KNOW WHERE IT LANDED.

THAT CAN'T BE. I DON'T DO TIME TRAVEL.

I NEED TO SHOW YOU SOMETHING...

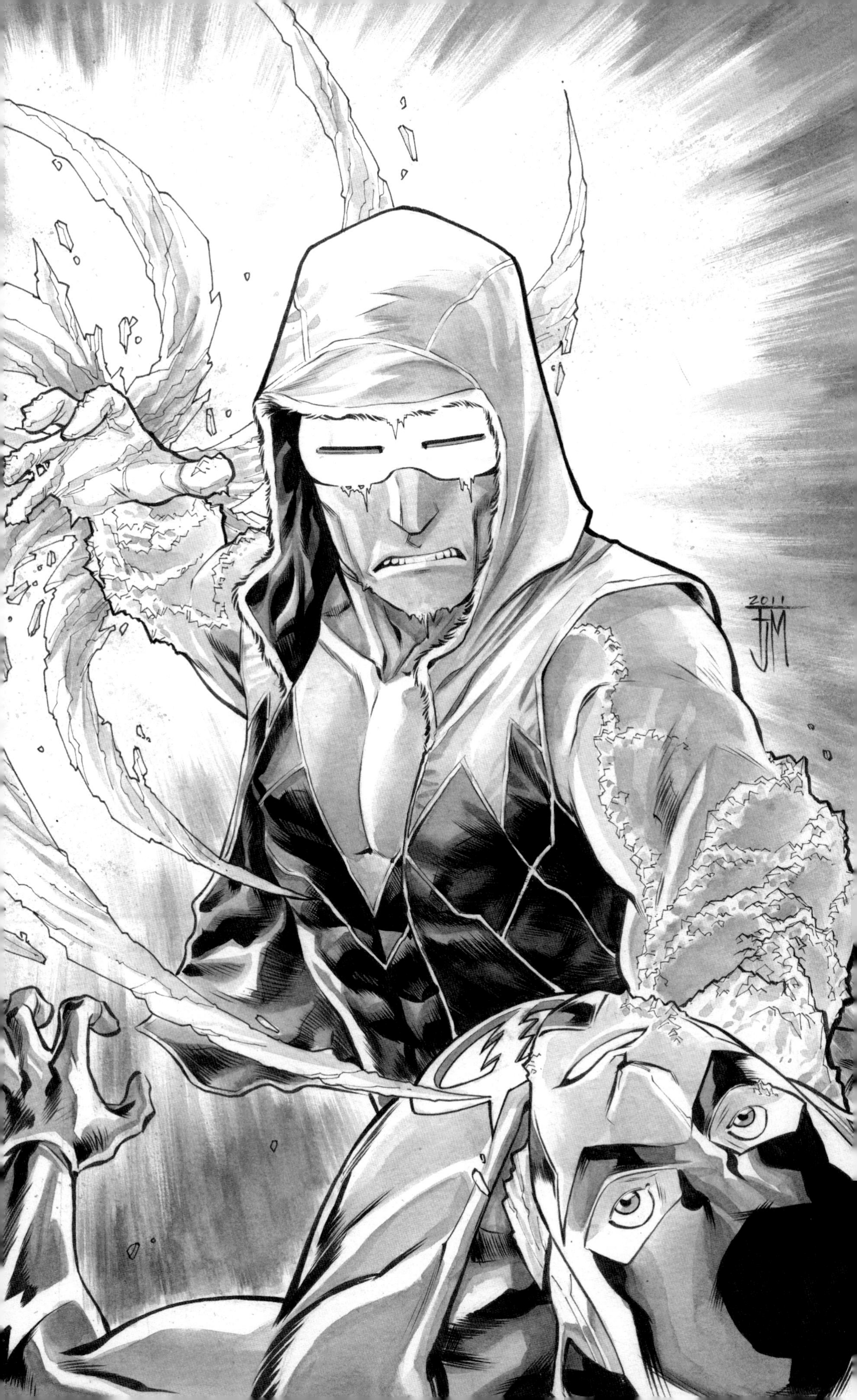
2011

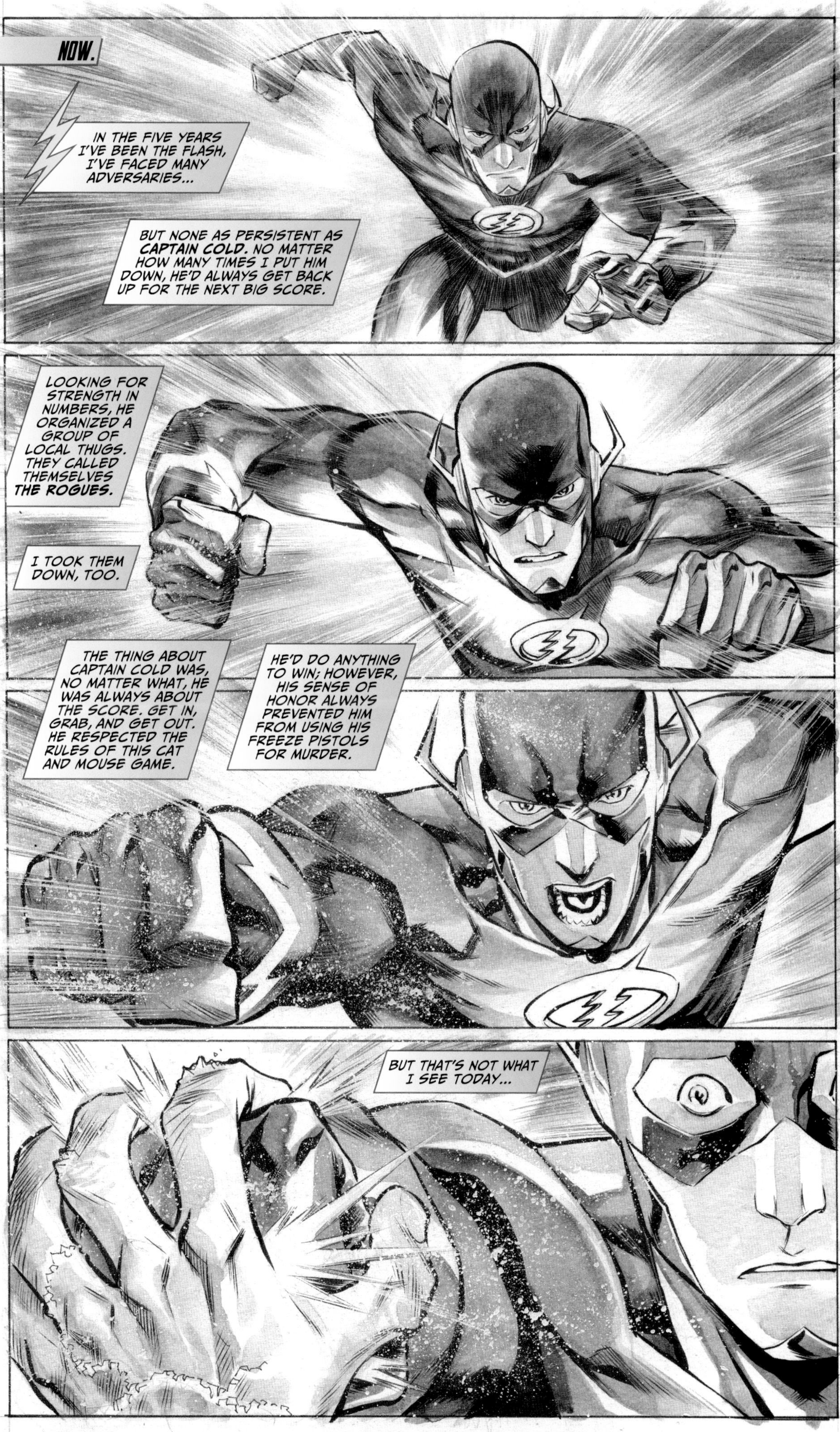
NOW.
IN THE FIVE YEARS I'VE BEEN THE FLASH, I'VE FACED MANY ADVERSARIES...
BUT NONE AS PERSISTENT AS CAPTAIN COLD. NO MATTER HOW MANY TIMES I PUT HIM DOWN, HE'D ALWAYS GET BACK UP FOR THE NEXT BIG SCORE.
LOOKING FOR STRENGTH IN NUMBERS, HE ORGANIZED A GROUP OF LOCAL THUGS. THEY CALLED THEMSELVES THE ROGUES.
I TOOK THEM DOWN, TOO.
THE THING ABOUT CAPTAIN COLD WAS, NO MATTER WHAT, HE WAS ALWAYS ABOUT THE SCORE. GET IN, GRAB, AND GET OUT. HE RESPECTED THE RULES OF THIS CAT AND MOUSE GAME.
HE'D DO ANYTHING TO WIN; HOWEVER, HIS SENSE OF HONOR ALWAYS PREVENTED HIM FROM USING HIS FREEZE PISTOLS FOR MURDER.
BUT THAT'S NOT WHAT I SEE TODAY...

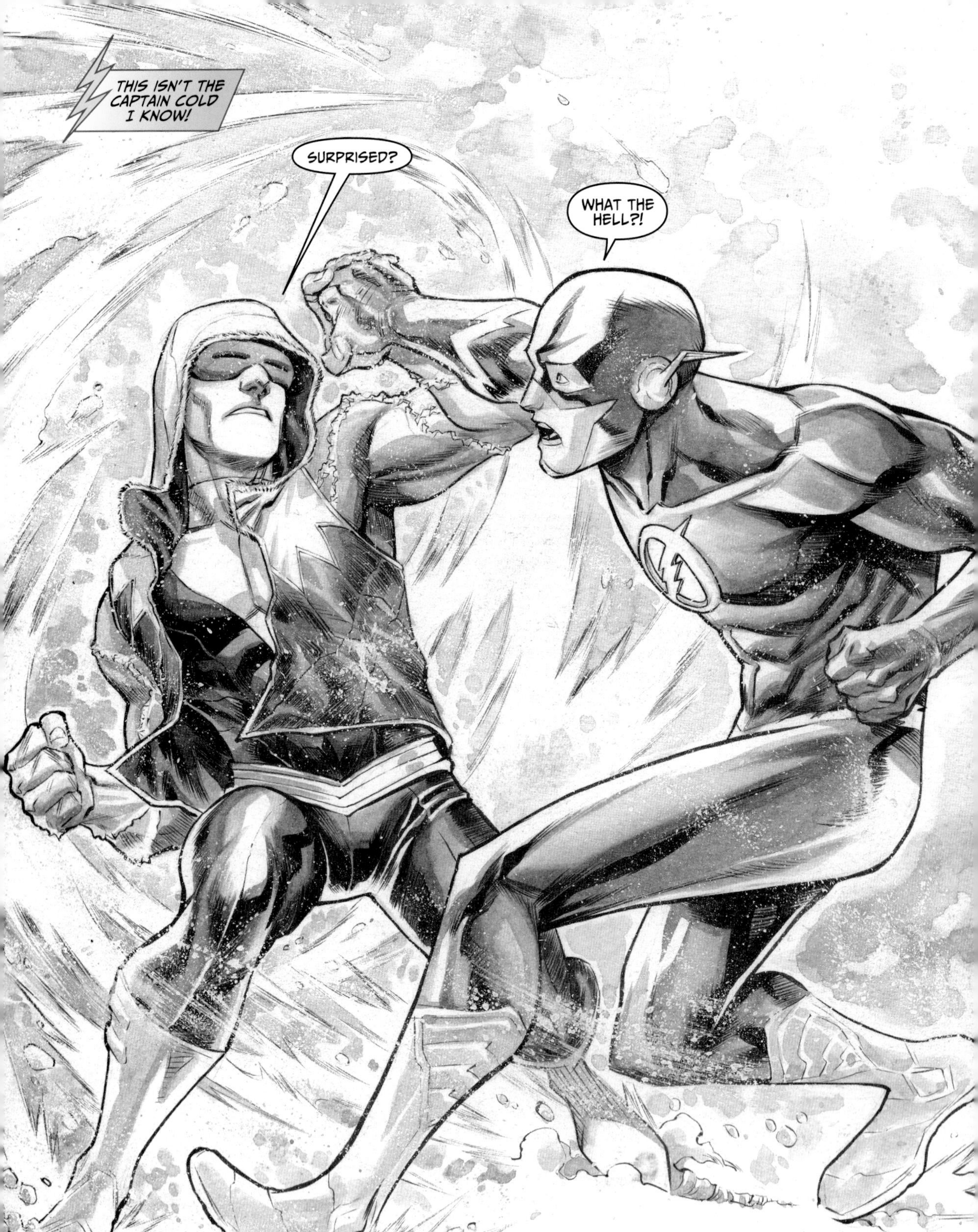
THIS ISN'T THE CAPTAIN COLD I KNOW!
SURPRISED?
WHAT THE HELL?!

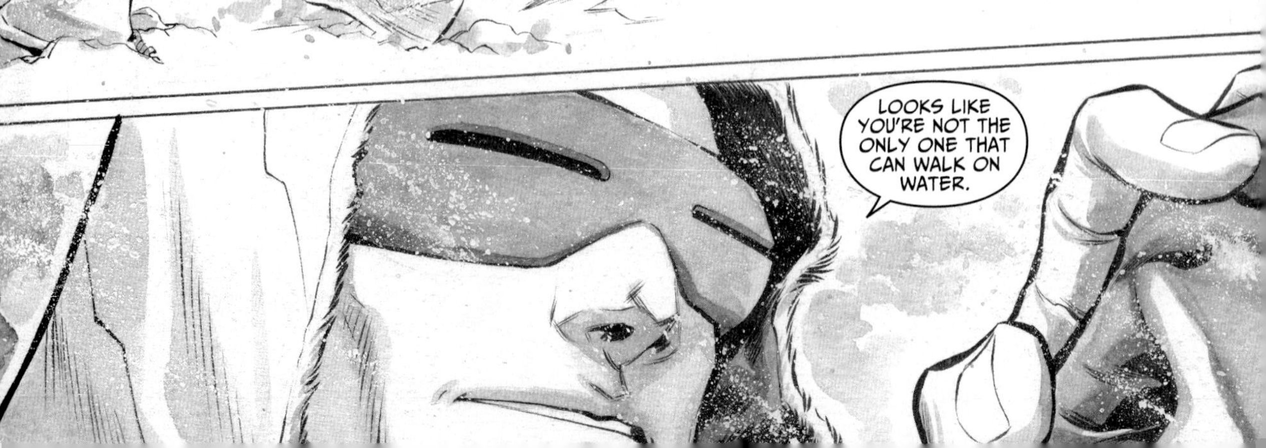
LOOKS LIKE YOU'RE NOT THE ONLY ONE THAT CAN WALK ON WATER.

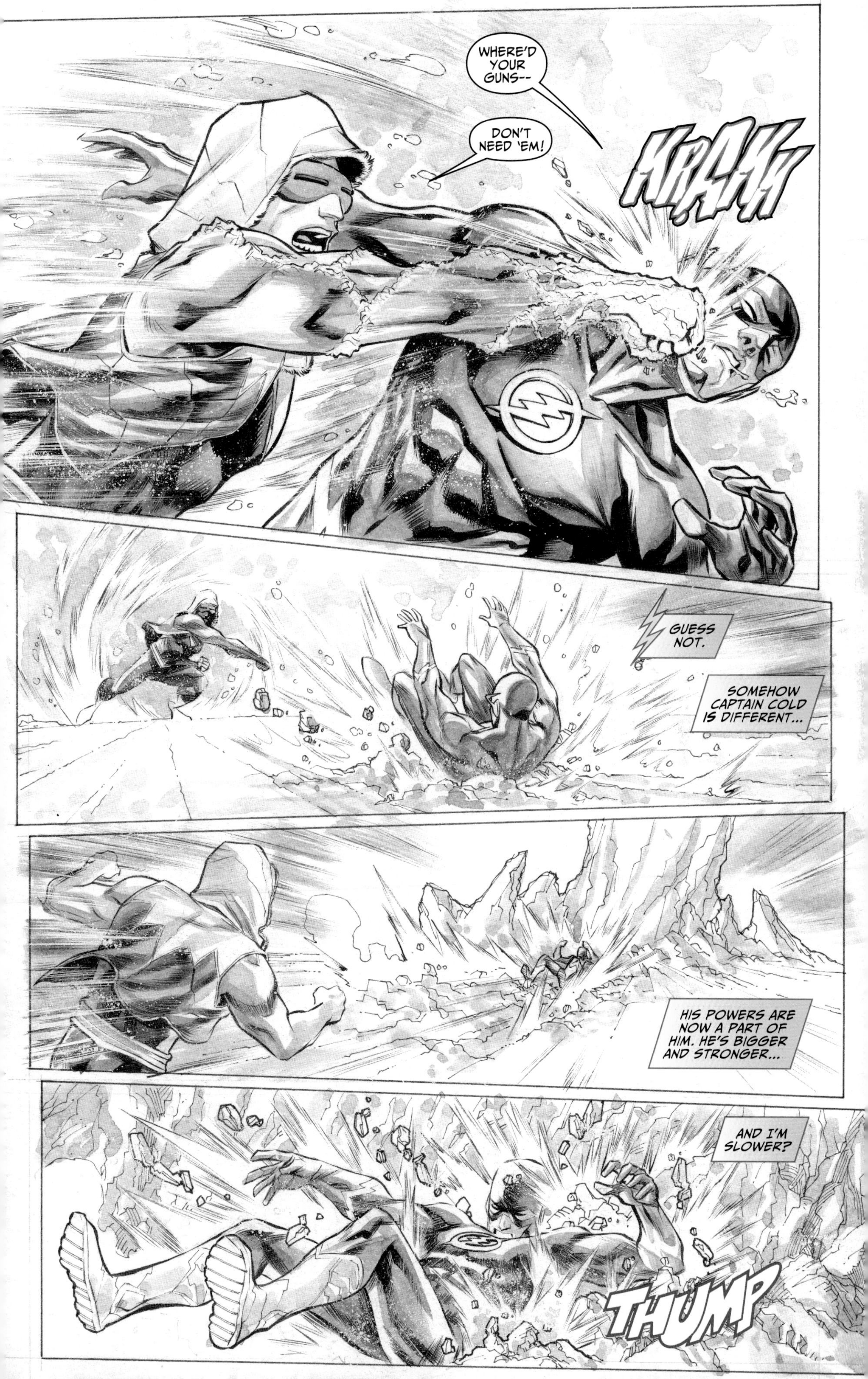
WHERE'D YOUR GUNS--
DON'T NEED 'EM!
KRAKK
GUESS NOT.
SOMEHOW CAPTAIN COLD IS DIFFERENT...
HIS POWERS ARE NOW A PART OF HIM. HE'S BIGGER AND STRONGER...
AND I'M SLOWER?
THUMP

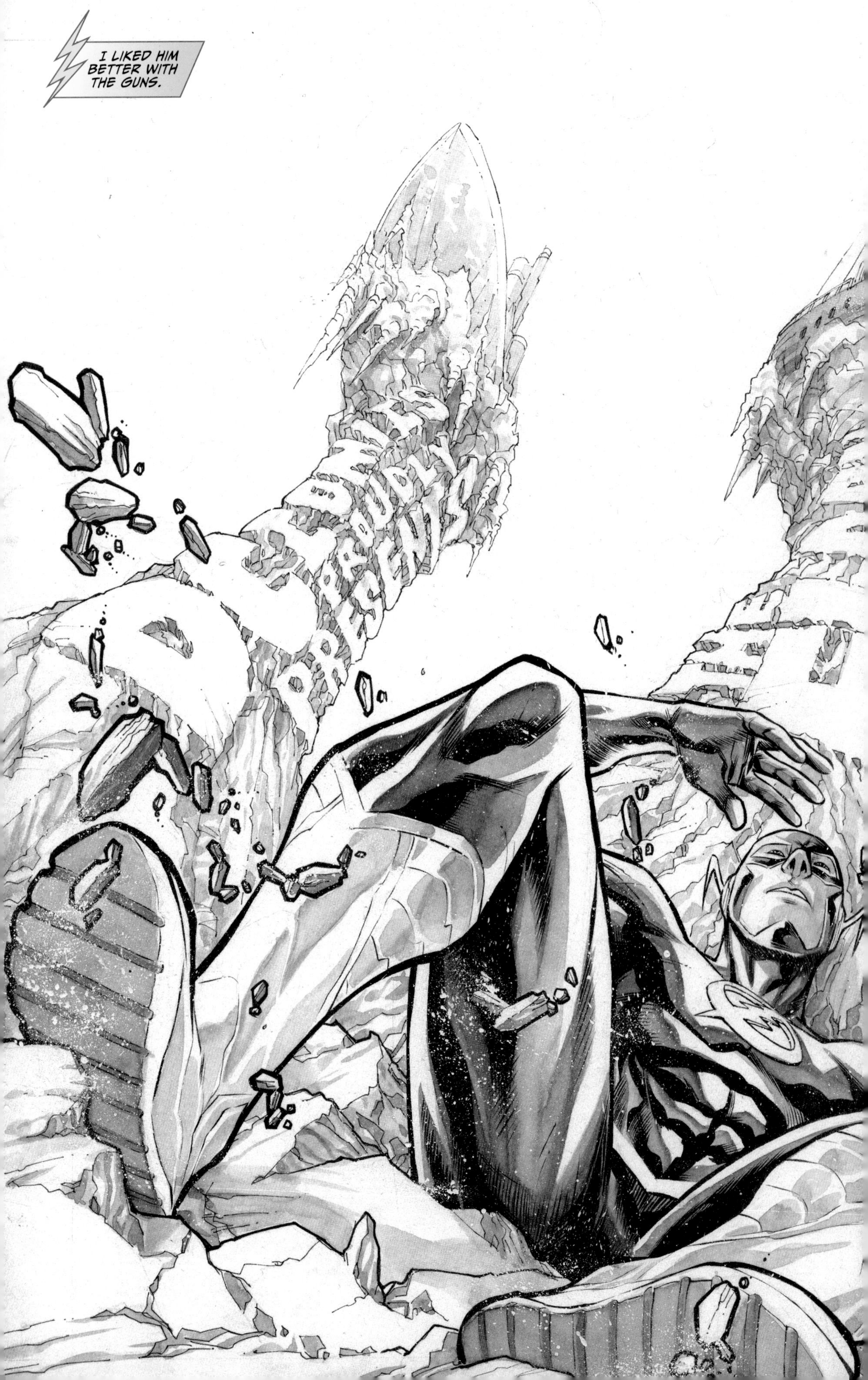
I LIKED HIM BETTER WITH THE GUNS.
PROUDLY PRESENTS

BEST SERVED COLD

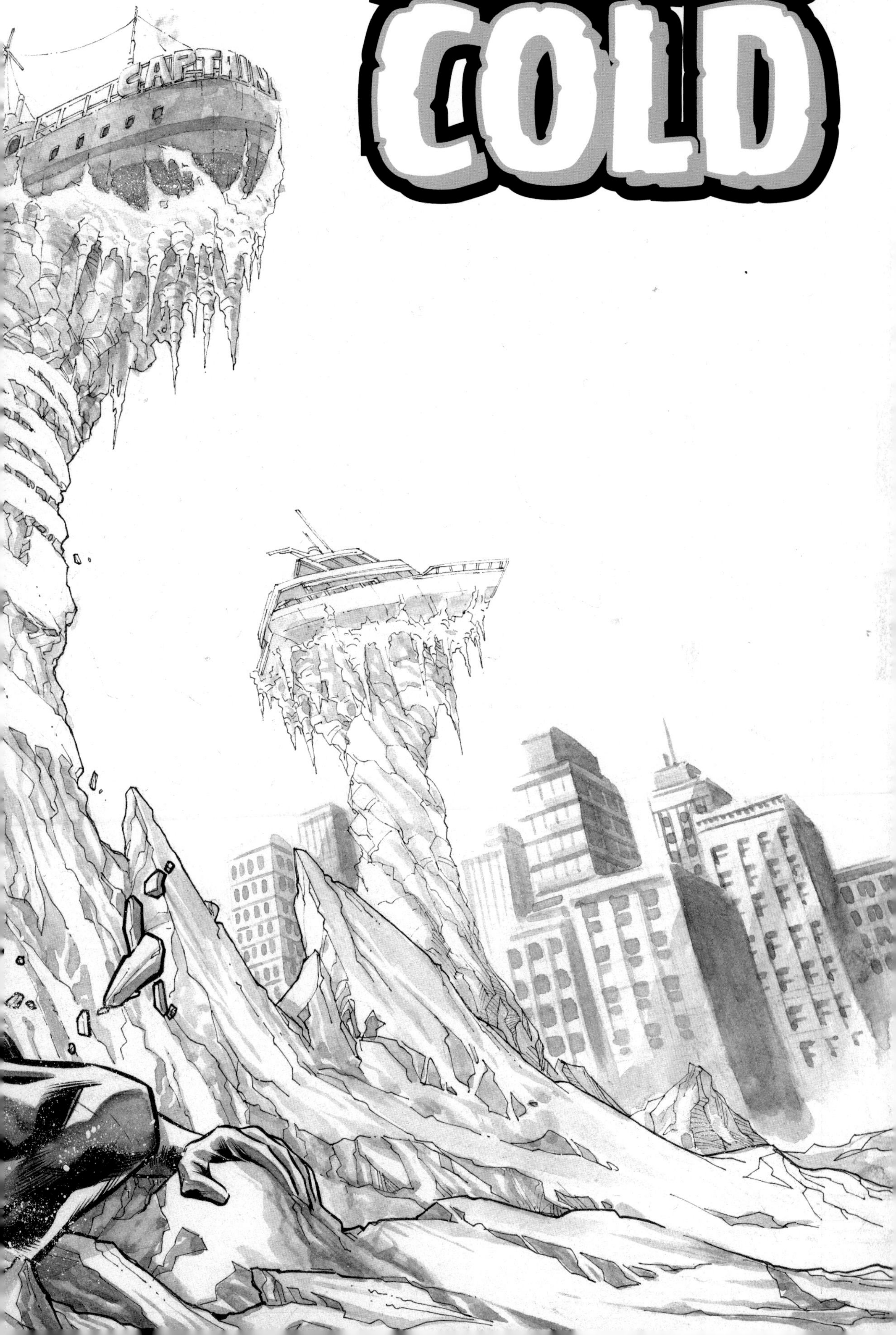

ZAP! ZAP!!

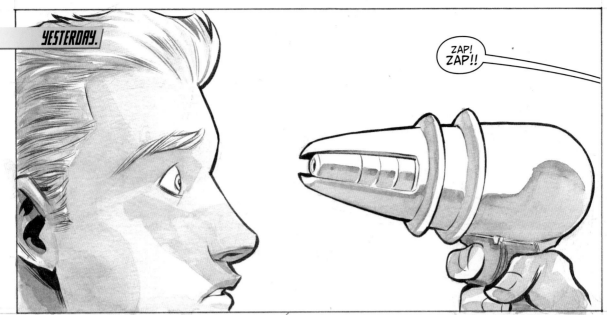

HEY...*NO FAIR!*

FINDERS KEEPERS!

I GOTTA ADMIT, PATTY...YOU WERE *RIGHT.* AFTER ALL THAT HAPPENED THE PAST TWO MONTHS, IT WAS SO NICE TO GET AWAY FOR A WEEKEND.

NO MOB RULE, NO E.M.P. BLASTS, NO LIFE-THREATENING CRISIS... JUST MY *GIRLFRIEND,* ROOM SERVICE AND CABLE TV. IT WAS AWESOME...

MAN, I'M GONNA MISS THAT *CABLE TV.*

...AND YOU ARE TOTALLY NOT LISTENING TO ME.

UHM...YES I WAS, BARRY. SOMETHING ABOUT CABLE TV.

COME ON, PATTY, YOU'VE BEEN HIDING THAT CASE FILE UNDER THERE FOR OVER AN *HOUR.*

AND I KNOW PART OF THE REASON WE WENT WAS TO FOLLOW UP ON THAT COLD CASE.

YOU DON'T HAVE TO HIDE THIS STUFF FROM ME.

I KNOW. BUT HOW ROMANTIC IS THAT? "LET'S GO ON THIS LITTLE GETAWAY! OH, AND BY THE WAY, IT JUST *HAPPENS* TO BE HOMETOWN TO THE CASE'S ONLY WITNESS."

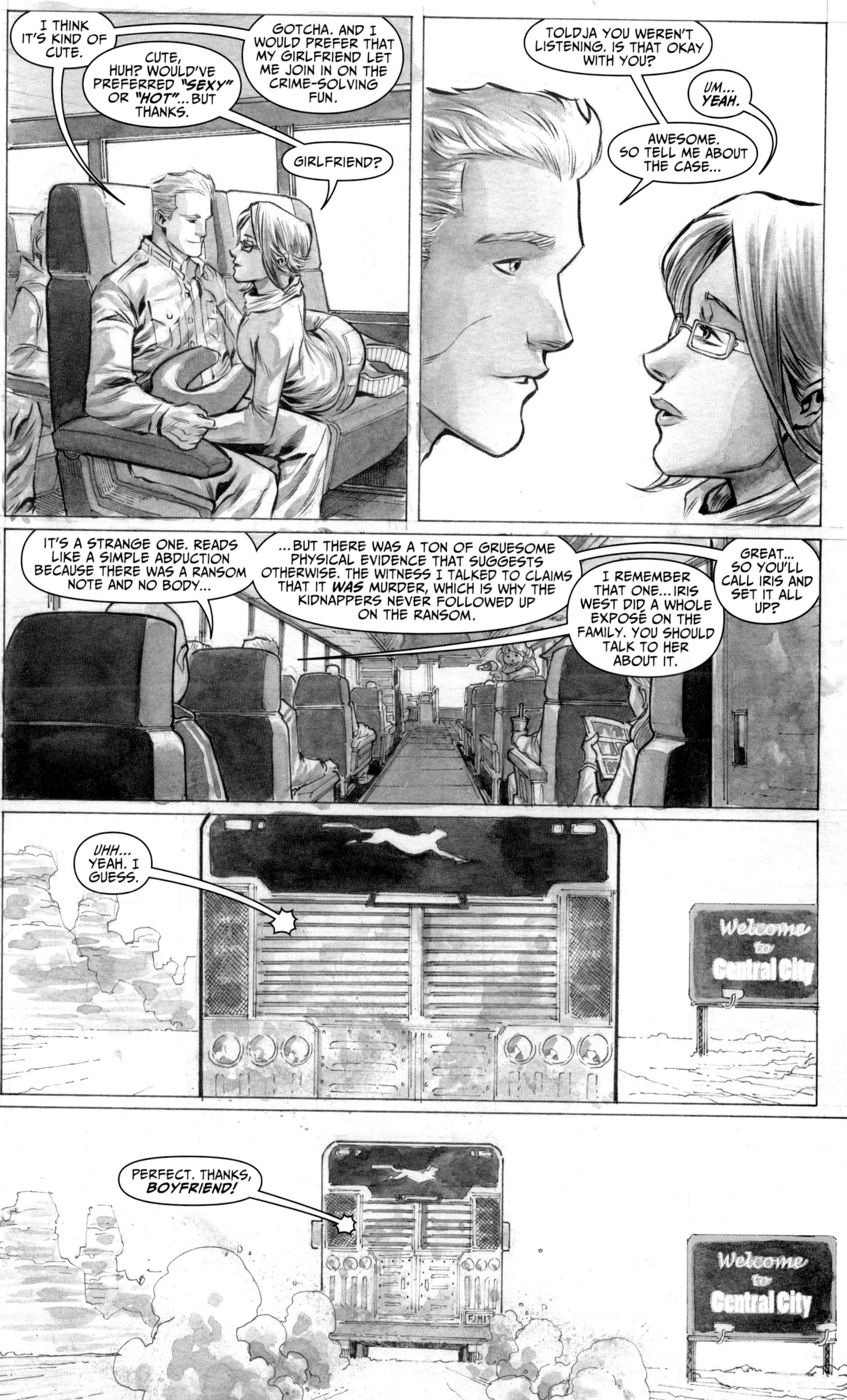
I THINK IT'S KIND OF CUTE.
CUTE, HUH? WOULD'VE PREFERRED "SEXY" OR "HOT"... BUT THANKS.
GOTCHA. AND I WOULD PREFER THAT MY GIRLFRIEND LET ME JOIN IN ON THE CRIME-SOLVING FUN.
GIRLFRIEND?
TOLDJA YOU WEREN'T LISTENING. IS THAT OKAY WITH YOU?
UM... YEAH.
AWESOME. SO TELL ME ABOUT THE CASE...
IT'S A STRANGE ONE. READS LIKE A SIMPLE ABDUCTION BECAUSE THERE WAS A RANSOM NOTE AND NO BODY...
...BUT THERE WAS A TON OF GRUESOME PHYSICAL EVIDENCE THAT SUGGESTS OTHERWISE. THE WITNESS I TALKED TO CLAIMS THAT IT WAS MURDER, WHICH IS WHY THE KIDNAPPERS NEVER FOLLOWED UP ON THE RANSOM.
I REMEMBER THAT ONE... IRIS WEST DID A WHOLE EXPOSÉ ON THE FAMILY. YOU SHOULD TALK TO HER ABOUT IT.
GREAT... SO YOU'LL CALL IRIS AND SET IT ALL UP?
UHH... YEAH. I GUESS.
Welcome to Central City
PERFECT. THANKS, BOYFRIEND!
Welcome to Central City

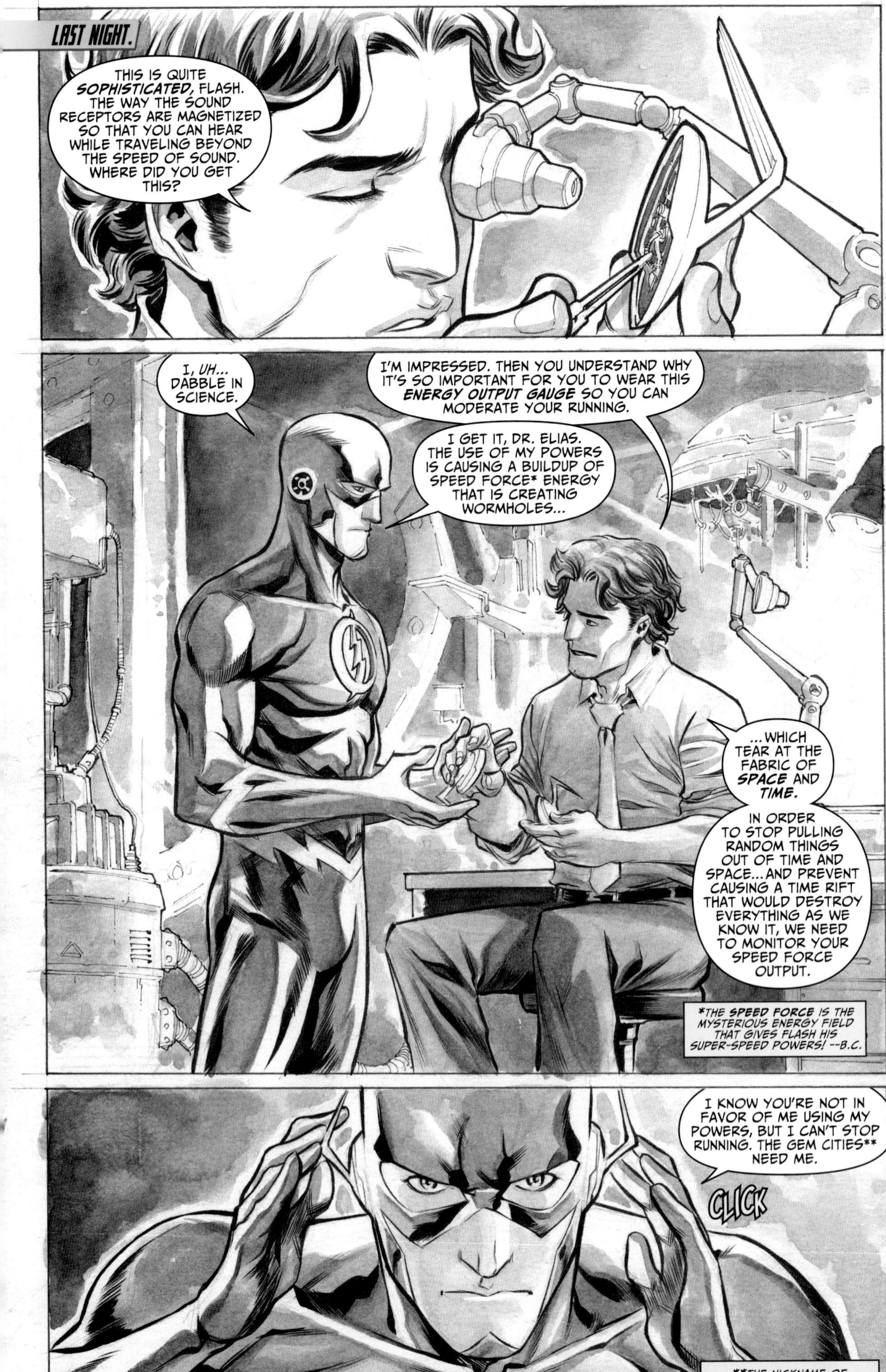
LAST NIGHT.
THIS IS QUITE SOPHISTICATED, FLASH. THE WAY THE SOUND RECEPTORS ARE MAGNETIZED SO THAT YOU CAN HEAR WHILE TRAVELING BEYOND THE SPEED OF SOUND. WHERE DID YOU GET THIS?
I, UH... DABBLE IN SCIENCE.
I'M IMPRESSED. THEN YOU UNDERSTAND WHY IT'S SO IMPORTANT FOR YOU TO WEAR THIS ENERGY OUTPUT GAUGE SO YOU CAN MODERATE YOUR RUNNING.
I GET IT, DR. ELIAS. THE USE OF MY POWERS IS CAUSING A BUILDUP OF SPEED FORCE* ENERGY THAT IS CREATING WORMHOLES...
...WHICH TEAR AT THE FABRIC OF SPACE AND TIME.
IN ORDER TO STOP PULLING RANDOM THINGS OUT OF TIME AND SPACE... AND PREVENT CAUSING A TIME RIFT THAT WOULD DESTROY EVERYTHING AS WE KNOW IT, WE NEED TO MONITOR YOUR SPEED FORCE OUTPUT.
*THE SPEED FORCE IS THE MYSTERIOUS ENERGY FIELD THAT GIVES FLASH HIS SUPER-SPEED POWERS! --B.C.
I KNOW YOU'RE NOT IN FAVOR OF ME USING MY POWERS, BUT I CAN'T STOP RUNNING. THE GEM CITIES** NEED ME.
CLICK
**THE NICKNAME OF NEIGHBORING CENTRAL CITY AND KEYSTONE CITY! --B.C.

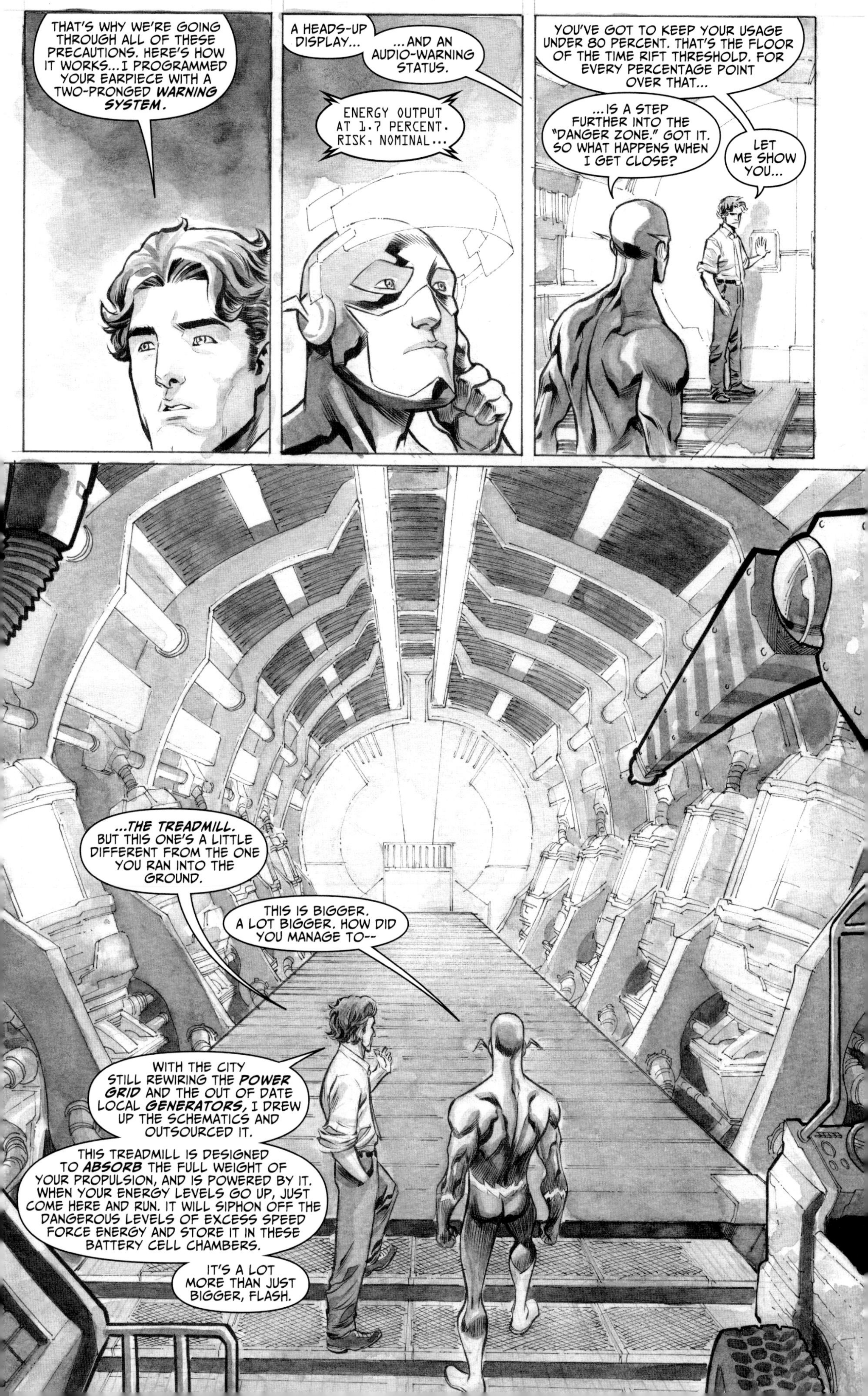
THAT'S WHY WE'RE GOING THROUGH ALL OF THESE PRECAUTIONS. HERE'S HOW IT WORKS...I PROGRAMMED YOUR EARPIECE WITH A TWO-PRONGED WARNING SYSTEM.
A HEADS-UP DISPLAY...
...AND AN AUDIO-WARNING STATUS.
ENERGY OUTPUT AT 1.7 PERCENT. RISK, NOMINAL...
YOU'VE GOT TO KEEP YOUR USAGE UNDER 80 PERCENT. THAT'S THE FLOOR OF THE TIME RIFT THRESHOLD. FOR EVERY PERCENTAGE POINT OVER THAT...
...IS A STEP FURTHER INTO THE "DANGER ZONE." GOT IT. SO WHAT HAPPENS WHEN I GET CLOSE?
LET ME SHOW YOU...
...THE TREADMILL. BUT THIS ONE'S A LITTLE DIFFERENT FROM THE ONE YOU RAN INTO THE GROUND.
THIS IS BIGGER. A LOT BIGGER. HOW DID YOU MANAGE TO--
WITH THE CITY STILL REWIRING THE POWER GRID AND THE OUT OF DATE LOCAL GENERATORS, I DREW UP THE SCHEMATICS AND OUTSOURCED IT.
THIS TREADMILL IS DESIGNED TO ABSORB THE FULL WEIGHT OF YOUR PROPULSION, AND IS POWERED BY IT. WHEN YOUR ENERGY LEVELS GO UP, JUST COME HERE AND RUN. IT WILL SIPHON OFF THE DANGEROUS LEVELS OF EXCESS SPEED FORCE ENERGY AND STORE IT IN THESE BATTERY CELL CHAMBERS.
IT'S A LOT MORE THAN JUST BIGGER, FLASH.

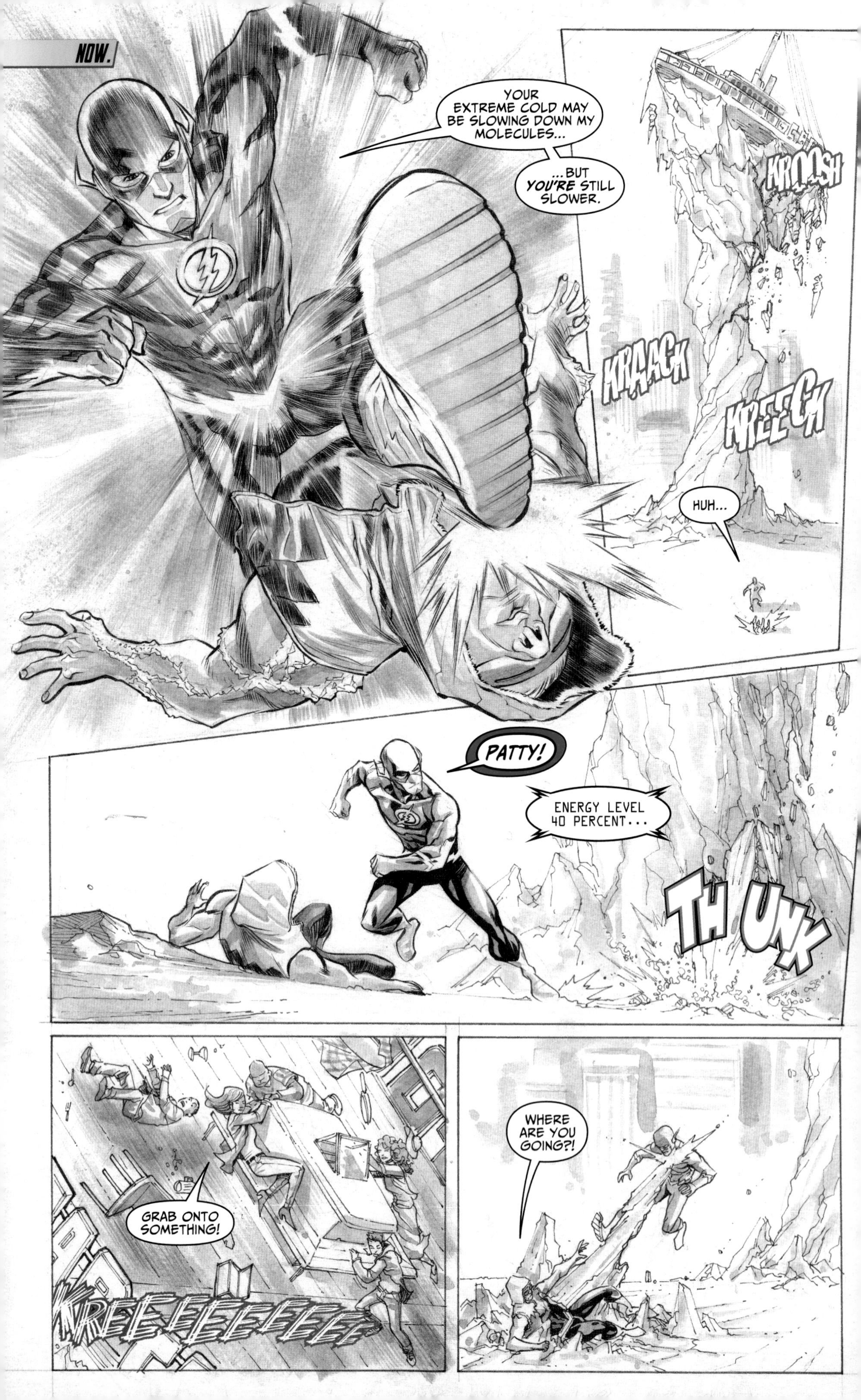
NOW.
YOUR EXTREME COLD MAY BE SLOWING DOWN MY MOLECULES...
...BUT YOU'RE STILL SLOWER.
KROOSH
KRAACK
KREECK
HUH...
PATTY!
ENERGY LEVEL 40 PERCENT...
THUNK
GRAB ONTO SOMETHING!
KREEEEEEEEEE
WHERE ARE YOU GOING?!

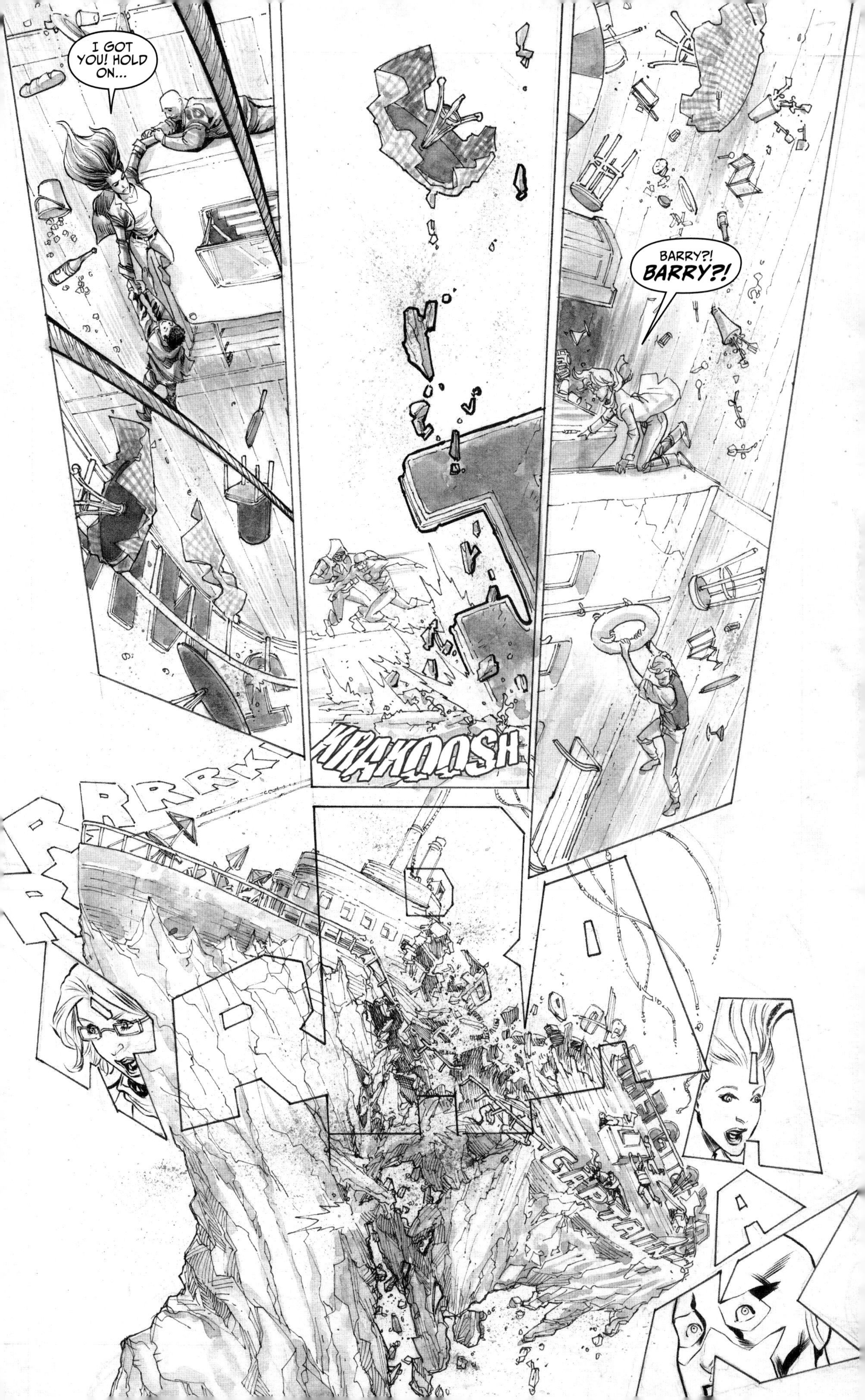

I GOT YOU! HOLD ON...
KRAKOOSH
BARRY?! BARRY?!

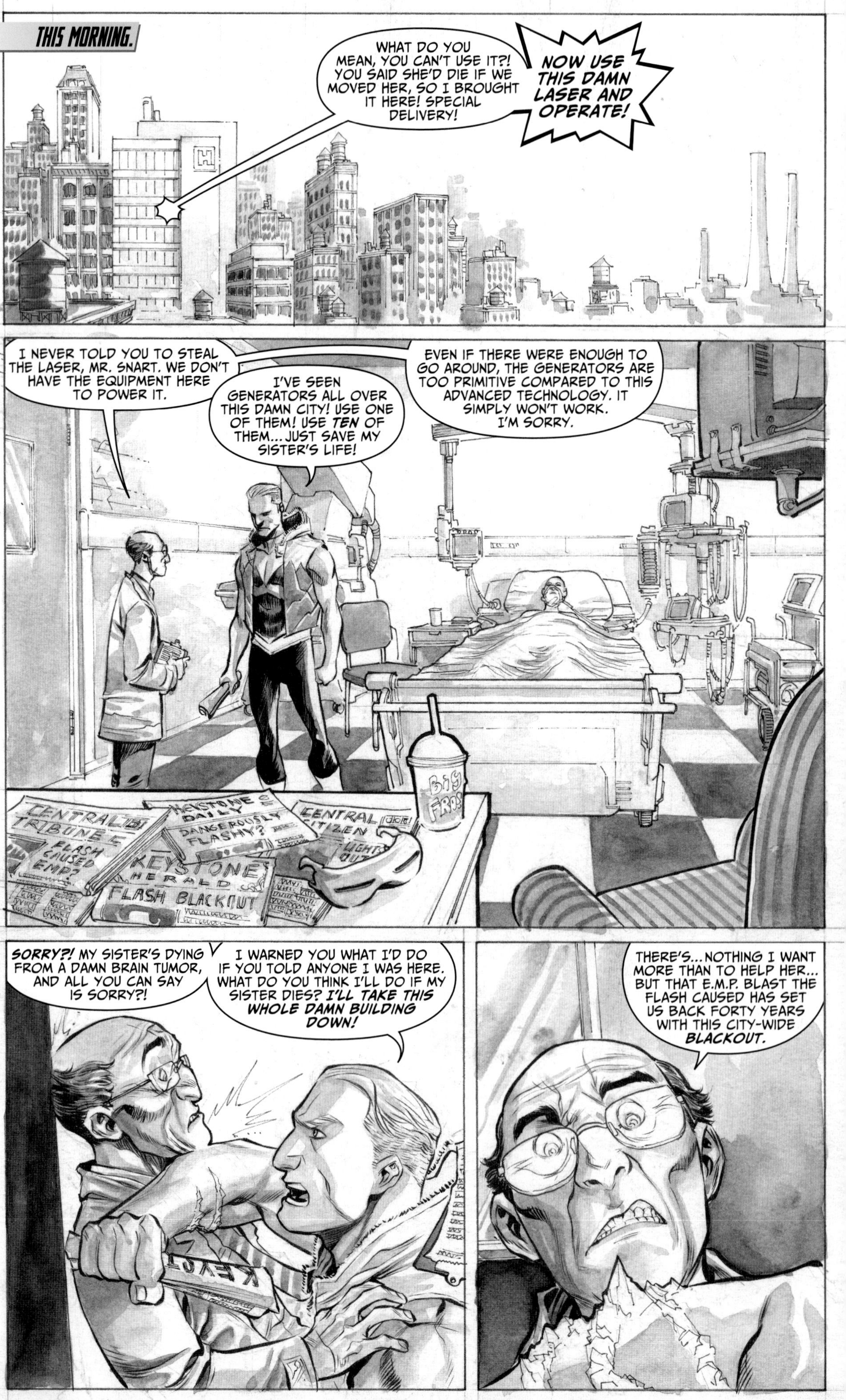
THIS MORNING.
WHAT DO YOU MEAN, YOU CAN'T USE IT?! YOU SAID SHE'D DIE IF WE MOVED HER, SO I BROUGHT IT HERE! SPECIAL DELIVERY!
NOW USE THIS DAMN LASER AND OPERATE!
I NEVER TOLD YOU TO STEAL THE LASER, MR. SNART. WE DON'T HAVE THE EQUIPMENT HERE TO POWER IT.
I'VE SEEN GENERATORS ALL OVER THIS DAMN CITY! USE ONE OF THEM! USE TEN OF THEM... JUST SAVE MY SISTER'S LIFE!
EVEN IF THERE WERE ENOUGH TO GO AROUND, THE GENERATORS ARE TOO PRIMITIVE COMPARED TO THIS ADVANCED TECHNOLOGY. IT SIMPLY WON'T WORK. I'M SORRY.
CENTRAL TRIBUNE
FLASH CAUSED EMP?
KEYSTONE DAILY
DANGEROUSLY FLASHY?
CENTRAL CITIZEN
LIGHTS OUT
KEYSTONE HERALD
FLASH BLACKOUT
SORRY?! MY SISTER'S DYING FROM A DAMN BRAIN TUMOR, AND ALL YOU CAN SAY IS SORRY?!
I WARNED YOU WHAT I'D DO IF YOU TOLD ANYONE I WAS HERE. WHAT DO YOU THINK I'LL DO IF MY SISTER DIES? I'LL TAKE THIS WHOLE DAMN BUILDING DOWN!
THERE'S... NOTHING I WANT MORE THAN TO HELP HER... BUT THAT E.M.P. BLAST THE FLASH CAUSED HAS SET US BACK FORTY YEARS WITH THIS CITY-WIDE BLACKOUT.

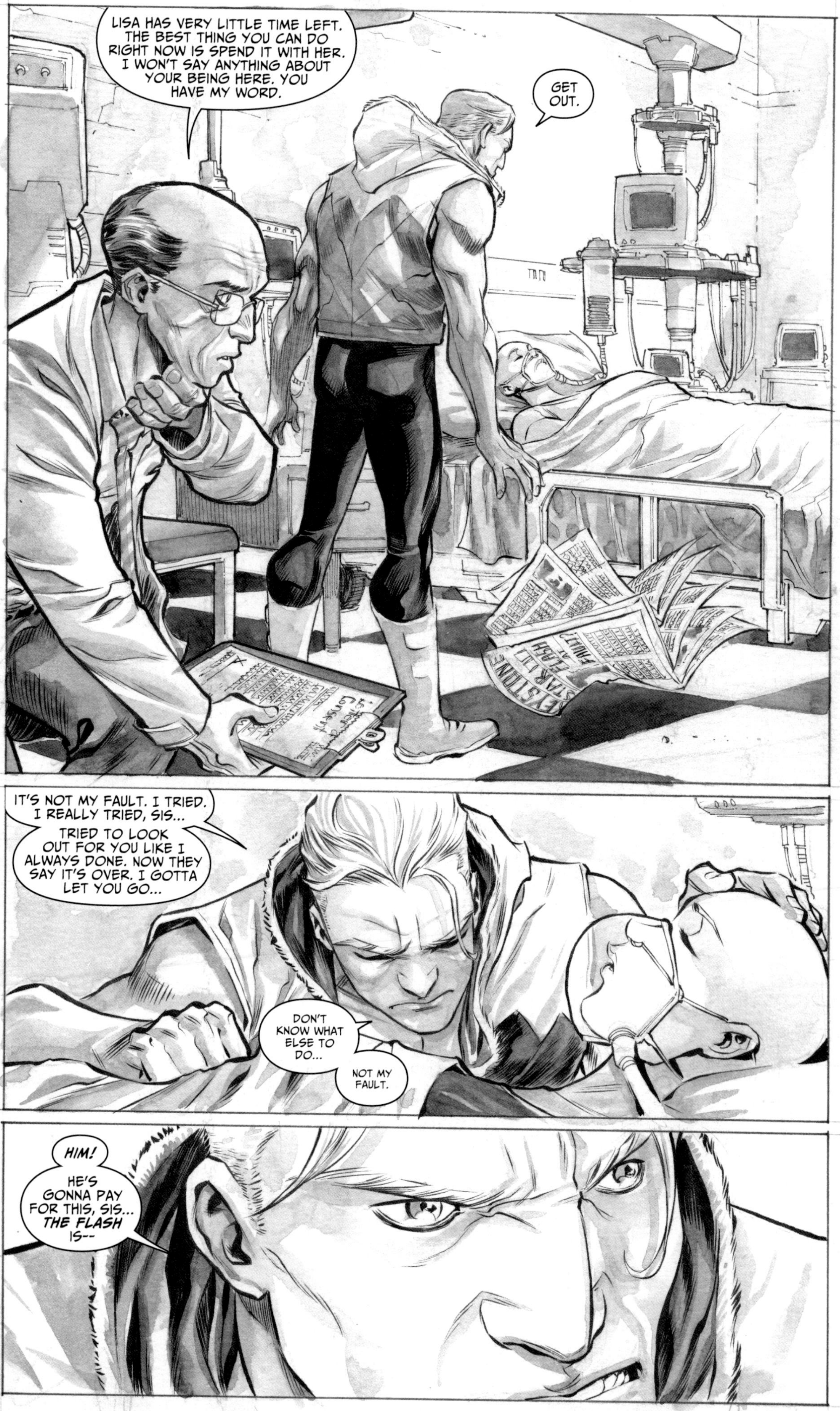
LISA HAS VERY LITTLE TIME LEFT. THE BEST THING YOU CAN DO RIGHT NOW IS SPEND IT WITH HER. I WON'T SAY ANYTHING ABOUT YOUR BEING HERE. YOU HAVE MY WORD.
GET OUT.
IT'S NOT MY FAULT. I TRIED. I REALLY TRIED, SIS...
TRIED TO LOOK OUT FOR YOU LIKE I ALWAYS DONE. NOW THEY SAY IT'S OVER. I GOTTA LET YOU GO...
DON'T KNOW WHAT ELSE TO DO...
NOT MY FAULT.
HIM!
HE'S GONNA PAY FOR THIS, SIS... *THE FLASH* IS--

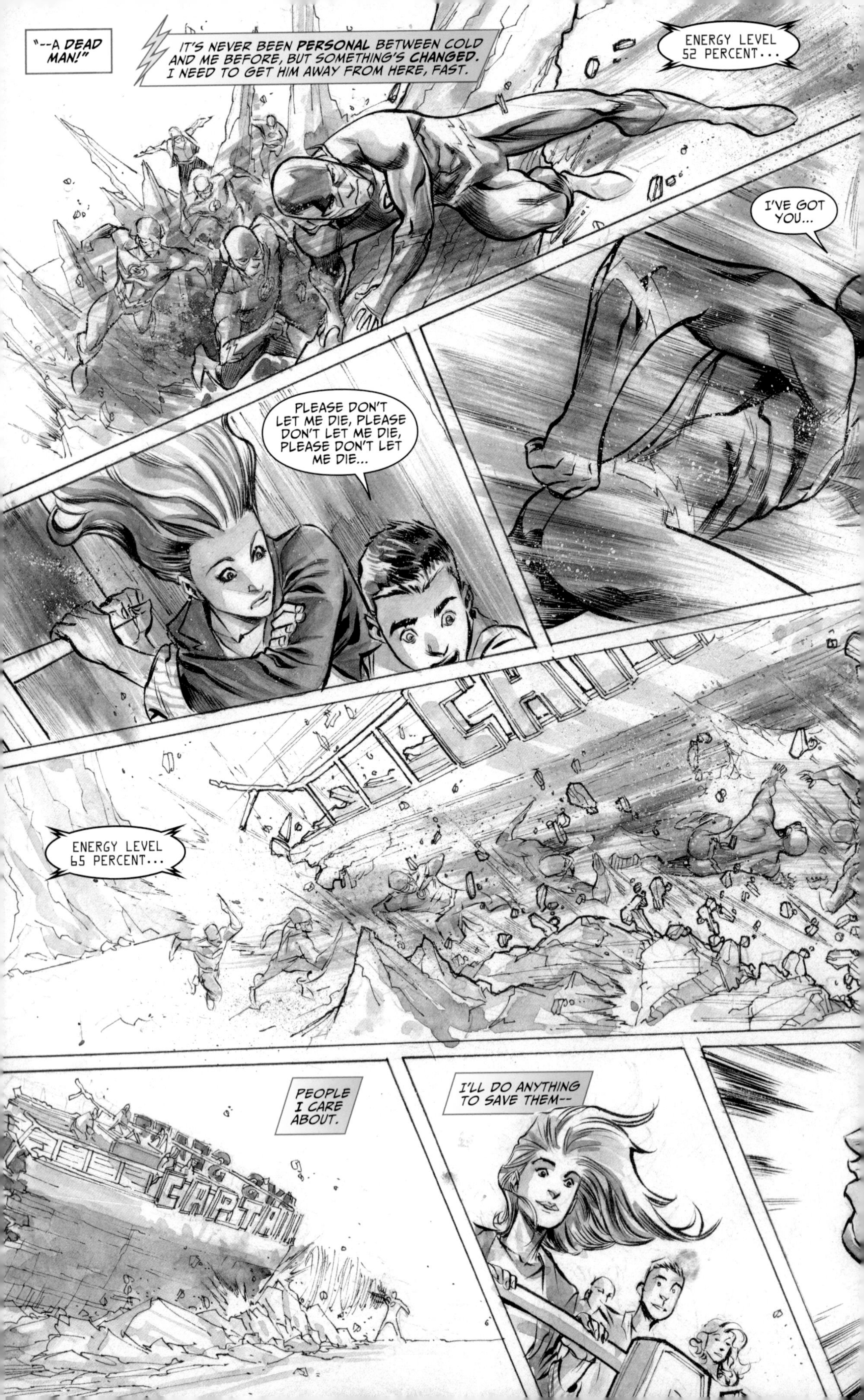
"--A DEAD MAN!"
IT'S NEVER BEEN PERSONAL BETWEEN COLD AND ME BEFORE, BUT SOMETHING'S CHANGED. I NEED TO GET HIM AWAY FROM HERE, FAST.
ENERGY LEVEL 52 PERCENT...
I'VE GOT YOU...
PLEASE DON'T LET ME DIE, PLEASE DON'T LET ME DIE, PLEASE DON'T LET ME DIE...
ENERGY LEVEL 65 PERCENT...
CAPTAIN
PEOPLE I CARE ABOUT.
I'LL DO ANYTHING TO SAVE THEM--

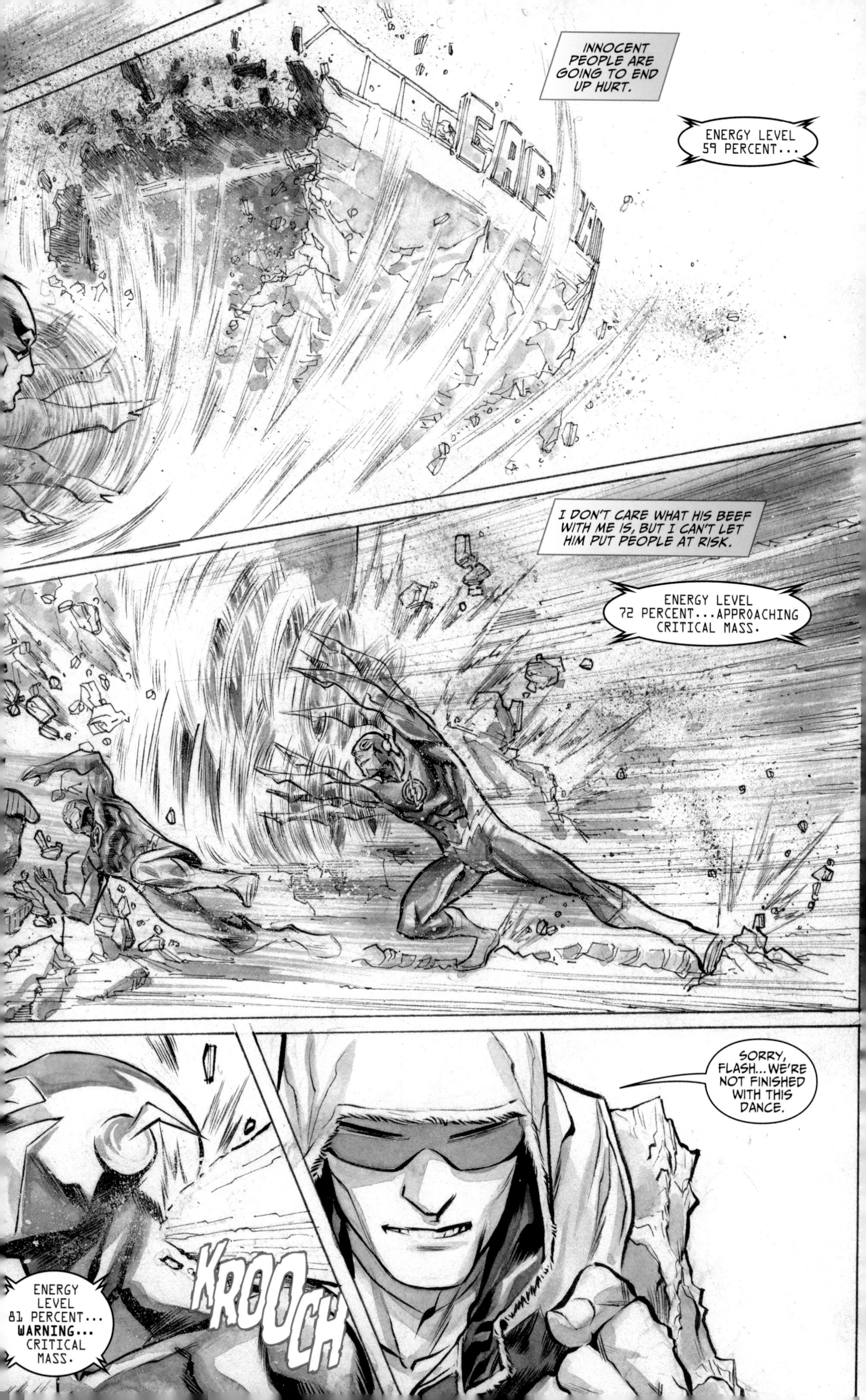
INNOCENT PEOPLE ARE GOING TO END UP HURT.
ENERGY LEVEL 59 PERCENT...
I DON'T CARE WHAT HIS BEEF WITH ME IS, BUT I CAN'T LET HIM PUT PEOPLE AT RISK.
ENERGY LEVEL 72 PERCENT...APPROACHING CRITICAL MASS.
SORRY, FLASH...WE'RE NOT FINISHED WITH THIS DANCE.
ENERGY LEVEL 81 PERCENT... **WARNING...** CRITICAL MASS.
KROOCH

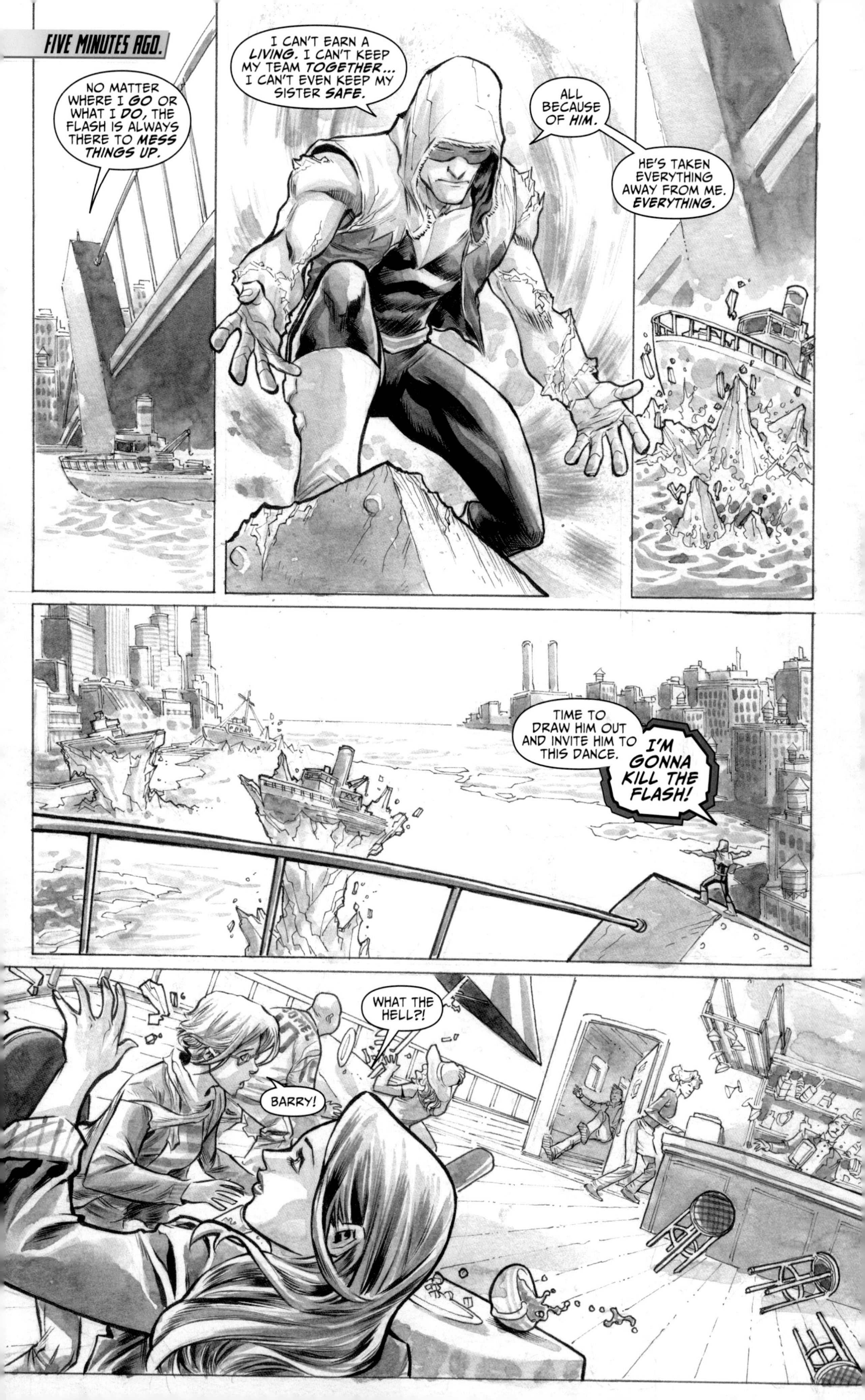
FIVE MINUTES AGO.
NO MATTER WHERE I GO OR WHAT I DO, THE FLASH IS ALWAYS THERE TO MESS THINGS UP.
I CAN'T EARN A LIVING. I CAN'T KEEP MY TEAM TOGETHER... I CAN'T EVEN KEEP MY SISTER SAFE.
ALL BECAUSE OF HIM.
HE'S TAKEN EVERYTHING AWAY FROM ME. EVERYTHING.
TIME TO DRAW HIM OUT AND INVITE HIM TO THIS DANCE.
I'M GONNA KILL THE FLASH!
WHAT THE HELL?!
BARRY!

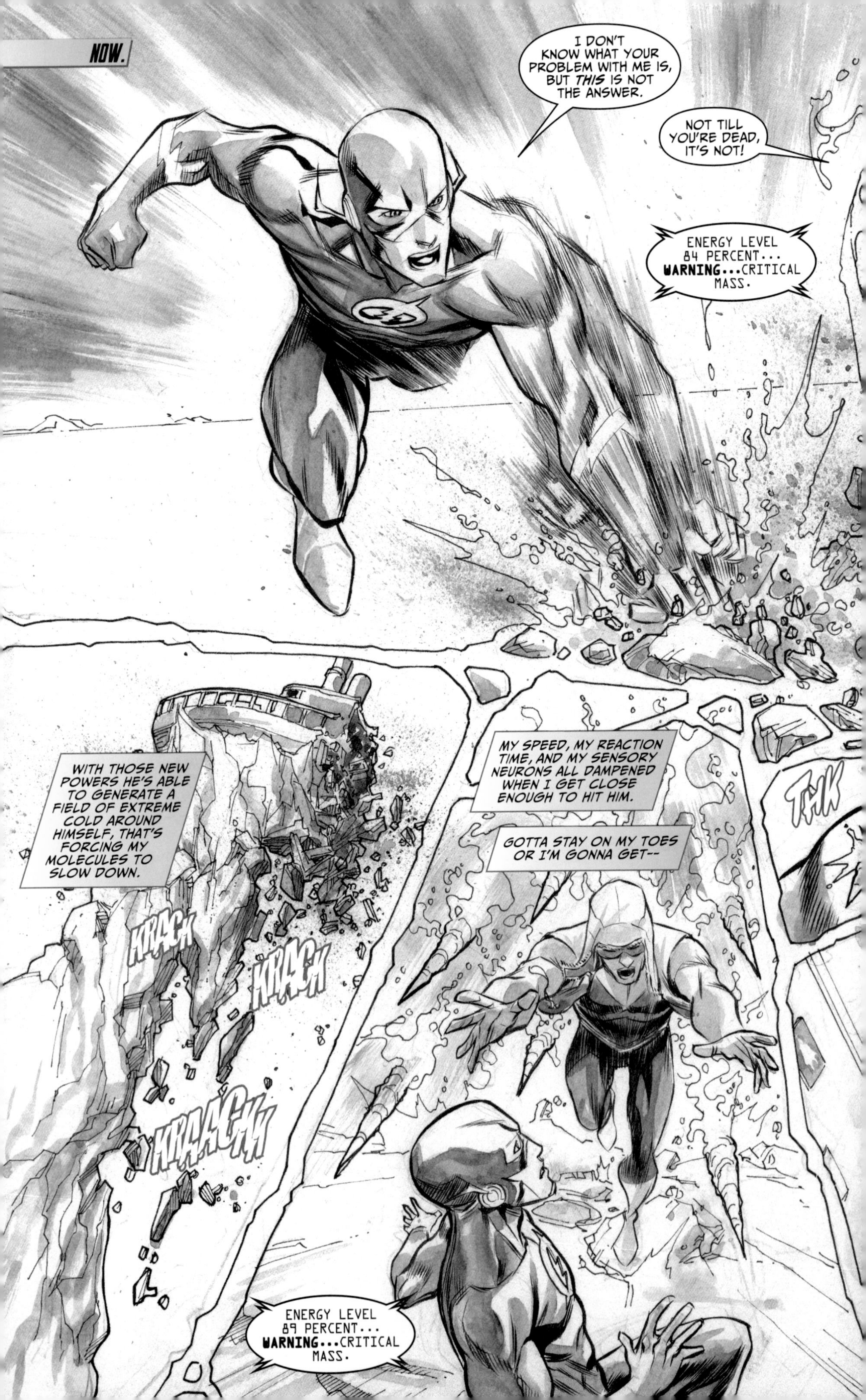
NOW.
I DON'T KNOW WHAT YOUR PROBLEM WITH ME IS, BUT *THIS* IS NOT THE ANSWER.
NOT TILL YOU'RE DEAD, IT'S NOT!
ENERGY LEVEL 84 PERCENT... **WARNING...** CRITICAL MASS.
WITH THOSE NEW POWERS HE'S ABLE TO GENERATE A FIELD OF EXTREME COLD AROUND HIMSELF, THAT'S FORCING MY MOLECULES TO SLOW DOWN.
KRACK
KRACK
KRAACKK
MY SPEED, MY REACTION TIME, AND MY SENSORY NEURONS ALL DAMPENED WHEN I GET CLOSE ENOUGH TO HIT HIM.
GOTTA STAY ON MY TOES OR I'M GONNA GET--
THK
ENERGY LEVEL 89 PERCENT... **WARNING...** CRITICAL MASS.

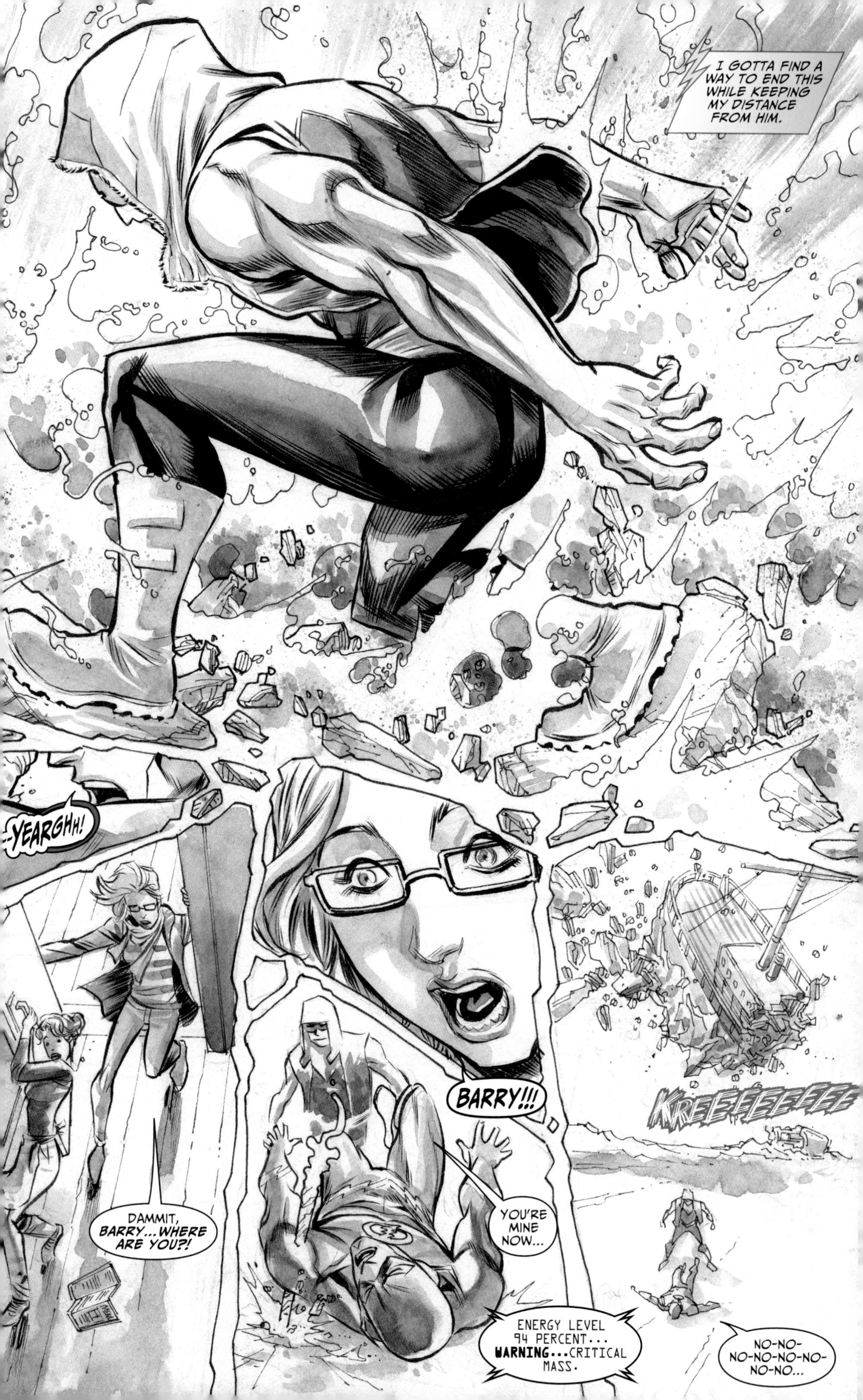
I GOTTA FIND A WAY TO END THIS WHILE KEEPING MY DISTANCE FROM HIM.
-YEARGHH!
BARRY!!!
KREEEEEEEE
DAMMIT, BARRY...WHERE ARE YOU?!
YOU'RE MINE NOW...
ENERGY LEVEL 94 PERCENT... WARNING...CRITICAL MASS.
NO-NO-NO-NO-NO-NO-NO-NO...

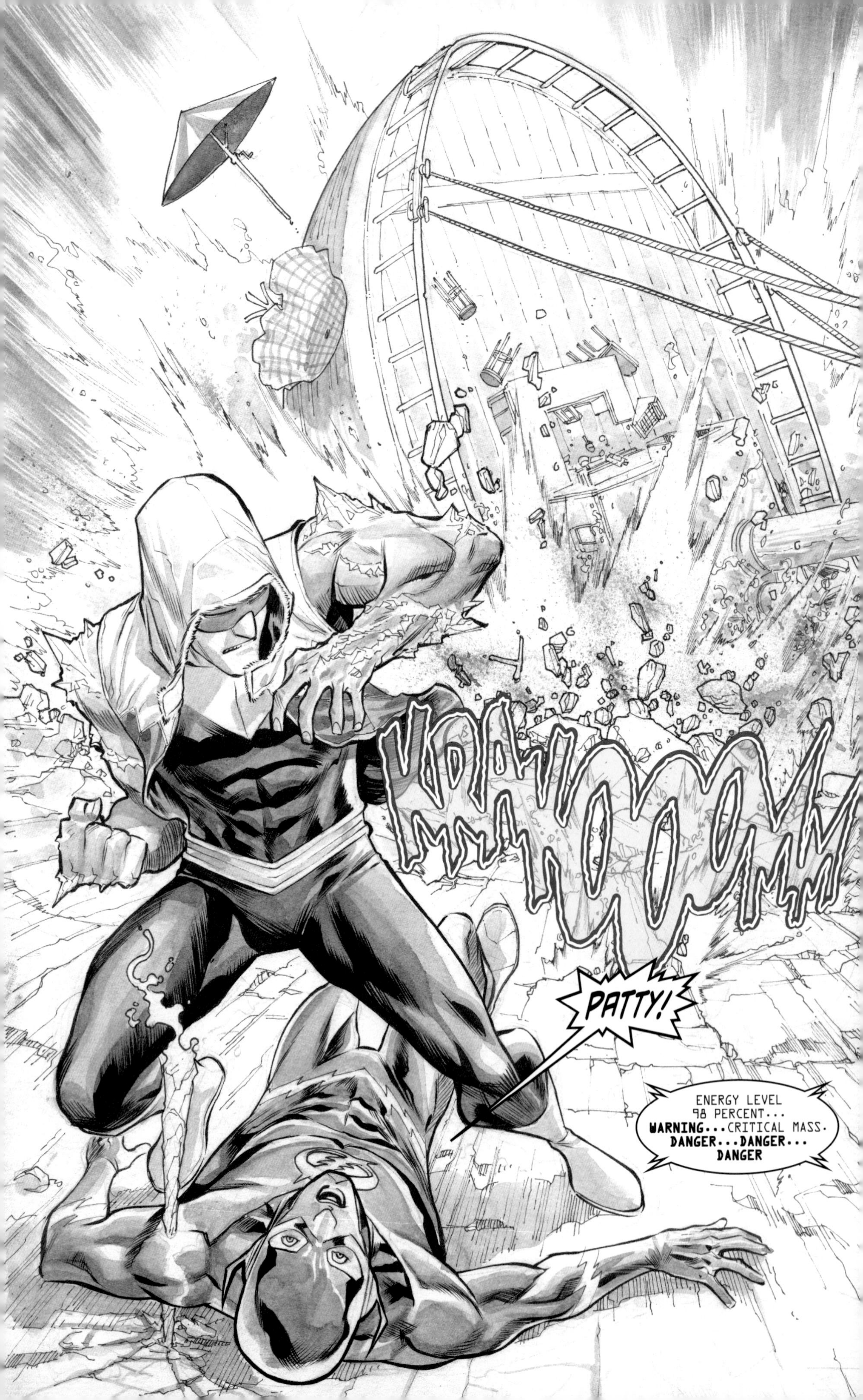
VRAWHOOOOM
PATTY!
ENERGY LEVEL 98 PERCENT... WARNING...CRITICAL MASS. DANGER...DANGER... DANGER

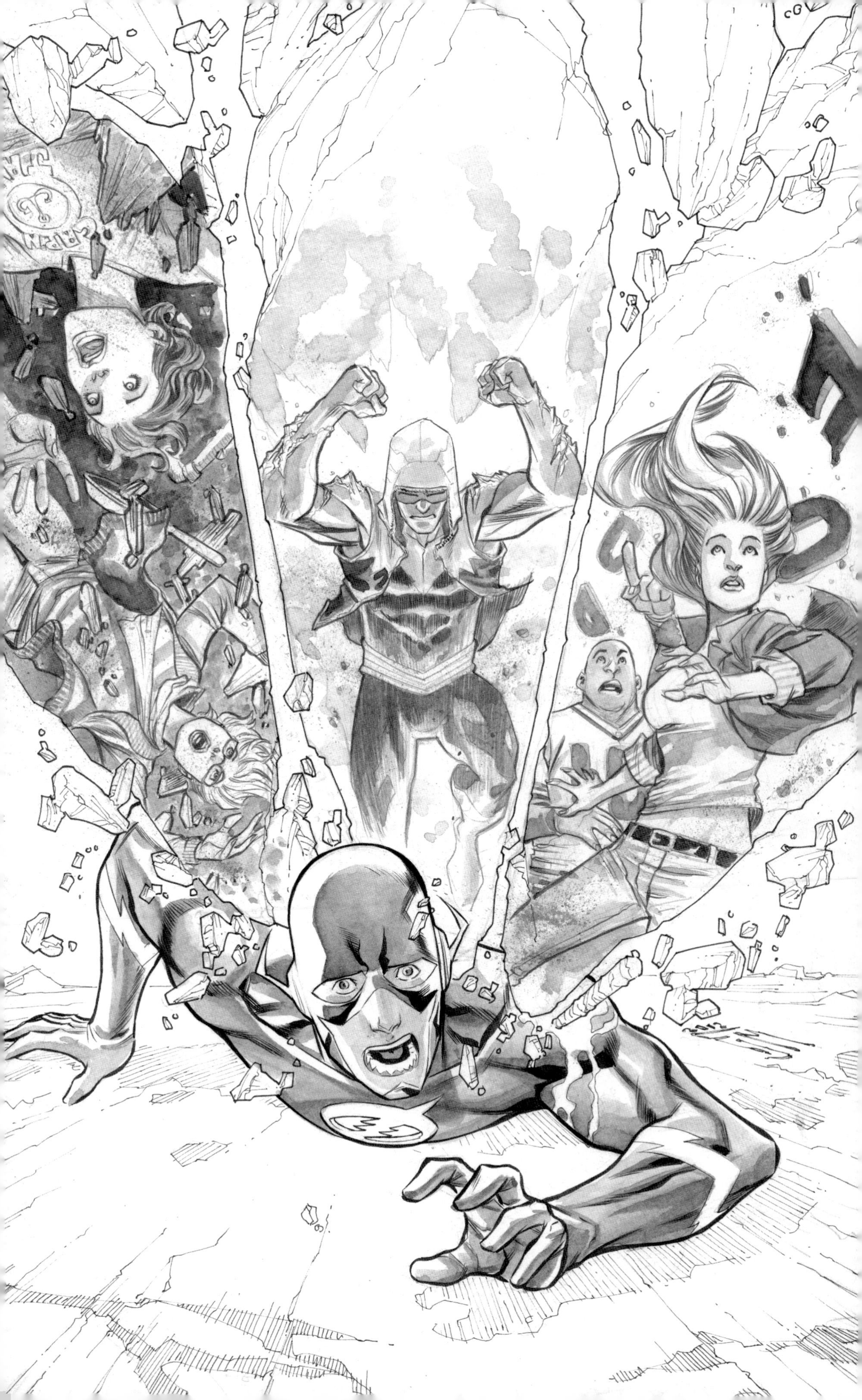

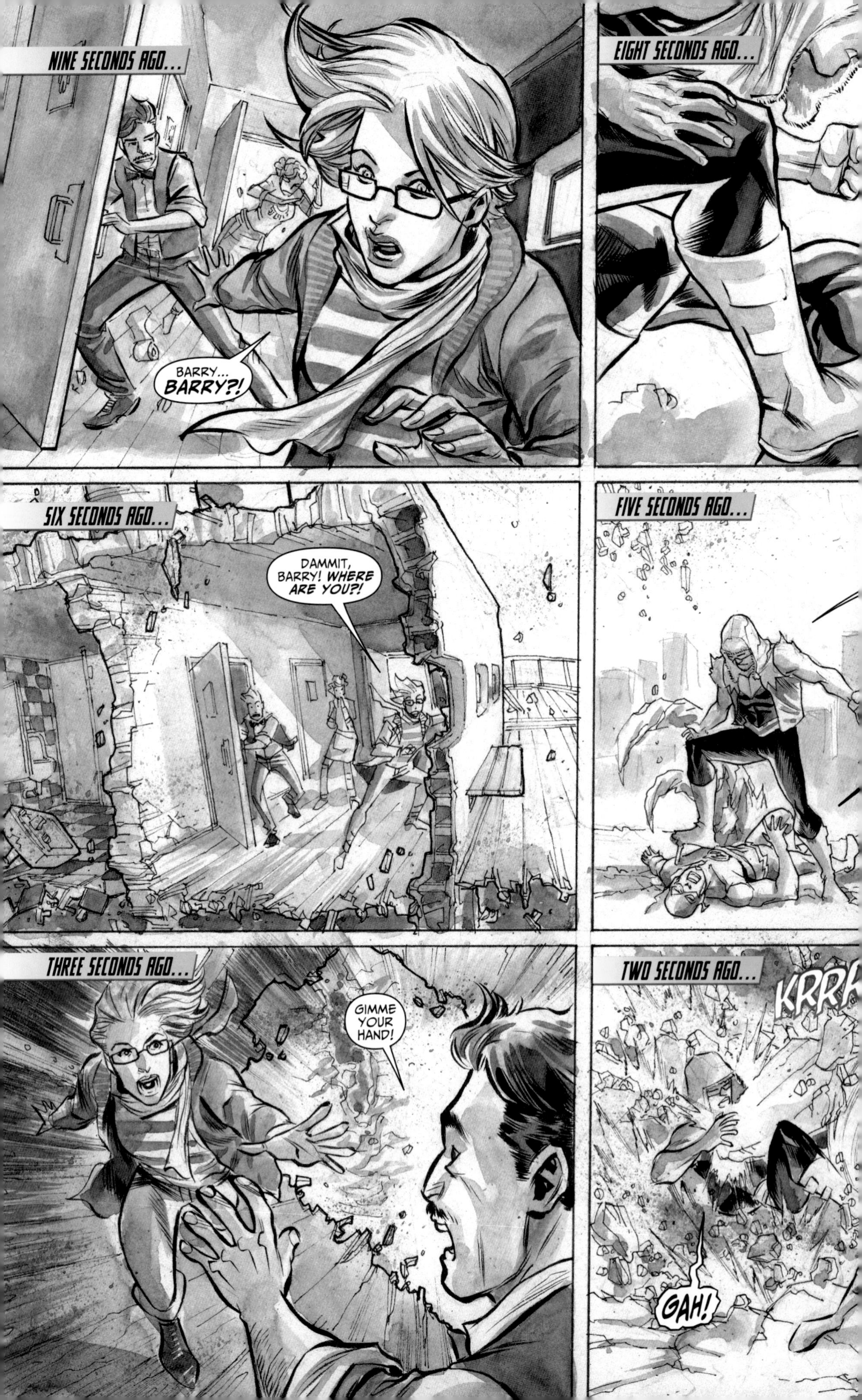

NINE SECONDS AGO...
BARRY... BARRY?!
EIGHT SECONDS AGO...
SIX SECONDS AGO...
DAMMIT, BARRY! WHERE ARE YOU?!
FIVE SECONDS AGO...
THREE SECONDS AGO...
GIMME YOUR HAND!
TWO SECONDS AGO...
KRRA
GAH!

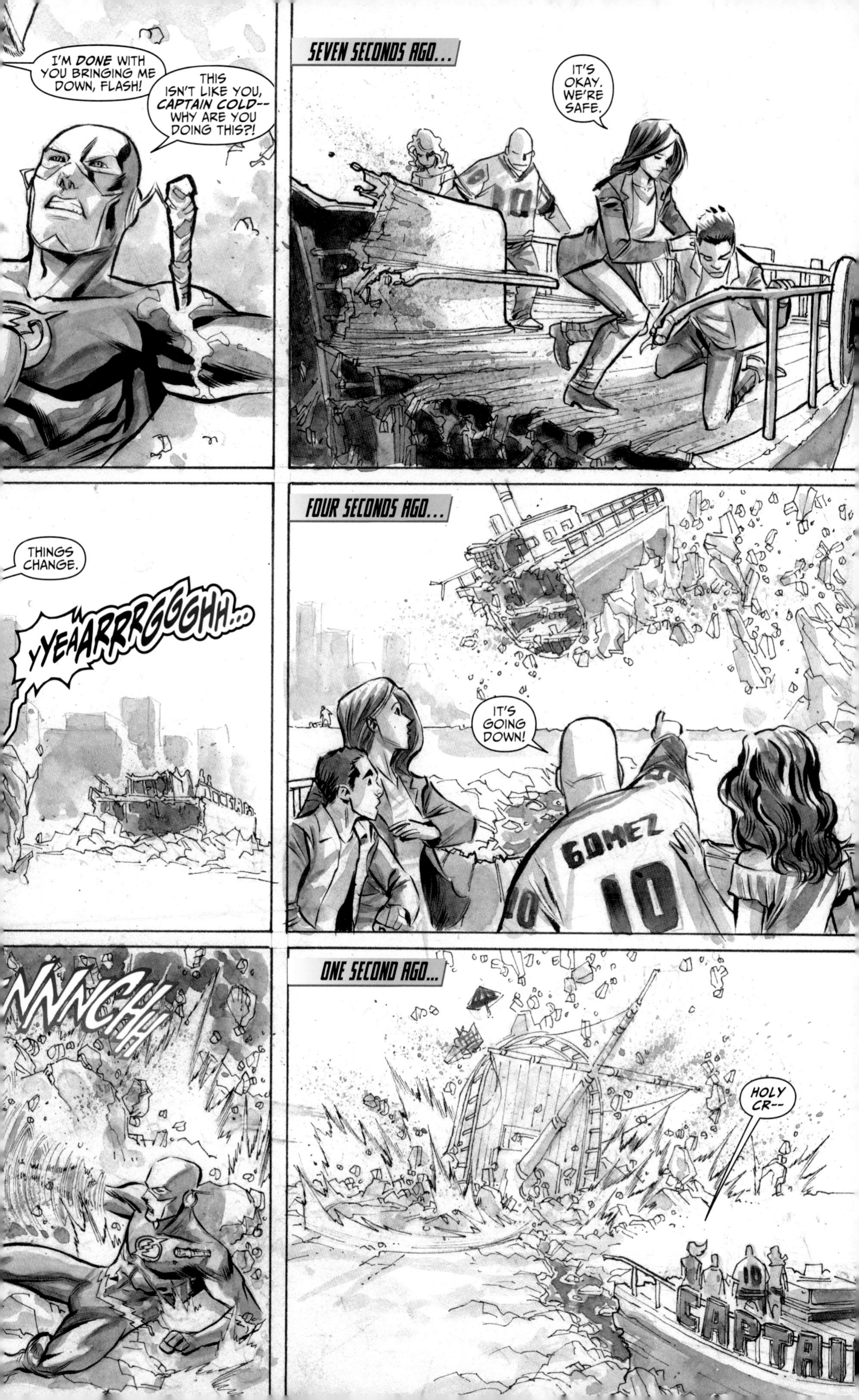
I'M DONE WITH YOU BRINGING ME DOWN, FLASH!
THIS ISN'T LIKE YOU, CAPTAIN COLD-- WHY ARE YOU DOING THIS?!
SEVEN SECONDS AGO...
IT'S OKAY. WE'RE SAFE.
THINGS CHANGE.
yYEAARRRGGGHH...
FOUR SECONDS AGO...
IT'S GOING DOWN!
GOMEZ
10
NNNCHH
ONE SECOND AGO...
HOLY CR--
CAPTAI

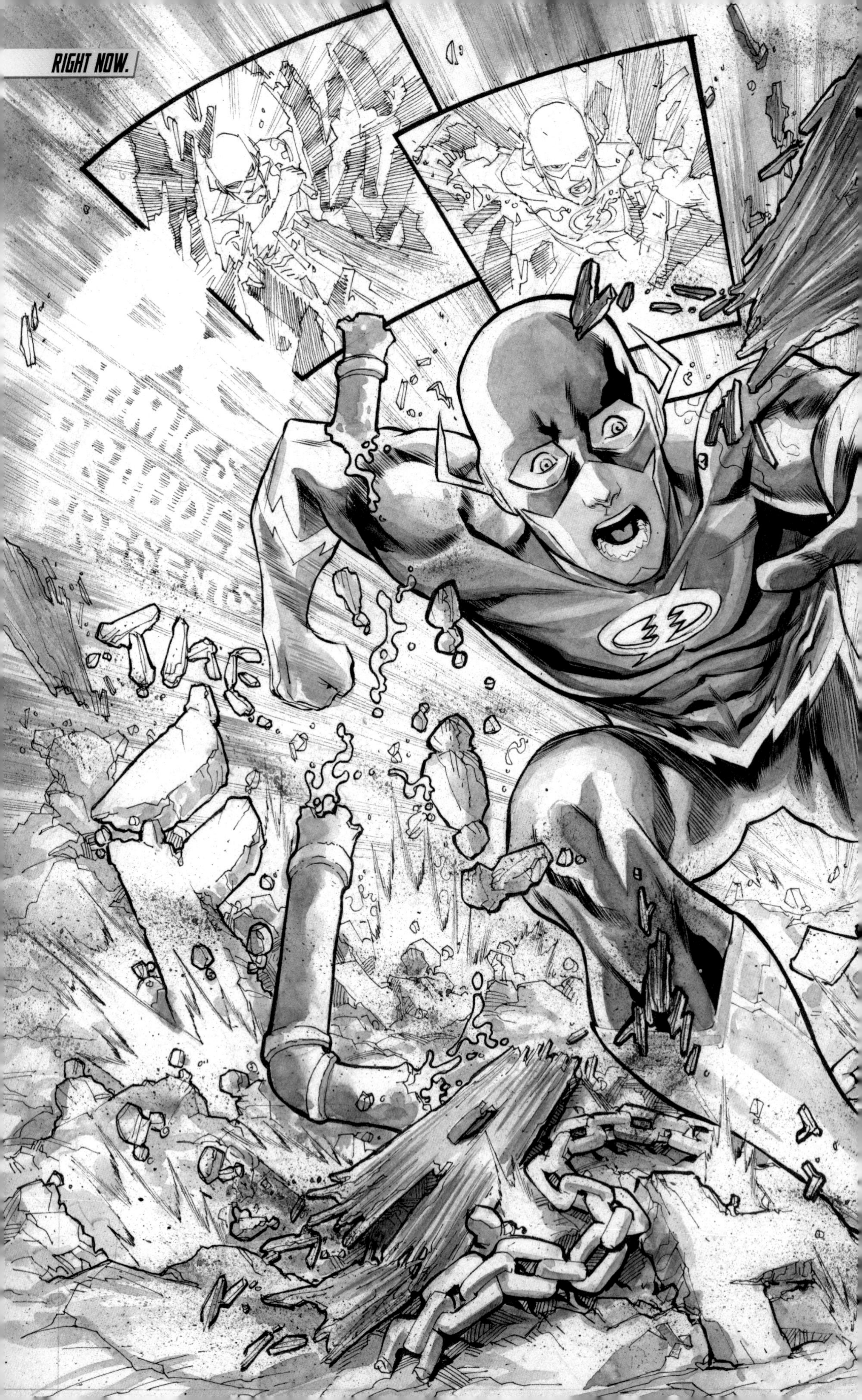
RIGHT NOW.

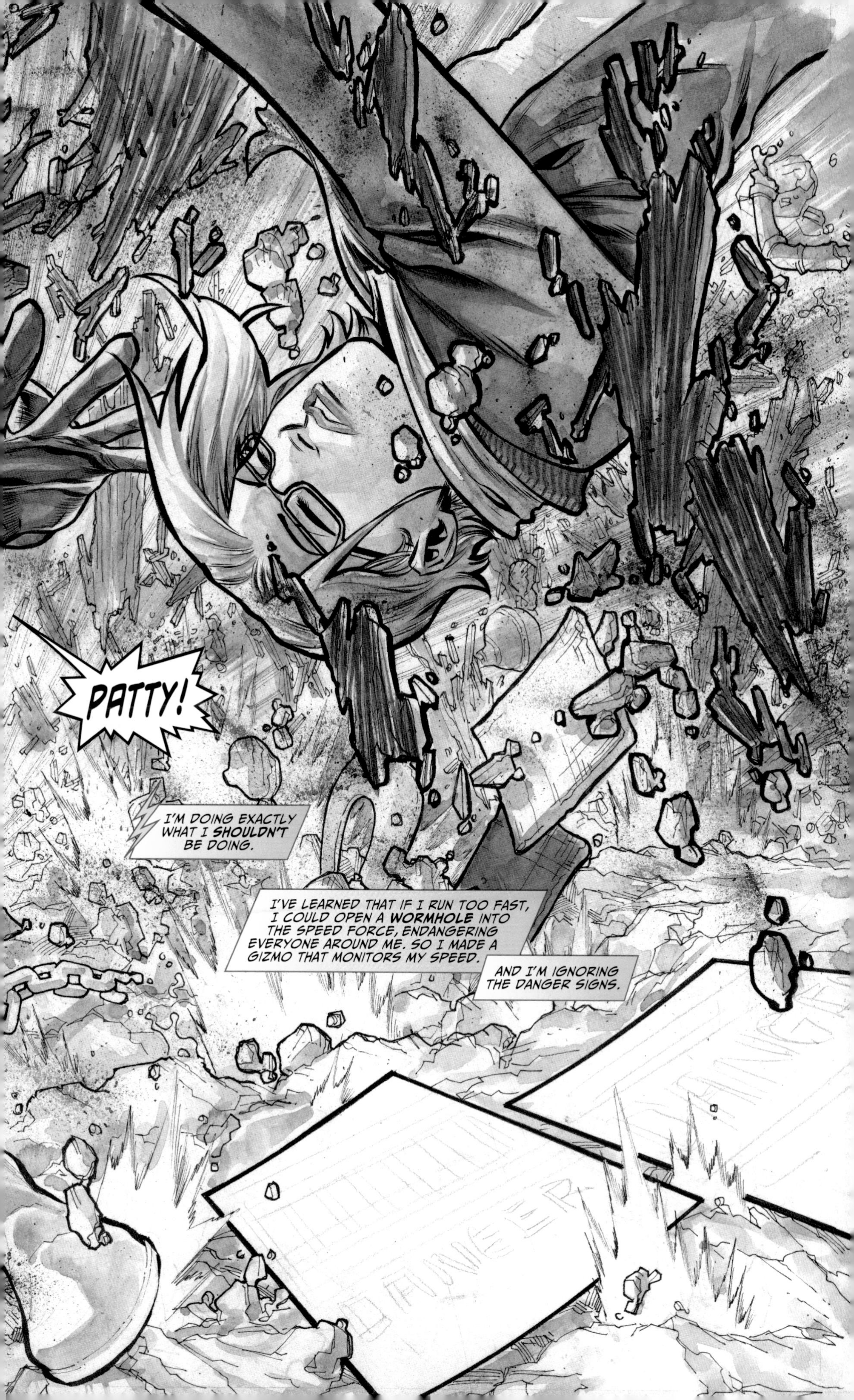
PATTY!
I'M DOING EXACTLY WHAT I SHOULDN'T BE DOING.
I'VE LEARNED THAT IF I RUN TOO FAST, I COULD OPEN A WORMHOLE INTO THE SPEED FORCE, ENDANGERING EVERYONE AROUND ME. SO I MADE A GIZMO THAT MONITORS MY SPEED.
AND I'M IGNORING THE DANGER SIGNS.
DANGER

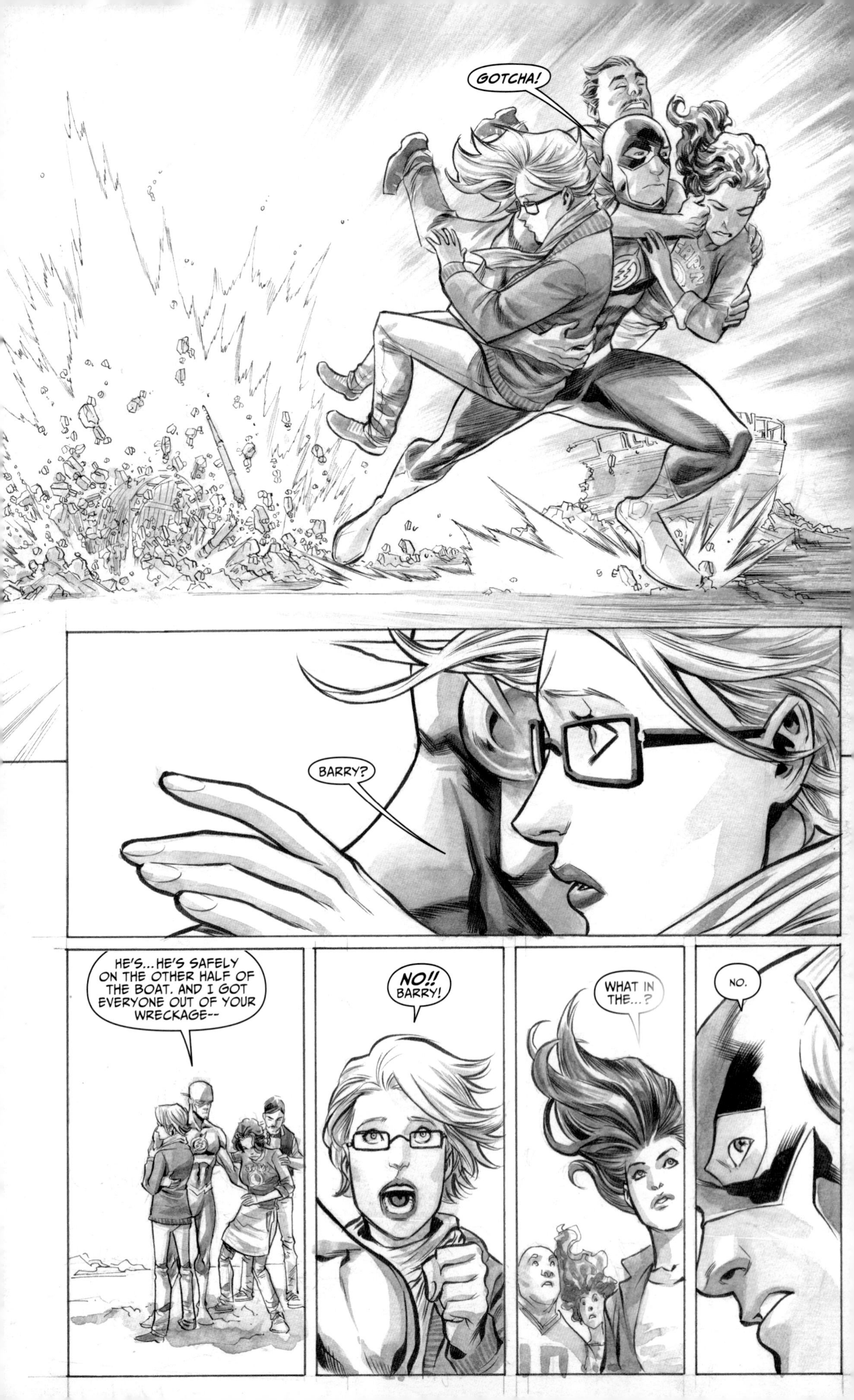
GOTCHA!
BARRY?
HE'S...HE'S SAFELY ON THE OTHER HALF OF THE BOAT. AND I GOT EVERYONE OUT OF YOUR WRECKAGE--
NO!! BARRY!
WHAT IN THE...?
NO.

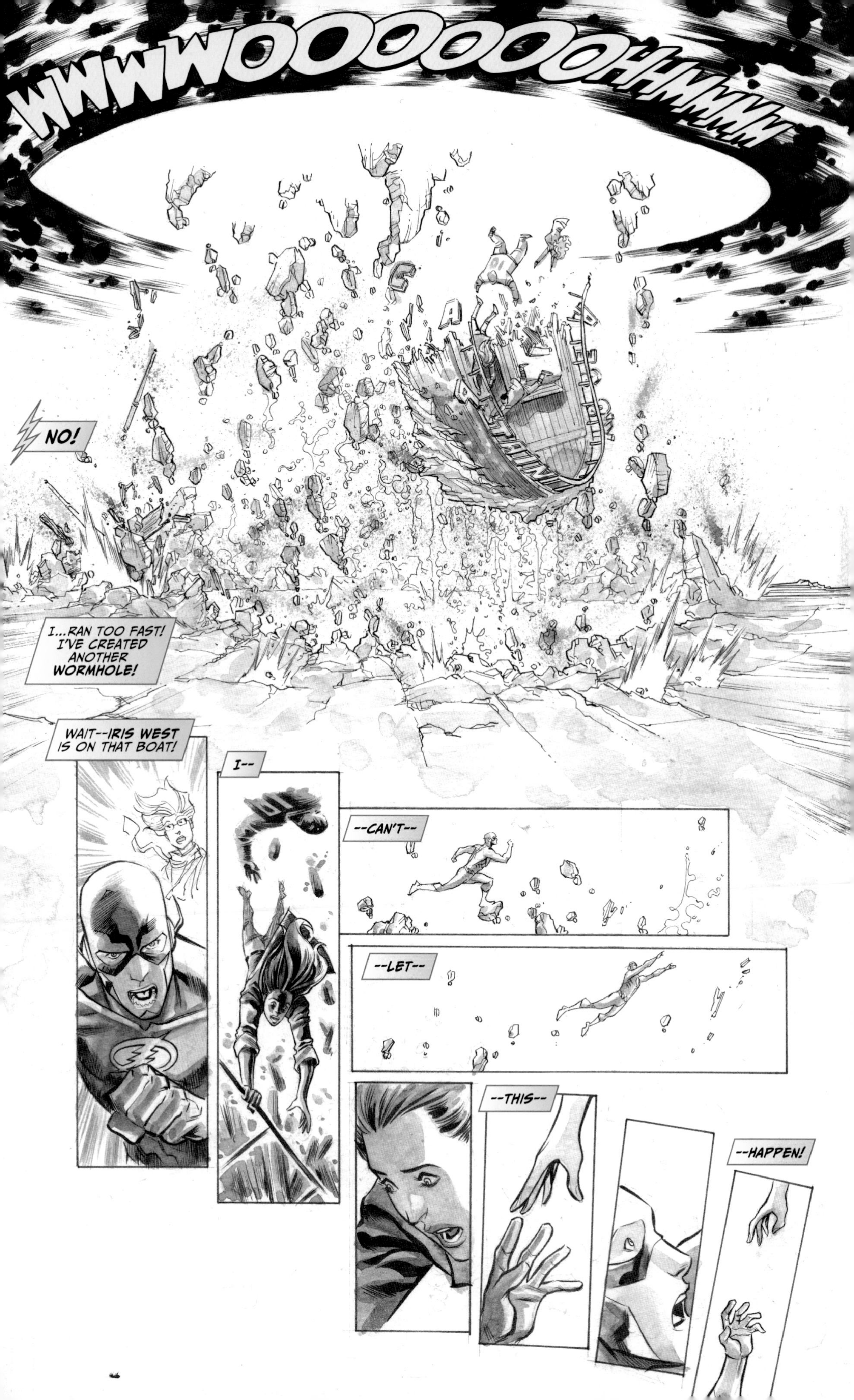
WWWWOOOOOOOHMMMM
NO!
I...RAN TOO FAST! I'VE CREATED ANOTHER WORMHOLE!
WAIT--IRIS WEST IS ON THAT BOAT!
I--
--CAN'T--
--LET--
--THIS--
--HAPPEN!

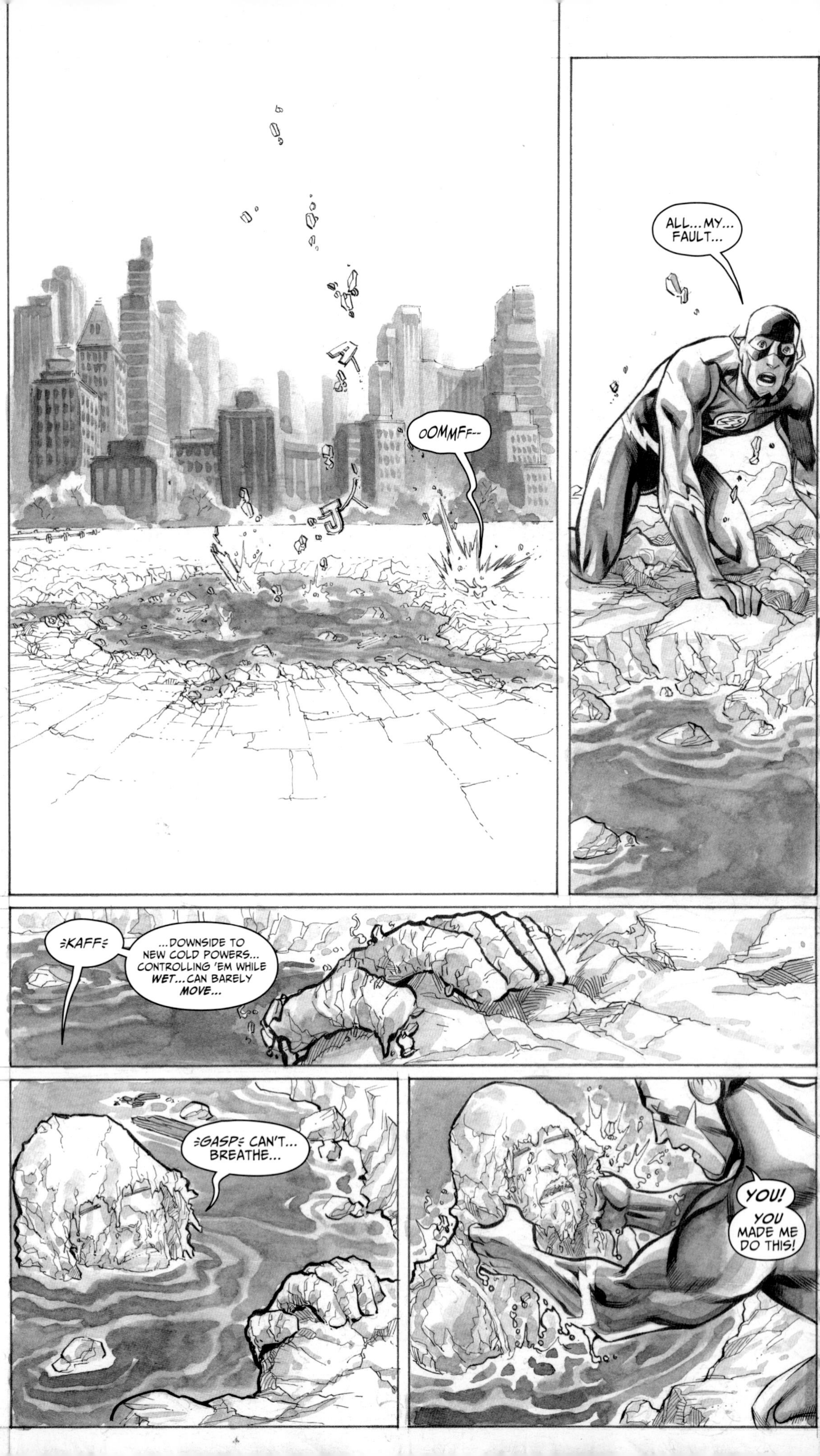
OOMMFF--
ALL... MY... FAULT...
KAFF
...DOWNSIDE TO NEW COLD POWERS... CONTROLLING 'EM WHILE WET...CAN BARELY MOVE...
GASP CAN'T... BREATHE...
YOU!
YOU MADE ME DO THIS!

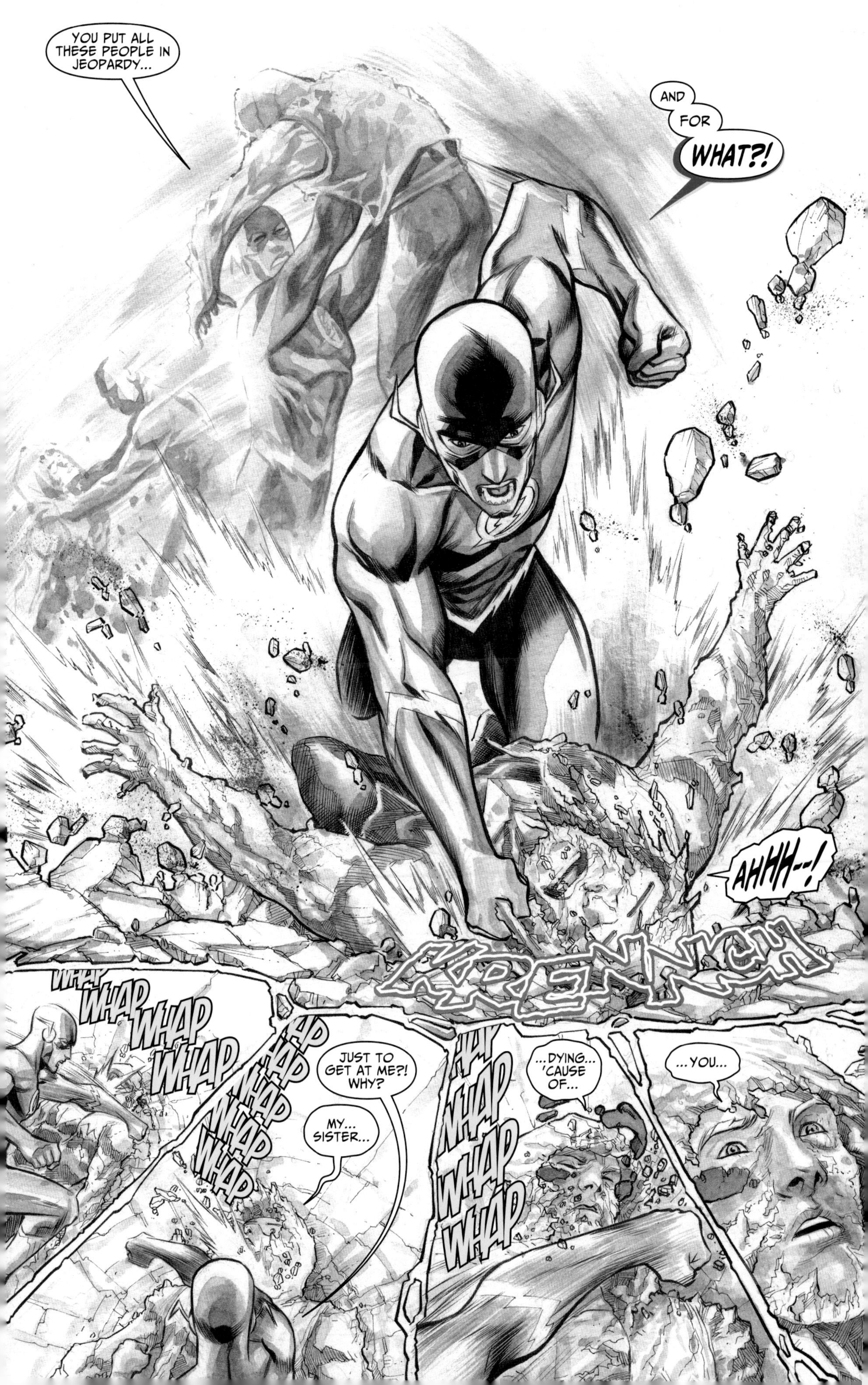
YOU PUT ALL THESE PEOPLE IN JEOPARDY...
AND FOR WHAT?!
AHHH--!
KRRRNNCH
WHAP WHAP WHAP WHAP
JUST TO GET AT ME?! WHY?
MY... SISTER...
...DYING... 'CAUSE OF...
...YOU...

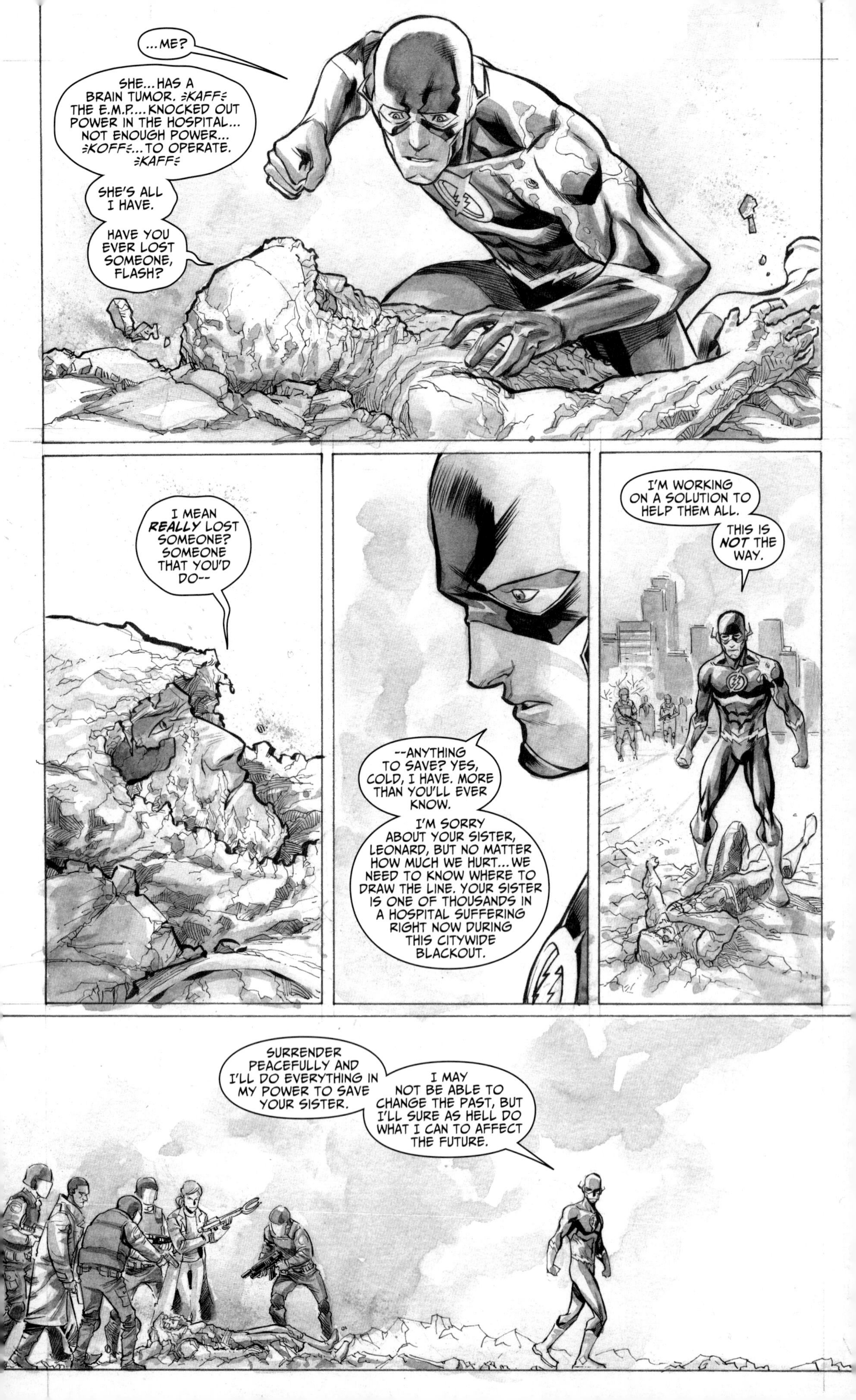
...ME?
SHE...HAS A BRAIN TUMOR. ≠KAFF≠ THE E.M.P....KNOCKED OUT POWER IN THE HOSPITAL... NOT ENOUGH POWER... ≠KOFF≠...TO OPERATE. ≠KAFF≠
SHE'S ALL I HAVE.
HAVE YOU EVER LOST SOMEONE, FLASH?
I MEAN REALLY LOST SOMEONE? SOMEONE THAT YOU'D DO--
--ANYTHING TO SAVE? YES, COLD, I HAVE. MORE THAN YOU'LL EVER KNOW.
I'M SORRY ABOUT YOUR SISTER, LEONARD, BUT NO MATTER HOW MUCH WE HURT...WE NEED TO KNOW WHERE TO DRAW THE LINE. YOUR SISTER IS ONE OF THOUSANDS IN A HOSPITAL SUFFERING RIGHT NOW DURING THIS CITYWIDE BLACKOUT.
I'M WORKING ON A SOLUTION TO HELP THEM ALL.
THIS IS NOT THE WAY.
SURRENDER PEACEFULLY AND I'LL DO EVERYTHING IN MY POWER TO SAVE YOUR SISTER.
I MAY NOT BE ABLE TO CHANGE THE PAST, BUT I'LL SURE AS HELL DO WHAT I CAN TO AFFECT THE FUTURE.

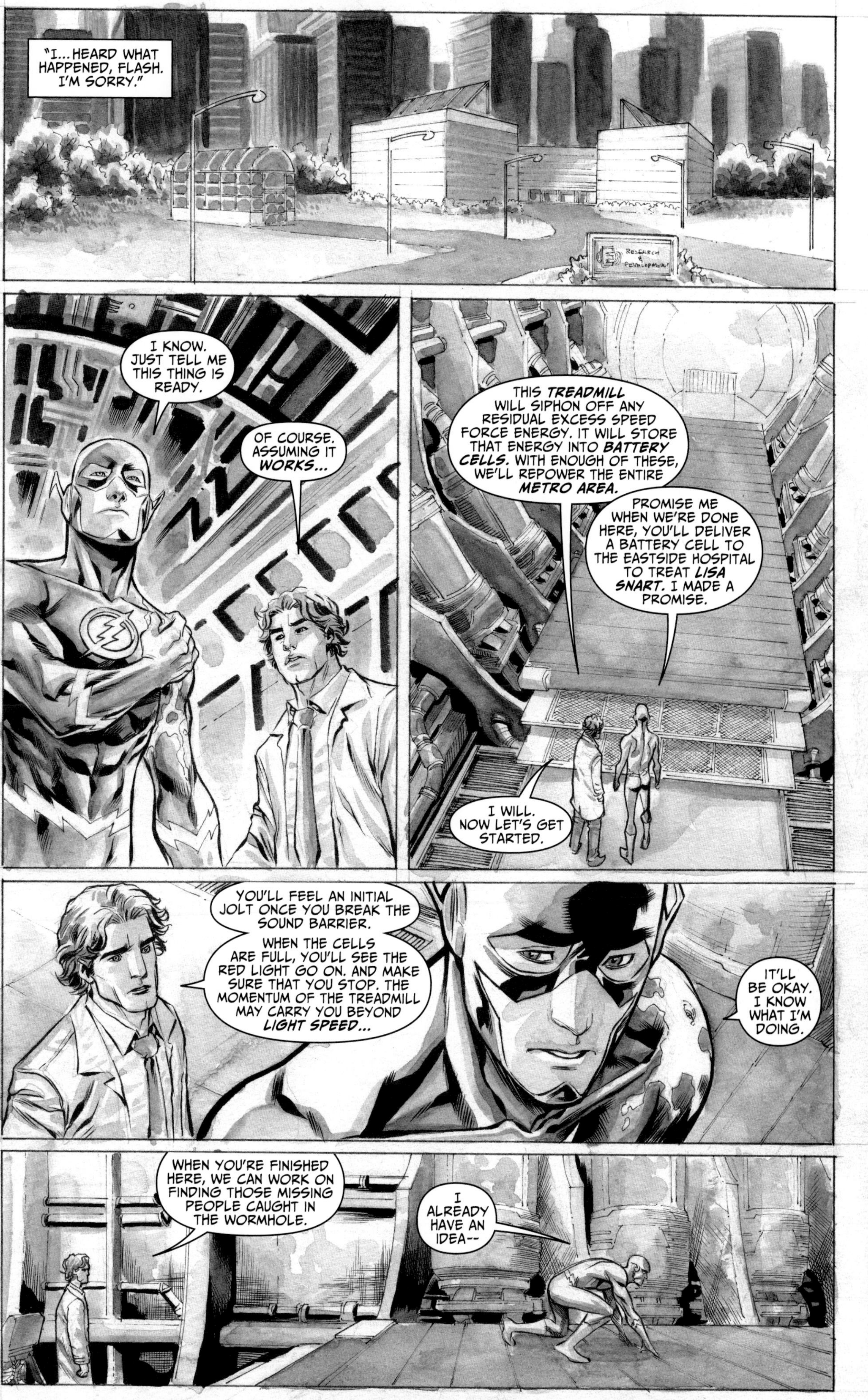
"I...HEARD WHAT HAPPENED, FLASH. I'M SORRY."
RESEARCH & DEVELOPMENT
I KNOW. JUST TELL ME THIS THING IS READY.
OF COURSE. ASSUMING IT WORKS...
THIS TREADMILL WILL SIPHON OFF ANY RESIDUAL EXCESS SPEED FORCE ENERGY. IT WILL STORE THAT ENERGY INTO BATTERY CELLS. WITH ENOUGH OF THESE, WE'LL REPOWER THE ENTIRE METRO AREA.
PROMISE ME WHEN WE'RE DONE HERE, YOU'LL DELIVER A BATTERY CELL TO THE EASTSIDE HOSPITAL TO TREAT LISA SNART. I MADE A PROMISE.
I WILL. NOW LET'S GET STARTED.
YOU'LL FEEL AN INITIAL JOLT ONCE YOU BREAK THE SOUND BARRIER.
WHEN THE CELLS ARE FULL, YOU'LL SEE THE RED LIGHT GO ON. AND MAKE SURE THAT YOU STOP. THE MOMENTUM OF THE TREADMILL MAY CARRY YOU BEYOND LIGHT SPEED...
IT'LL BE OKAY. I KNOW WHAT I'M DOING.
WHEN YOU'RE FINISHED HERE, WE CAN WORK ON FINDING THOSE MISSING PEOPLE CAUGHT IN THE WORMHOLE.
I ALREADY HAVE AN IDEA--

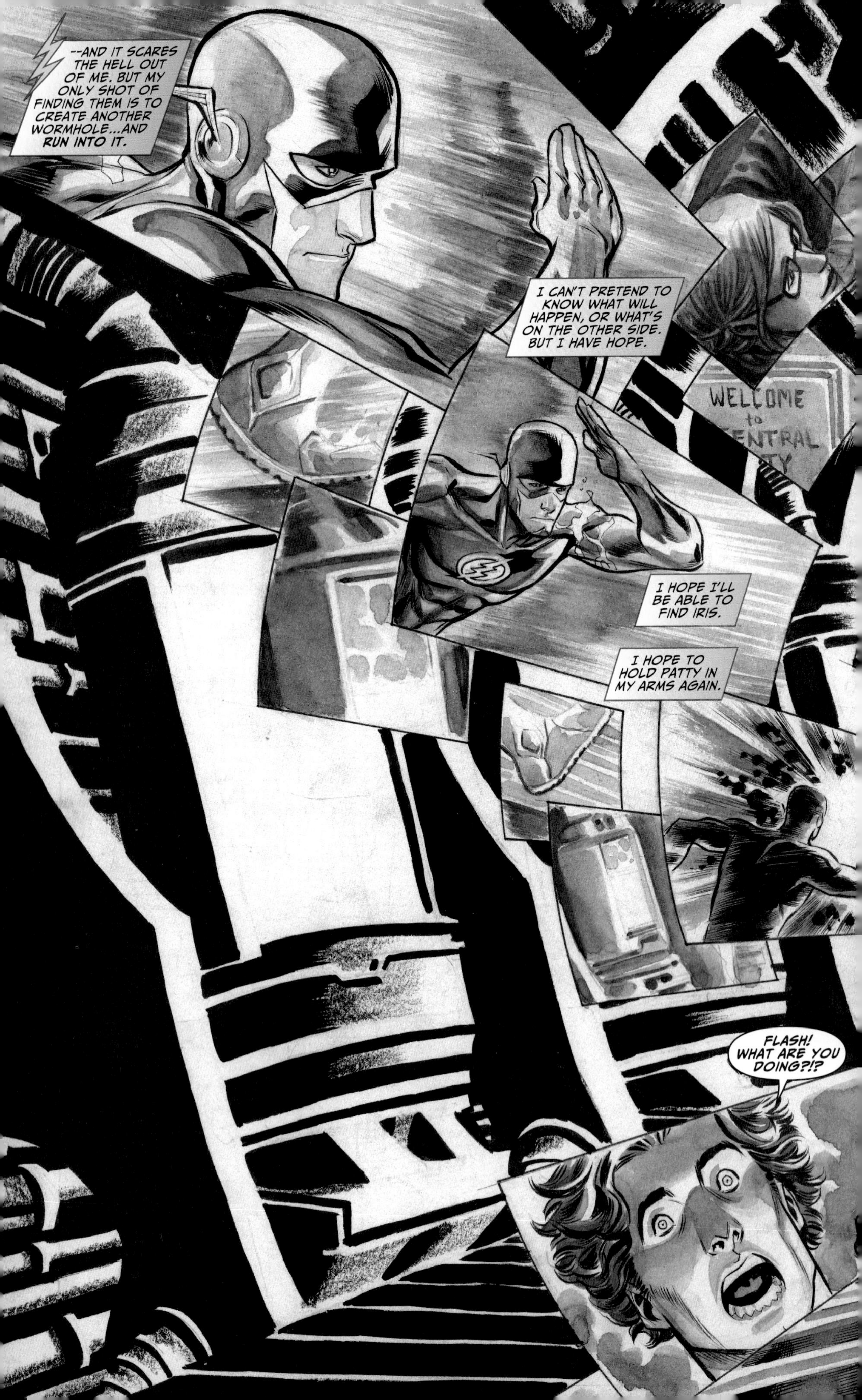
--AND IT SCARES THE HELL OUT OF ME. BUT MY ONLY SHOT OF FINDING THEM IS TO CREATE ANOTHER WORMHOLE...AND RUN INTO IT.
I CAN'T PRETEND TO KNOW WHAT WILL HAPPEN, OR WHAT'S ON THE OTHER SIDE. BUT I HAVE HOPE.
WELCOME to
I HOPE I'LL BE ABLE TO FIND IRIS.
I HOPE TO HOLD PATTY IN MY ARMS AGAIN.
FLASH! WHAT ARE YOU DOING?!?

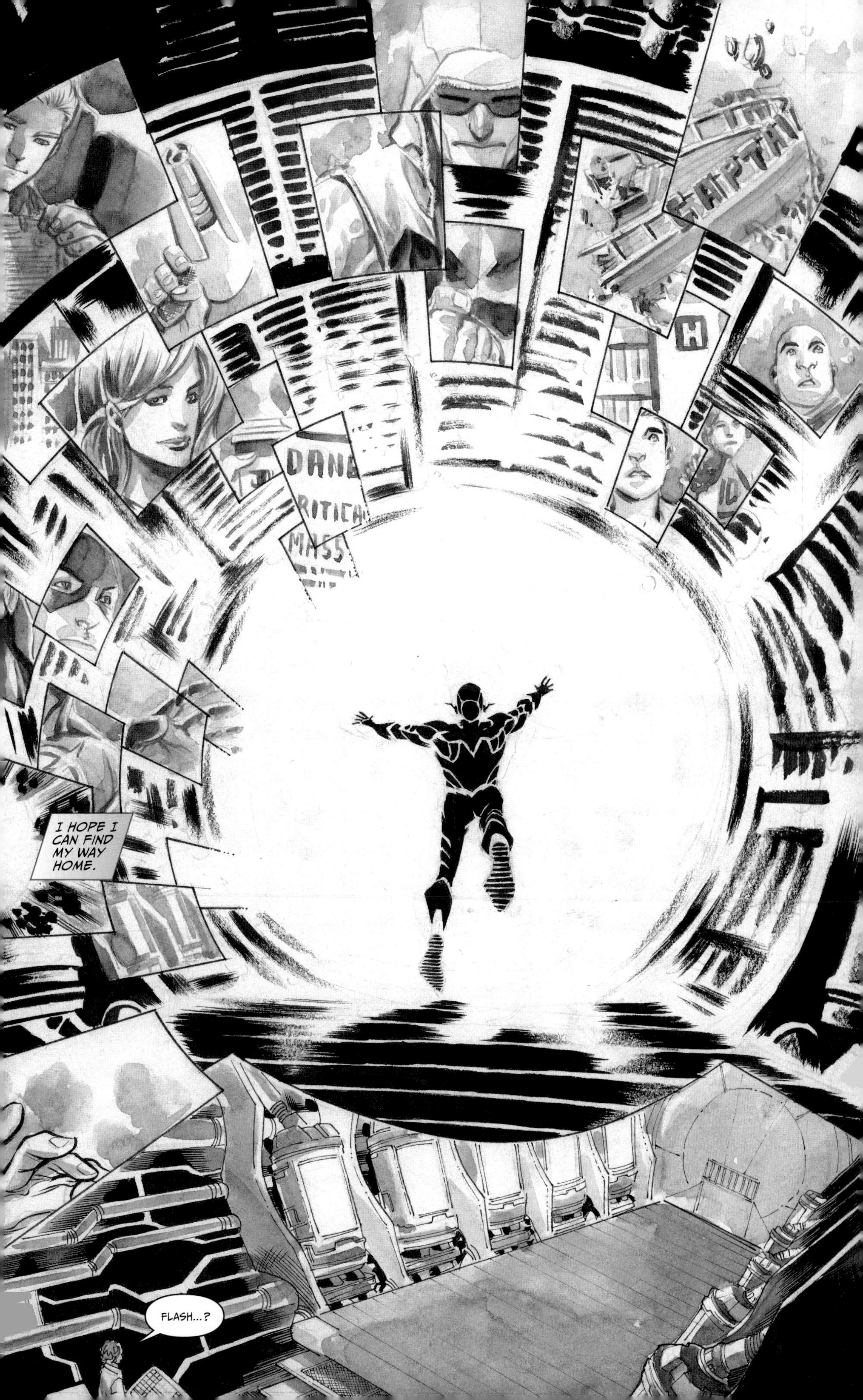
I HOPE I CAN FIND MY WAY HOME.
FLASH...?

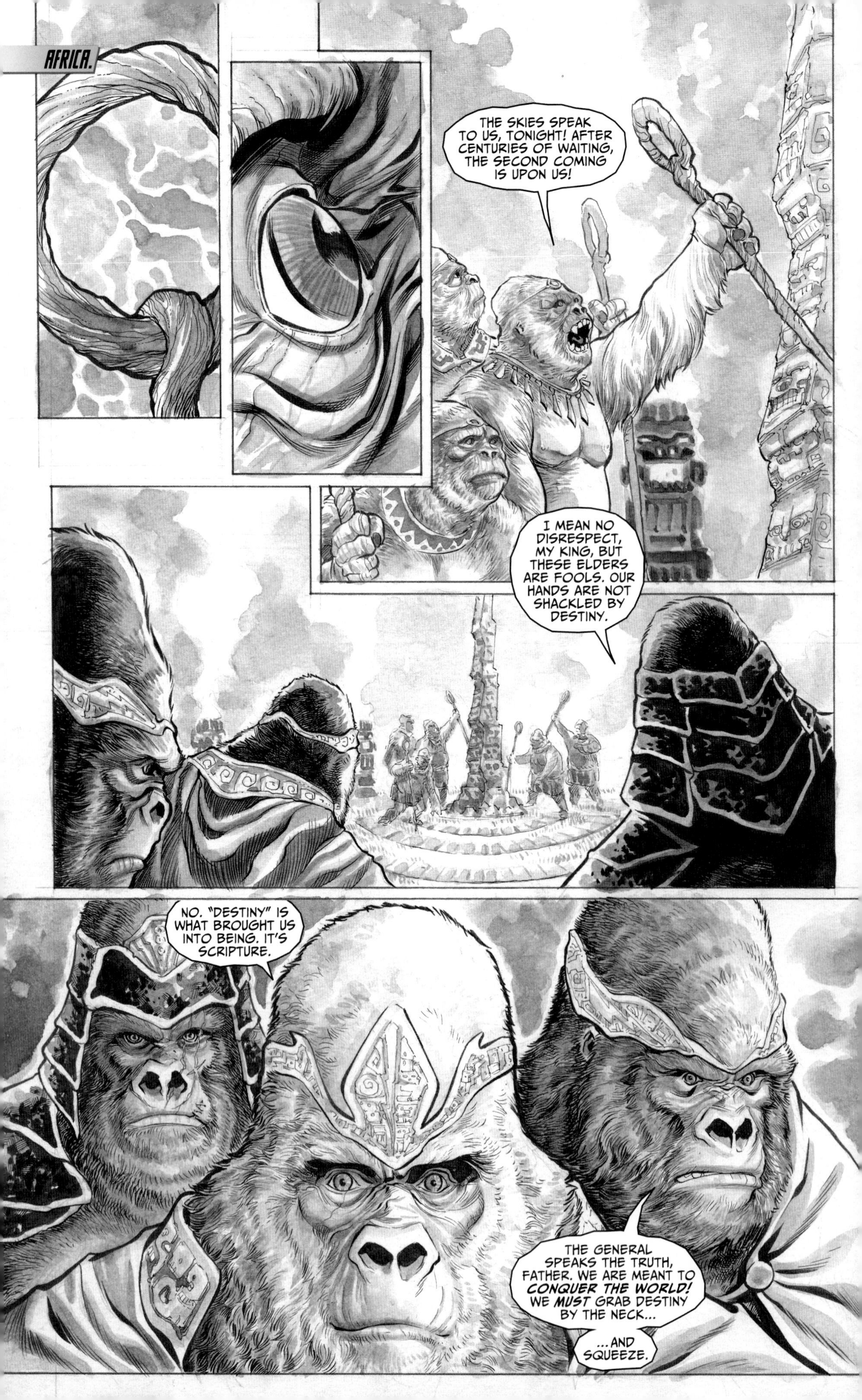
AFRICA.
THE SKIES SPEAK TO US, TONIGHT! AFTER CENTURIES OF WAITING, THE SECOND COMING IS UPON US!
I MEAN NO DISRESPECT, MY KING, BUT THESE ELDERS ARE FOOLS. OUR HANDS ARE NOT SHACKLED BY DESTINY.
NO. "DESTINY" IS WHAT BROUGHT US INTO BEING. IT'S SCRIPTURE.
THE GENERAL SPEAKS THE TRUTH, FATHER. WE ARE MEANT TO ***CONQUER THE WORLD!*** WE ***MUST*** GRAB DESTINY BY THE NECK...
...AND SQUEEZE.

"MY SISTER... SHE'S REALLY GONNA BE OKAY?"

YES. THANKS TO DR. ELIAS'S POWER CELL WE USED THE LASER TO ISOLATE AND DESTROY THE TUMOR ON HER BRAIN. SHE HAS *FULL COGNITIVE FUNCTIONS.* HOWEVER...

...THERE WAS SOME *DAMAGE* TO HER NERVOUS SYSTEM. I'M...NOT SURE IF SHE'LL EVER WALK AGAIN.

UUUUHHH...

LISA! I'M HERE, SIS...I'M RIGHT HERE.

L...LE... LEN? IS THAT YOU?

IT'S ME, SIS... OH, GOD, I THOUGHT I LOST YOU...

YOU... AFTER WHAT YOU *DID* TO US...TO ME...

...YOU SHOULD'VE *LET ME DIE.*

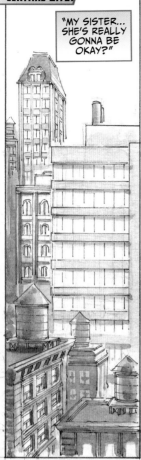

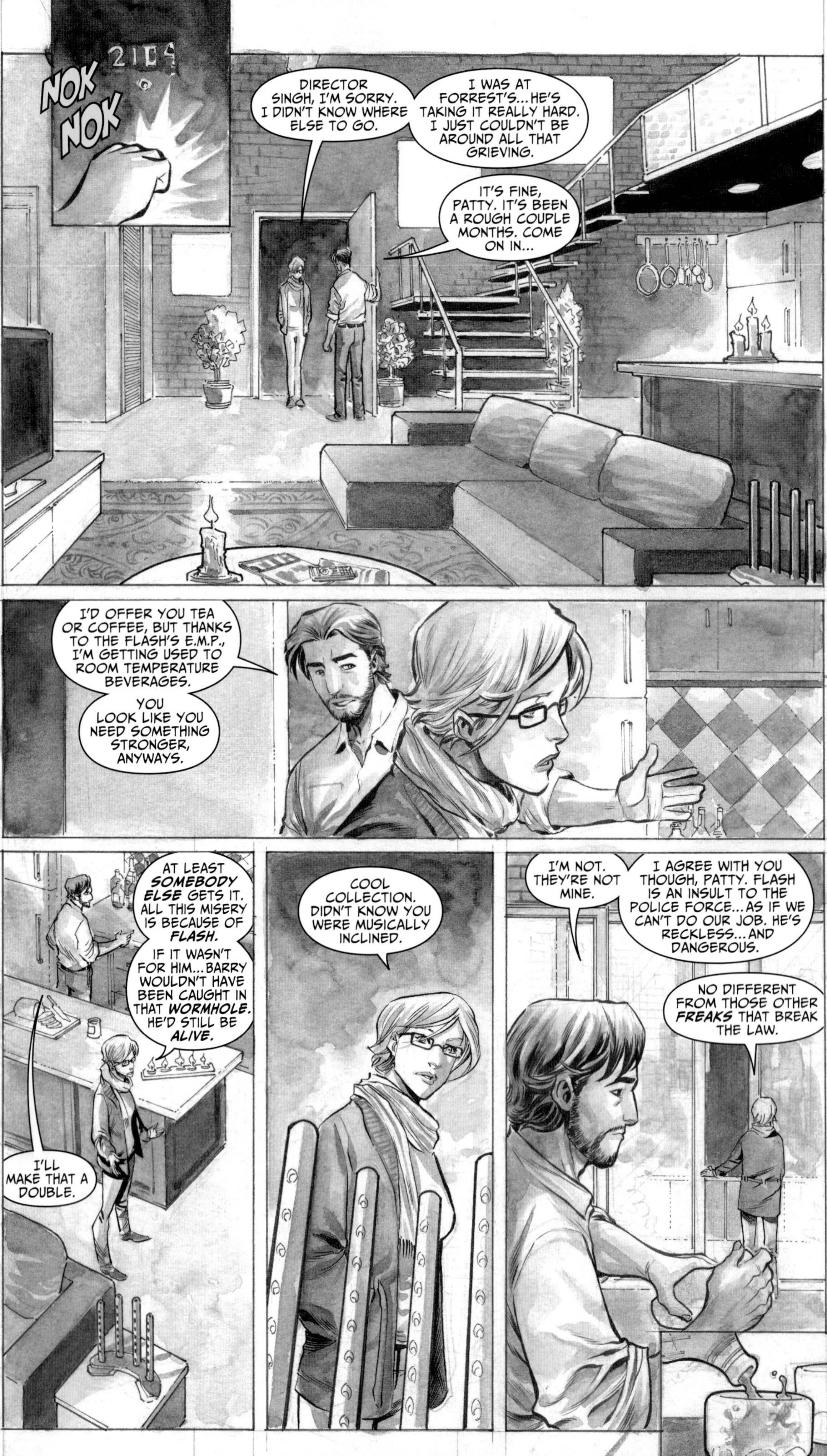
2109
NOK NOK
DIRECTOR SINGH, I'M SORRY. I DIDN'T KNOW WHERE ELSE TO GO.
I WAS AT FORREST'S...HE'S TAKING IT REALLY HARD. I JUST COULDN'T BE AROUND ALL THAT GRIEVING.
IT'S FINE, PATTY. IT'S BEEN A ROUGH COUPLE MONTHS. COME ON IN...
I'D OFFER YOU TEA OR COFFEE, BUT THANKS TO THE FLASH'S E.M.P., I'M GETTING USED TO ROOM TEMPERATURE BEVERAGES.
YOU LOOK LIKE YOU NEED SOMETHING STRONGER, ANYWAYS.
AT LEAST SOMEBODY ELSE GETS IT. ALL THIS MISERY IS BECAUSE OF FLASH.
IF IT WASN'T FOR HIM...BARRY WOULDN'T HAVE BEEN CAUGHT IN THAT WORMHOLE. HE'D STILL BE ALIVE.
I'LL MAKE THAT A DOUBLE.
COOL COLLECTION. DIDN'T KNOW YOU WERE MUSICALLY INCLINED.
I'M NOT. THEY'RE NOT MINE.
I AGREE WITH YOU THOUGH, PATTY. FLASH IS AN INSULT TO THE POLICE FORCE...AS IF WE CAN'T DO OUR JOB. HE'S RECKLESS...AND DANGEROUS.
NO DIFFERENT FROM THOSE OTHER FREAKS THAT BREAK THE LAW.

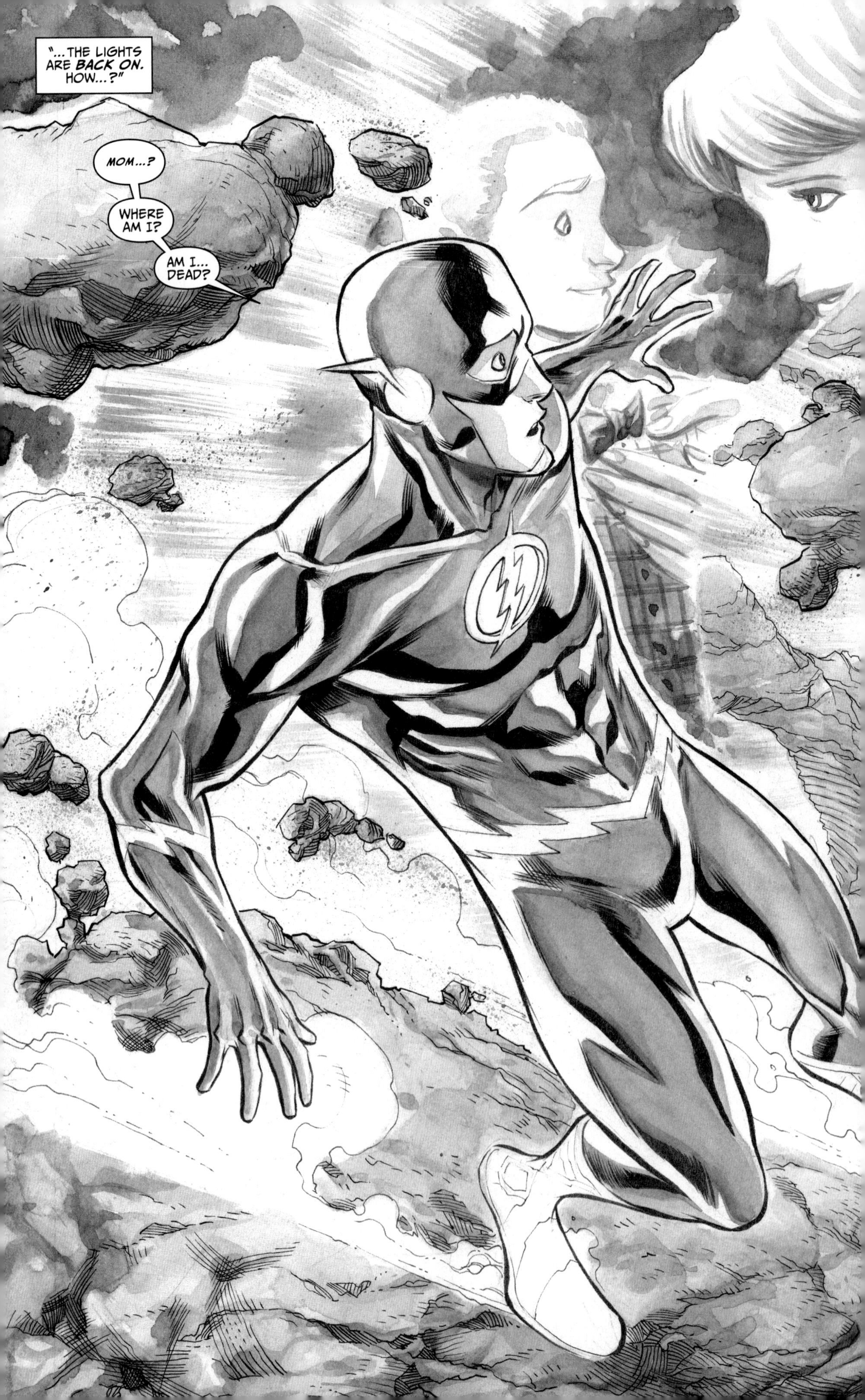
"...THE LIGHTS ARE BACK ON. HOW...?"
MOM...?
WHERE AM I?
AM I... DEAD?

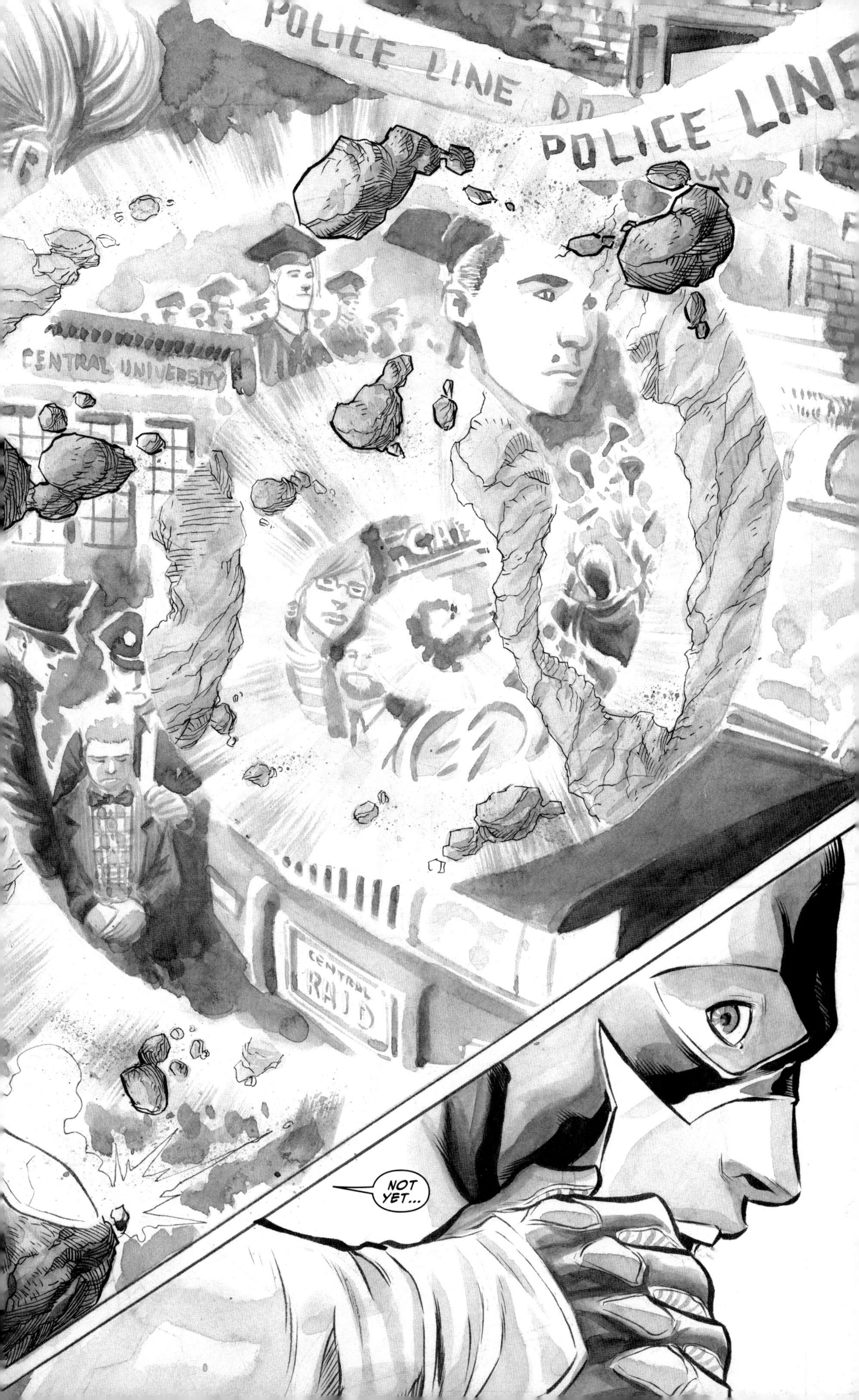
POLICE LINE
POLICE LINE
CENTRAL UNIVERSITY
NOT YET...

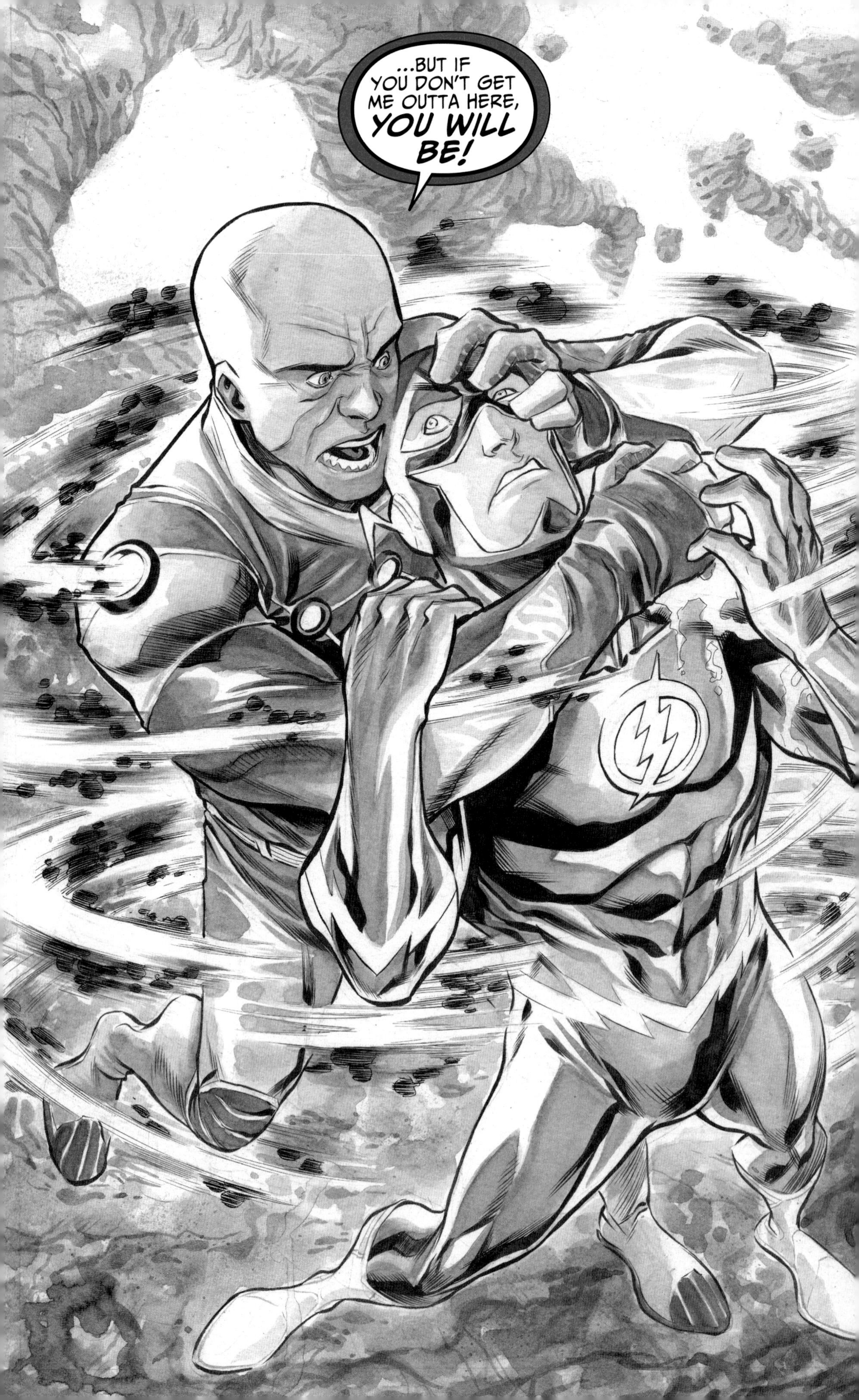
...BUT IF YOU DON'T GET ME OUTTA HERE, YOU WILL BE!

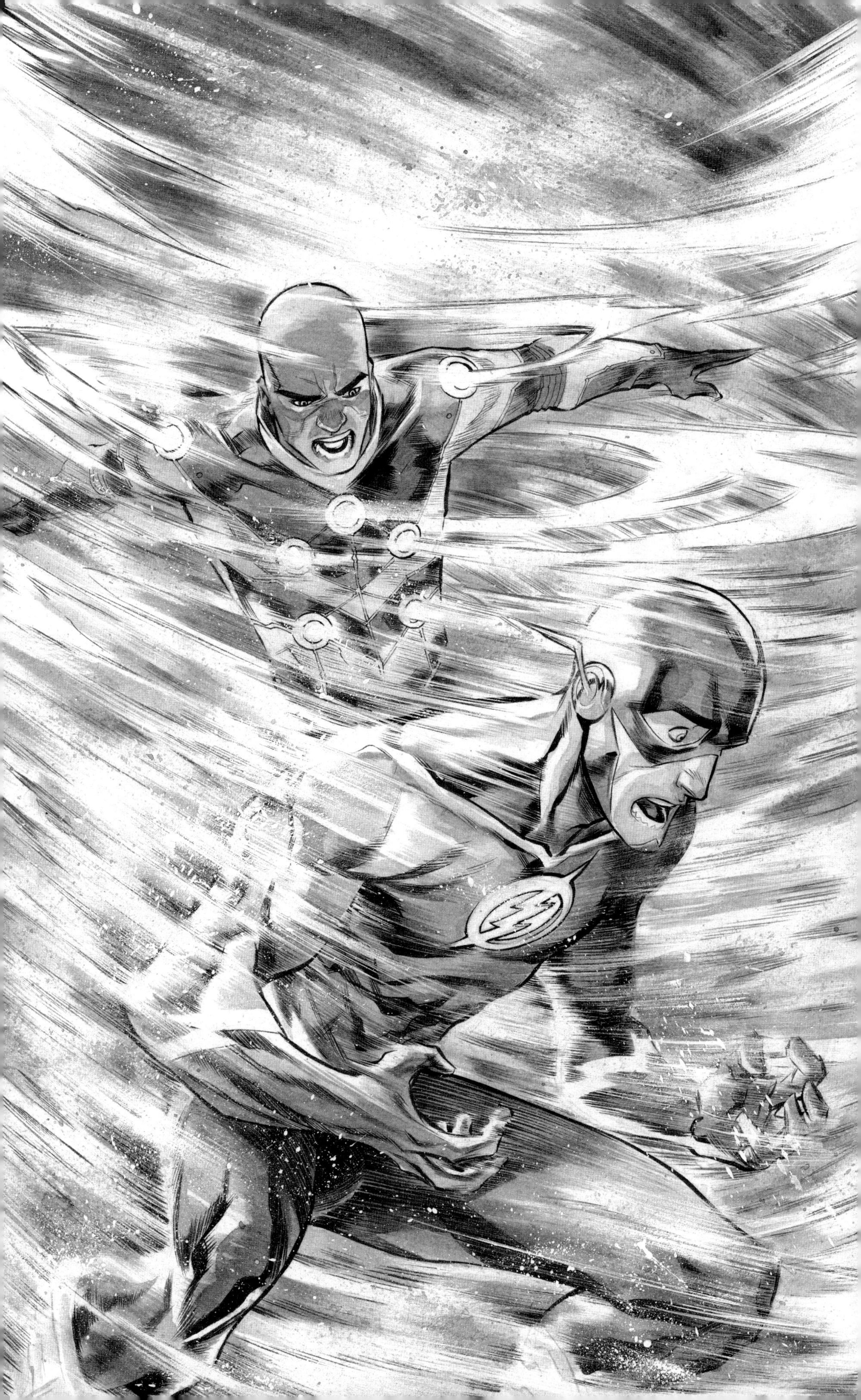

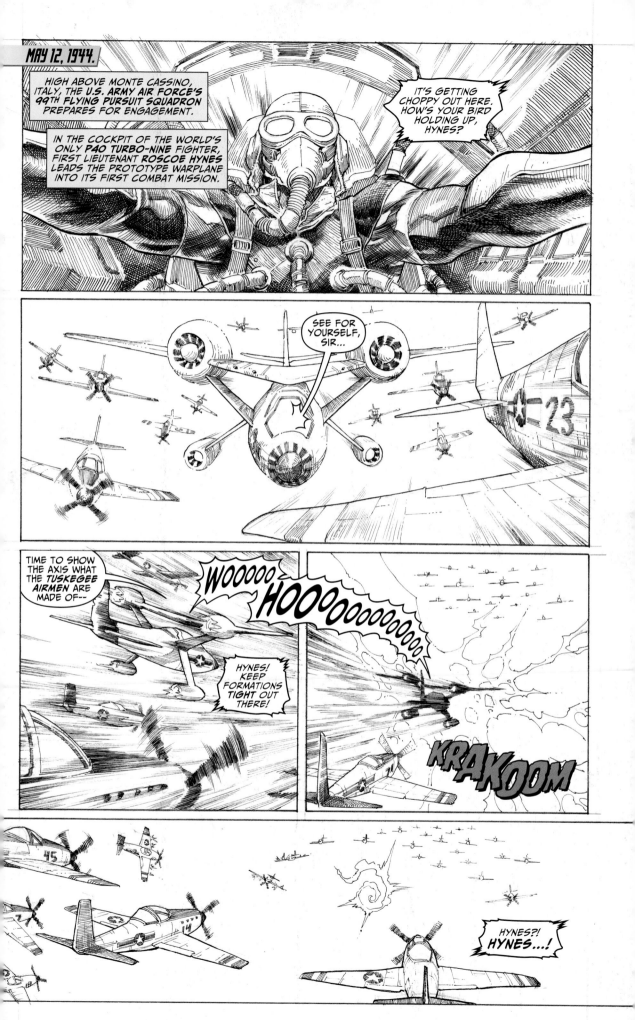

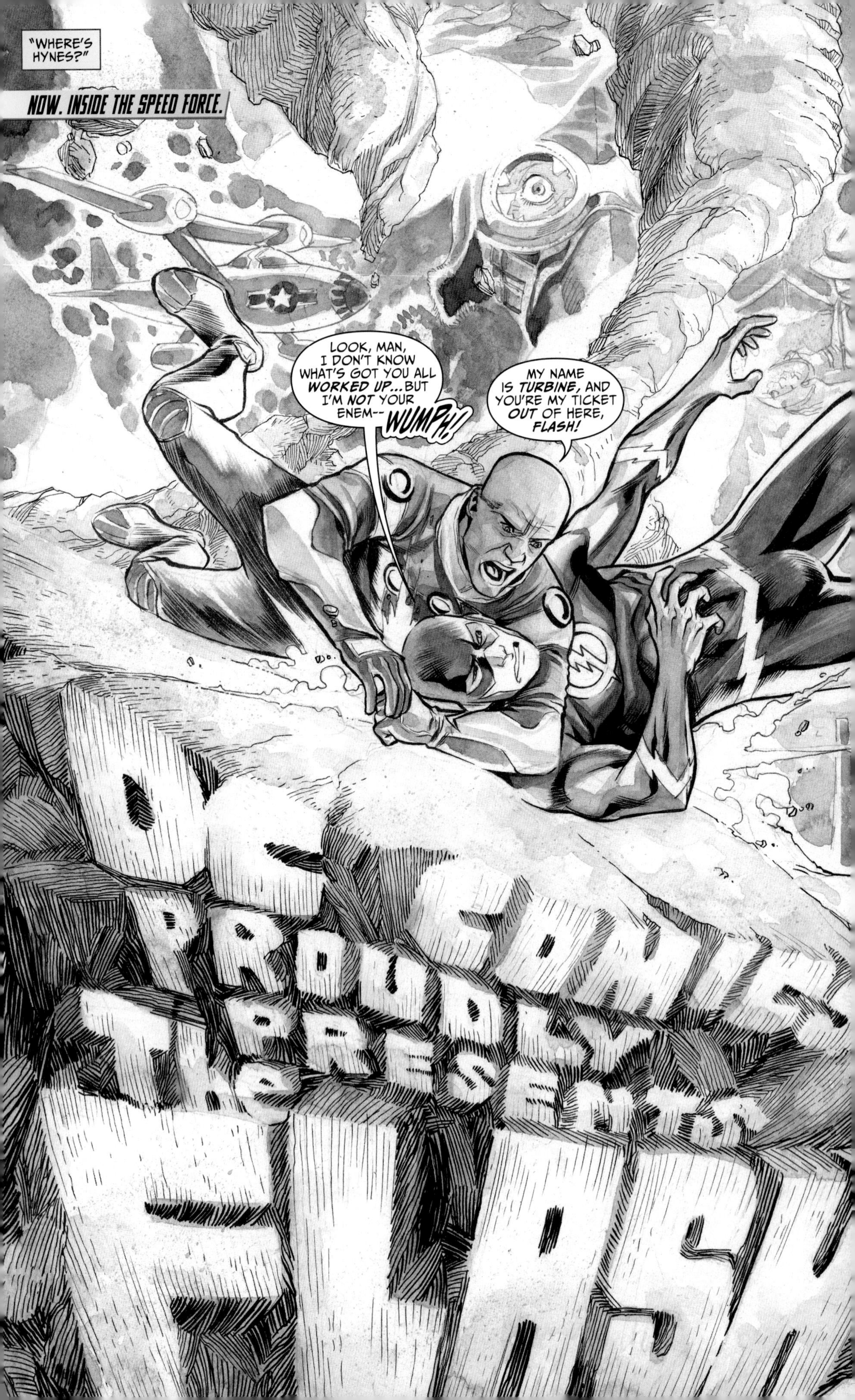
"WHERE'S HYNES?"
NOW. INSIDE THE SPEED FORCE.
LOOK, MAN, I DON'T KNOW WHAT'S GOT YOU ALL WORKED UP... BUT I'M NOT YOUR ENEM-- WUMPH!
MY NAME IS TURBINE, AND YOU'RE MY TICKET OUT OF HERE, FLASH!
PROUDLY
PRESENTS

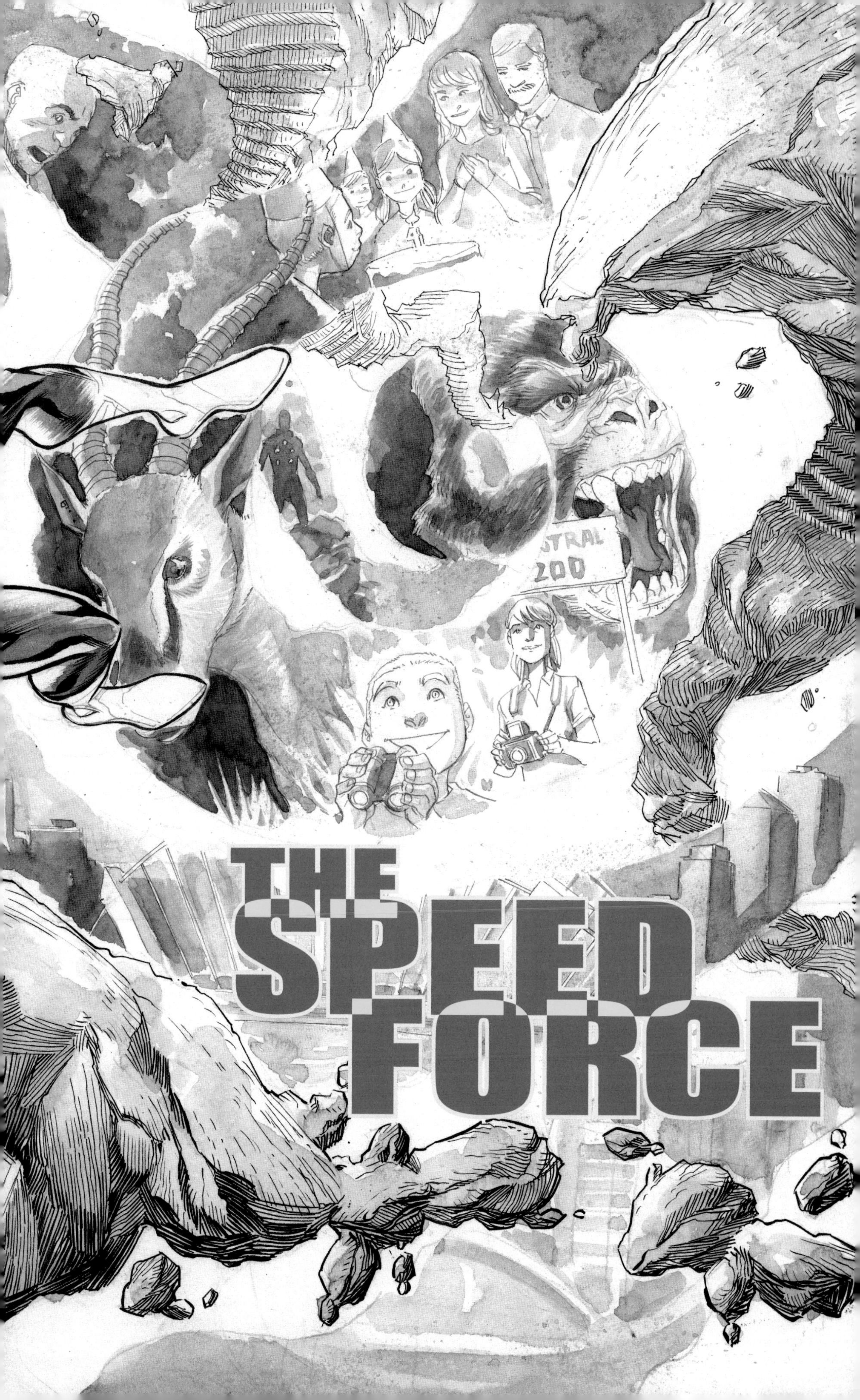
THE SPEED FORCE

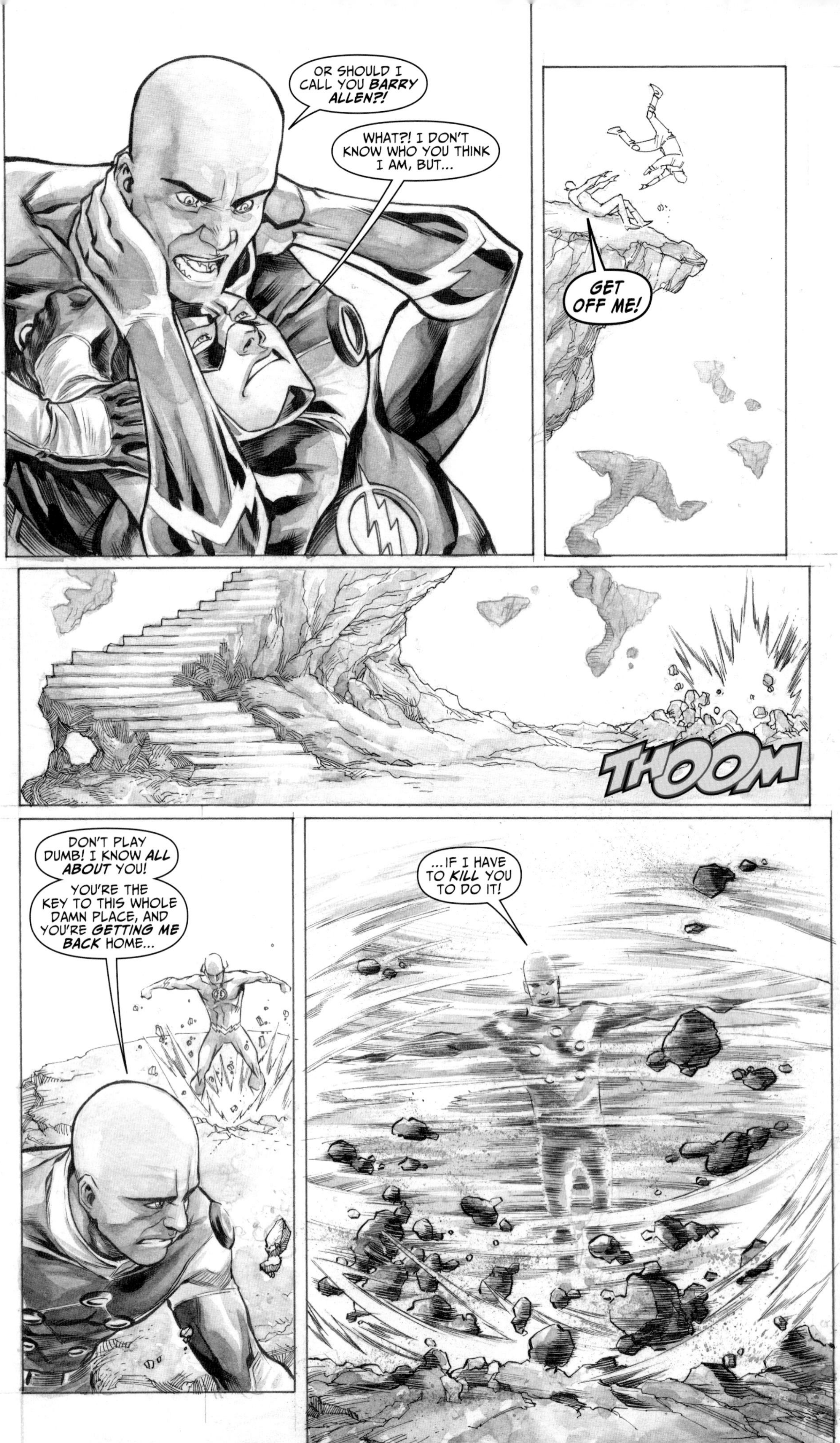
OR SHOULD I CALL YOU BARRY ALLEN?!
WHAT?! I DON'T KNOW WHO YOU THINK I AM, BUT...
GET OFF ME!
THOOM
DON'T PLAY DUMB! I KNOW ALL ABOUT YOU!
YOU'RE THE KEY TO THIS WHOLE DAMN PLACE, AND YOU'RE GETTING ME BACK HOME...
...IF I HAVE TO KILL YOU TO DO IT!

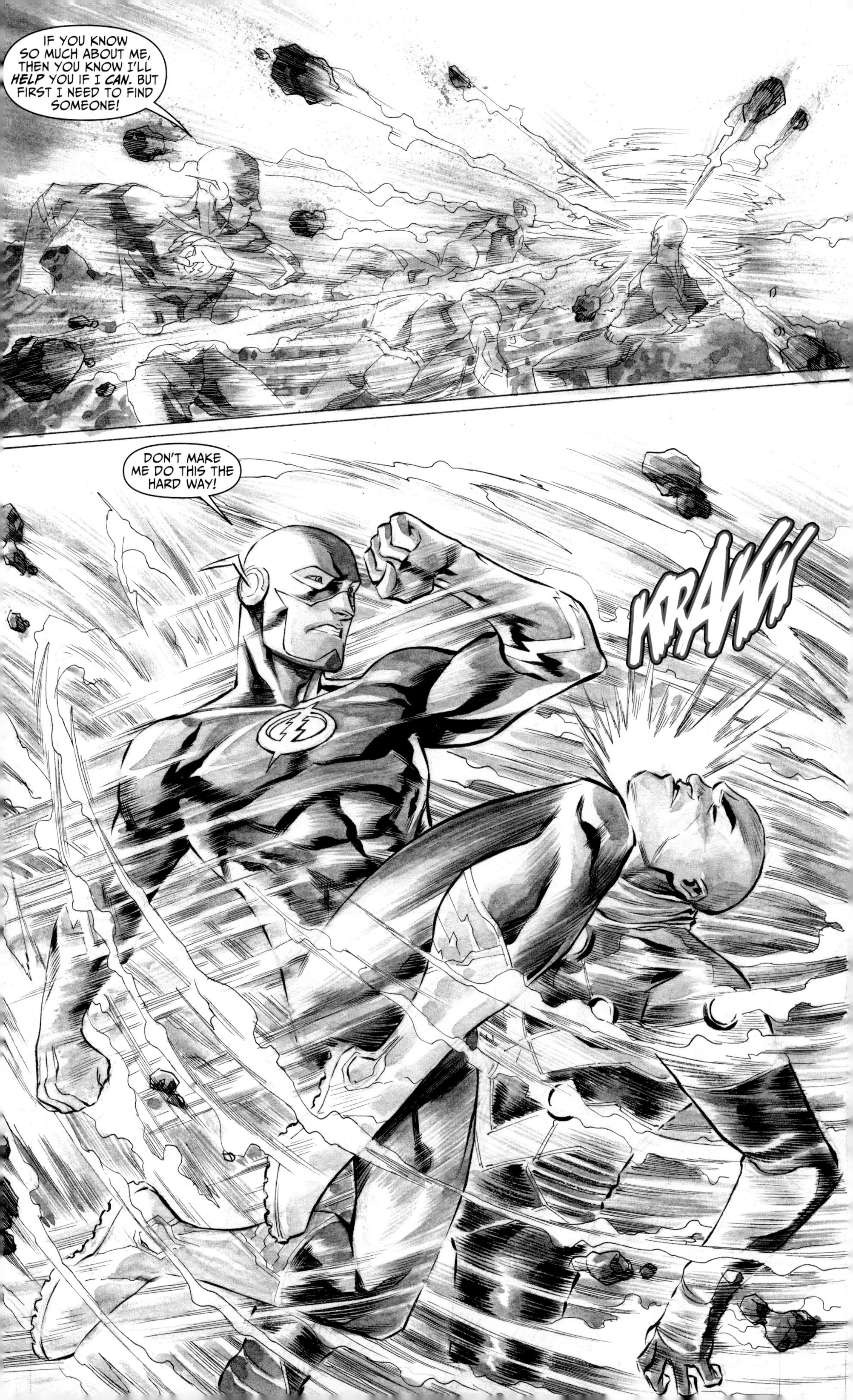
IF YOU KNOW SO MUCH ABOUT ME, THEN YOU KNOW I'LL HELP YOU IF I CAN. BUT FIRST I NEED TO FIND SOMEONE!
DON'T MAKE ME DO THIS THE HARD WAY!
KRANK

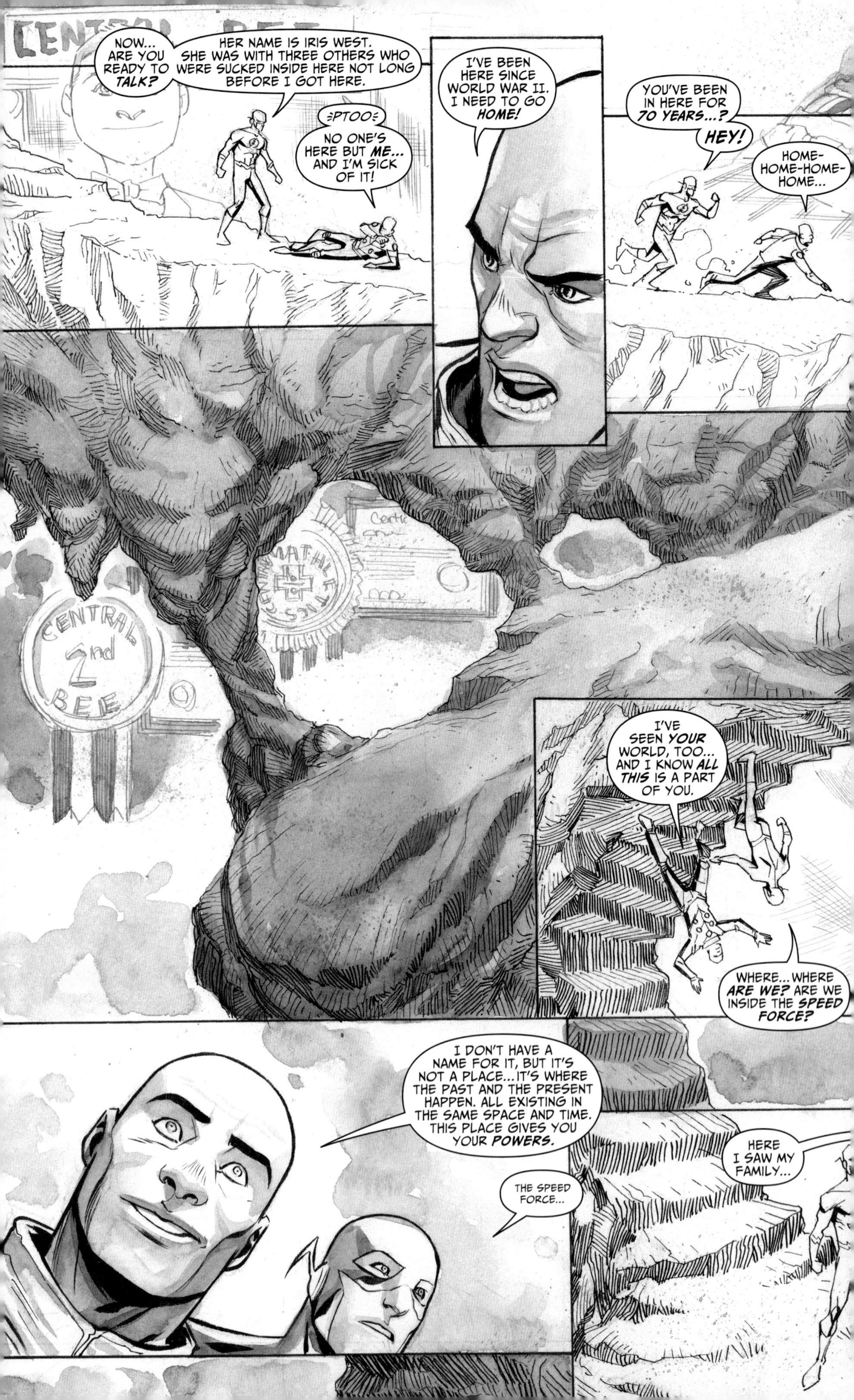
NOW... ARE YOU READY TO *TALK?*
HER NAME IS IRIS WEST. SHE WAS WITH THREE OTHERS WHO WERE SUCKED INSIDE HERE NOT LONG BEFORE I GOT HERE.
PTOO
NO ONE'S HERE BUT *ME...* AND I'M SICK OF IT!
I'VE BEEN HERE SINCE WORLD WAR II. I NEED TO GO *HOME!*
YOU'VE BEEN IN HERE FOR *70 YEARS...?*
HEY!
HOME-HOME-HOME-HOME...
I'VE SEEN *YOUR* WORLD, TOO... AND I KNOW *ALL THIS* IS A PART OF YOU.
WHERE... WHERE *ARE WE?* ARE WE INSIDE THE *SPEED FORCE?*
I DON'T HAVE A NAME FOR IT, BUT IT'S NOT A PLACE... IT'S WHERE THE PAST AND THE PRESENT HAPPEN. ALL EXISTING IN THE SAME SPACE AND TIME. THIS PLACE GIVES YOU YOUR *POWERS.*
THE SPEED FORCE...
HERE I SAW MY FAMILY...

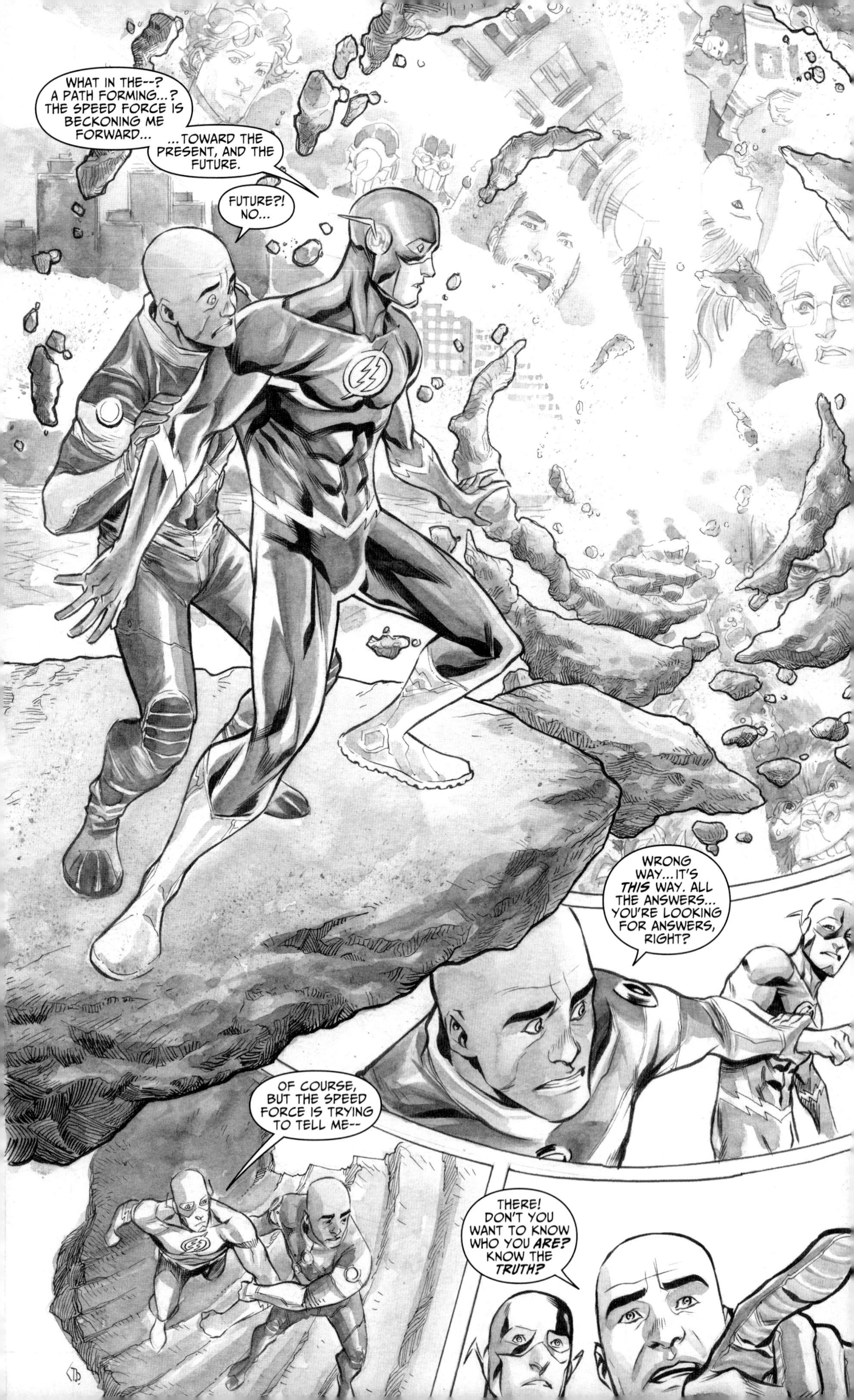
WHAT IN THE--? A PATH FORMING...? THE SPEED FORCE IS BECKONING ME FORWARD...
...TOWARD THE PRESENT, AND THE FUTURE.
FUTURE?! NO...
WRONG WAY...IT'S THIS WAY. ALL THE ANSWERS... YOU'RE LOOKING FOR ANSWERS, RIGHT?
OF COURSE, BUT THE SPEED FORCE IS TRYING TO TELL ME--
THERE! DON'T YOU WANT TO KNOW WHO YOU ARE? KNOW THE TRUTH?

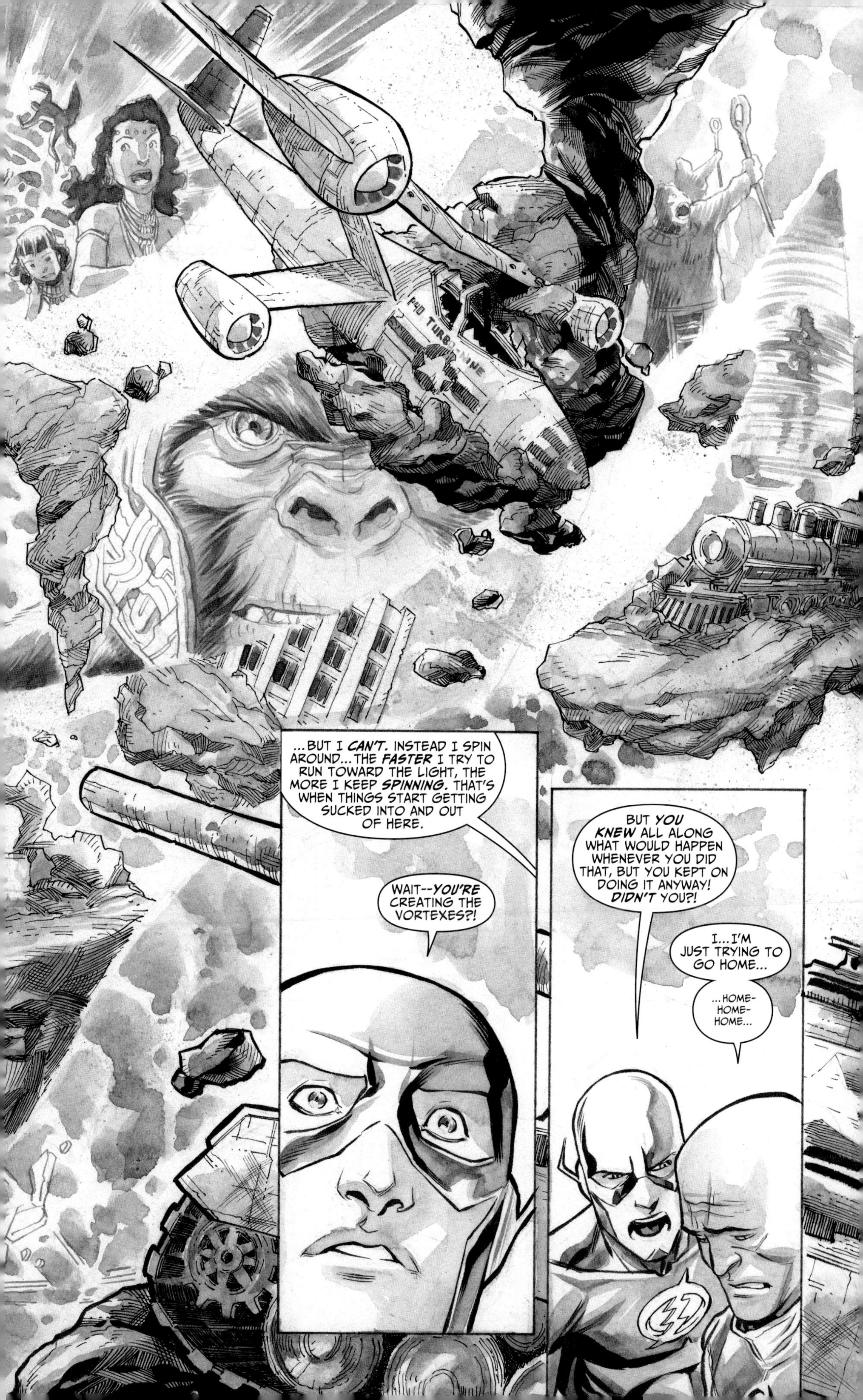
...BUT I CAN'T. INSTEAD I SPIN AROUND...THE FASTER I TRY TO RUN TOWARD THE LIGHT, THE MORE I KEEP SPINNING. THAT'S WHEN THINGS START GETTING SUCKED INTO AND OUT OF HERE.
WAIT--YOU'RE CREATING THE VORTEXES?!
BUT YOU KNEW ALL ALONG WHAT WOULD HAPPEN WHENEVER YOU DID THAT, BUT YOU KEPT ON DOING IT ANYWAY! DIDN'T YOU?!
I...I'M JUST TRYING TO GO HOME...
...HOME-HOME-HOME...

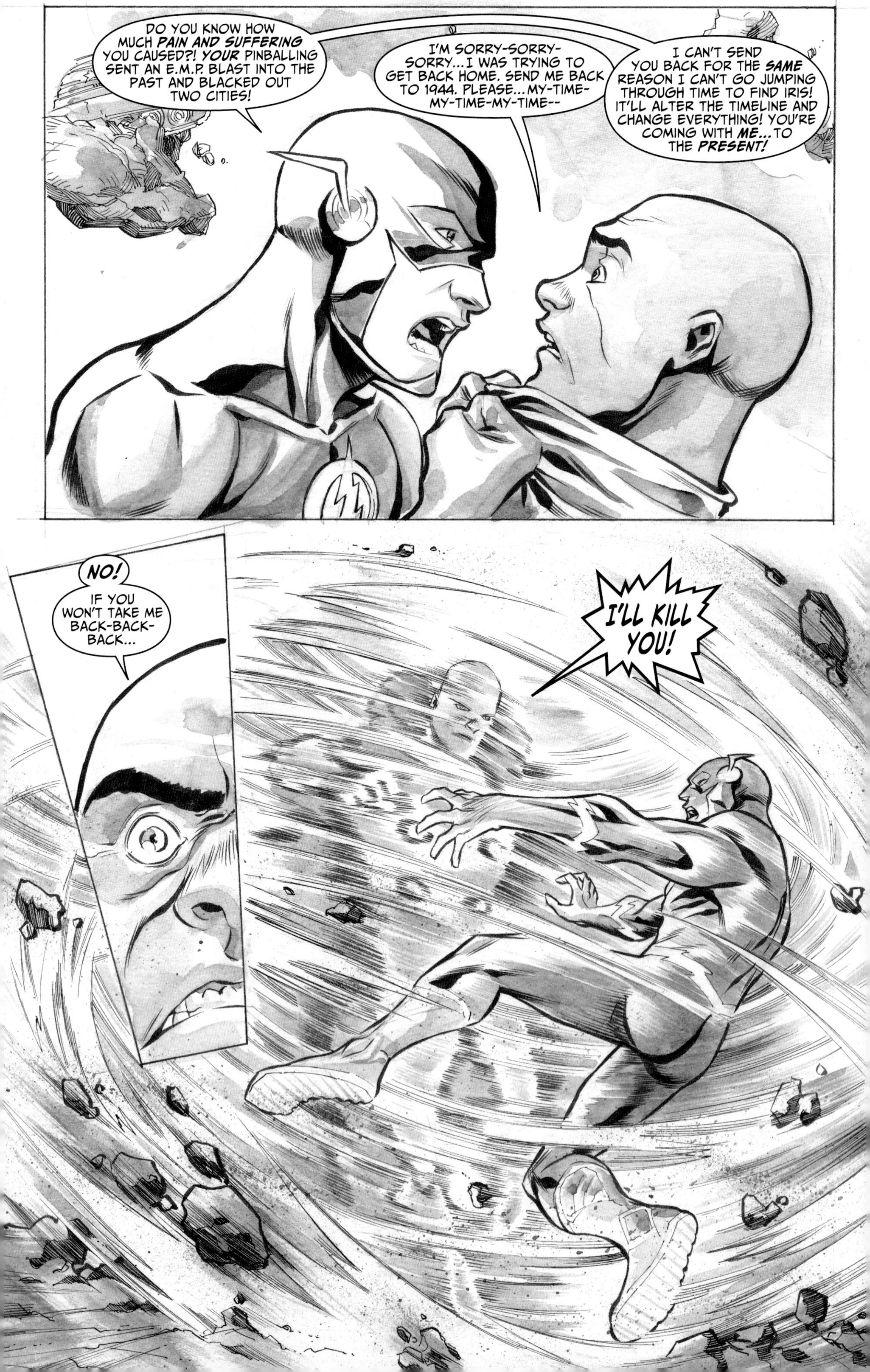
DO YOU KNOW HOW MUCH **PAIN AND SUFFERING** YOU CAUSED?! **YOUR** PINBALLING SENT AN E.M.P. BLAST INTO THE PAST AND BLACKED OUT TWO CITIES!
I'M SORRY-SORRY-SORRY... I WAS TRYING TO GET BACK HOME. SEND ME BACK TO 1944. PLEASE... MY-TIME-MY-TIME-MY-TIME--
I CAN'T SEND YOU BACK FOR THE **SAME** REASON I CAN'T GO JUMPING THROUGH TIME TO FIND IRIS! IT'LL ALTER THE TIMELINE AND CHANGE EVERYTHING! YOU'RE COMING WITH **ME...** TO THE **PRESENT!**
NO!
IF YOU WON'T TAKE ME BACK-BACK-BACK...
I'LL KILL YOU!

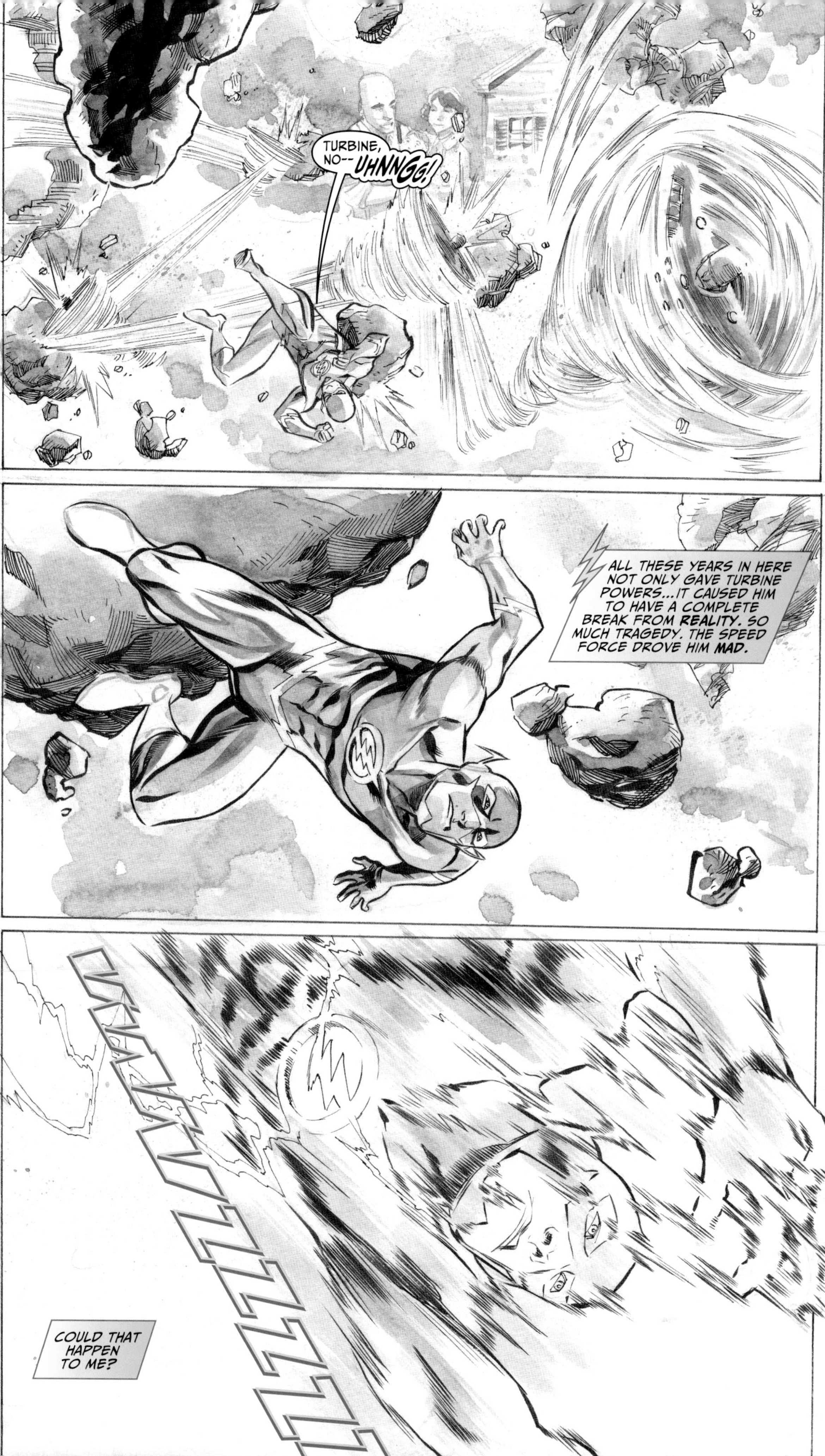

TURBINE, NO-- UHNNGG!
ALL THESE YEARS IN HERE NOT ONLY GAVE TURBINE POWERS...IT CAUSED HIM TO HAVE A COMPLETE BREAK FROM **REALITY**. SO MUCH TRAGEDY. THE SPEED FORCE DROVE HIM **MAD**.
COULD THAT HAPPEN TO ME?

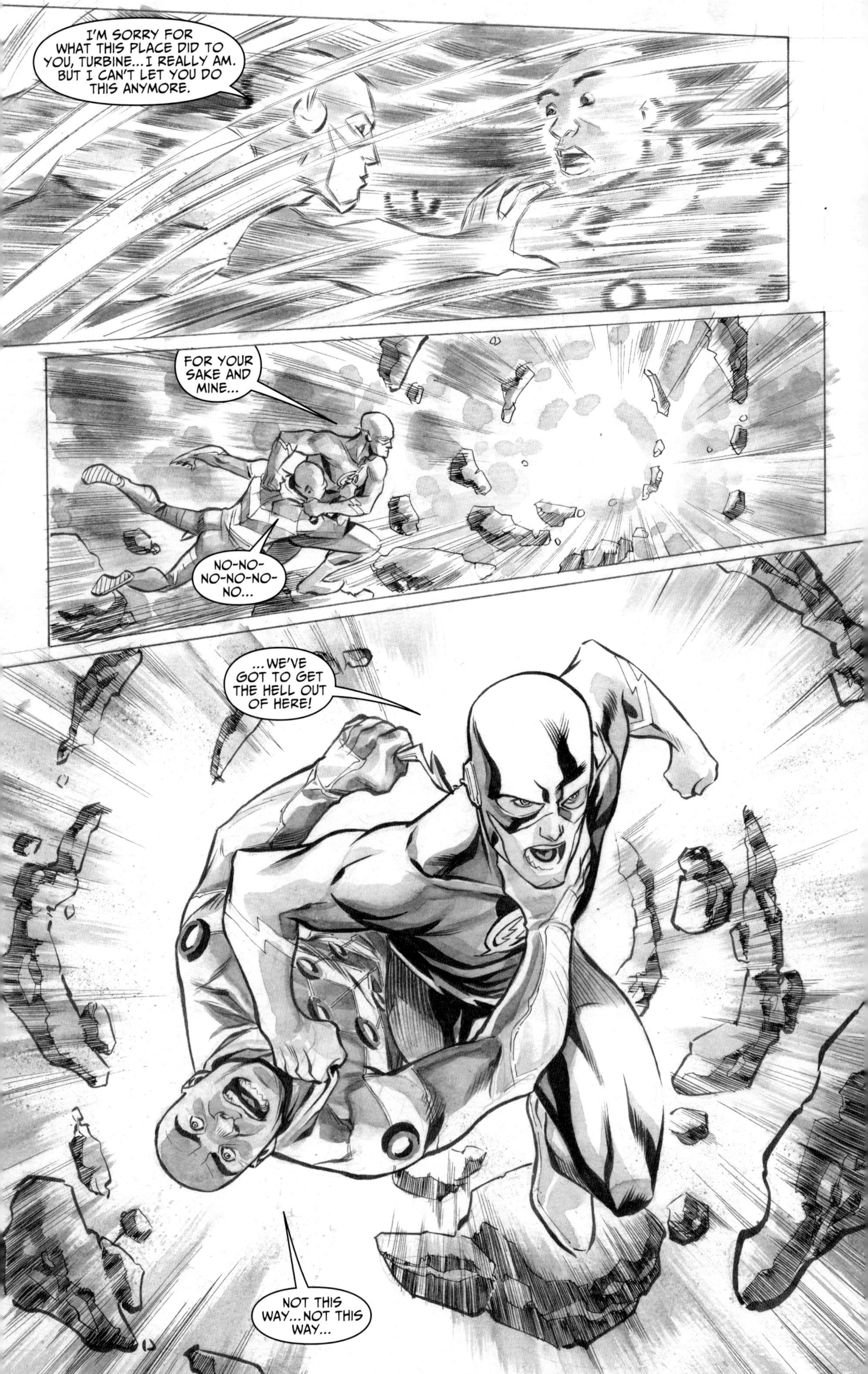

I'M SORRY FOR WHAT THIS PLACE DID TO YOU, TURBINE...I REALLY AM. BUT I CAN'T LET YOU DO THIS ANYMORE.
FOR YOUR SAKE AND MINE...
NO-NO-NO-NO-NO-NO...
...WE'VE GOT TO GET THE HELL OUT OF HERE!
NOT THIS WAY...NOT THIS WAY...

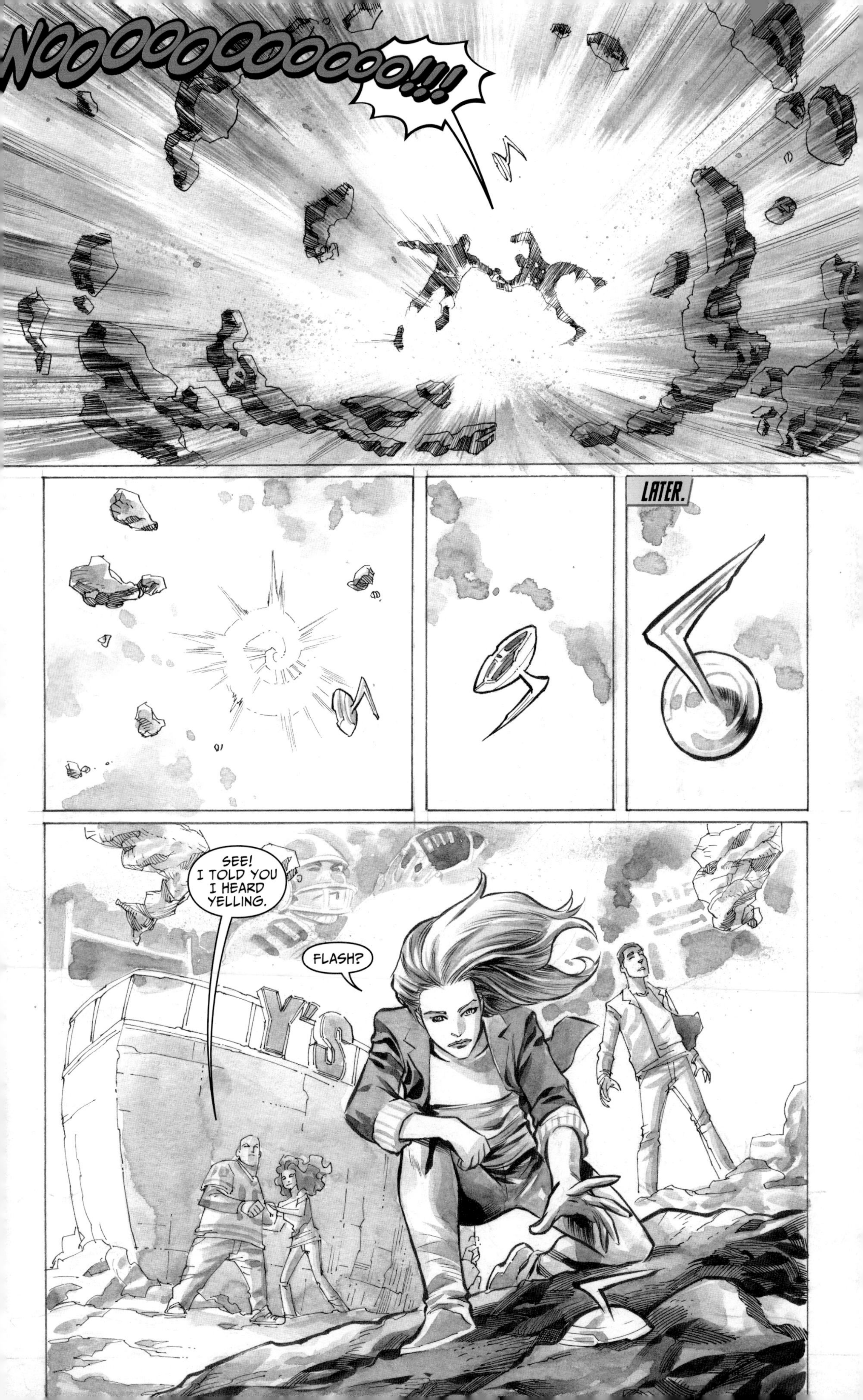
NOOOOOOOOOOOOO!!!
LATER.
SEE! I TOLD YOU I HEARD YELLING.
FLASH?

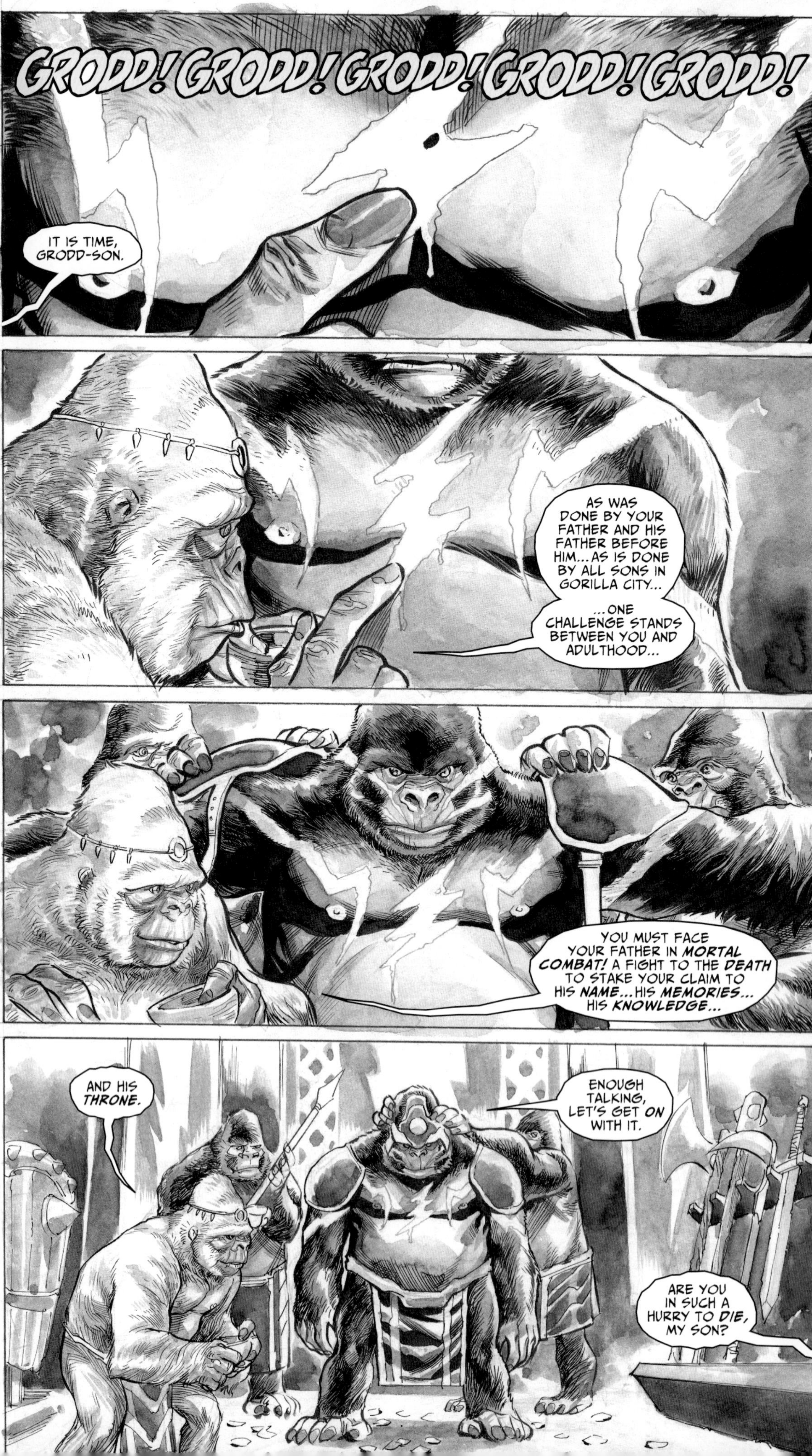
GRODD! GRODD! GRODD! GRODD! GRODD!
IT IS TIME, GRODD-SON.
AS WAS DONE BY YOUR FATHER AND HIS FATHER BEFORE HIM... AS IS DONE BY ALL SONS IN GORILLA CITY...
...ONE CHALLENGE STANDS BETWEEN YOU AND ADULTHOOD...
YOU MUST FACE YOUR FATHER IN MORTAL COMBAT! A FIGHT TO THE DEATH TO STAKE YOUR CLAIM TO HIS NAME... HIS MEMORIES... HIS KNOWLEDGE...
AND HIS THRONE.
ENOUGH TALKING, LET'S GET ON WITH IT.
ARE YOU IN SUCH A HURRY TO DIE, MY SON?

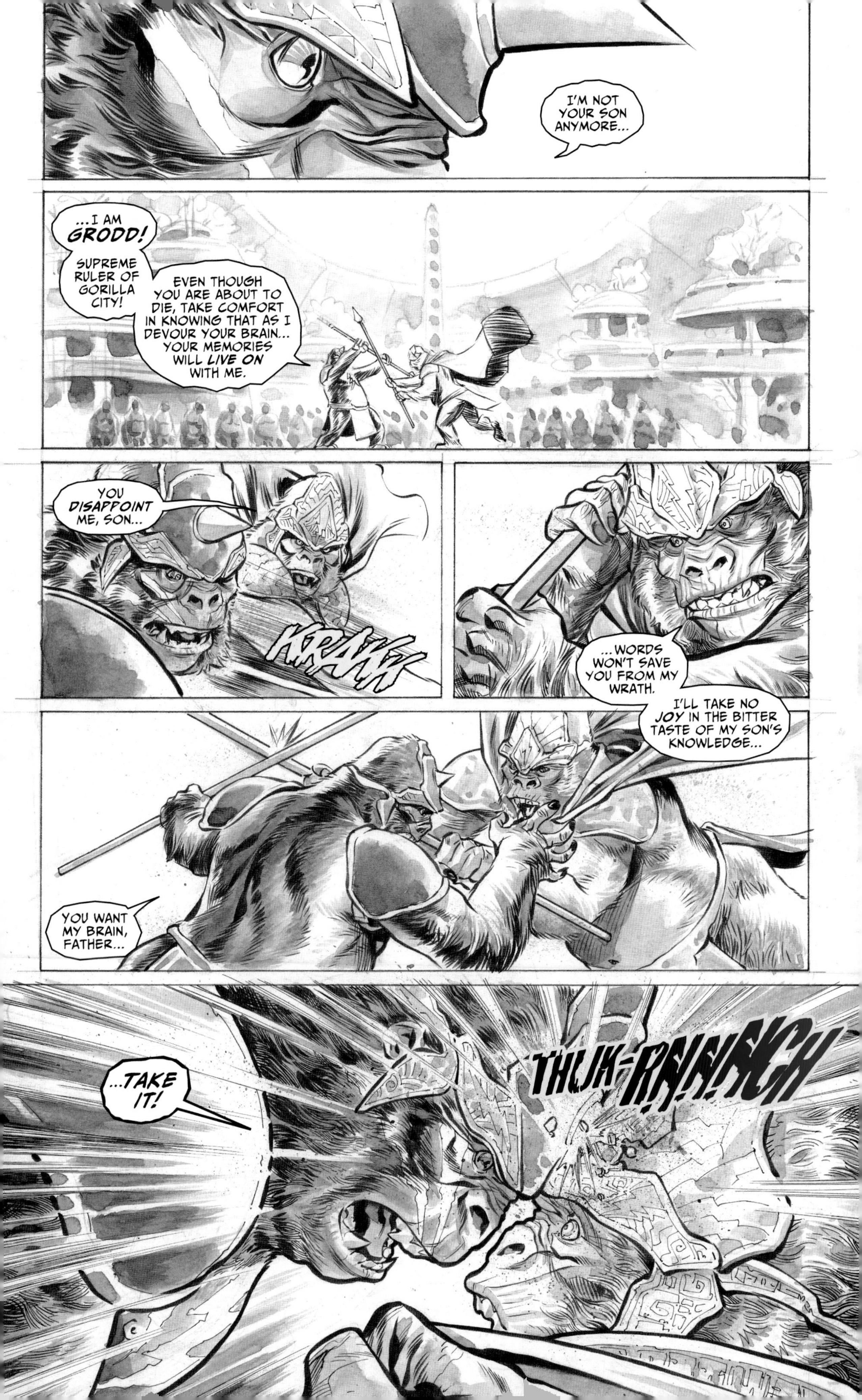
I'M NOT YOUR SON ANYMORE...
...I AM GRODD!
SUPREME RULER OF GORILLA CITY!
EVEN THOUGH YOU ARE ABOUT TO DIE, TAKE COMFORT IN KNOWING THAT AS I DEVOUR YOUR BRAIN... YOUR MEMORIES WILL LIVE ON WITH ME.
YOU DISAPPOINT ME, SON...
KRAKK
...WORDS WON'T SAVE YOU FROM MY WRATH.
I'LL TAKE NO JOY IN THE BITTER TASTE OF MY SON'S KNOWLEDGE...
YOU WANT MY BRAIN, FATHER...
...TAKE IT!
THUK-RAAACH

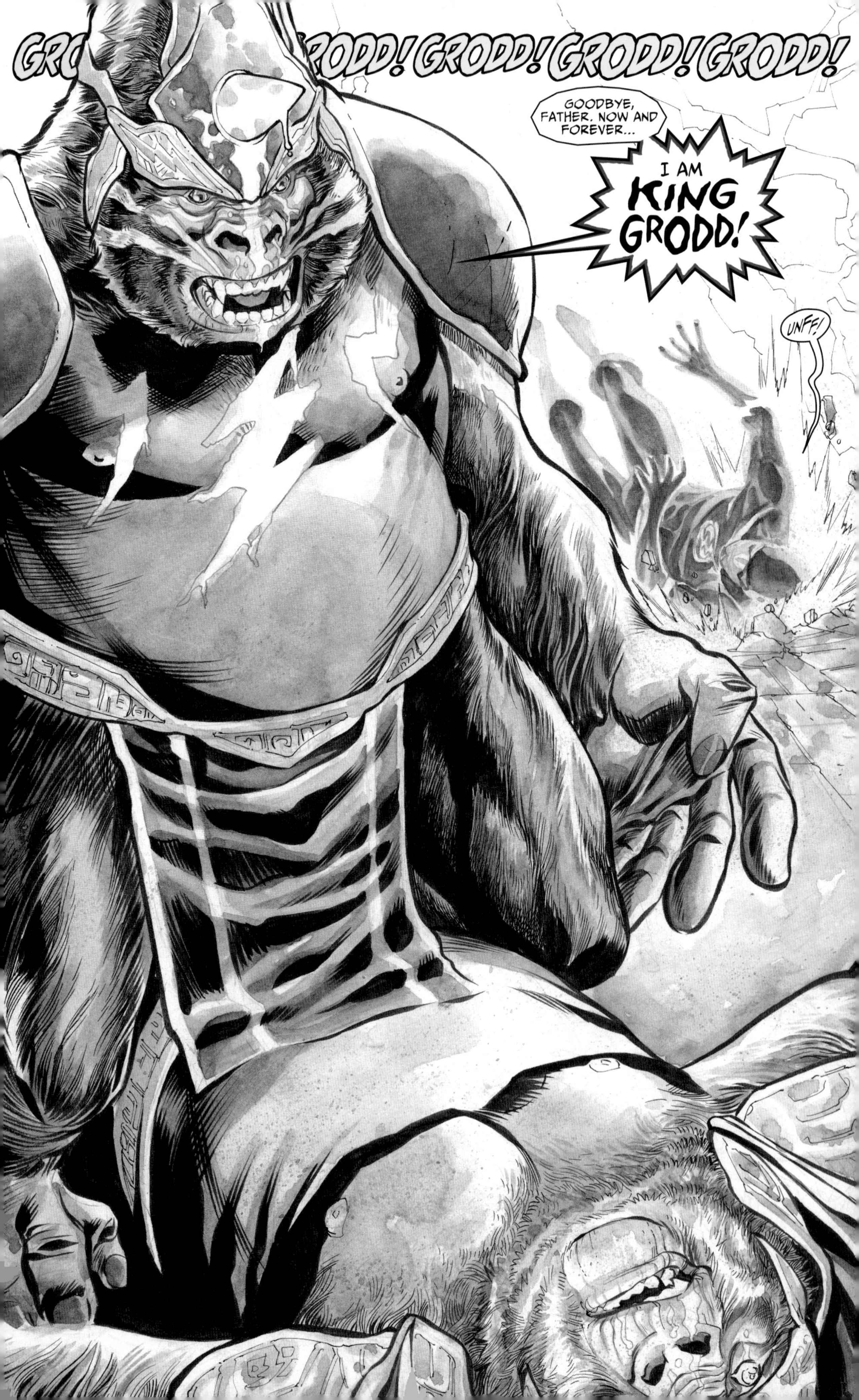
GRODD! GRODD! GRODD! GRODD!
GOODBYE, FATHER. NOW AND FOREVER...
I AM KING GRODD!
UNFF!

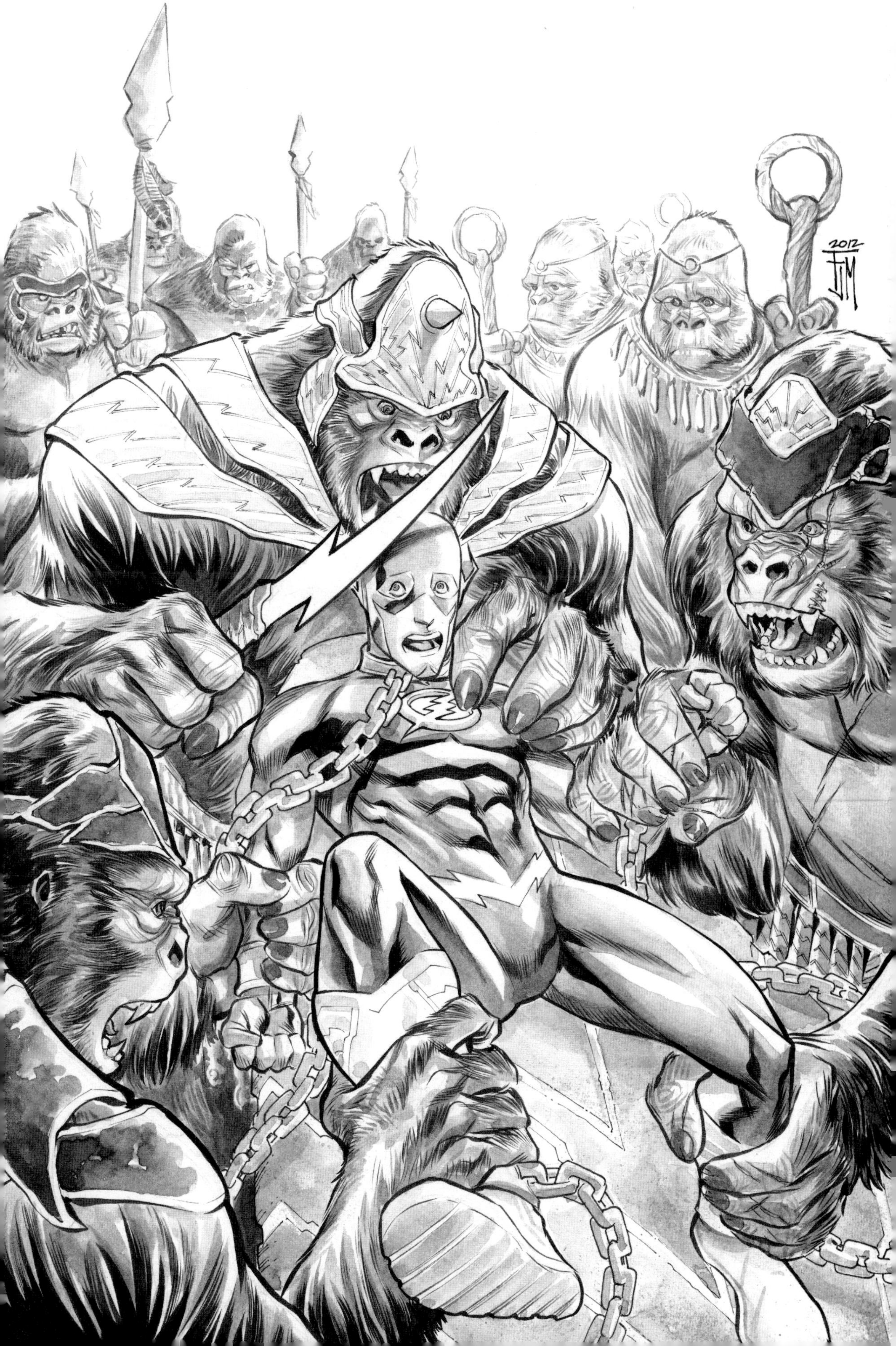
2012

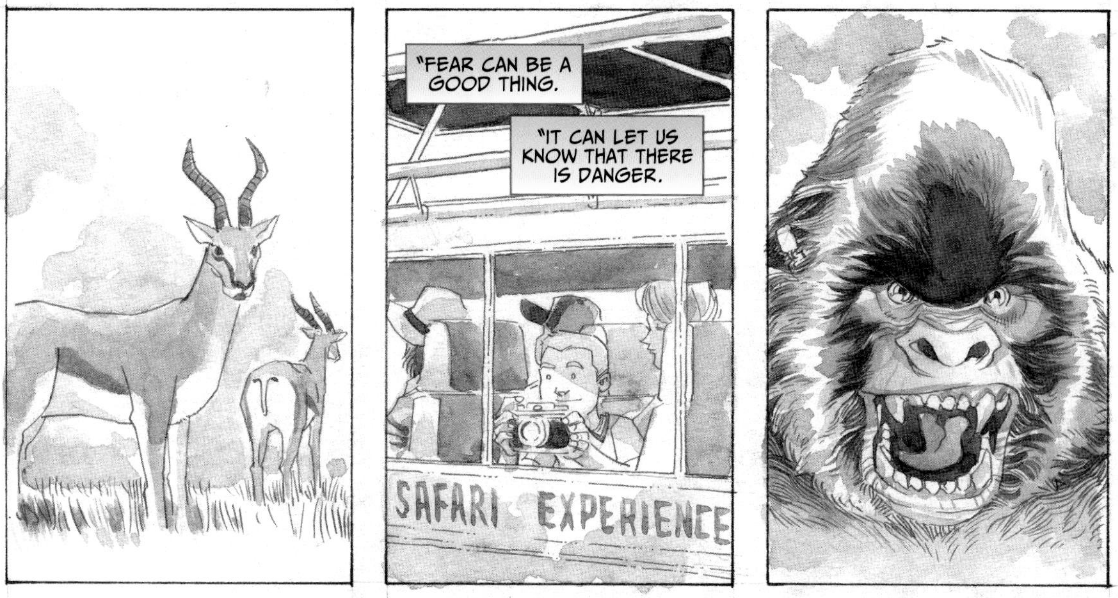
"FEAR CAN BE A GOOD THING.
"IT CAN LET US KNOW THAT THERE IS DANGER.
SAFARI EXPERIENCE

DC COMICS

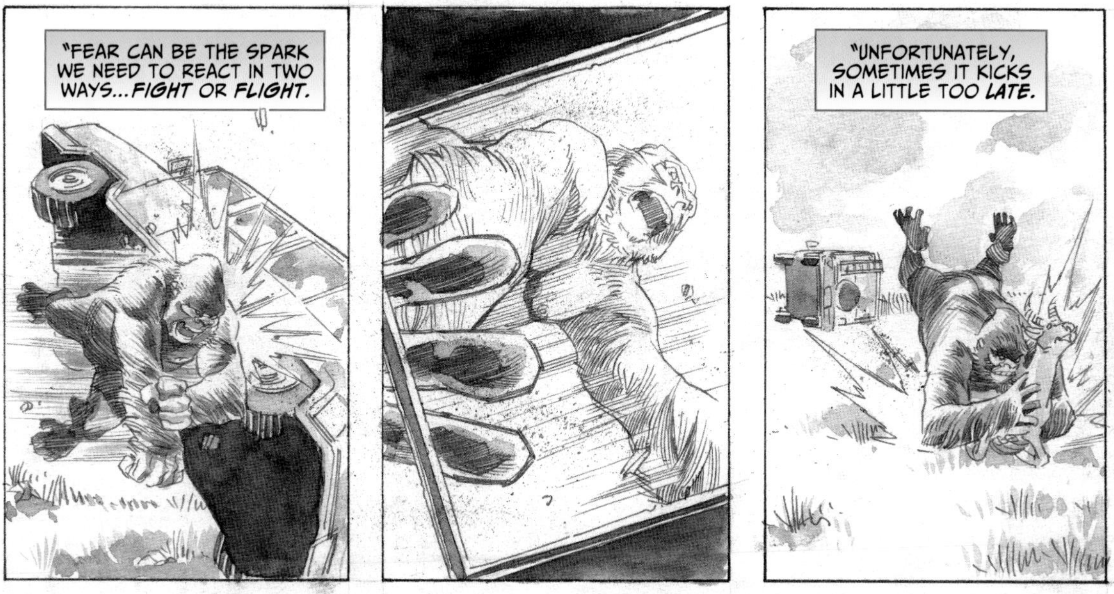
"FEAR CAN BE THE SPARK WE NEED TO REACT IN TWO WAYS...*FIGHT* OR *FLIGHT*.
"UNFORTUNATELY, SOMETIMES IT KICKS IN A LITTLE TOO *LATE*.

PROUDLY PRESENTS

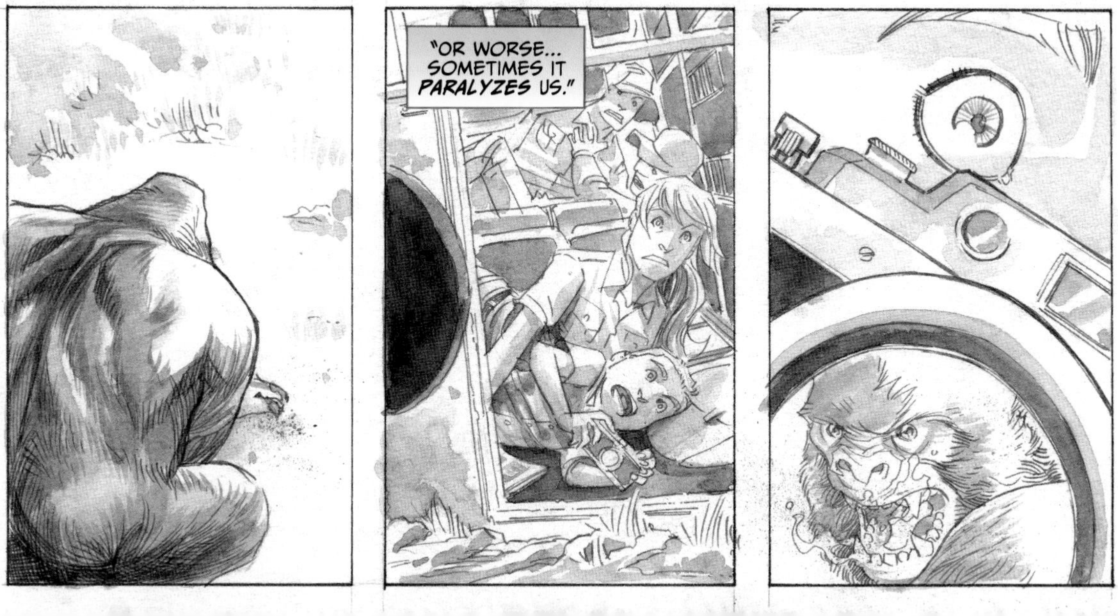
"OR WORSE... SOMETIMES IT *PARALYZES* US."

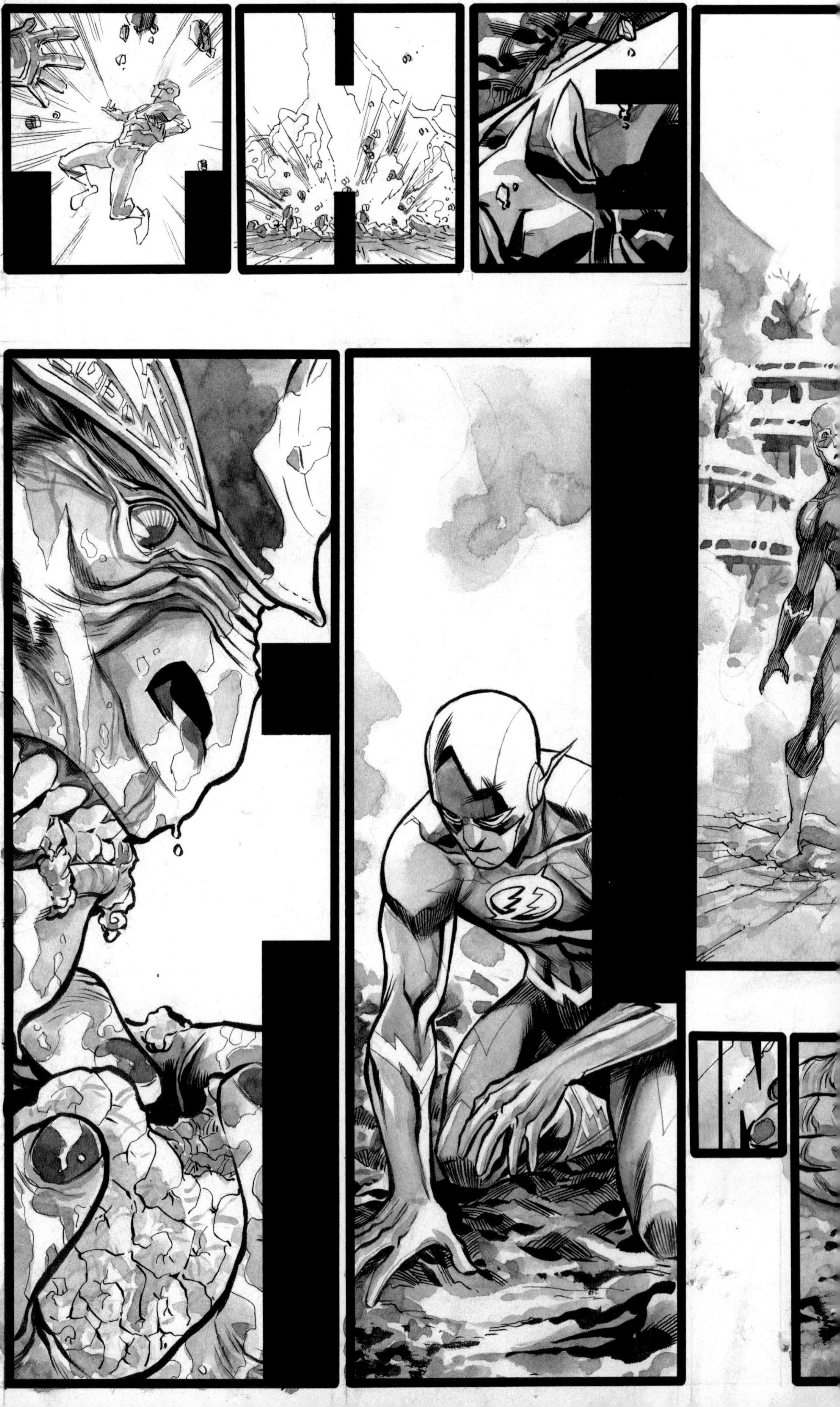

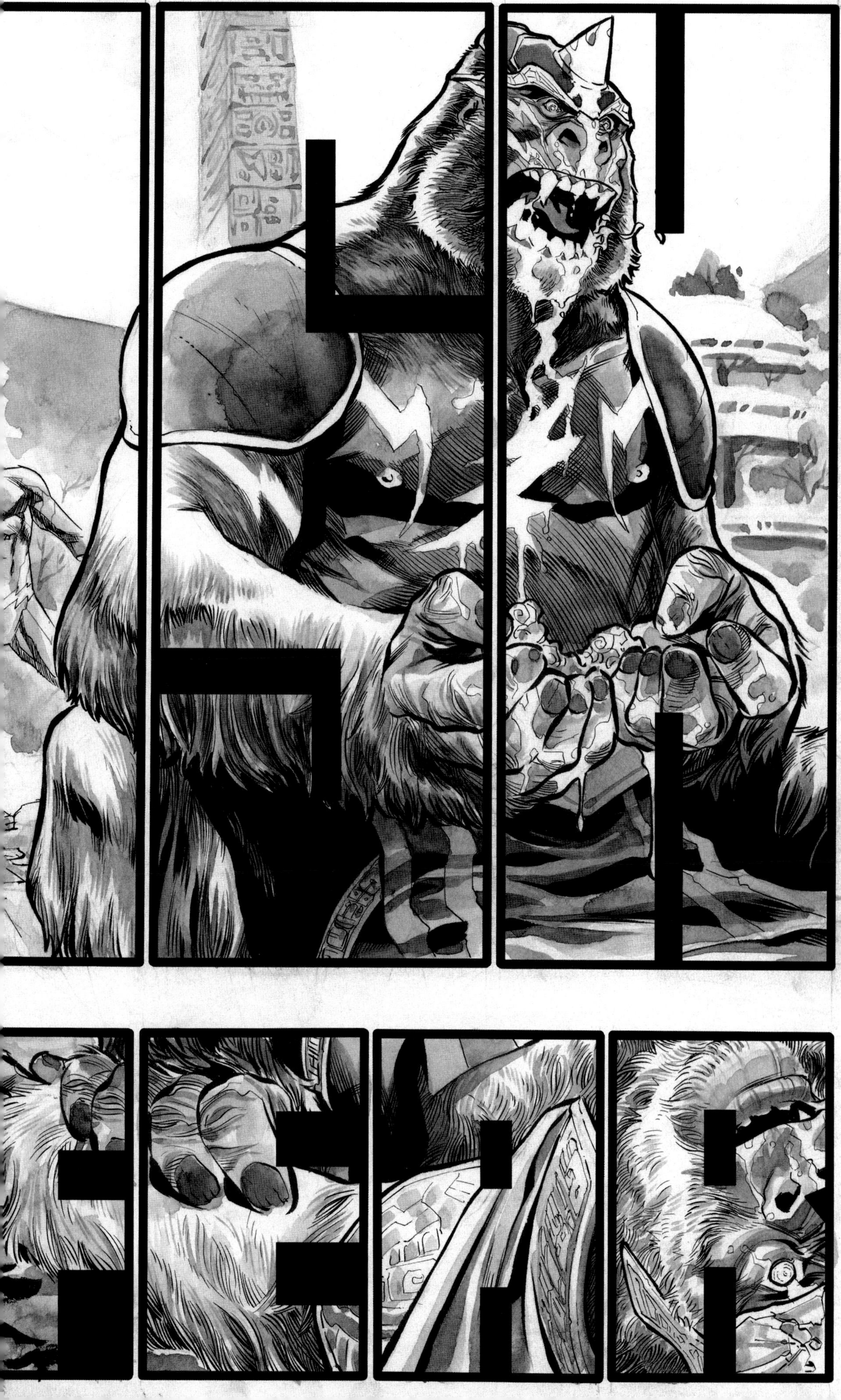

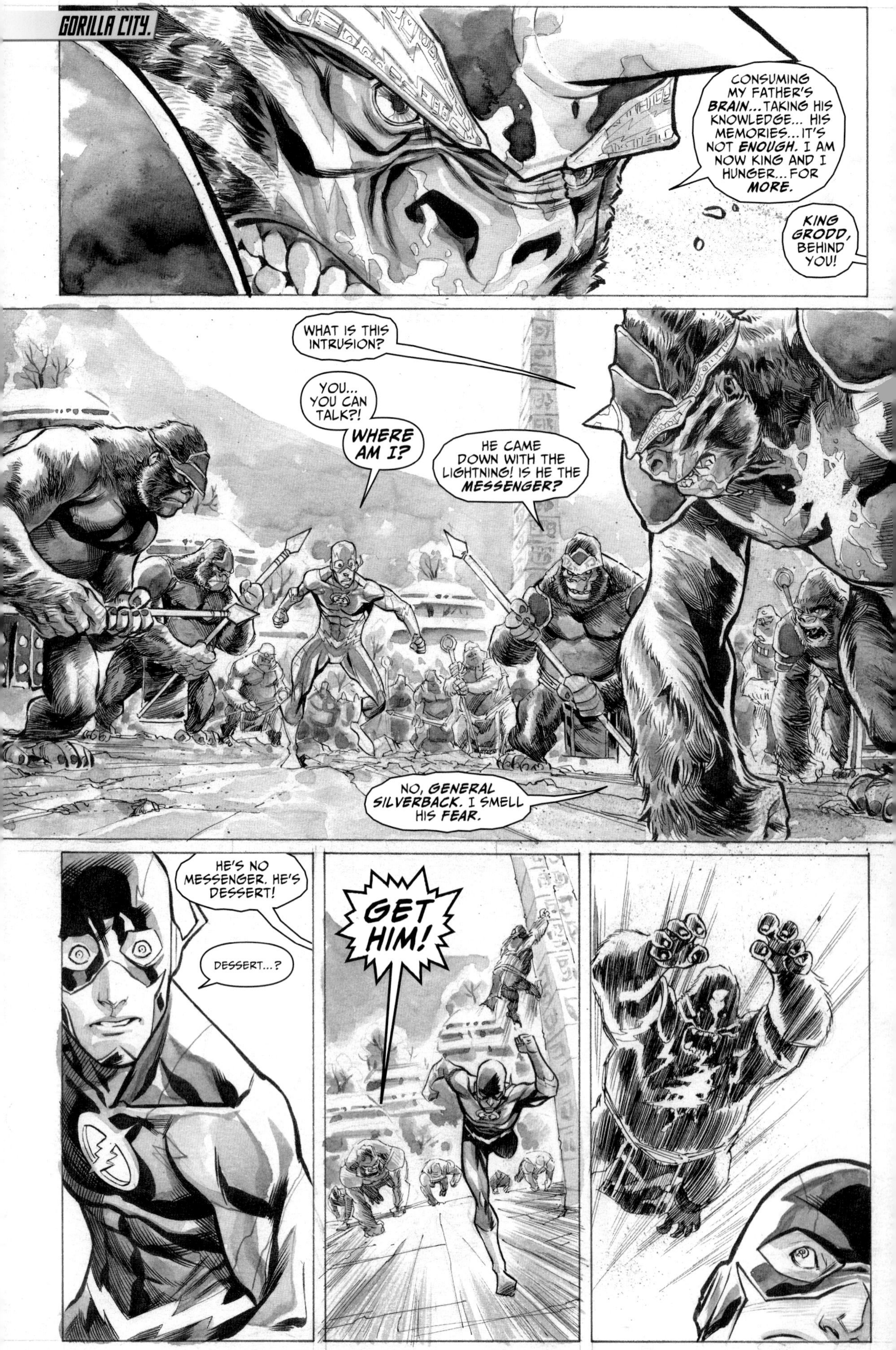
GORILLA CITY.
CONSUMING MY FATHER'S BRAIN... TAKING HIS KNOWLEDGE... HIS MEMORIES... IT'S NOT ENOUGH. I AM NOW KING AND I HUNGER... FOR MORE.
KING GRODD, BEHIND YOU!
WHAT IS THIS INTRUSION?
YOU... YOU CAN TALK?!
WHERE AM I?
HE CAME DOWN WITH THE LIGHTNING! IS HE THE MESSENGER?
NO, GENERAL SILVERBACK. I SMELL HIS FEAR.
HE'S NO MESSENGER. HE'S DESSERT!
DESSERT...?
GET HIM!

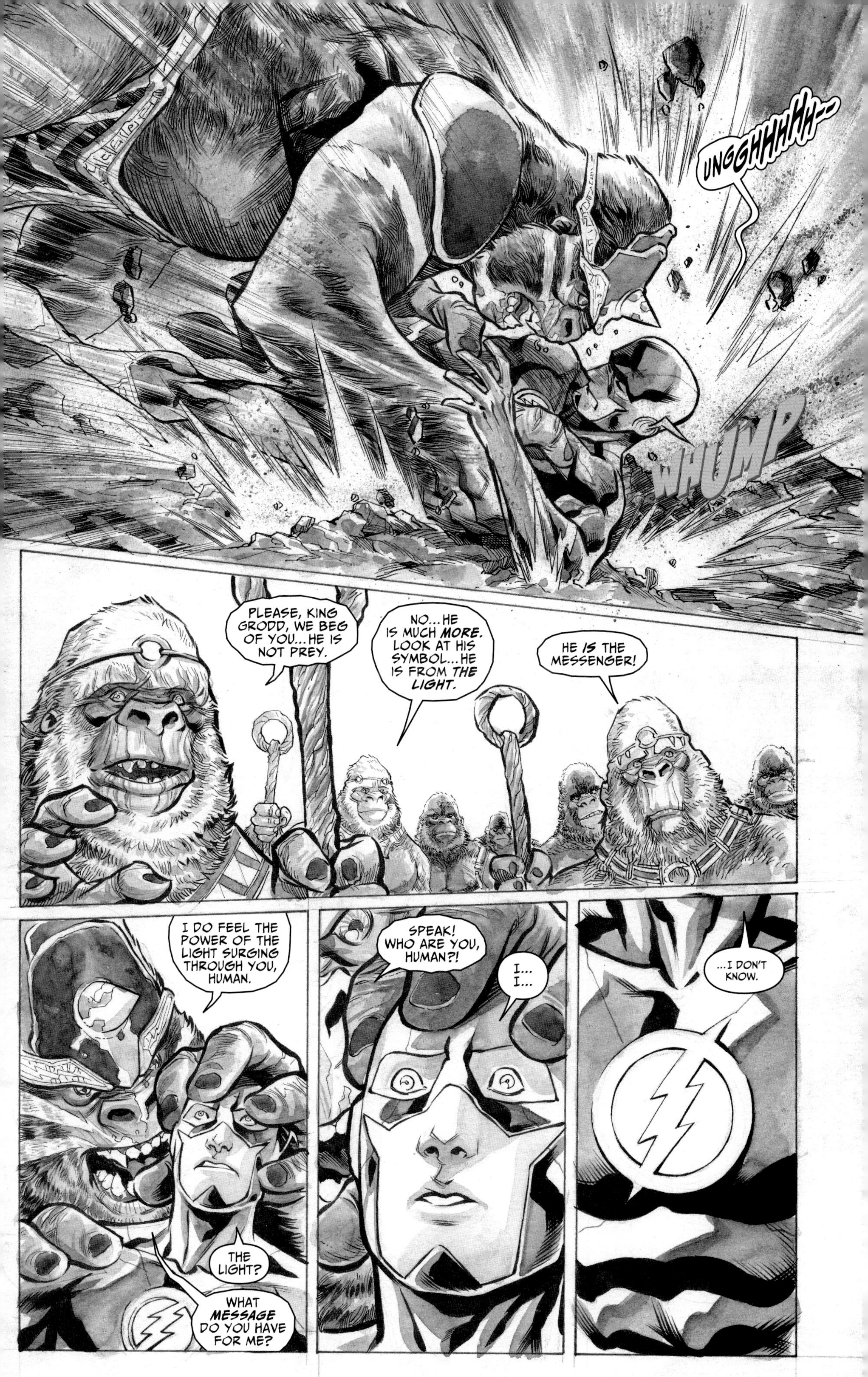
UNGGHHHHH--
WHUMP
PLEASE, KING GRODD, WE BEG OF YOU...HE IS NOT PREY.
NO...HE IS MUCH MORE. LOOK AT HIS SYMBOL...HE IS FROM THE LIGHT.
HE IS THE MESSENGER!
I DO FEEL THE POWER OF THE LIGHT SURGING THROUGH YOU, HUMAN.
THE LIGHT?
WHAT MESSAGE DO YOU HAVE FOR ME?
SPEAK! WHO ARE YOU, HUMAN?!
I... I...
...I DON'T KNOW.

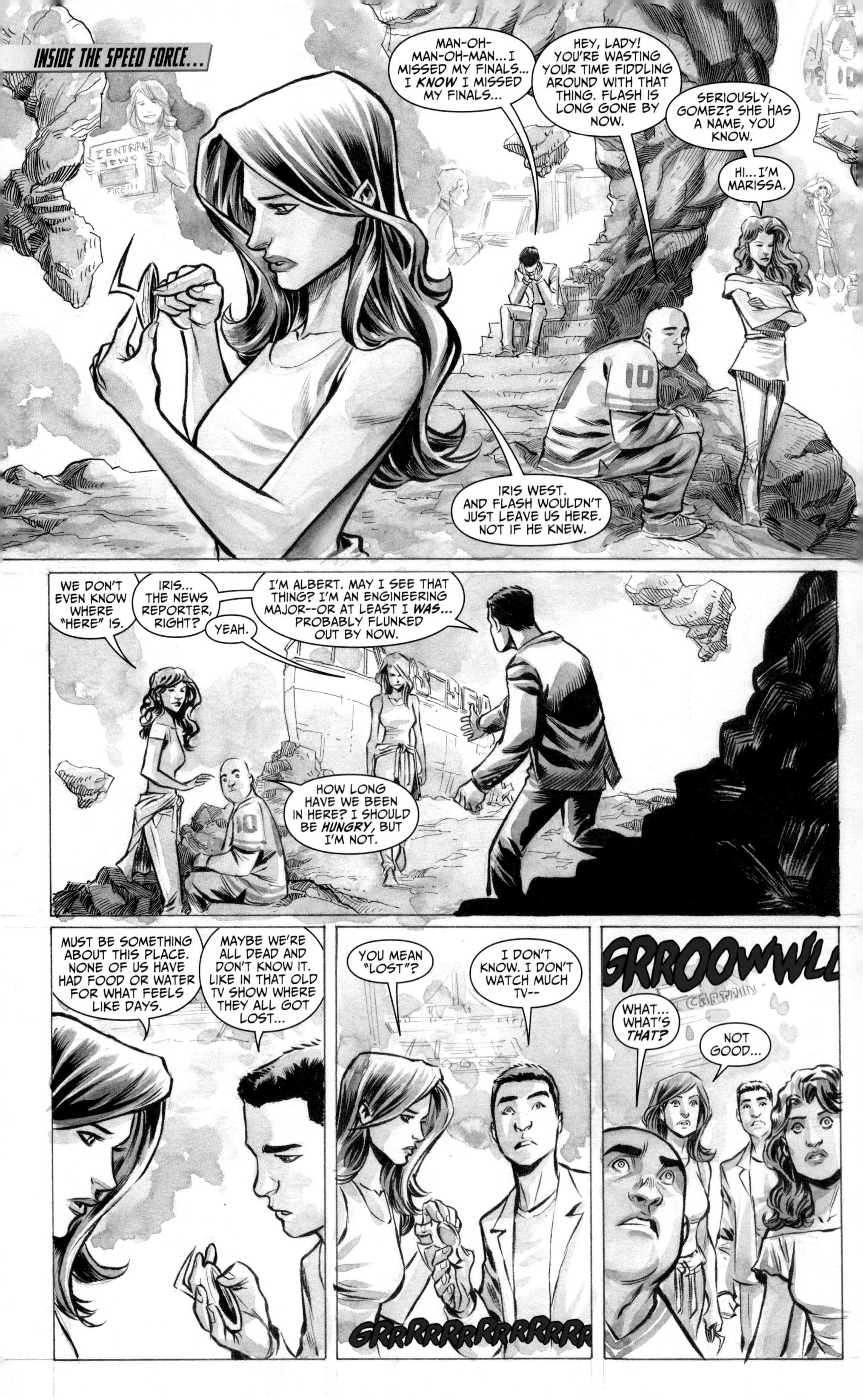
INSIDE THE SPEED FORCE...
CENTRAL NEWS
MAN-OH-MAN-OH-MAN... I MISSED MY FINALS... I KNOW I MISSED MY FINALS...
HEY, LADY! YOU'RE WASTING YOUR TIME FIDDLING AROUND WITH THAT THING. FLASH IS LONG GONE BY NOW.
SERIOUSLY, GOMEZ? SHE HAS A NAME, YOU KNOW.
HI... I'M MARISSA.
IRIS WEST. AND FLASH WOULDN'T JUST LEAVE US HERE. NOT IF HE KNEW.
WE DON'T EVEN KNOW WHERE "HERE" IS.
IRIS... THE NEWS REPORTER, RIGHT?
YEAH.
I'M ALBERT. MAY I SEE THAT THING? I'M AN ENGINEERING MAJOR--OR AT LEAST I WAS... PROBABLY FLUNKED OUT BY NOW.
HOW LONG HAVE WE BEEN IN HERE? I SHOULD BE HUNGRY, BUT I'M NOT.
MUST BE SOMETHING ABOUT THIS PLACE. NONE OF US HAVE HAD FOOD OR WATER FOR WHAT FEELS LIKE DAYS.
MAYBE WE'RE ALL DEAD AND DON'T KNOW IT. LIKE IN THAT OLD TV SHOW WHERE THEY ALL GOT LOST...
YOU MEAN "LOST"?
I DON'T KNOW. I DON'T WATCH MUCH TV--
GRRRRRRRRRRRRRRR
GRROOWWLL
WHAT... WHAT'S THAT?
NOT GOOD...

"...NOT GOOD AT *ALL*."

CENTRAL CITY POLICE STATION.

YOU'RE KIDDING, RIGHT? THEY'RE ALREADY HOLDING PUBLIC DEMONSTRATIONS DENOUNCING ONE VIGILANTE. NOW *YOU* WANT TO GO BACK OUT THERE AND PLAY HERO?

THE DEMONSTRATIONS ARE *WHY* I WANT TO DO THIS. AND IT'S NOT A GAME. WITH FLASH MISSING, CENTRAL CITY *NEEDS* ME. IT NEEDS *THE PIED PIPER*.

THIS CITY DOES *NOT* NEED ANOTHER VIGILANTE. AND I DON'T NEED YOU SHOWING UP HERE WHERE PEOPLE CAN SEE US.

HARTLEY, IT'S BAD ENOUGH YOU SHOW UP AT MY *WORK*...BUT NOW YOU DROP *THIS* ON ME?

WHAT ARE YOU *AFRAID* OF?

SO THAT'S WHAT THIS IS ABOUT. YOU'RE WORRIED THAT PEOPLE WILL START *TALKING*.

THAT'S *NOT* IT. IT DOESN'T LOOK GOOD TO HAVE A PUBLICLY ACKNOWLEDGED *VIGILANTE* SHOWING UP--

STOP.

STOP TRYING TO MAKE THIS ABOUT THE PIED PIPER. THIS IS ABOUT *US.* YOU AND ME.

IF *YOU* CAN'T ACCEPT OUR RELATIONSHIP, HOW WILL ANYONE *ELSE*?

NOK NOK

I'M SORRY TO INTERRUPT, DIRECTOR--IT'S JUST THAT... I WAS HOPING YOU COULD SIGN OFF ON THIS *LEAVE OF ABSENCE*.

UH...IS THIS A BAD TIME?

NO...NO... WHATEVER YOU NEED, PATTY. UHM... JUST LEAVE IT HERE AND I'LL SIGN IT.

FINE, DAVID...KEEP YOUR *SECRETS*...

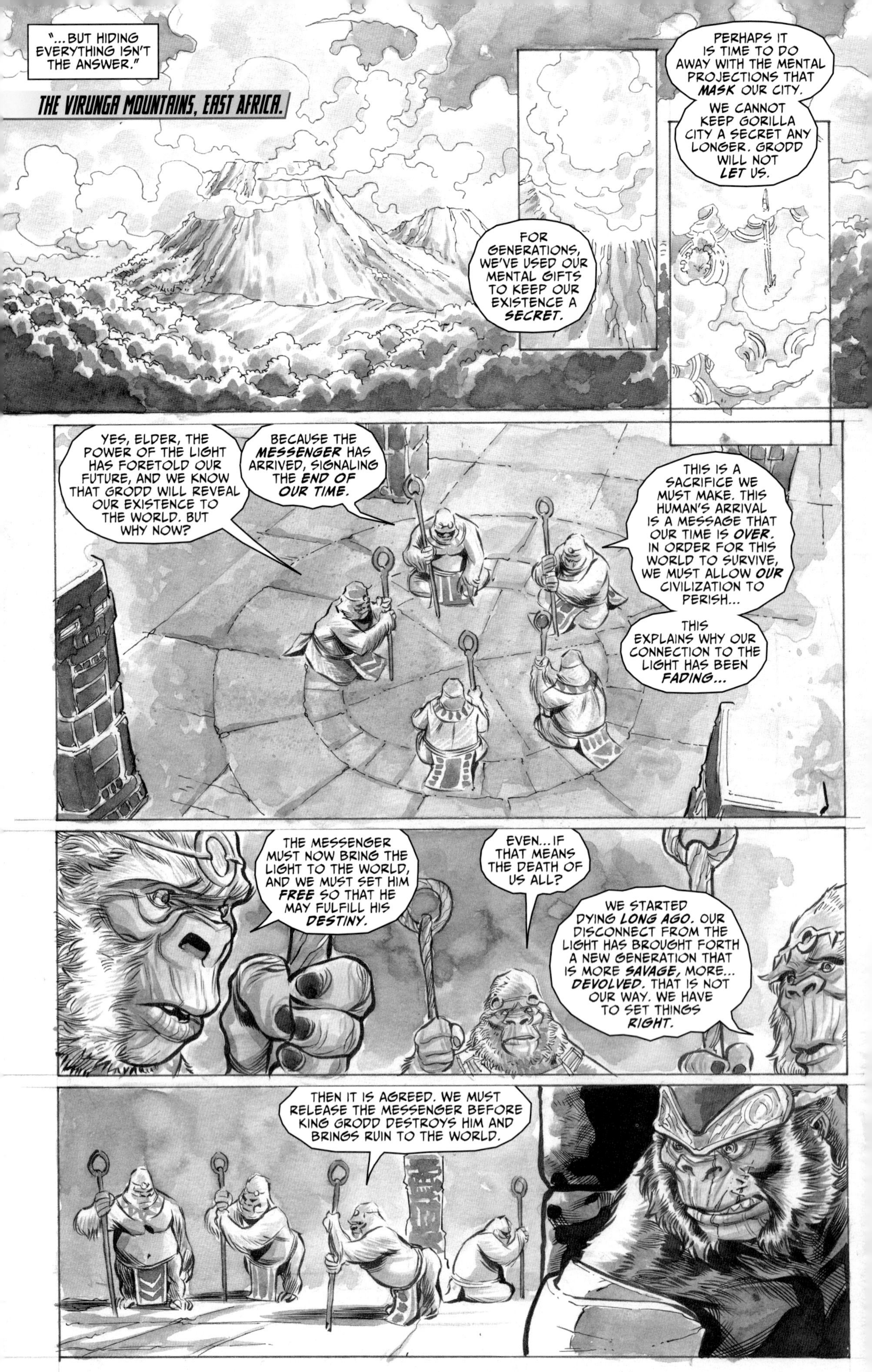
"...BUT HIDING EVERYTHING ISN'T THE ANSWER."
THE VIRUNGA MOUNTAINS, EAST AFRICA.
FOR GENERATIONS, WE'VE USED OUR MENTAL GIFTS TO KEEP OUR EXISTENCE A SECRET.
PERHAPS IT IS TIME TO DO AWAY WITH THE MENTAL PROJECTIONS THAT MASK OUR CITY.
WE CANNOT KEEP GORILLA CITY A SECRET ANY LONGER. GRODD WILL NOT LET US.
YES, ELDER, THE POWER OF THE LIGHT HAS FORETOLD OUR FUTURE, AND WE KNOW THAT GRODD WILL REVEAL OUR EXISTENCE TO THE WORLD. BUT WHY NOW?
BECAUSE THE MESSENGER HAS ARRIVED, SIGNALING THE END OF OUR TIME.
THIS IS A SACRIFICE WE MUST MAKE. THIS HUMAN'S ARRIVAL IS A MESSAGE THAT OUR TIME IS OVER. IN ORDER FOR THIS WORLD TO SURVIVE, WE MUST ALLOW OUR CIVILIZATION TO PERISH...
THIS EXPLAINS WHY OUR CONNECTION TO THE LIGHT HAS BEEN FADING...
THE MESSENGER MUST NOW BRING THE LIGHT TO THE WORLD, AND WE MUST SET HIM FREE SO THAT HE MAY FULFILL HIS DESTINY.
EVEN...IF THAT MEANS THE DEATH OF US ALL?
WE STARTED DYING LONG AGO. OUR DISCONNECT FROM THE LIGHT HAS BROUGHT FORTH A NEW GENERATION THAT IS MORE SAVAGE, MORE... DEVOLVED. THAT IS NOT OUR WAY. WE HAVE TO SET THINGS RIGHT.
THEN IT IS AGREED. WE MUST RELEASE THE MESSENGER BEFORE KING GRODD DESTROYS HIM AND BRINGS RUIN TO THE WORLD.

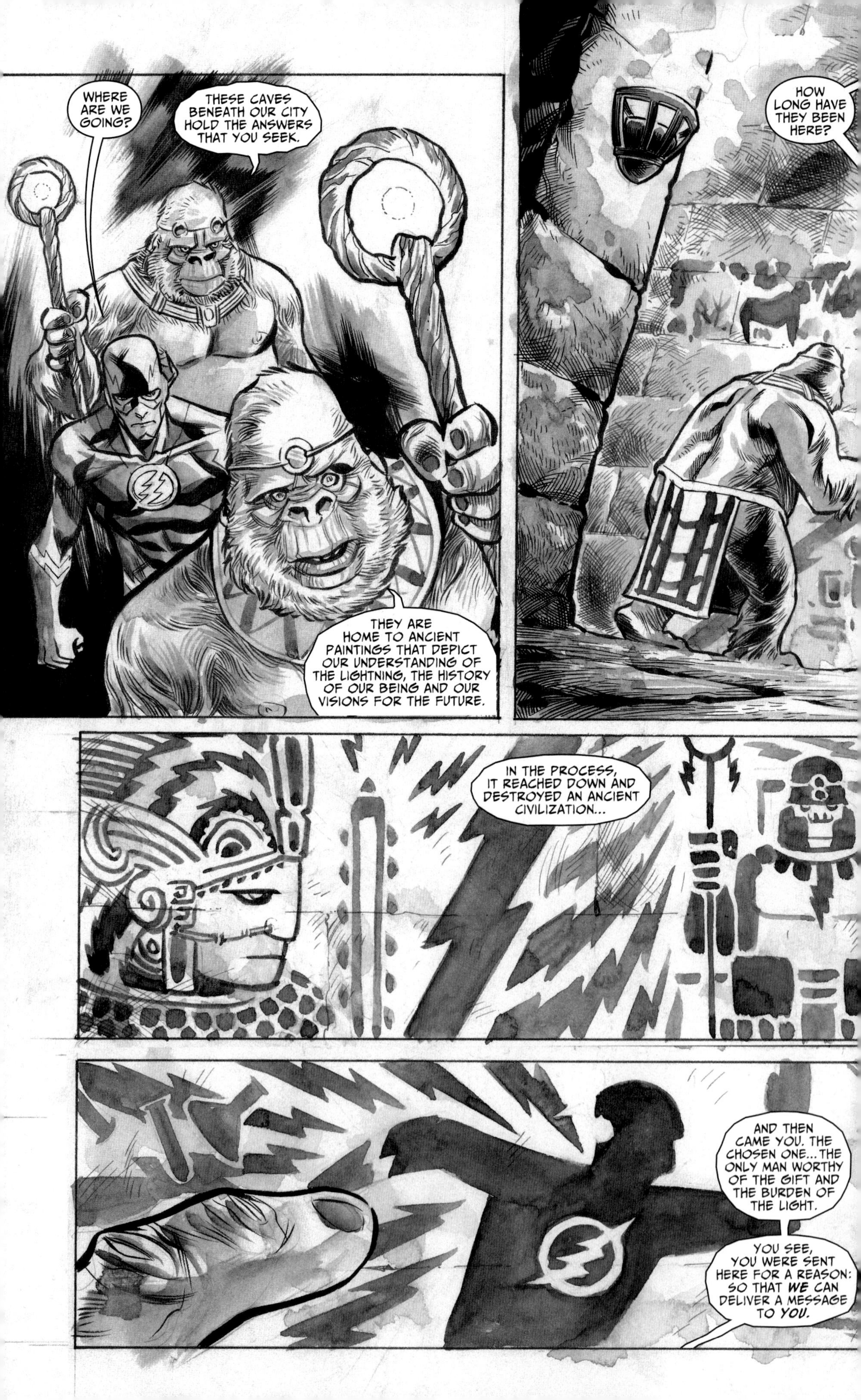
WHERE ARE WE GOING?
THESE CAVES BENEATH OUR CITY HOLD THE ANSWERS THAT YOU SEEK.
THEY ARE HOME TO ANCIENT PAINTINGS THAT DEPICT OUR UNDERSTANDING OF THE LIGHTNING, THE HISTORY OF OUR BEING AND OUR VISIONS FOR THE FUTURE.
HOW LONG HAVE THEY BEEN HERE?
IN THE PROCESS, IT REACHED DOWN AND DESTROYED AN ANCIENT CIVILIZATION...
AND THEN CAME YOU. THE CHOSEN ONE...THE ONLY MAN WORTHY OF THE GIFT AND THE BURDEN OF THE LIGHT.
YOU SEE, YOU WERE SENT HERE FOR A REASON: SO THAT *WE* CAN DELIVER A MESSAGE TO *YOU.*

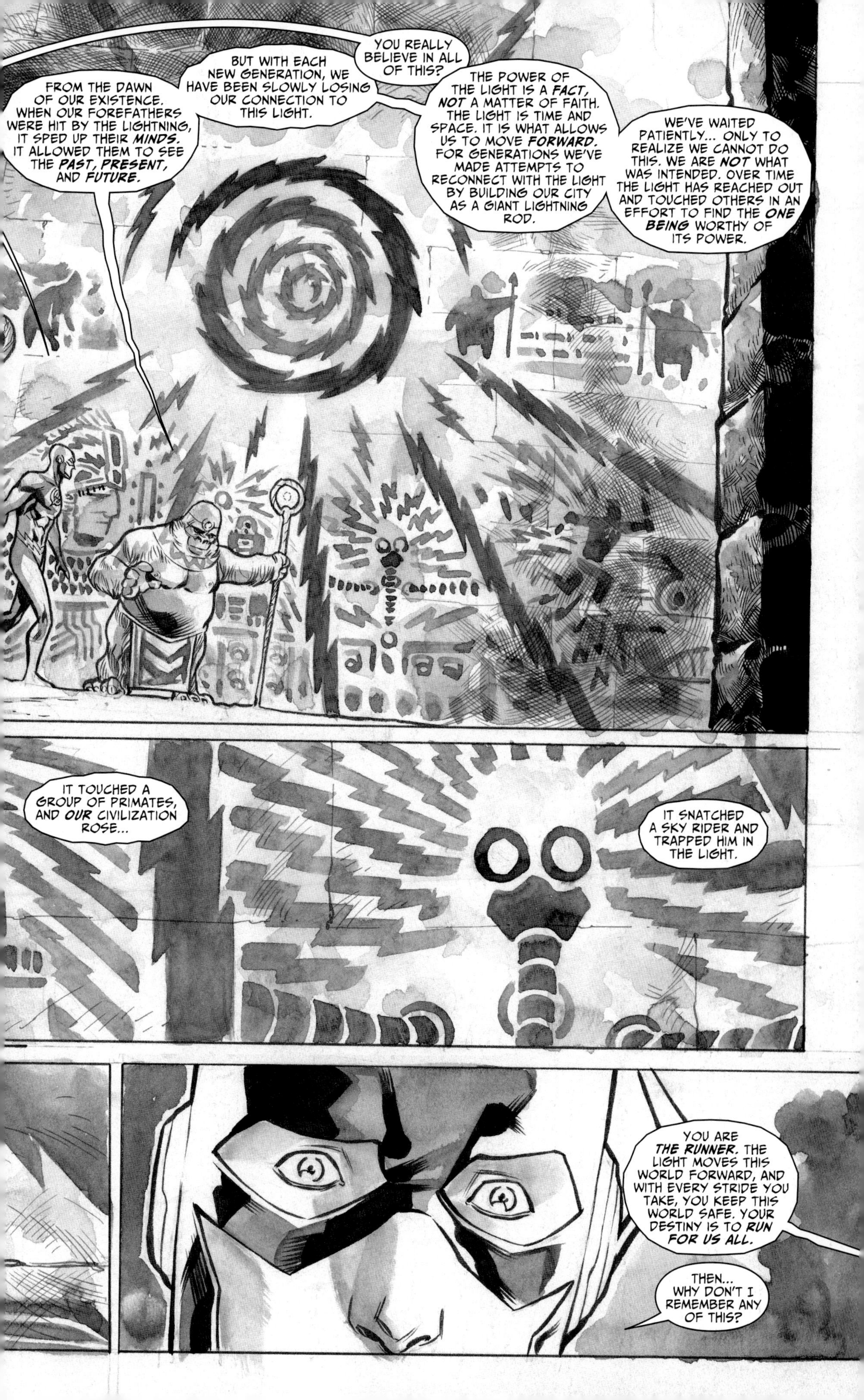
FROM THE DAWN OF OUR EXISTENCE. WHEN OUR FOREFATHERS WERE HIT BY THE LIGHTNING, IT SPED UP THEIR *MINDS.* IT ALLOWED THEM TO SEE THE *PAST, PRESENT,* AND *FUTURE.*
BUT WITH EACH NEW GENERATION, WE HAVE BEEN SLOWLY LOSING OUR CONNECTION TO THIS LIGHT.
YOU REALLY BELIEVE IN ALL OF THIS?
THE POWER OF THE LIGHT IS A *FACT, NOT* A MATTER OF FAITH. THE LIGHT IS TIME AND SPACE. IT IS WHAT ALLOWS US TO MOVE *FORWARD.* FOR GENERATIONS WE'VE MADE ATTEMPTS TO RECONNECT WITH THE LIGHT BY BUILDING OUR CITY AS A GIANT LIGHTNING ROD.
WE'VE WAITED PATIENTLY... ONLY TO REALIZE WE CANNOT DO THIS. WE ARE *NOT* WHAT WAS INTENDED. OVER TIME THE LIGHT HAS REACHED OUT AND TOUCHED OTHERS IN AN EFFORT TO FIND THE *ONE BEING* WORTHY OF ITS POWER.
IT TOUCHED A GROUP OF PRIMATES, AND *OUR* CIVILIZATION ROSE...
IT SNATCHED A SKY RIDER AND TRAPPED HIM IN THE LIGHT.
YOU ARE *THE RUNNER.* THE LIGHT MOVES THIS WORLD FORWARD, AND WITH EVERY STRIDE YOU TAKE, YOU KEEP THIS WORLD SAFE. YOUR DESTINY IS TO *RUN FOR US ALL.*
THEN... WHY DON'T I REMEMBER ANY OF THIS?

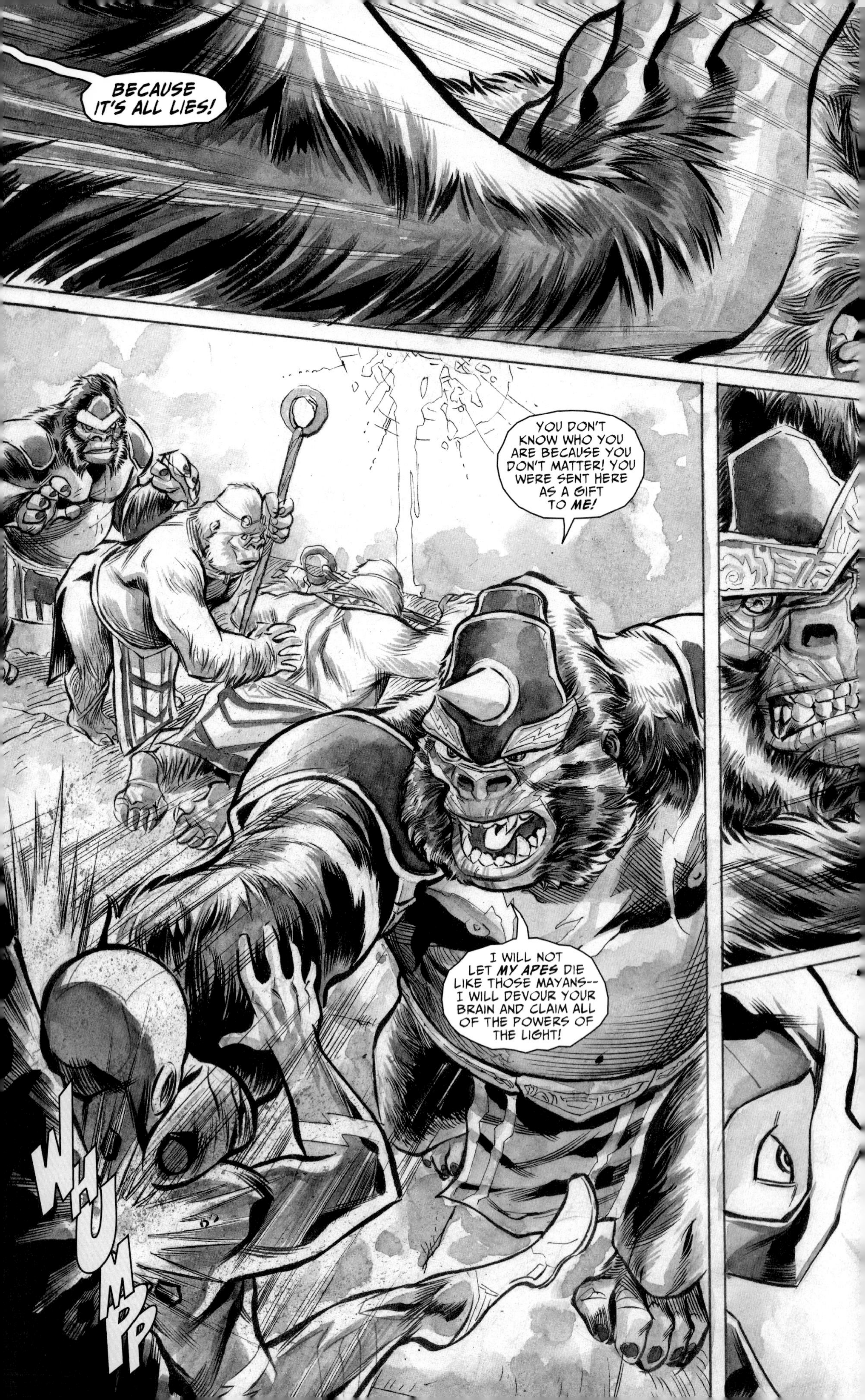
BECAUSE IT'S ALL LIES!
YOU DON'T KNOW WHO YOU ARE BECAUSE YOU DON'T MATTER! YOU WERE SENT HERE AS A GIFT TO ME!
I WILL NOT LET MY APES DIE LIKE THOSE MAYANS-- I WILL DEVOUR YOUR BRAIN AND CLAIM ALL OF THE POWERS OF THE LIGHT!
WHUMPP

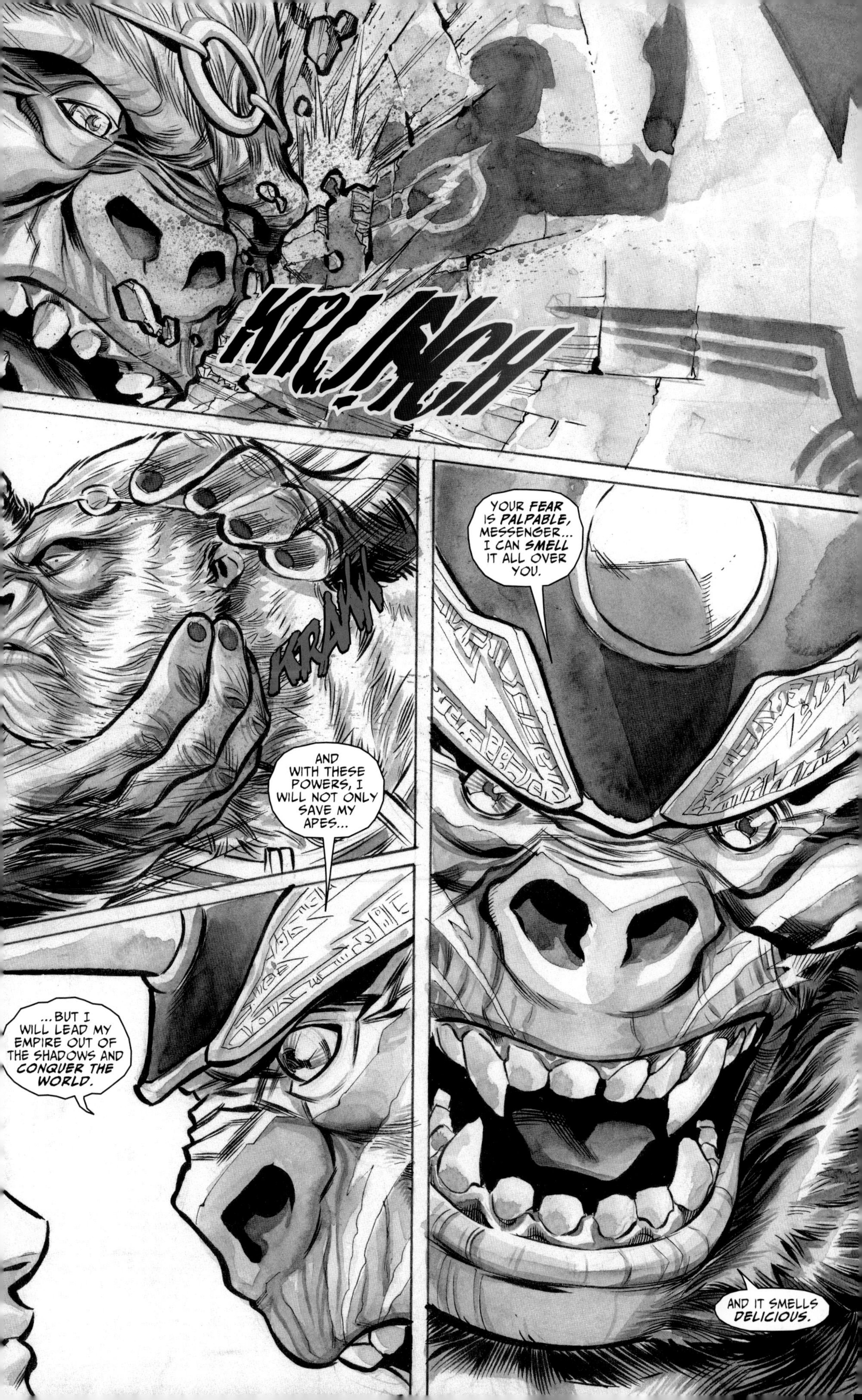

KRUNCH
KRAKK
YOUR FEAR IS PALPABLE, MESSENGER... I CAN SMELL IT ALL OVER YOU.
AND WITH THESE POWERS, I WILL NOT ONLY SAVE MY APES...
...BUT I WILL LEAD MY EMPIRE OUT OF THE SHADOWS AND CONQUER THE WORLD.
AND IT SMELLS DELICIOUS.

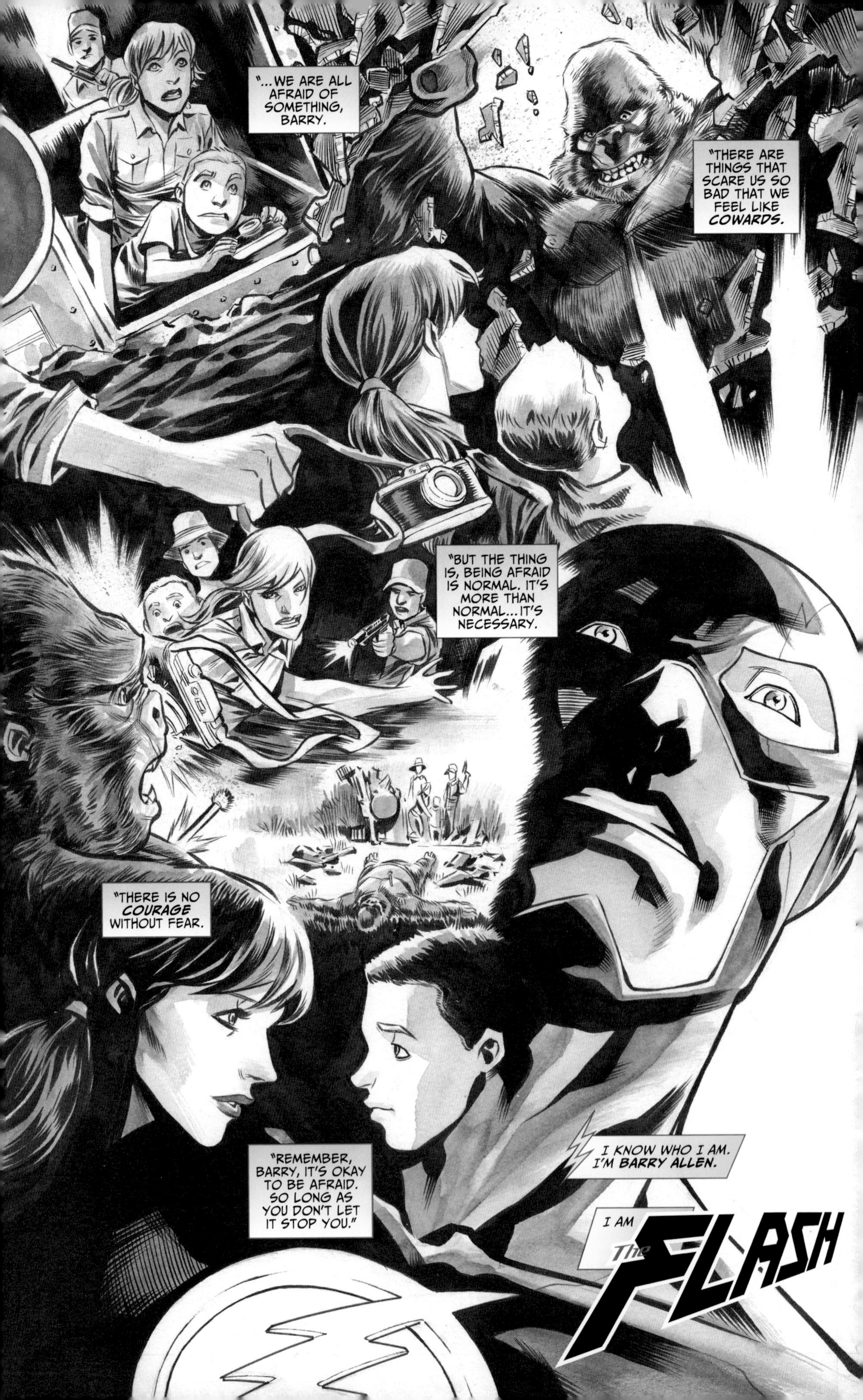
"...WE ARE ALL AFRAID OF SOMETHING, BARRY.
"THERE ARE THINGS THAT SCARE US SO BAD THAT WE FEEL LIKE *COWARDS.*
"BUT THE THING IS, BEING AFRAID IS NORMAL. IT'S MORE THAN NORMAL...IT'S NECESSARY.
"THERE IS NO *COURAGE* WITHOUT FEAR.
"REMEMBER, BARRY, IT'S OKAY TO BE AFRAID. SO LONG AS YOU DON'T LET IT STOP YOU."
I KNOW WHO I AM. I'M *BARRY ALLEN.*
I AM
The FLASH

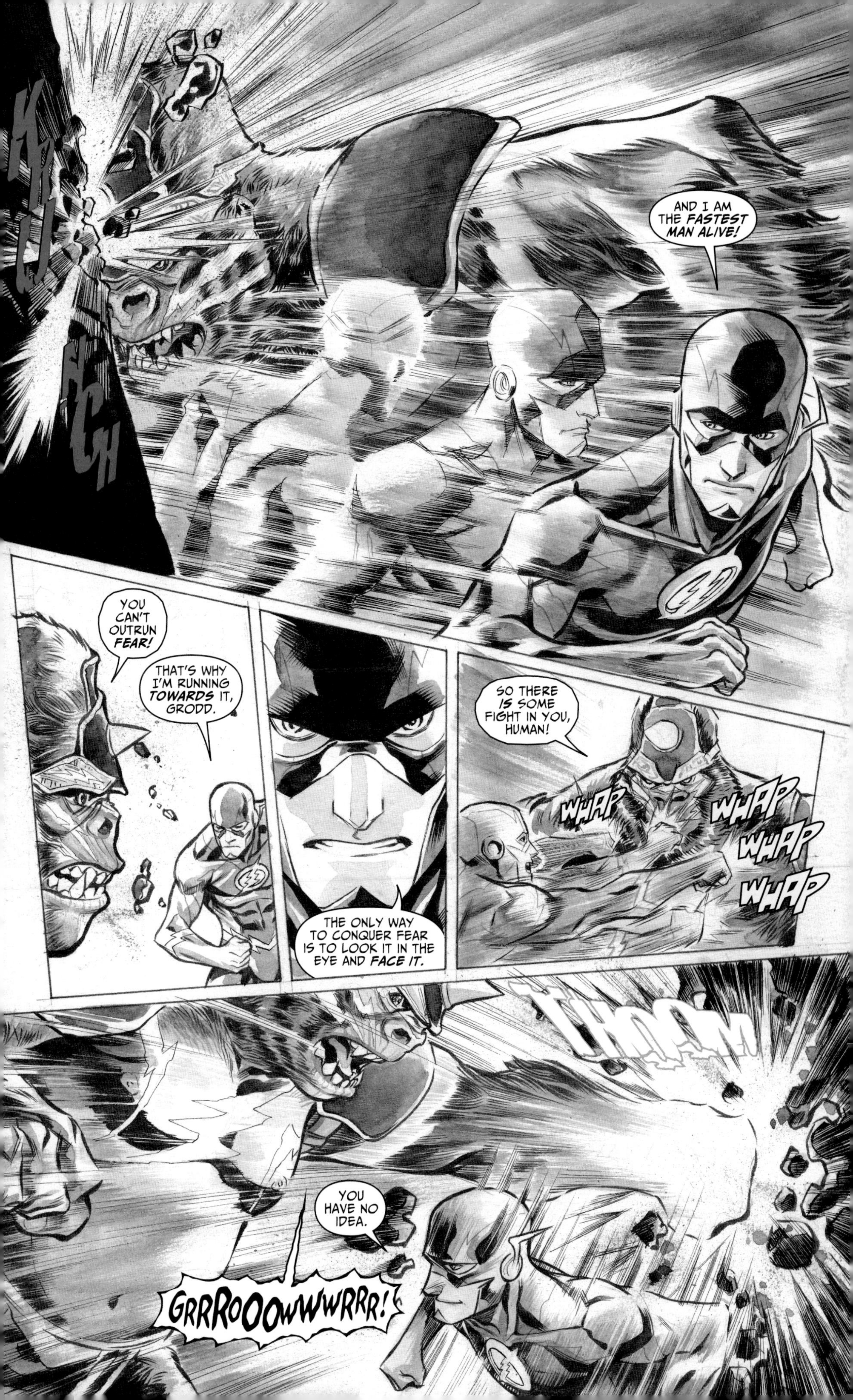
KRUNCH
AND I AM THE FASTEST MAN ALIVE!
YOU CAN'T OUTRUN FEAR!
THAT'S WHY I'M RUNNING TOWARDS IT, GRODD.
THE ONLY WAY TO CONQUER FEAR IS TO LOOK IT IN THE EYE AND FACE IT.
SO THERE IS SOME FIGHT IN YOU, HUMAN!
WHAP
WHAP
WHAP
WHAP
THOOM
YOU HAVE NO IDEA.
GRRROOOWWWRRR!

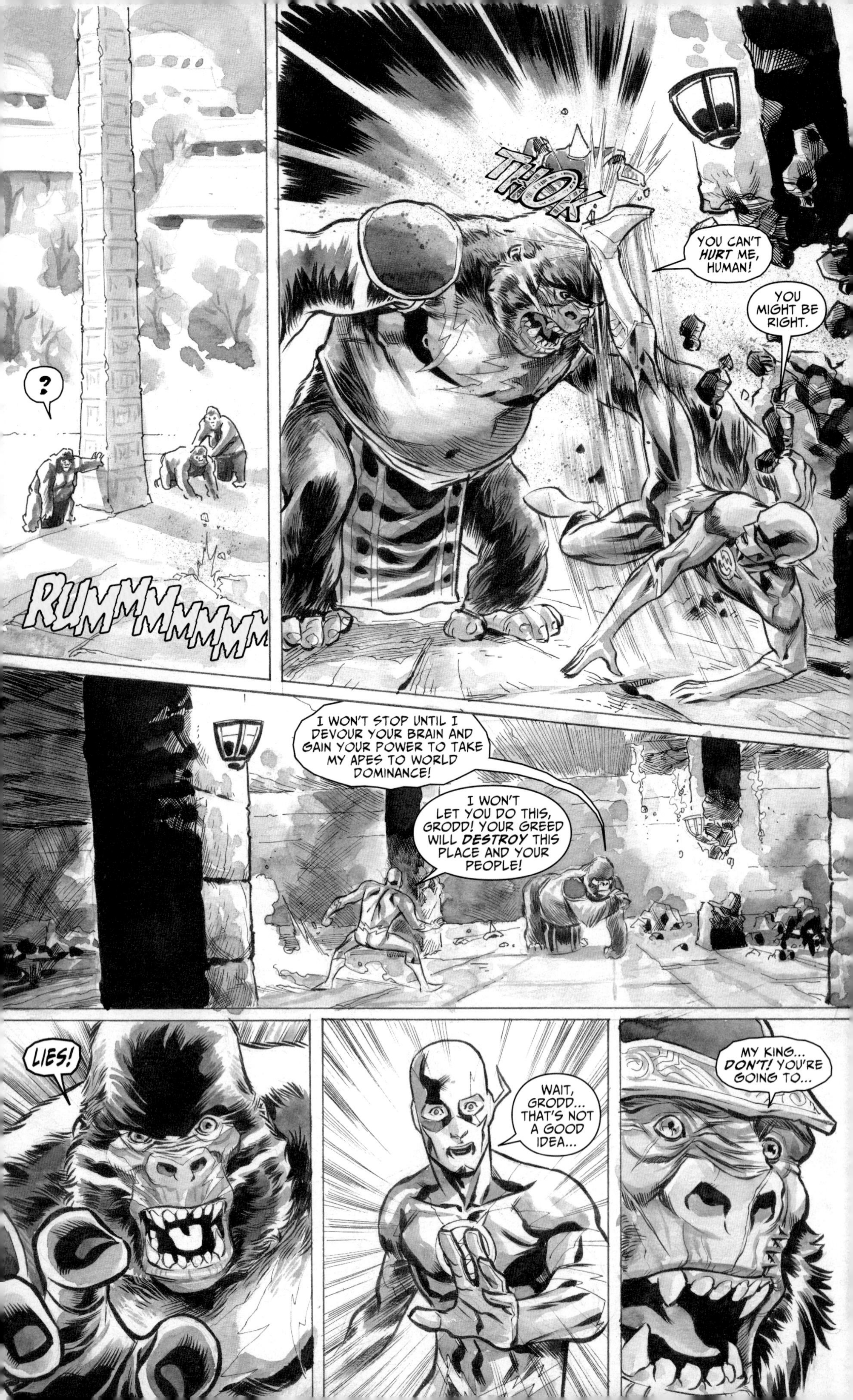
?
RUMMMMMMMMM
THOK
YOU CAN'T HURT ME, HUMAN!
YOU MIGHT BE RIGHT.
I WON'T STOP UNTIL I DEVOUR YOUR BRAIN AND GAIN YOUR POWER TO TAKE MY APES TO WORLD DOMINANCE!
I WON'T LET YOU DO THIS, GRODD! YOUR GREED WILL DESTROY THIS PLACE AND YOUR PEOPLE!
LIES!
WAIT, GRODD... THAT'S NOT A GOOD IDEA...
MY KING... DON'T! YOU'RE GOING TO...

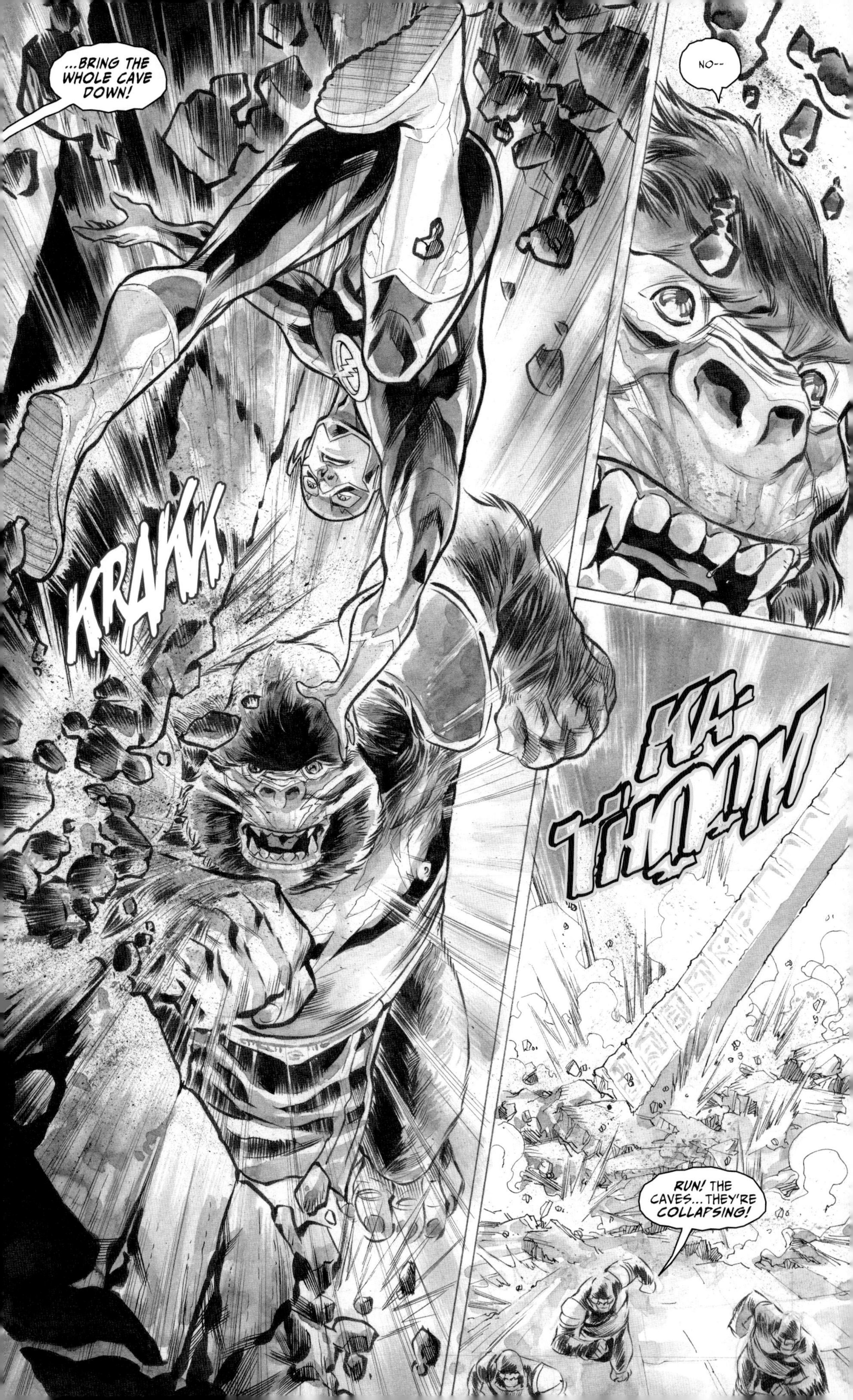
...BRING THE WHOLE CAVE DOWN!
NO--
KRAKK
KA-THOOM
RUN! THE CAVES... THEY'RE COLLAPSING!

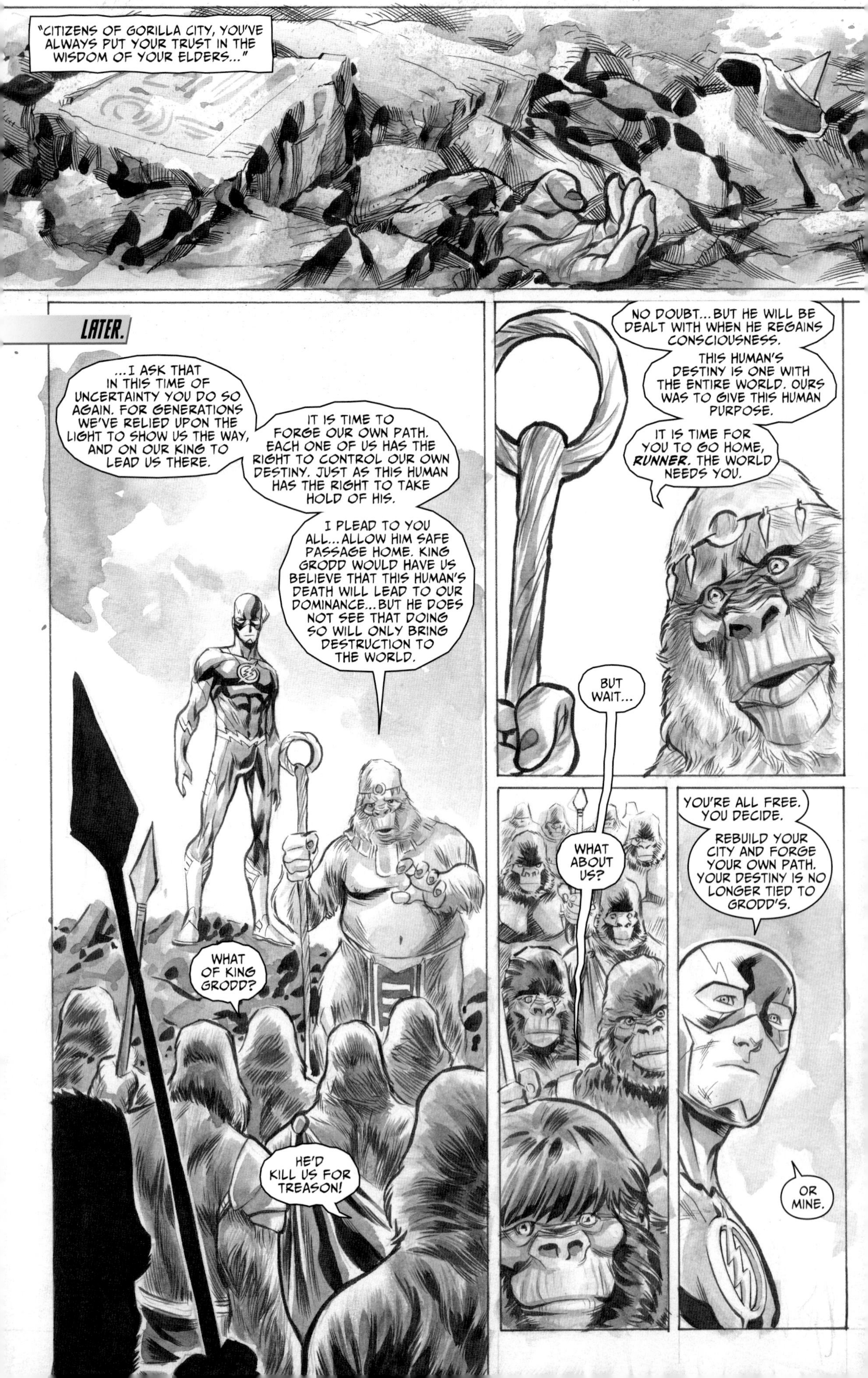

"CITIZENS OF GORILLA CITY, YOU'VE ALWAYS PUT YOUR TRUST IN THE WISDOM OF YOUR ELDERS..."
LATER.
...I ASK THAT IN THIS TIME OF UNCERTAINTY YOU DO SO AGAIN. FOR GENERATIONS WE'VE RELIED UPON THE LIGHT TO SHOW US THE WAY, AND ON OUR KING TO LEAD US THERE.
IT IS TIME TO FORGE OUR OWN PATH. EACH ONE OF US HAS THE RIGHT TO CONTROL OUR OWN DESTINY. JUST AS THIS HUMAN HAS THE RIGHT TO TAKE HOLD OF HIS.
I PLEAD TO YOU ALL...ALLOW HIM SAFE PASSAGE HOME. KING GRODD WOULD HAVE US BELIEVE THAT THIS HUMAN'S DEATH WILL LEAD TO OUR DOMINANCE...BUT HE DOES NOT SEE THAT DOING SO WILL ONLY BRING DESTRUCTION TO THE WORLD.
WHAT OF KING GRODD?
HE'D KILL US FOR TREASON!
NO DOUBT...BUT HE WILL BE DEALT WITH WHEN HE REGAINS CONSCIOUSNESS.
THIS HUMAN'S DESTINY IS ONE WITH THE ENTIRE WORLD. OURS WAS TO GIVE THIS HUMAN PURPOSE.
IT IS TIME FOR YOU TO GO HOME, RUNNER. THE WORLD NEEDS YOU.
BUT WAIT...
WHAT ABOUT US?
YOU'RE ALL FREE. YOU DECIDE.
REBUILD YOUR CITY AND FORGE YOUR OWN PATH. YOUR DESTINY IS NO LONGER TIED TO GRODD'S.
OR MINE.

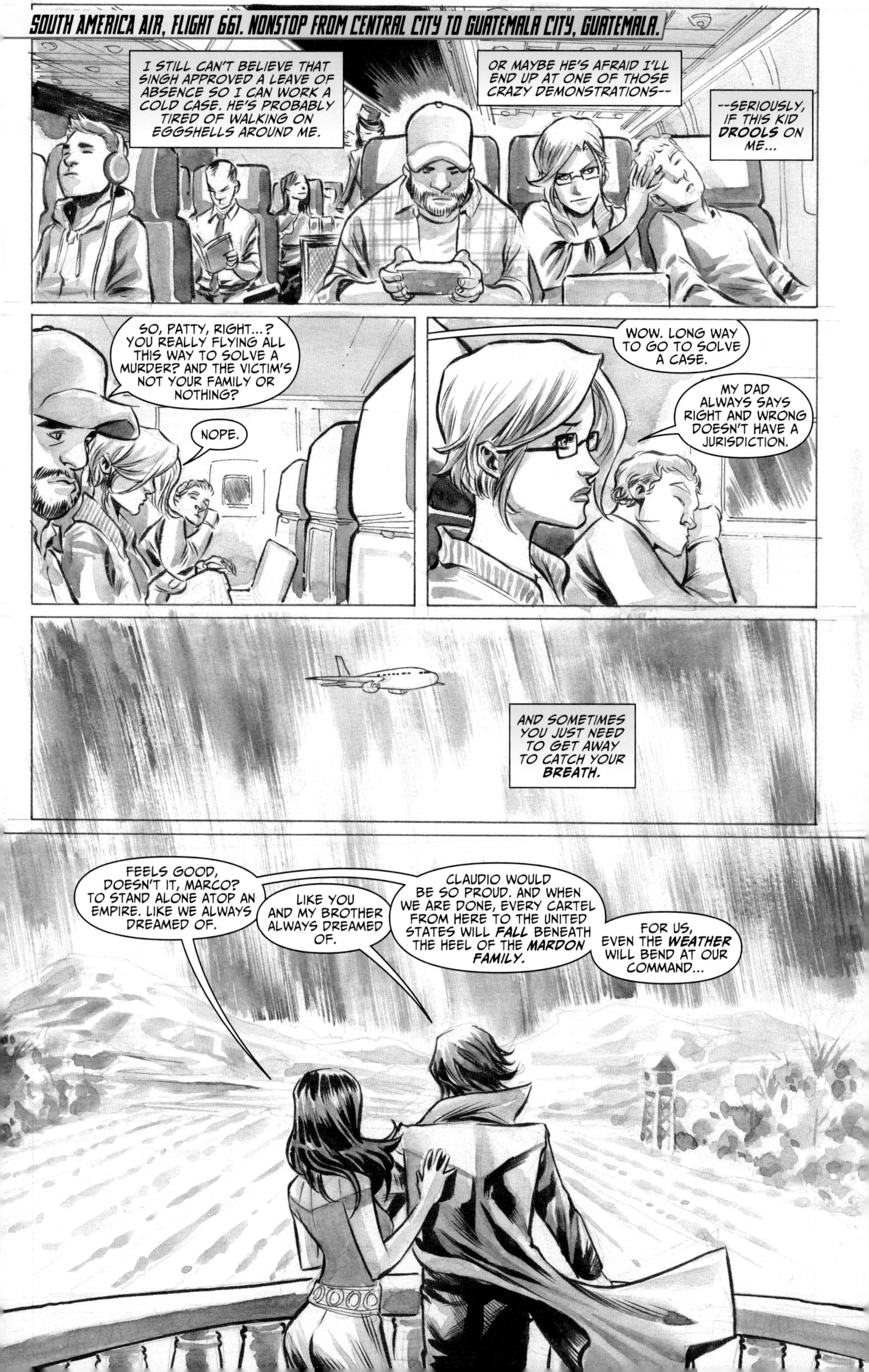

SOUTH AMERICA AIR, FLIGHT 661. NONSTOP FROM CENTRAL CITY TO GUATEMALA CITY, GUATEMALA.
I STILL CAN'T BELIEVE THAT SINGH APPROVED A LEAVE OF ABSENCE SO I CAN WORK A COLD CASE. HE'S PROBABLY TIRED OF WALKING ON EGGSHELLS AROUND ME.
OR MAYBE HE'S AFRAID I'LL END UP AT ONE OF THOSE CRAZY DEMONSTRATIONS--
--SERIOUSLY, IF THIS KID DROOLS ON ME...
SO, PATTY, RIGHT...? YOU REALLY FLYING ALL THIS WAY TO SOLVE A MURDER? AND THE VICTIM'S NOT YOUR FAMILY OR NOTHING?
NOPE.
WOW. LONG WAY TO GO TO SOLVE A CASE.
MY DAD ALWAYS SAYS RIGHT AND WRONG DOESN'T HAVE A JURISDICTION.
AND SOMETIMES YOU JUST NEED TO GET AWAY TO CATCH YOUR BREATH.
FEELS GOOD, DOESN'T IT, MARCO? TO STAND ALONE ATOP AN EMPIRE. LIKE WE ALWAYS DREAMED OF.
LIKE YOU AND MY BROTHER ALWAYS DREAMED OF.
CLAUDIO WOULD BE SO PROUD. AND WHEN WE ARE DONE, EVERY CARTEL FROM HERE TO THE UNITED STATES WILL FALL BENEATH THE HEEL OF THE MARDON FAMILY.
FOR US, EVEN THE WEATHER WILL BEND AT OUR COMMAND...

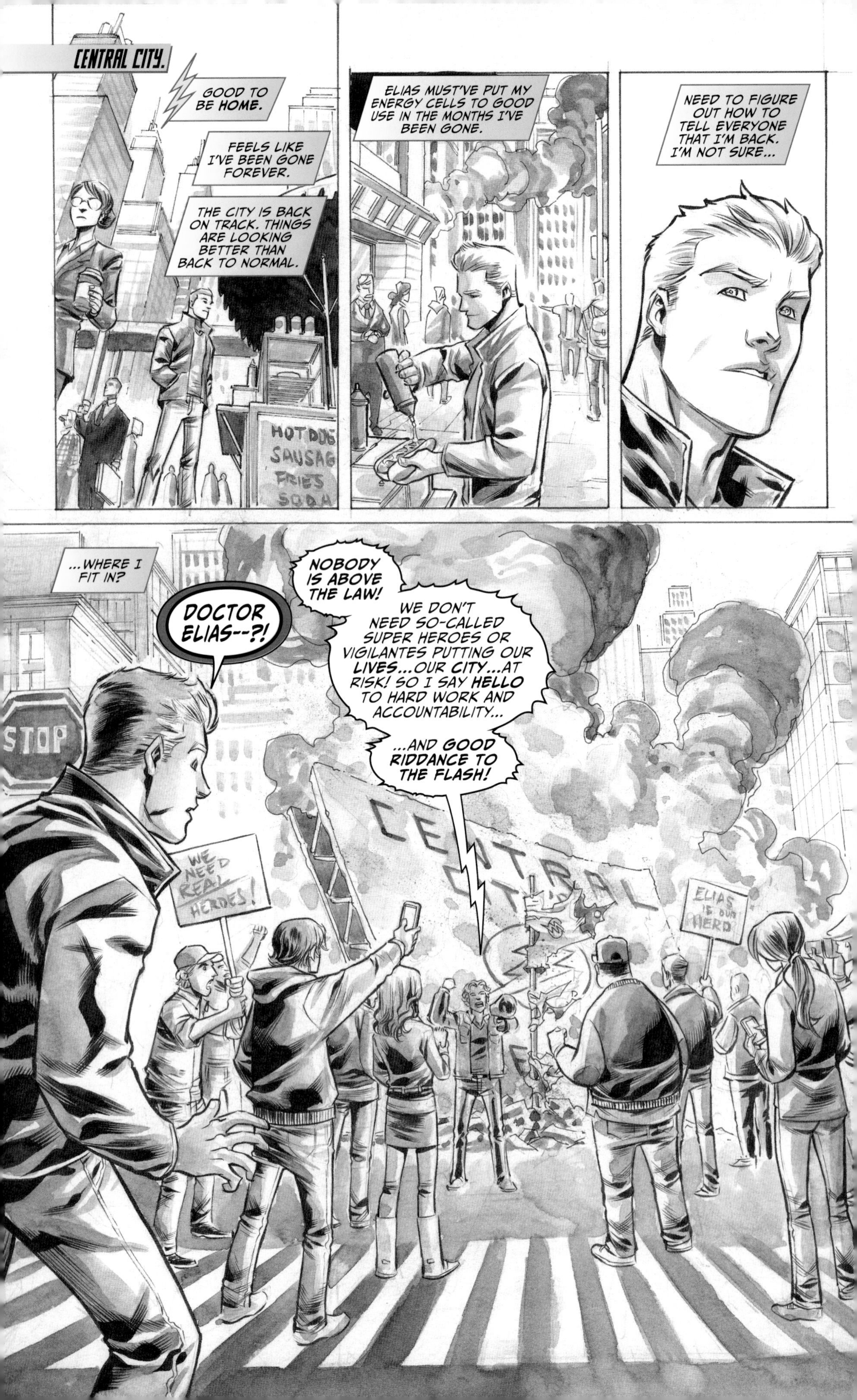
CENTRAL CITY.
GOOD TO BE HOME.
FEELS LIKE I'VE BEEN GONE FOREVER.
THE CITY IS BACK ON TRACK. THINGS ARE LOOKING BETTER THAN BACK TO NORMAL.
HOT DOG SAUSAG FRIES SODA
ELIAS MUST'VE PUT MY ENERGY CELLS TO GOOD USE IN THE MONTHS I'VE BEEN GONE.
NEED TO FIGURE OUT HOW TO TELL EVERYONE THAT I'M BACK. I'M NOT SURE...
...WHERE I FIT IN?
DOCTOR ELIAS--?!
NOBODY IS ABOVE THE LAW!
WE DON'T NEED SO-CALLED SUPER HEROES OR VIGILANTES PUTTING OUR LIVES...OUR CITY...AT RISK! SO I SAY HELLO TO HARD WORK AND ACCOUNTABILITY...
...AND GOOD RIDDANCE TO THE FLASH!
STOP
WE NEED REAL HEROES!
CENTRAL CITY
ELIAS IS OUR HERO

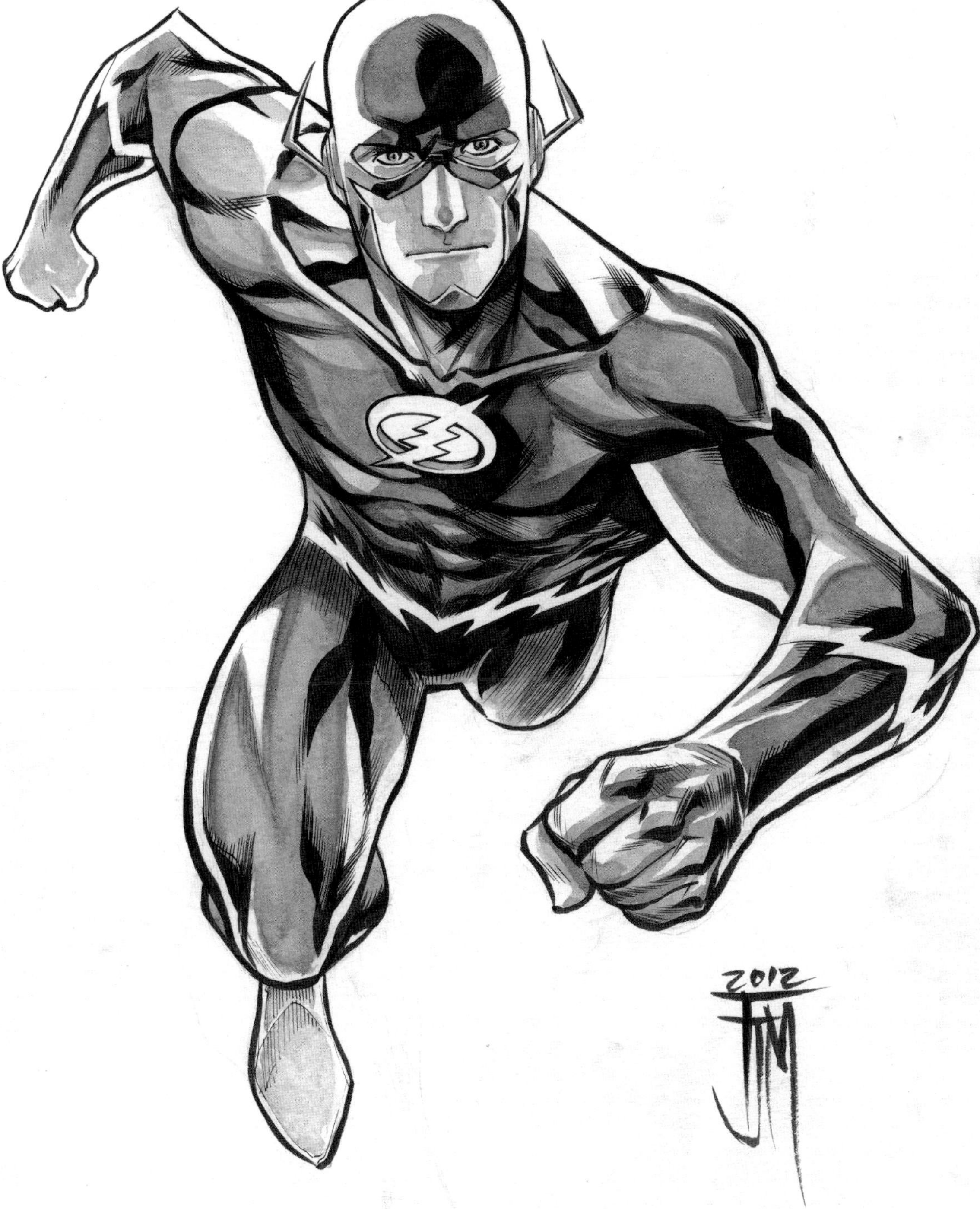
2012

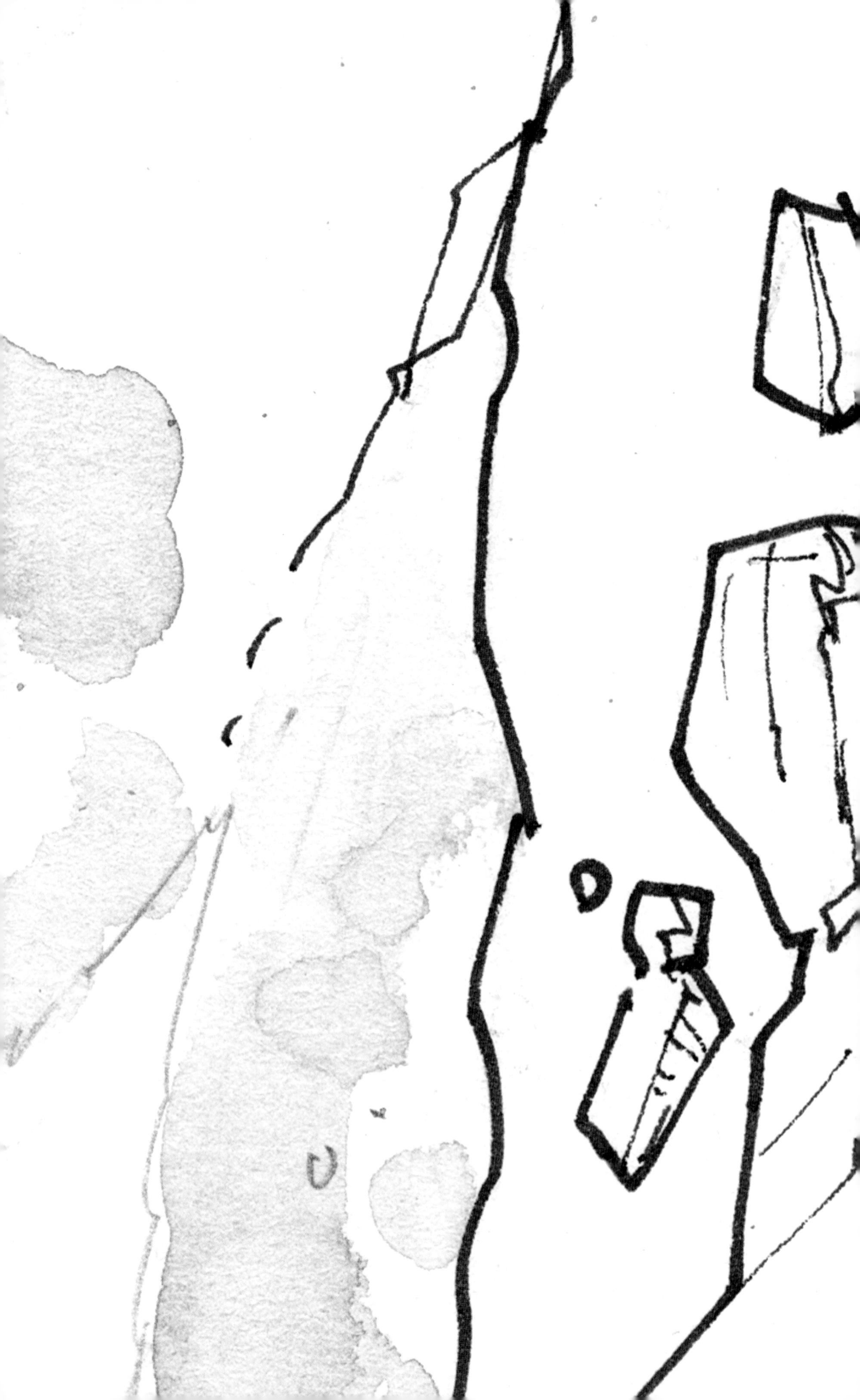

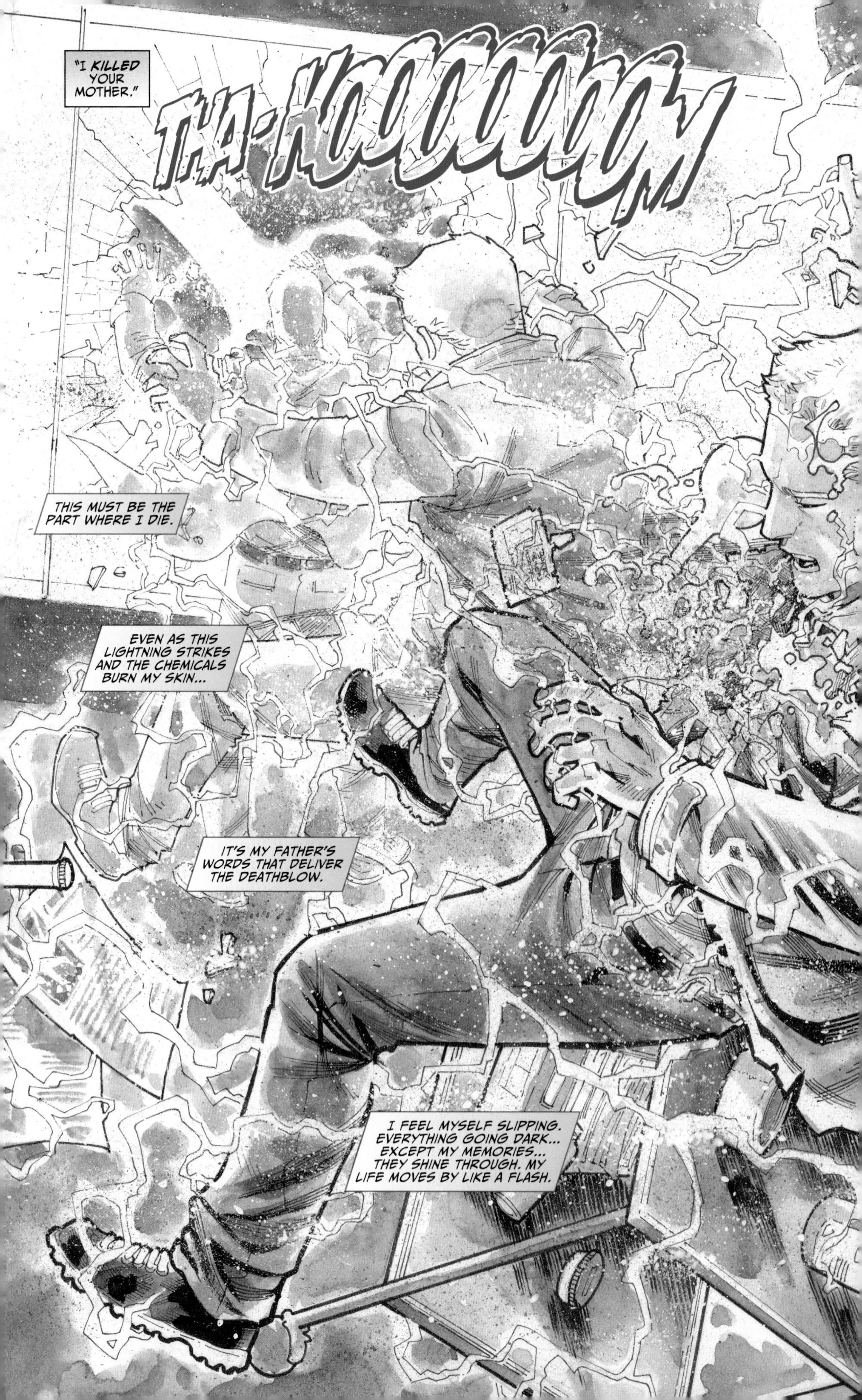
"I KILLED YOUR MOTHER."
TA-KOOOOOOM
THIS MUST BE THE PART WHERE I DIE.
EVEN AS THIS LIGHTNING STRIKES AND THE CHEMICALS BURN MY SKIN...
IT'S MY FATHER'S WORDS THAT DELIVER THE DEATHBLOW.
I FEEL MYSELF SLIPPING. EVERYTHING GOING DARK... EXCEPT MY MEMORIES... THEY SHINE THROUGH. MY LIFE MOVES BY LIKE A FLASH.

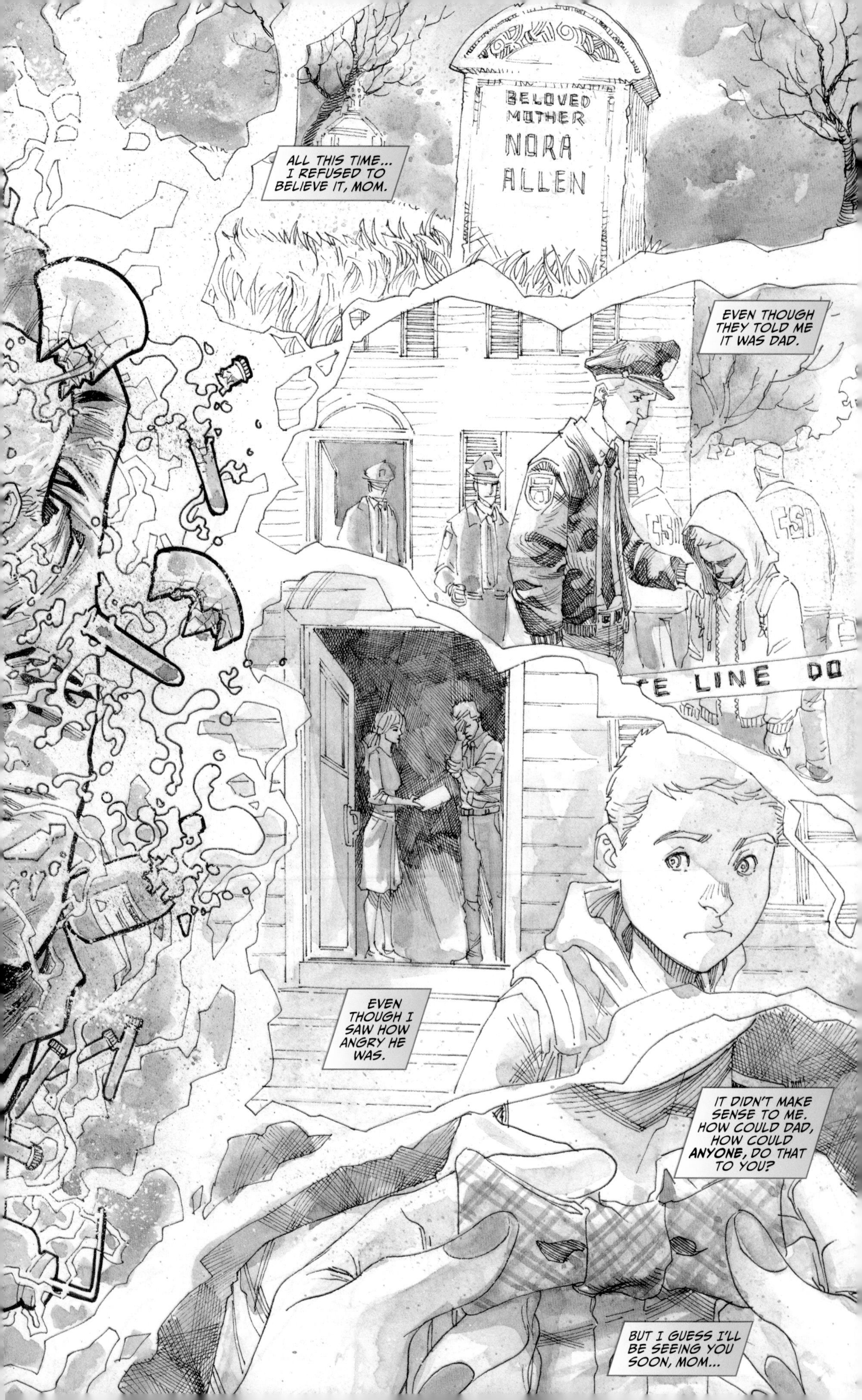
BELOVED MOTHER NORA ALLEN
ALL THIS TIME... I REFUSED TO BELIEVE IT, MOM.
EVEN THOUGH THEY TOLD ME IT WAS DAD.
CSI
CSI
E LINE DO
EVEN THOUGH I SAW HOW ANGRY HE WAS.
IT DIDN'T MAKE SENSE TO ME. HOW COULD DAD, HOW COULD ANYONE, DO THAT TO YOU?
BUT I GUESS I'LL BE SEEING YOU SOON, MOM...

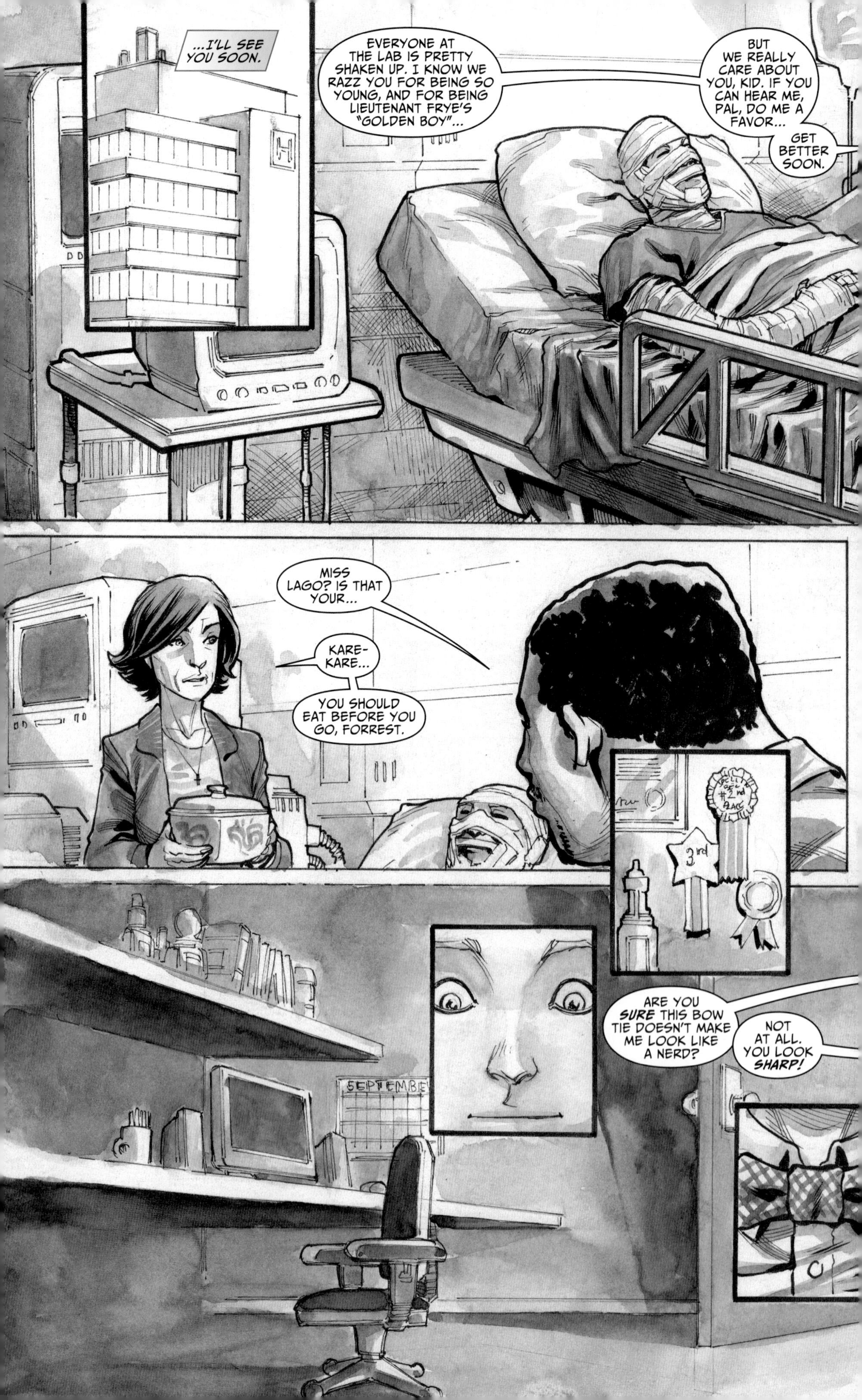
...I'LL SEE YOU SOON.
EVERYONE AT THE LAB IS PRETTY SHAKEN UP. I KNOW WE RAZZ YOU FOR BEING SO YOUNG, AND FOR BEING LIEUTENANT FRYE'S "GOLDEN BOY"...
BUT WE REALLY CARE ABOUT YOU, KID. IF YOU CAN HEAR ME, PAL, DO ME A FAVOR...
GET BETTER SOON.
MISS LAGO? IS THAT YOUR...
KARE-KARE...
YOU SHOULD EAT BEFORE YOU GO, FORREST.
3rd
ARE YOU SURE THIS BOW TIE DOESN'T MAKE ME LOOK LIKE A NERD?
NOT AT ALL. YOU LOOK SHARP!

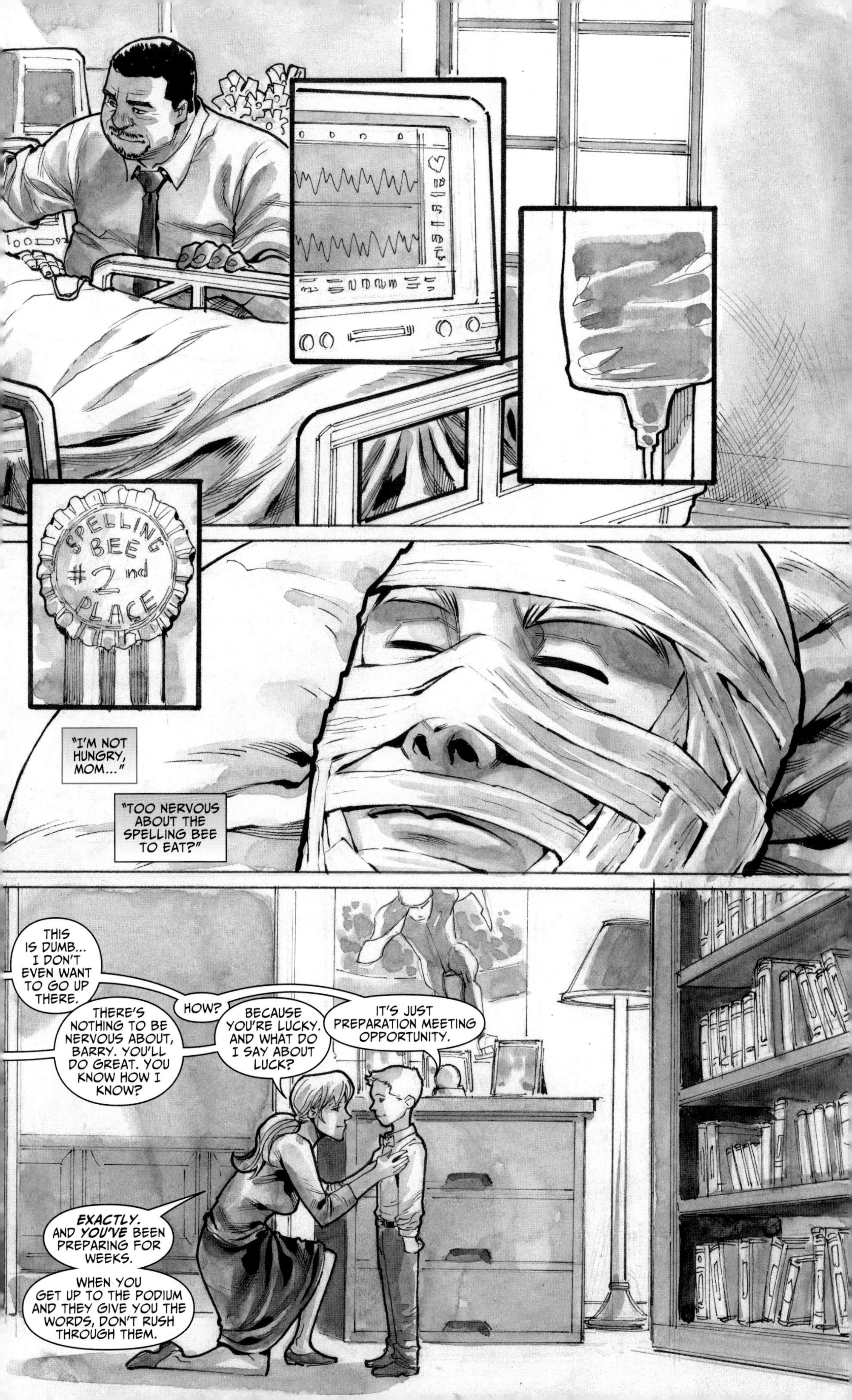
SPELLING BEE #2nd PLACE
"I'M NOT HUNGRY, MOM..."
"TOO NERVOUS ABOUT THE SPELLING BEE TO EAT?"
THIS IS DUMB... I DON'T EVEN WANT TO GO UP THERE.
THERE'S NOTHING TO BE NERVOUS ABOUT, BARRY. YOU'LL DO GREAT. YOU KNOW HOW I KNOW?
HOW?
BECAUSE YOU'RE LUCKY. AND WHAT DO I SAY ABOUT LUCK?
IT'S JUST PREPARATION MEETING OPPORTUNITY.
EXACTLY. AND YOU'VE BEEN PREPARING FOR WEEKS.
WHEN YOU GET UP TO THE PODIUM AND THEY GIVE YOU THE WORDS, DON'T RUSH THROUGH THEM.

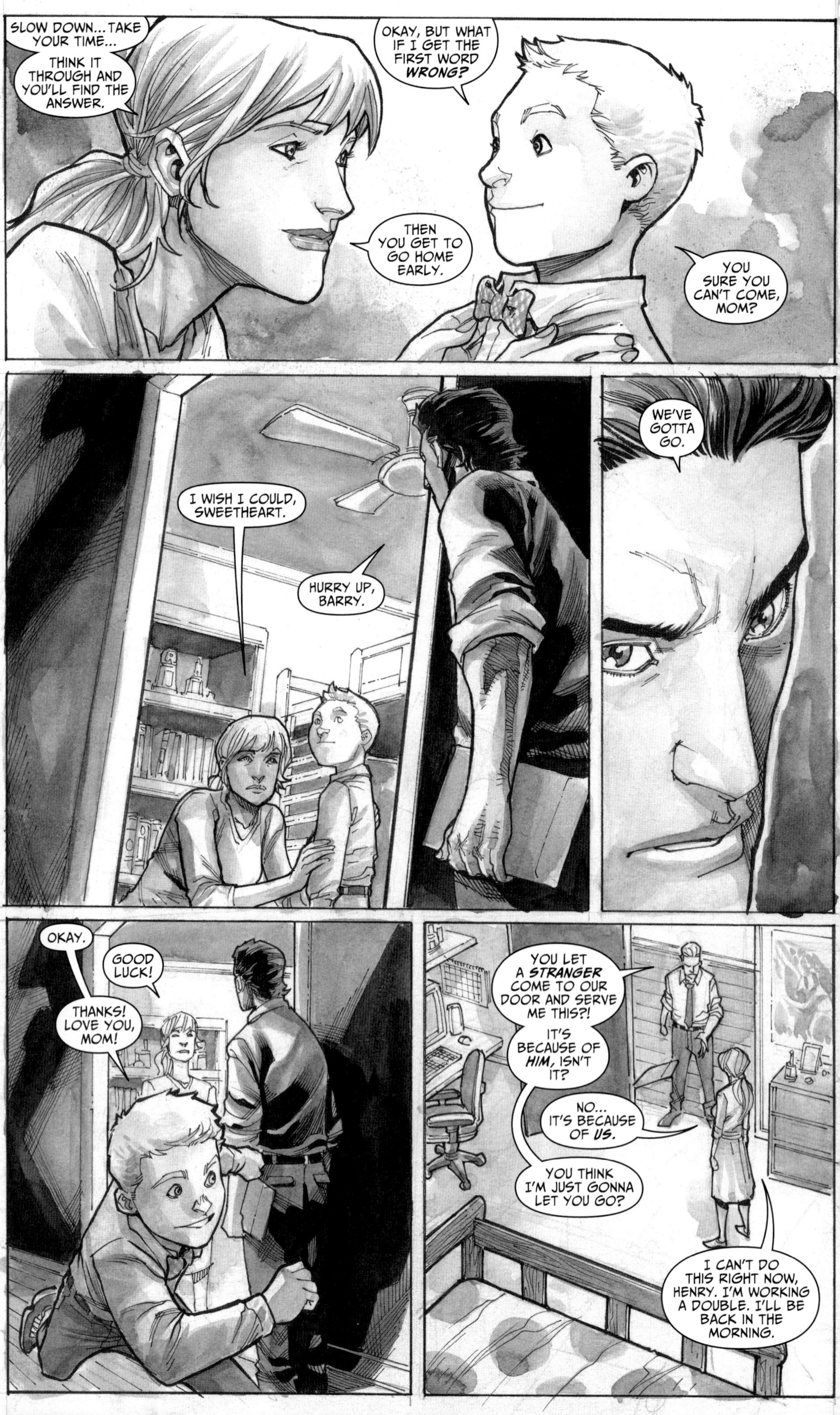
SLOW DOWN...TAKE YOUR TIME...
THINK IT THROUGH AND YOU'LL FIND THE ANSWER.
OKAY, BUT WHAT IF I GET THE FIRST WORD WRONG?
THEN YOU GET TO GO HOME EARLY.
YOU SURE YOU CAN'T COME, MOM?
I WISH I COULD, SWEETHEART.
HURRY UP, BARRY.
WE'VE GOTTA GO.
OKAY.
GOOD LUCK!
THANKS! LOVE YOU, MOM!
YOU LET A STRANGER COME TO OUR DOOR AND SERVE ME THIS?!
IT'S BECAUSE OF HIM, ISN'T IT?
NO... IT'S BECAUSE OF US.
YOU THINK I'M JUST GONNA LET YOU GO?
I CAN'T DO THIS RIGHT NOW, HENRY. I'M WORKING A DOUBLE. I'LL BE BACK IN THE MORNING.

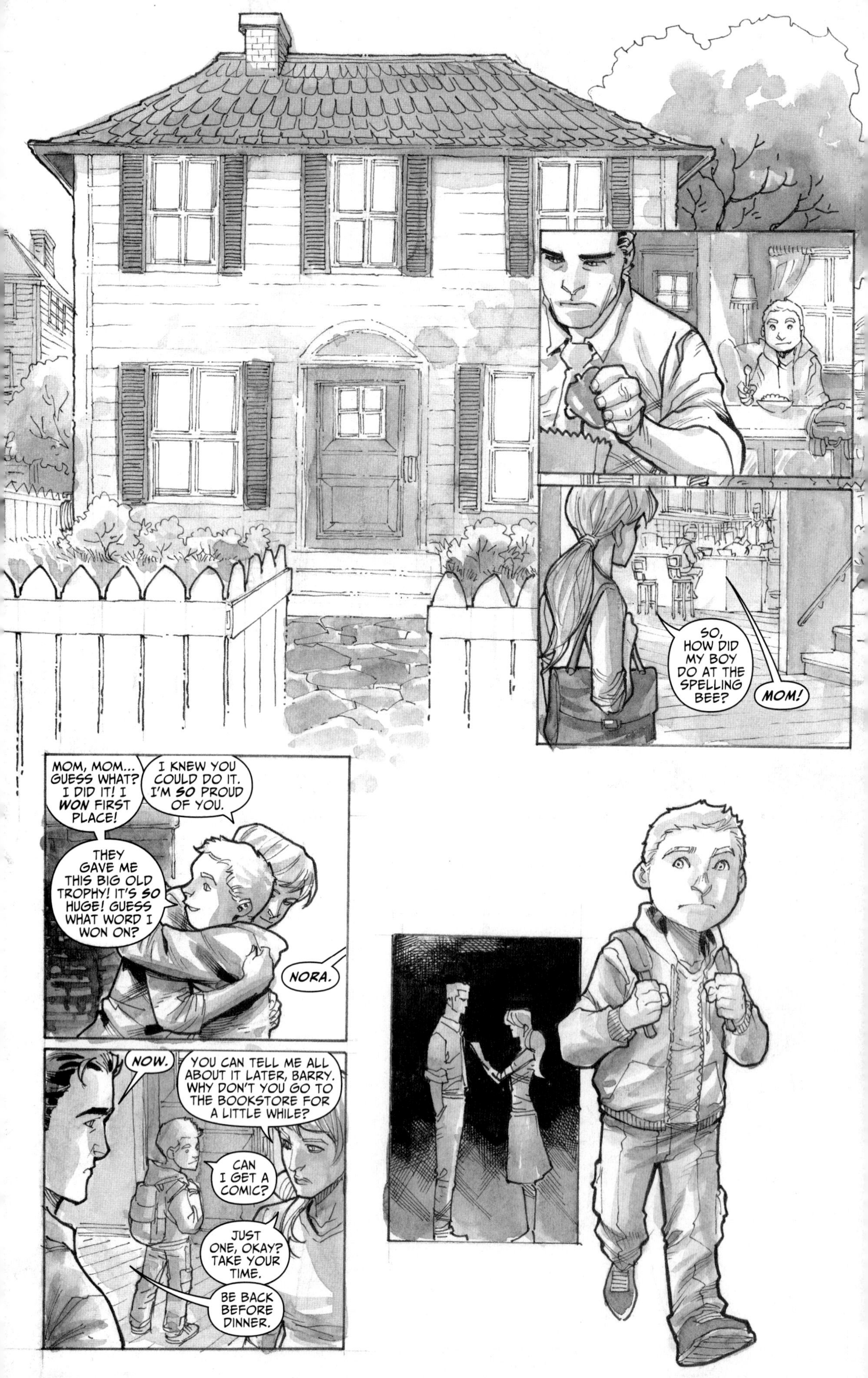
SO, HOW DID MY BOY DO AT THE SPELLING BEE?
MOM!
MOM, MOM... GUESS WHAT? I DID IT! I WON FIRST PLACE!
I KNEW YOU COULD DO IT. I'M SO PROUD OF YOU.
THEY GAVE ME THIS BIG OLD TROPHY! IT'S SO HUGE! GUESS WHAT WORD I WON ON?
NORA.
NOW.
YOU CAN TELL ME ALL ABOUT IT LATER, BARRY. WHY DON'T YOU GO TO THE BOOKSTORE FOR A LITTLE WHILE?
CAN I GET A COMIC?
JUST ONE, OKAY? TAKE YOUR TIME.
BE BACK BEFORE DINNER.

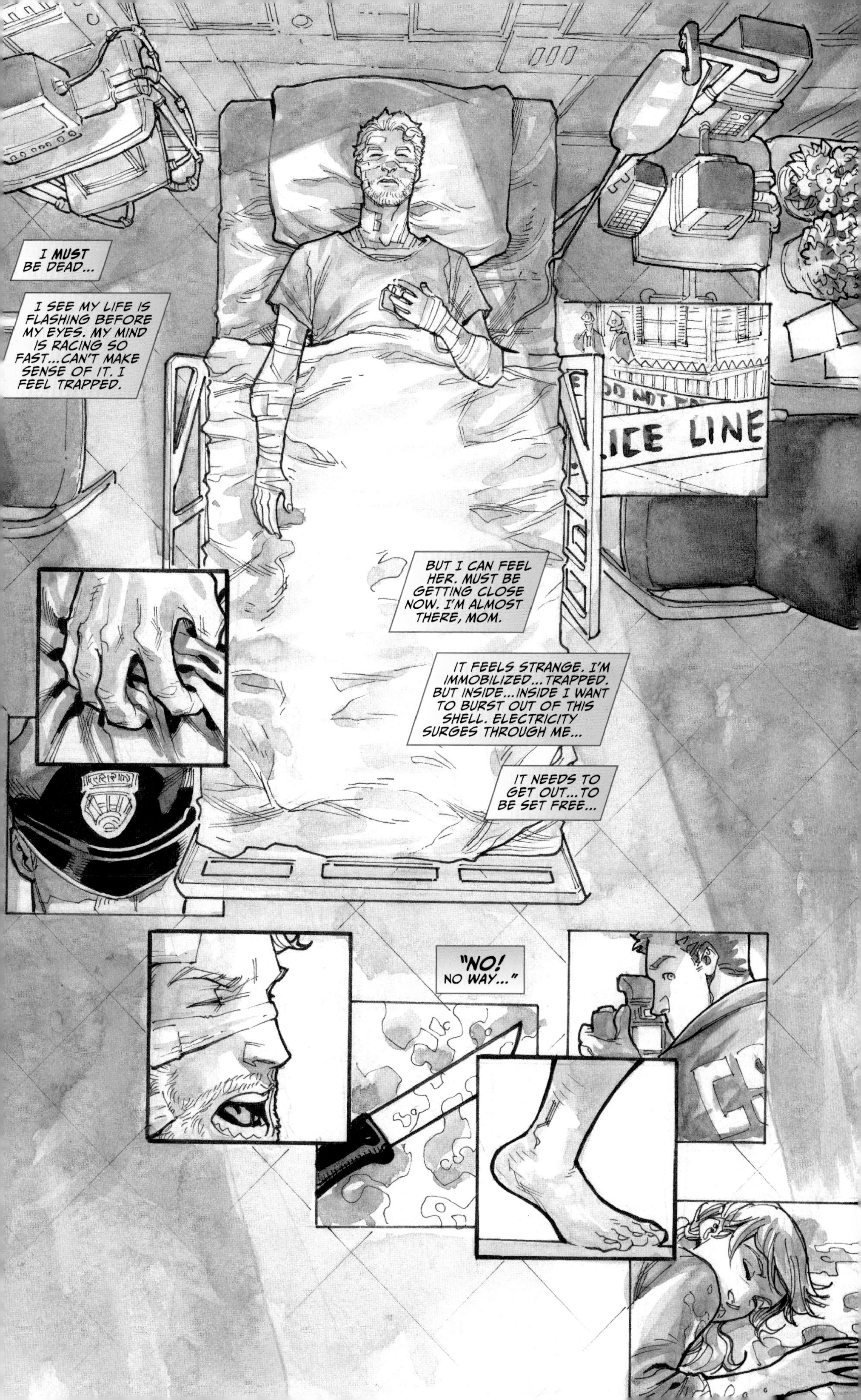
I MUST BE DEAD...
I SEE MY LIFE IS FLASHING BEFORE MY EYES. MY MIND IS RACING SO FAST...CAN'T MAKE SENSE OF IT. I FEEL TRAPPED.
BUT I CAN FEEL HER. MUST BE GETTING CLOSE NOW. I'M ALMOST THERE, MOM.
IT FEELS STRANGE. I'M IMMOBILIZED...TRAPPED. BUT INSIDE...INSIDE I WANT TO BURST OUT OF THIS SHELL. ELECTRICITY SURGES THROUGH ME...
IT NEEDS TO GET OUT...TO BE SET FREE...
"NO! NO WAY..."
ICE LINE

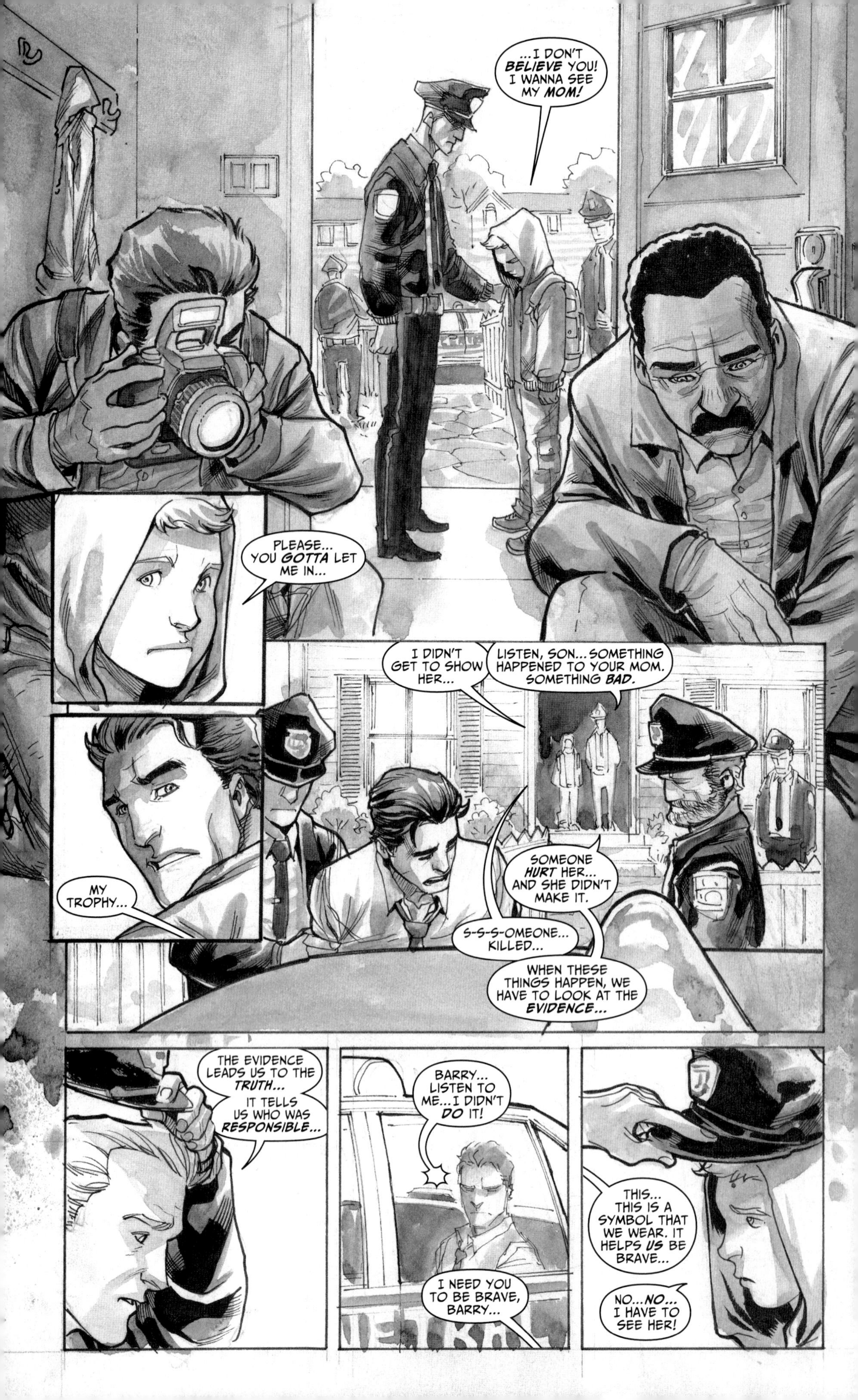
...I DON'T BELIEVE YOU! I WANNA SEE MY MOM!
PLEASE... YOU GOTTA LET ME IN...
MY TROPHY...
I DIDN'T GET TO SHOW HER...
LISTEN, SON... SOMETHING HAPPENED TO YOUR MOM. SOMETHING BAD.
SOMEONE HURT HER... AND SHE DIDN'T MAKE IT.
S-S-S-OMEONE... KILLED...
WHEN THESE THINGS HAPPEN, WE HAVE TO LOOK AT THE EVIDENCE...
THE EVIDENCE LEADS US TO THE TRUTH...
IT TELLS US WHO WAS RESPONSIBLE...
BARRY... LISTEN TO ME... I DIDN'T DO IT!
I NEED YOU TO BE BRAVE, BARRY...
THIS... THIS IS A SYMBOL THAT WE WEAR. IT HELPS US BE BRAVE...
NO...NO... I HAVE TO SEE HER!

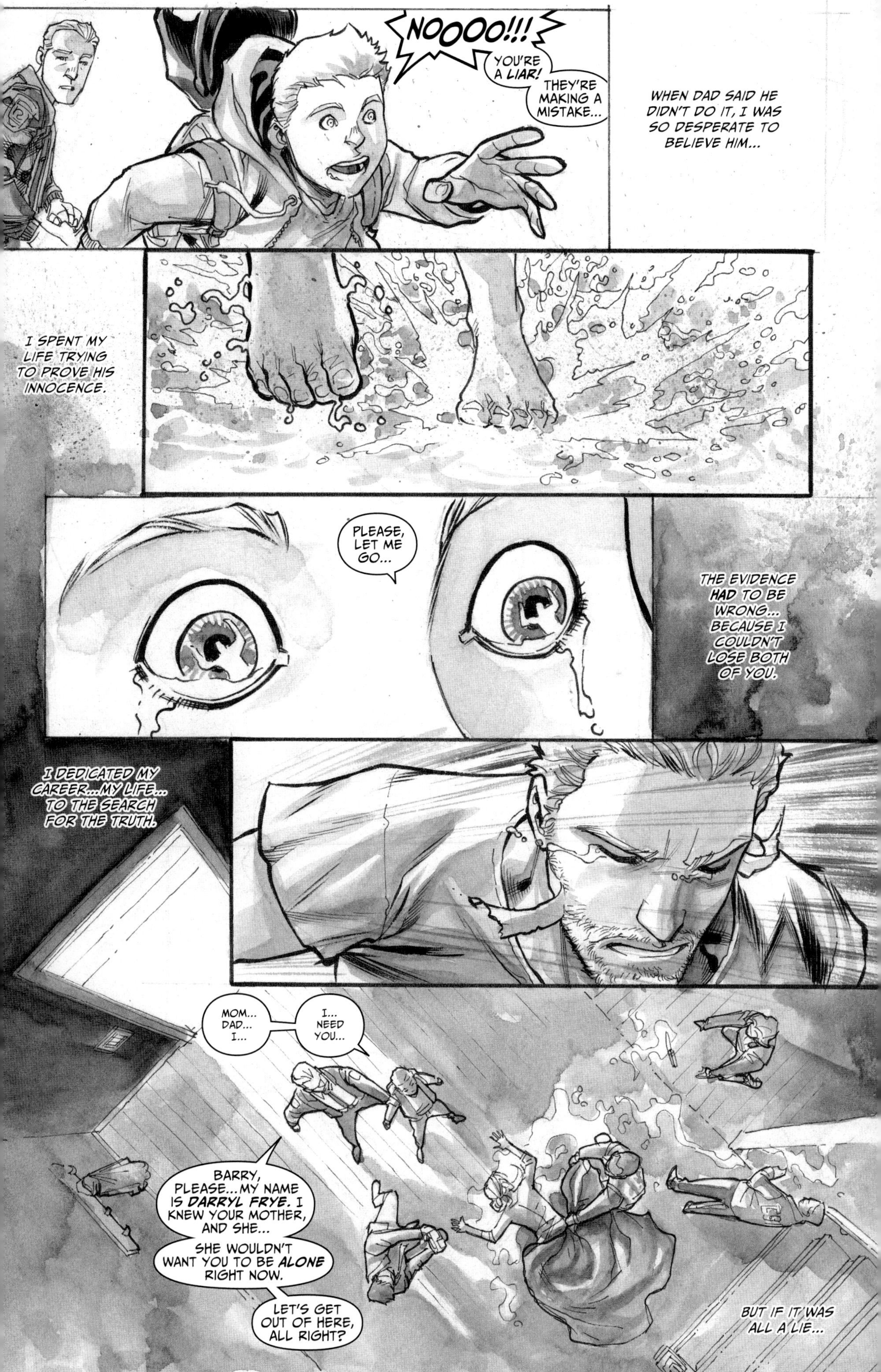
NOOOO!!!
YOU'RE A LIAR!
THEY'RE MAKING A MISTAKE...
WHEN DAD SAID HE DIDN'T DO IT, I WAS SO DESPERATE TO BELIEVE HIM...
I SPENT MY LIFE TRYING TO PROVE HIS INNOCENCE.
PLEASE, LET ME GO...
THE EVIDENCE HAD TO BE WRONG... BECAUSE I COULDN'T LOSE BOTH OF YOU.
I DEDICATED MY CAREER...MY LIFE... TO THE SEARCH FOR THE TRUTH.
MOM... DAD... I...
I... NEED YOU...
BARRY, PLEASE...MY NAME IS DARRYL FRYE. I KNEW YOUR MOTHER, AND SHE...
SHE WOULDN'T WANT YOU TO BE ALONE RIGHT NOW.
LET'S GET OUT OF HERE, ALL RIGHT?
BUT IF IT WAS ALL A LIE...

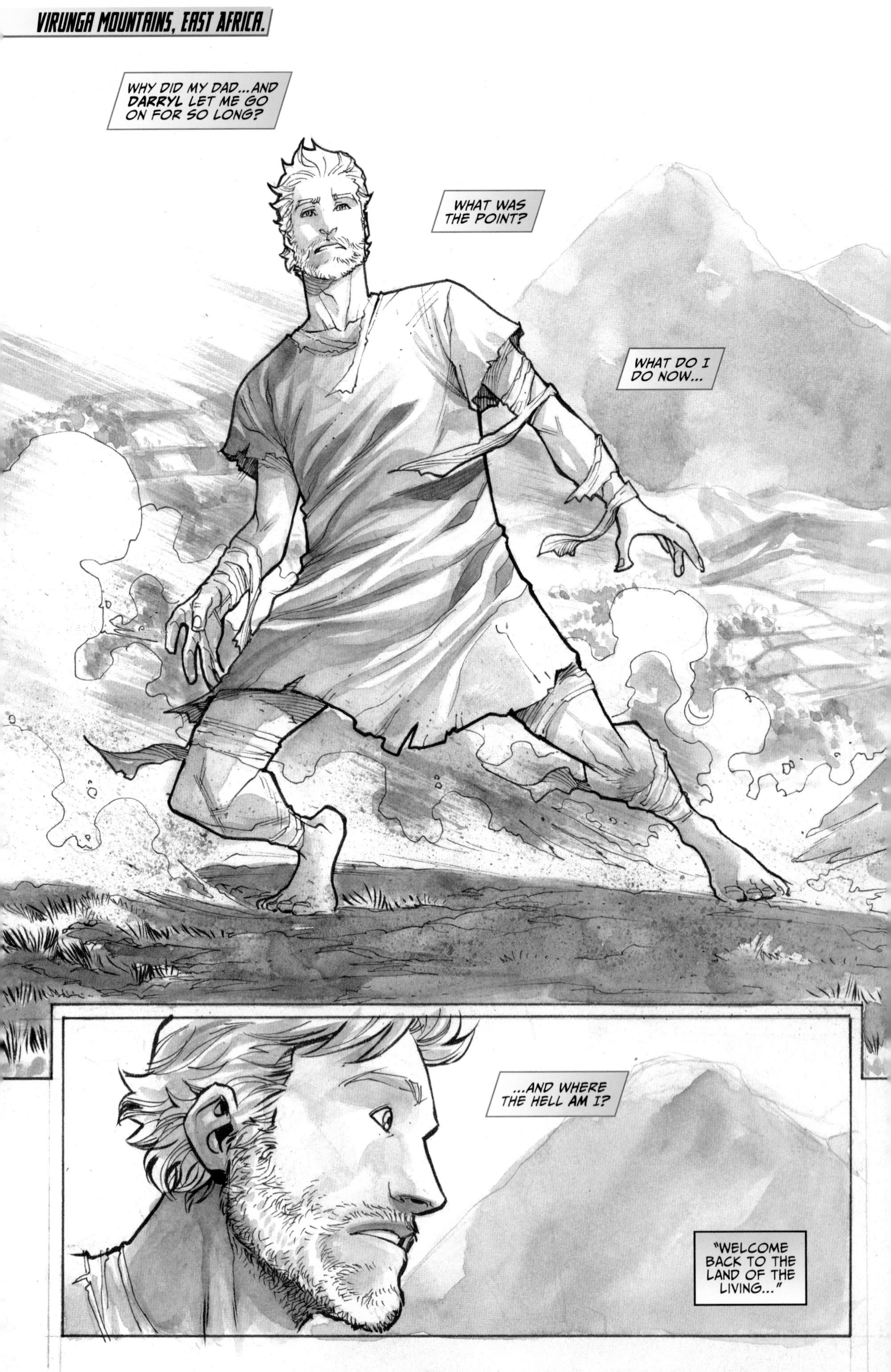
VIRUNGA MOUNTAINS, EAST AFRICA.
WHY DID MY DAD...AND DARRYL LET ME GO ON FOR SO LONG?
WHAT WAS THE POINT?
WHAT DO I DO NOW...
...AND WHERE THE HELL AM I?
"WELCOME BACK TO THE LAND OF THE LIVING..."

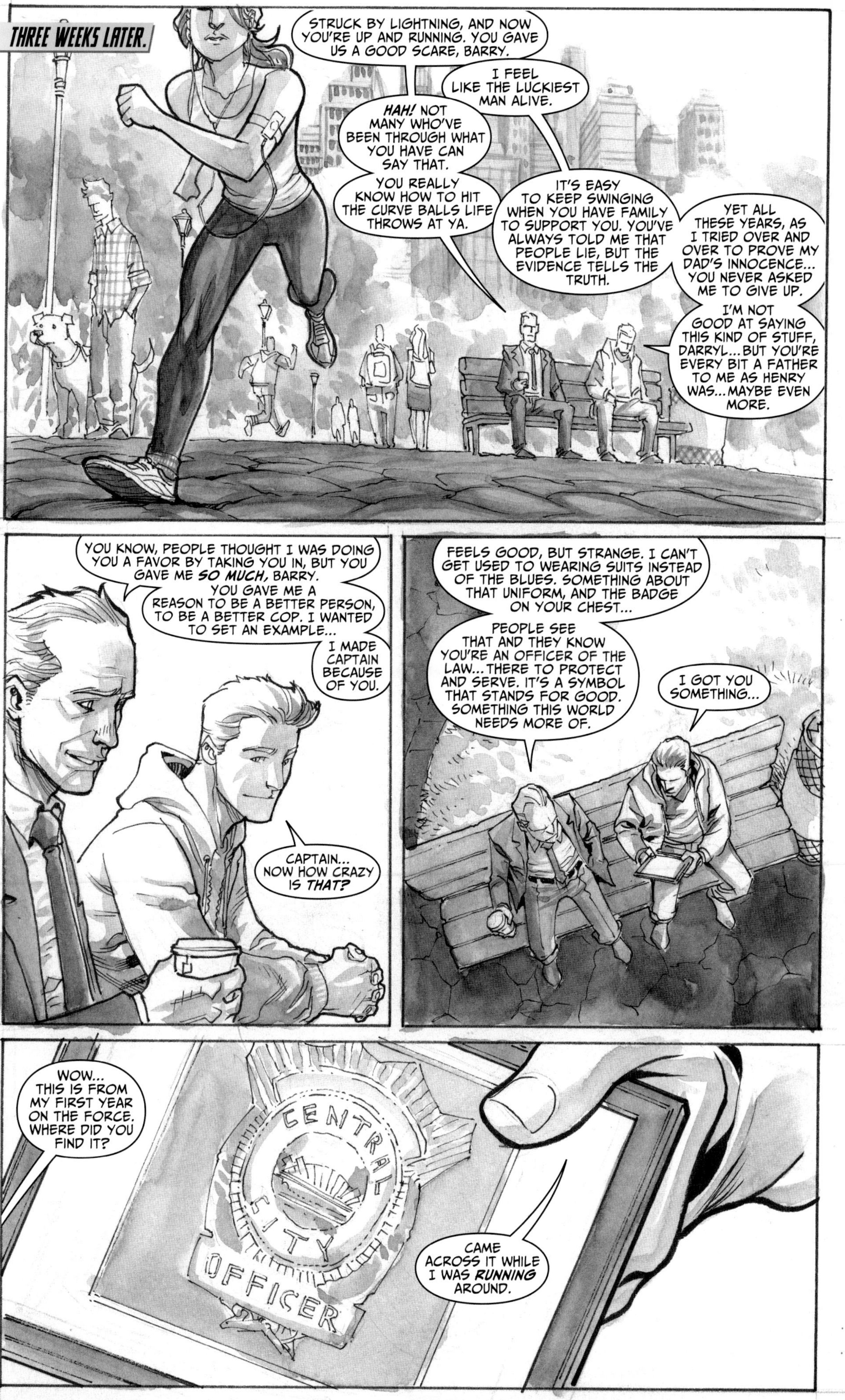
THREE WEEKS LATER.
STRUCK BY LIGHTNING, AND NOW YOU'RE UP AND RUNNING. YOU GAVE US A GOOD SCARE, BARRY.
I FEEL LIKE THE LUCKIEST MAN ALIVE.
HAH! NOT MANY WHO'VE BEEN THROUGH WHAT YOU HAVE CAN SAY THAT.
YOU REALLY KNOW HOW TO HIT THE CURVE BALLS LIFE THROWS AT YA.
IT'S EASY TO KEEP SWINGING WHEN YOU HAVE FAMILY TO SUPPORT YOU. YOU'VE ALWAYS TOLD ME THAT PEOPLE LIE, BUT THE EVIDENCE TELLS THE TRUTH.
YET ALL THESE YEARS, AS I TRIED OVER AND OVER TO PROVE MY DAD'S INNOCENCE... YOU NEVER ASKED ME TO GIVE UP.
I'M NOT GOOD AT SAYING THIS KIND OF STUFF, DARRYL... BUT YOU'RE EVERY BIT A FATHER TO ME AS HENRY WAS... MAYBE EVEN MORE.
YOU KNOW, PEOPLE THOUGHT I WAS DOING YOU A FAVOR BY TAKING YOU IN, BUT YOU GAVE ME SO MUCH, BARRY.
YOU GAVE ME A REASON TO BE A BETTER PERSON, TO BE A BETTER COP. I WANTED TO SET AN EXAMPLE...
I MADE CAPTAIN BECAUSE OF YOU.
CAPTAIN... NOW HOW CRAZY IS THAT?
FEELS GOOD, BUT STRANGE. I CAN'T GET USED TO WEARING SUITS INSTEAD OF THE BLUES. SOMETHING ABOUT THAT UNIFORM, AND THE BADGE ON YOUR CHEST...
PEOPLE SEE THAT AND THEY KNOW YOU'RE AN OFFICER OF THE LAW... THERE TO PROTECT AND SERVE. IT'S A SYMBOL THAT STANDS FOR GOOD. SOMETHING THIS WORLD NEEDS MORE OF.
I GOT YOU SOMETHING...
WOW... THIS IS FROM MY FIRST YEAR ON THE FORCE. WHERE DID YOU FIND IT?
CENTRAL CITY OFFICER
CAME ACROSS IT WHILE I WAS RUNNING AROUND.

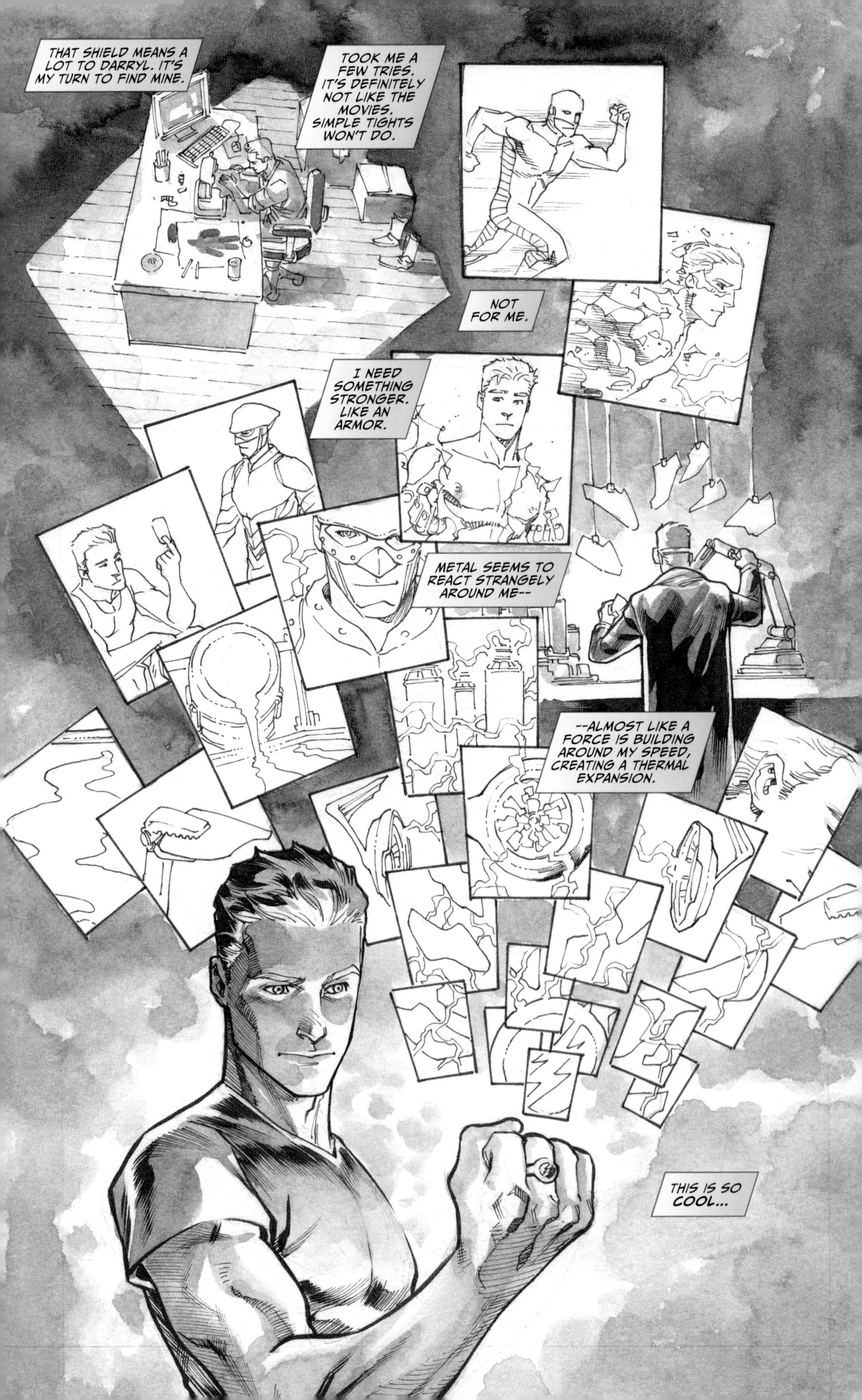
THAT SHIELD MEANS A LOT TO DARRYL. IT'S MY TURN TO FIND MINE.
TOOK ME A FEW TRIES. IT'S DEFINITELY NOT LIKE THE MOVIES. SIMPLE TIGHTS WON'T DO.
NOT FOR ME.
I NEED SOMETHING STRONGER. LIKE AN ARMOR.
METAL SEEMS TO REACT STRANGELY AROUND ME--
--ALMOST LIKE A FORCE IS BUILDING AROUND MY SPEED, CREATING A THERMAL EXPANSION.
THIS IS SO COOL...

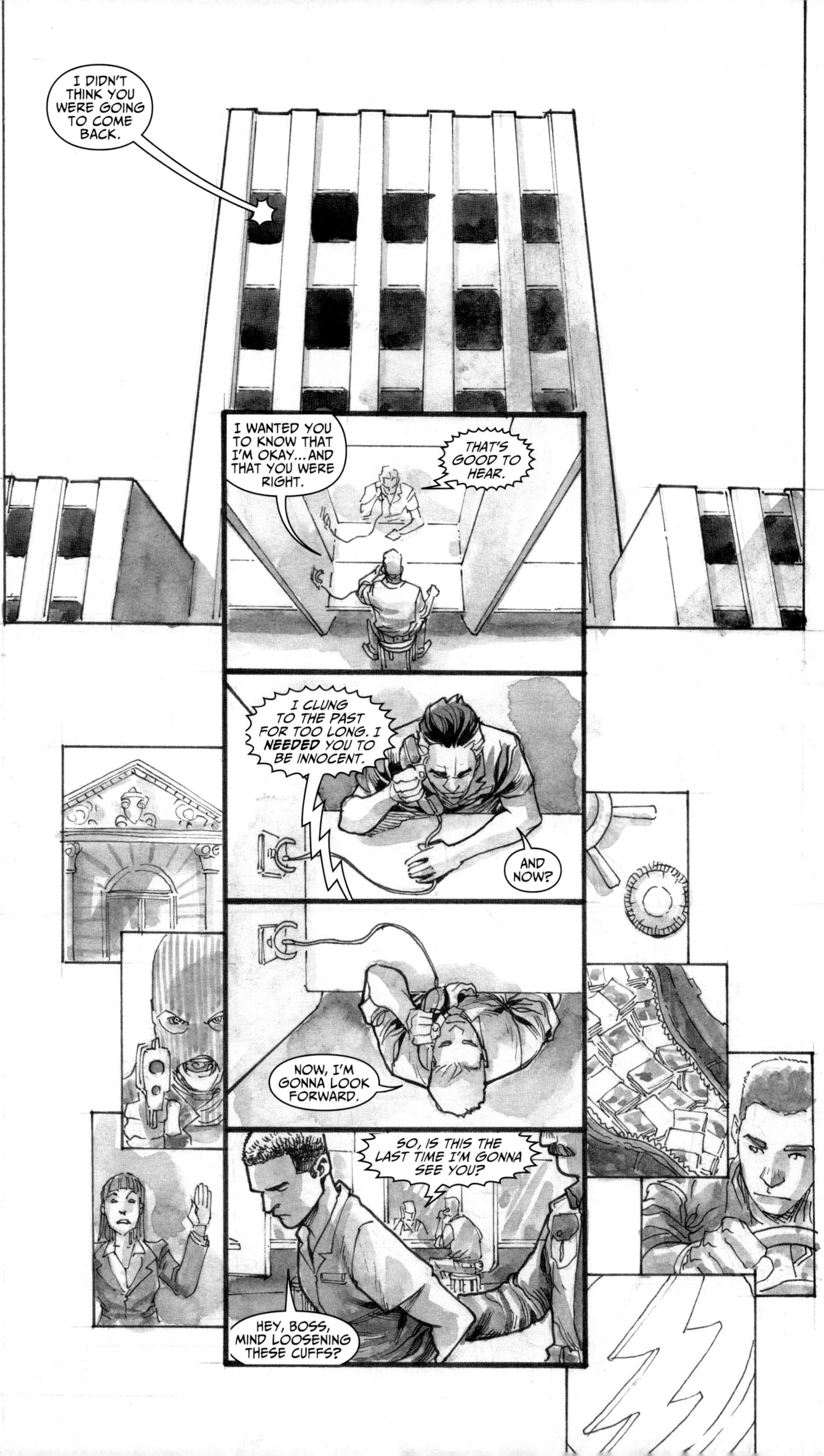
I DIDN'T THINK YOU WERE GOING TO COME BACK.
I WANTED YOU TO KNOW THAT I'M OKAY...AND THAT YOU WERE RIGHT.
THAT'S GOOD TO HEAR.
I CLUNG TO THE PAST FOR TOO LONG. I NEEDED YOU TO BE INNOCENT.
AND NOW?
NOW, I'M GONNA LOOK FORWARD.
SO, IS THIS THE LAST TIME I'M GONNA SEE YOU?
HEY, BOSS, MIND LOOSENING THESE CUFFS?

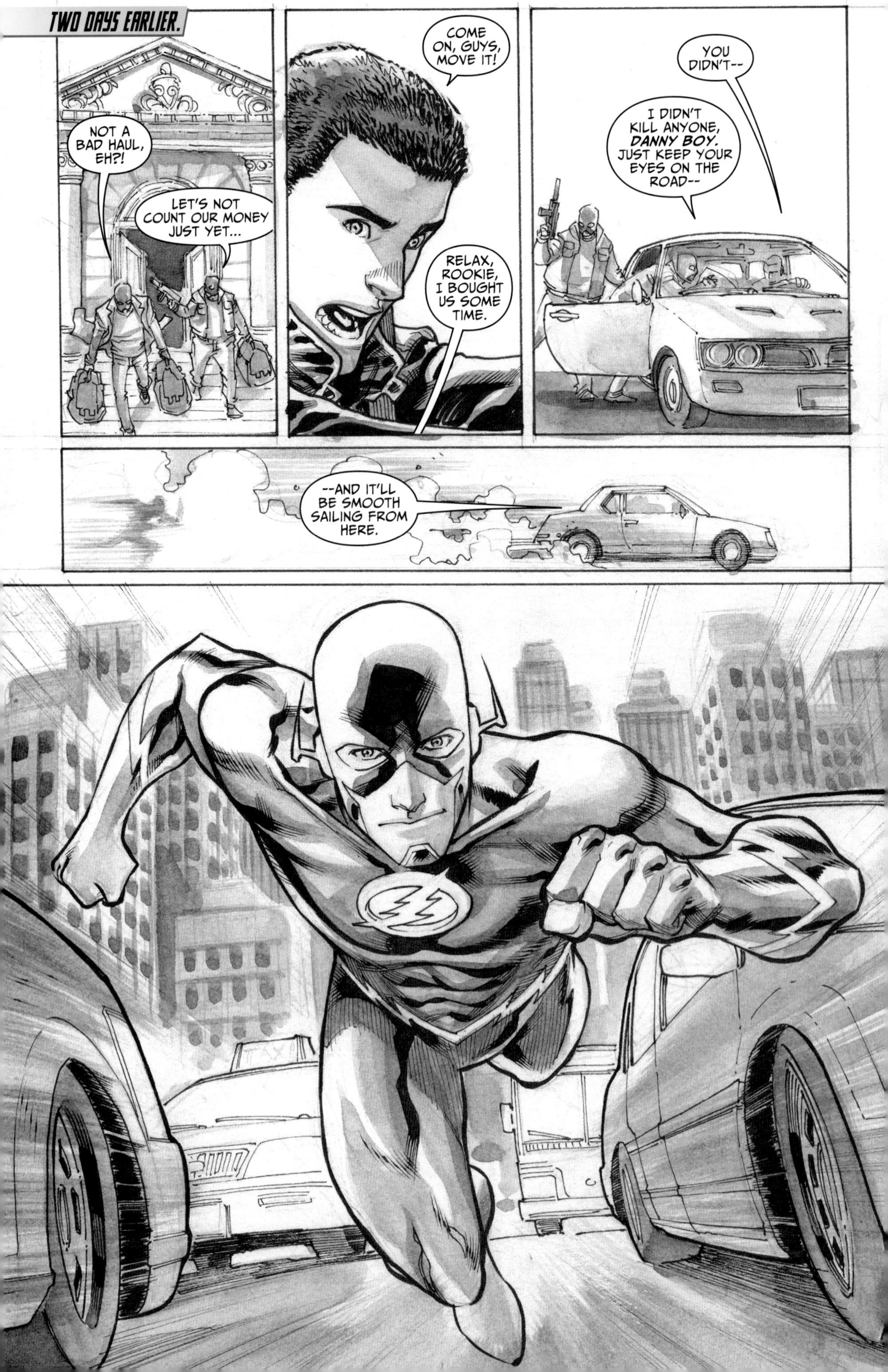
TWO DAYS EARLIER.
NOT A BAD HAUL, EH?!
LET'S NOT COUNT OUR MONEY JUST YET...
COME ON, GUYS, MOVE IT!
RELAX, ROOKIE, I BOUGHT US SOME TIME.
YOU DIDN'T--
I DIDN'T KILL ANYONE, DANNY BOY. JUST KEEP YOUR EYES ON THE ROAD--
--AND IT'LL BE SMOOTH SAILING FROM HERE.

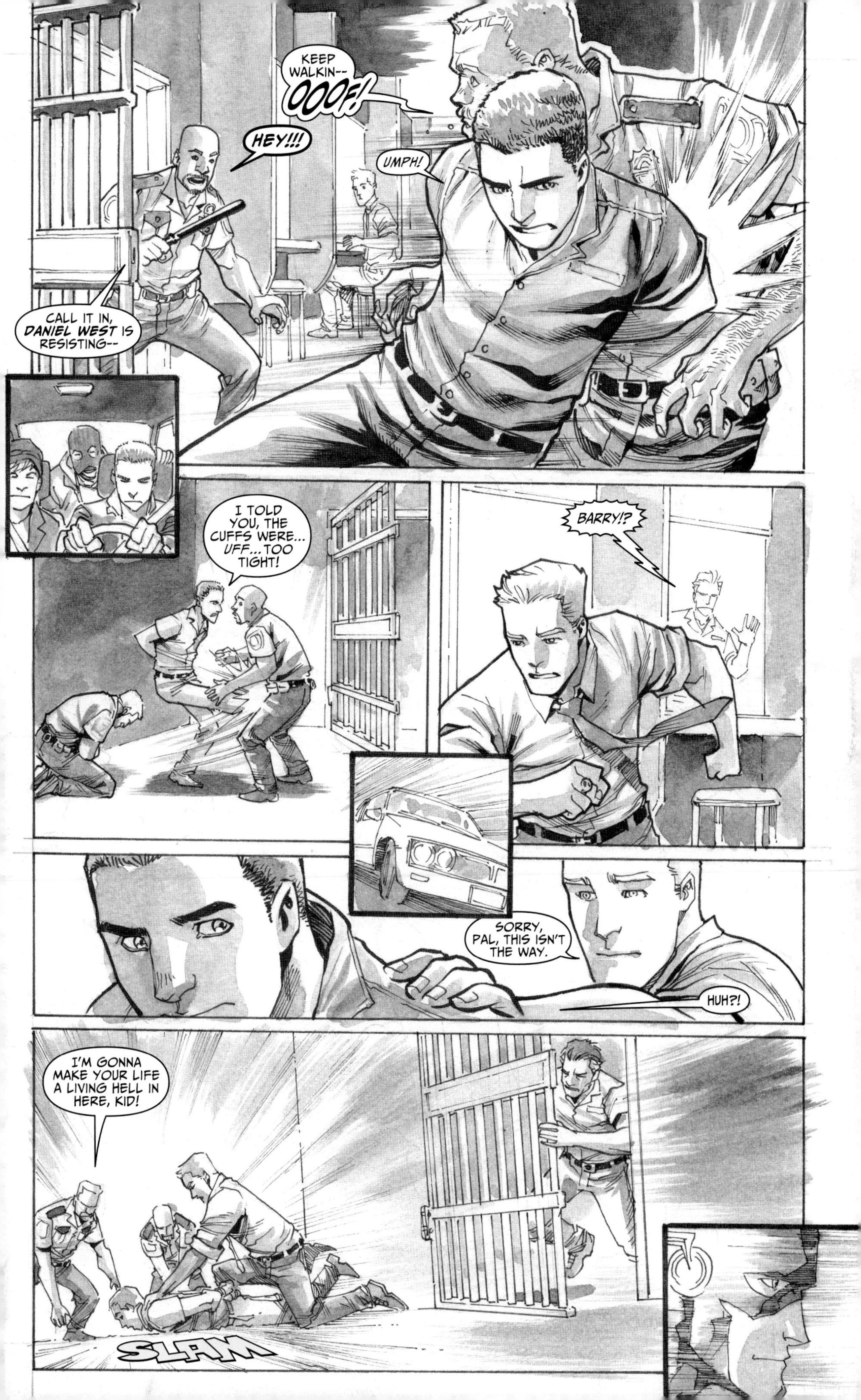
KEEP WALKIN-- OOOF!
HEY!!!
UMPH!
CALL IT IN, DANIEL WEST IS RESISTING--
I TOLD YOU, THE CUFFS WERE... UFF...TOO TIGHT!
BARRY!?
SORRY, PAL, THIS ISN'T THE WAY.
HUH?!
I'M GONNA MAKE YOUR LIFE A LIVING HELL IN HERE, KID!
SLAM

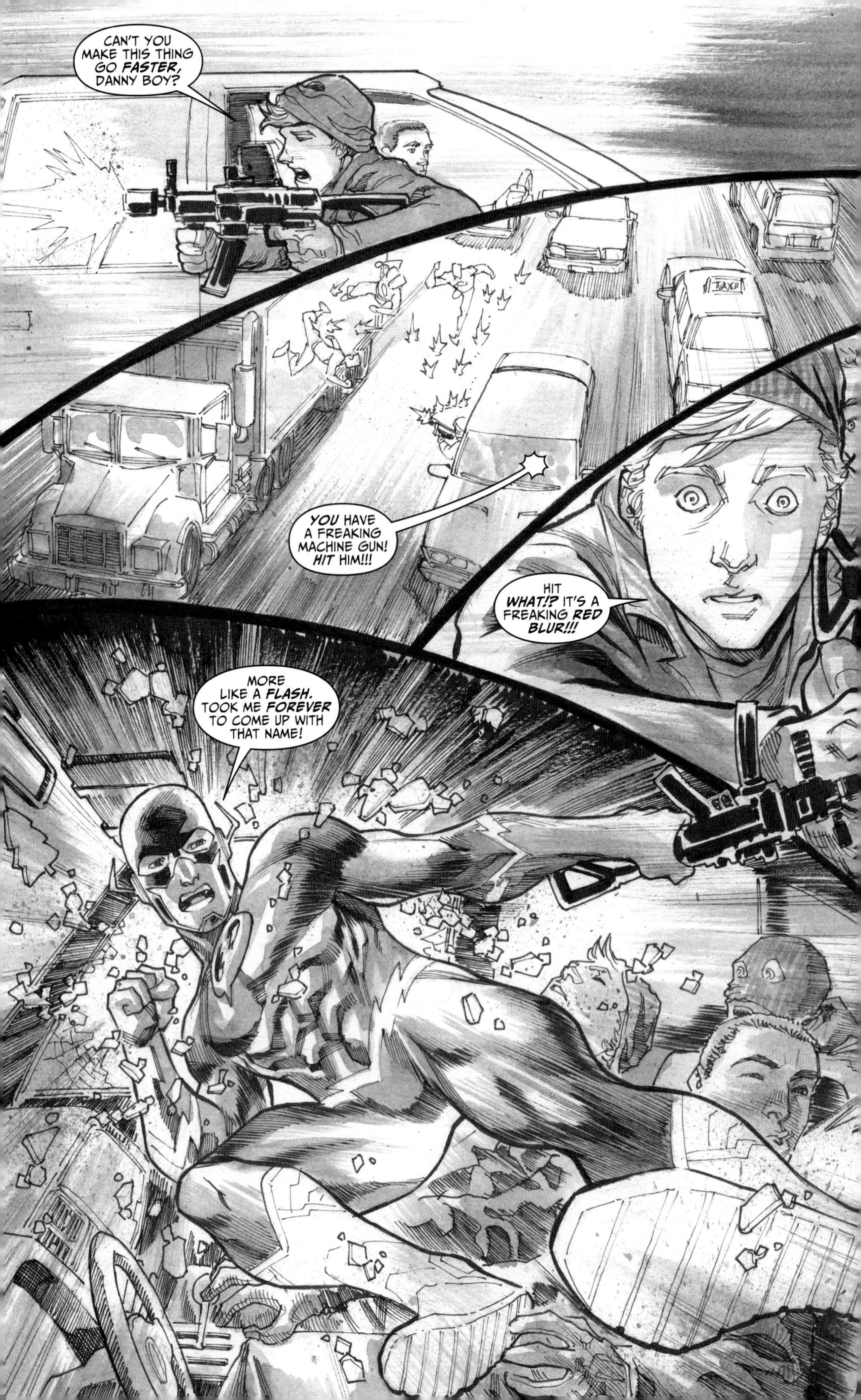
CAN'T YOU MAKE THIS THING GO FASTER, DANNY BOY?
YOU HAVE A FREAKING MACHINE GUN! HIT HIM!!!
HIT WHAT!? IT'S A FREAKING RED BLUR!!!
MORE LIKE A FLASH. TOOK ME FOREVER TO COME UP WITH THAT NAME!

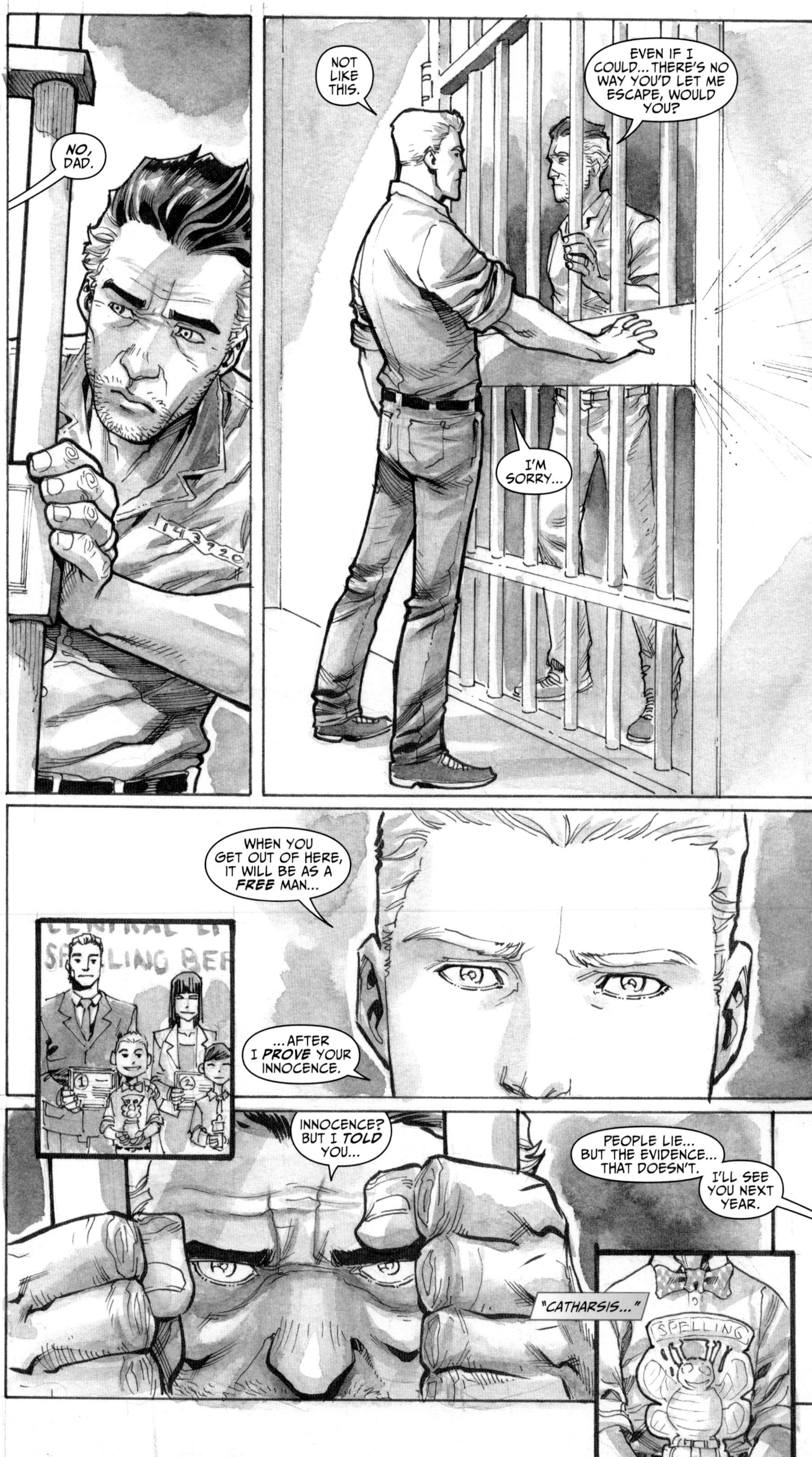
NO, DAD.
NOT LIKE THIS.
EVEN IF I COULD... THERE'S NO WAY YOU'D LET ME ESCAPE, WOULD YOU?
I'M SORRY...
143920
WHEN YOU GET OUT OF HERE, IT WILL BE AS A FREE MAN...
...AFTER I PROVE YOUR INNOCENCE.
INNOCENCE? BUT I TOLD YOU...
PEOPLE LIE... BUT THE EVIDENCE... THAT DOESN'T.
I'LL SEE YOU NEXT YEAR.
"CATHARSIS..."
SPELLING